2008

FOUNDATIONS OF
PASTORAL CARE

BRUCE L. PETERSEN

BEACON HILL PRESS
OF KANSAS CITY

ISBN-13: 978-0-8341-2305-2
ISBN-10: 0-8341-2305-3

Printed in
China

Cover Design: Brandon Hill
Interior Design: Sharon Page

Library of Congress Cataloging-in-Publication Data

Petersen, Bruce L., 1942-
    Foundations of pastoral care / Bruce L. Petersen.
        p. cm.
    Includes bibliographical references.
    ISBN-13: 978-0-8341-2305-2 (hardcover)
    ISBN-10: 0-8341-2305-3 (hardcover)
    1. Pastoral care. I. Title.

    BV4011.3.P48 2007
    253—dc22

                                                                        200700

10 9 8 7 6 5 4

DEDICATION

To my wife, Jackie,
who was willing to sacrifice
some of our personal and vacation time
as a couple so this book could be finished.

To my students, past and present.
You constantly inspire me
to do my best in the classroom.
Knowing you gives me faith in the
Church of the near and distant future,
as you take over leadership in ministry.
Above everything else, aspire to be
shepherds of your flock.

CONTENTS

ACKNOWLEDGMENTS

I am most grateful to the many people who helped me in completing this project. Thank you, Tim Pusey, Jeren Rowell, Judith Schwanz, Eddie Estep, and Tim Swanson, for reading the manuscript and making so many helpful suggestions. Bonnie Perry and Richard Buckner of Beacon Hill Press of Kansas City, you have given encouragement throughout the process. I have especially appreciated the guidance of my colleague and friend, Alex Varughese, managing editor of the Centennial Initiative. The dean of the School of Theology and Philosophy, Jeanne Serrão, and my faculty friends at Mount Vernon Nazarene University have continually offered words of encouragement. I felt the support of President LeBron Fairbanks at each stage of the project. Without such good friends this book would not have been completed.

I feel special gratitude to the churches I pastored. Thank you for your patience as you taught me what it meant to live in community. I beg your forgiveness for the times I didn't fully put into practice the principles I write about here. You have all enriched my life.

UNIT 1

PASTORAL CARE FOUNDATIONS

ONE

AN INTRODUCTION
TO PASTORAL CARE

Bill and Denise Reynolds could not have been more excited. A church had actually selected them to be their parsonage family. Now, here came the rented truck, driven by an old friend, arriving with all their earthly possessions. A half dozen people from their new church helped unload their furniture and clothing into the parsonage next to the church. Then they carried boxes of books into Bill's tiny study.

After a long afternoon of hard work, Bill thanked all the helpers. Then he stood for a few minutes staring at the study door. There at eye level hung a black nameplate, announcing him to the world as PASTOR.

The reality hit him with such force that Bill walked around the old metal desk and collapsed on the ancient wooden swivel chair. From the time he was fifteen and felt the call of God, he had known this moment would come. He had completed his educational training, and once he fulfilled his required practical experience here at the church, he would be ordained for a lifetime of ministry in the Church of Jesus Christ. But now, sitting in his first office, Bill felt overwhelmed by a feeling of panic. What do I do now?

He knew he would have to prepare at least one sermon every week. That thought excited him. He always enjoyed letting a Bible passage come alive in his heart as he prepared to preach. But what will I do with the rest of the week, *he thought? People in this congregation would be depending on him to help them face difficult situations. And what about those needy people out on the streets and in the homes near the church? They would need his attention too.*

Some of the members who had helped with the unloading had called him Pastor Bill or Pastor Reynolds. He told Denise later he felt a bit uncomfortable with the title. It sounded so pretentious. He didn't feel more significant than anyone else. Deep down he wasn't sure he understood what it meant to be a pastor anyway.

The first thing that came to Bill's mind when he heard the title pastor was an image of a shepherd leaning on a staff while sheep grazed in clusters on a green hillside. That certainly didn't fit his suburban setting. His new church was surrounded by 2 million people. Even the idea of sheep was ludicrous. Bill smiled as he thought. A lost sheep in these parts would be cornered by the department of animal control if it weren't first flattened by a big rig on the freeway.

Perhaps the pastor-shepherd was simply a holdover from a simpler agrarian age. Perhaps Bill needed to see himself more as the chief executive officer over a

Christian organization or a spiritual social worker trying to help people through their difficult circumstances. As he was about to begin his ministerial career he realized he would soon learn the answer to this question: What does it mean to be a real pastor to people in the twenty-first century?

▶ TODAY'S ROLE MODELS

It's safe to assume that most pastors want to have an effective, growing congregation. One may think that the easiest way to achieve that goal is to find a successful pastor or church and then copy the methodology. There are indeed many powerful images of ministry shaping the thinking of both the person desiring to serve a church and the congregation that will be served.

Who are the popular role models today?

THE TELEVISION PERSONALITY

Perhaps the most significant influencer at the present time is television. A century ago a minister could gain national notoriety by publishing a book or writing a newspaper column. People today are using their eyes less for reading and more for watching. For some pastors, television has become a tool for building a church with international recognition. No longer do religious broadcasters try to buy expensive time on network television. Satellite television, with its ability to cover the globe with coverage, has spawned an abundance of large churches broadcasting weekly worship services to a worldwide audience.

However, such churches tend to cultivate a following of spectators who participate in isolation. Viewers may vicariously feel a part of the weekly celebration. However, they receive no personal encouragement, fellowship, or compassion from a television church that may be located thousands of miles away.

THE MEGACHURCH VISIONARY PASTOR

Many young pastors become conference junkies, hoping that they will finally discover the secret ingredient that will cause their congregation to explode with growth.

There is no question that some megachurch pastors have altered the landscape of the evangelical church in North America. But most pastors fail to recognize the personal impact these visionary leaders exert on a specific community through their unique pastoral personality. It's impossible to simply clone Willow Creek Church in Prairie City, Nebraska, or Saddleback Church in Pleasantville, Vermont. Even with their large pastoral staffs and vast resources, these superchurches face the constant struggle of finding effective ways to provide pastoral care for the people who are part of their congregations.

THE PULPIT GIANT

Some pastors and churches believe that the key to a growing church is a strong pulpit. They are convinced that if a minister can preach in a dynamic fashion, people will flock to the church. Pastors hear the recorded sermons of Chuck Swindoll, Thomas Long, or Haddon Robinson and say to themselves, *If I could only preach like that . . .*

Interestingly, pastors used to be called *Preacher* by members of the congregation. Not too many years ago people might ask when moving to a new community, "Where is the best preaching in town?" Today they ask who has the best worship music or who offers the best programs for children and youth. Many churches are starved spiritually because of the lack of biblical preaching. Every pastor needs to be willing to invest the time necessary each week in preparation to be the best preacher possible. And yet, preaching alone will not create a strong, healthy, caring congregation.

And last but not least—

THE PASTOR

The imagery of pastor as a valid model for ministry is again gaining acceptance after a period where the Church emphasized management and efficiency over caring and compassion. Today people, both inside and outside the Church, are becoming more interested in the importance of relating to others. Pastors both initiate and help facilitate those relationships within the Church.

The word *pastor* is not so much a title as a role—the role of being a shepherd to a flock of people. In fact, the word *pastor* comes from the Latin word *pascere* or *shepherd*. It means "to feed." It suggests a holistic approach to ministry that is both ancient and contemporary.

The term *pastor* is only found one time in the New Testament scriptures to identify the person who takes on the responsibility of spiritual leadership for a local Body of Believers. Ephesians 4:11-12 says, "It was he who gave some to be apostles, some to be prophets, some to be evangelists, and some to be *pastors* and teachers, to prepare God's people for works of service, so that the body of Christ may be built up" (italics added). However, the metaphor of the Spiritual leader as a shepherd is found many times throughout Scripture.

Nowhere is the model for ministry stated more clearly than in the image Peter creates for us in 1 Pet. 5:1-4:

To the elders among you, I appeal as a fellow elder, a witness of Christ's sufferings and one who also will share in the glory to be revealed: *be shepherds of God's flock that is under your care,* serving as overseers—not because you must, but because you are willing, as God wants you to be; not greedy for money, but eager to serve; not lording it over those entrusted to you, but being examples to the flock. And when the Chief Shepherd appears, you will receive the crown of glory that will never fade away *(italics added).*

Notice Peter did not call them to be overseers, teachers, prophets, or evangelists. His primary metaphor for the elders of the local church was "shepherds of God's flock."

Other world religions do not use the word *pastor.* Even the Jewish faith, which has a rich heritage built around the pastor-shepherd motif, does not refer to their rabbis in this way. The term *pastor* has become a uniquely Christian title for one in professional ministry. And yet it has been ignored by many who are looking for more contemporary icons. Various titles have been used across the centuries for those in Christian ministry, such as *elder, parson, preacher, minister, evangelist, clergy, priest, reverend,* or *chaplain.* But no name or title better describes the role and responsibility of ministry better than the term *pastor-shepherd.*

Pastor E. Glenn Wagner argues for a return to an emphasis on pastoral concern by the clergy.

Like Esau, we pastors have sold our biblical birthright as shepherds called by God for the pottage of skills and gimmicks designed by humans. We have misunderstood the role of pastor and defined it incorrectly. We have left our biblical and theological moorings.[1]

Another pastor, David Wiersbe, agrees with this new emphasis on pastoral concern. "Pastors need to be with people. Any approach to ministry that reduces or eliminates a pastor's contact with a wide cross section of the congregation is off the biblical path."[2] Could it be that the best model or image for ministry today is still found in the biblical word *pastor?*

You cannot understand the role of Christian ministry without examining the life of Jesus. Thomas Oden says:

From the earthly ministry of Jesus of Nazareth, we learn the rudiments of Christian ministry. Jesus' vision and practice of ministry is significant for all Christian vision and practice of ministry. If ministry cannot be clearly established as the continuation of Jesus' own intention and practice, we lose its central theological premise.[3]

From Jesus' own identification as "the good shepherd" (John 10:11), to his example of compassion and concern for people in the gospel accounts, he provides an inspiring example of pastoral care. The subject of shepherding will be discussed in greater detail in chapter 6.

▶ THE HISTORICAL DEVELOPMENT OF PASTORAL CARE

Early in the development of the primitive church in Acts the apostles appointed people to be set apart to lead local congregations. Paul lists the spiritual gifts given to those who would give leadership and direction to the church in Eph. 4:11-12: "It was he who gave some to be apostles, some to be prophets, some to be evangelists, and some to be pastors and teachers, to prepare God's people for works of service, so that the body of Christ may be built up." Robb Redman says, "The primary modes of pastoral care in the New Testament consist of mutual edification *(oikodomē)*, encouragement *(paraklēsis)*, and a mutual discipline (Matt. 18:15-17). The work of pastoral care is here recognized as the work of the whole people of God. . . . On the other hand, the New Testament also recognizes the unique calling of pastors, elders, and bishops, who are given a ministry of oversight and supervision."[4] The apostle Paul wrote the books of 1 and 2 Timothy and Titus specifically to instruct pastors and overseers how to care for people in the Church.

As the centuries passed, the Church continued to place an emphasis on the shepherding ministry. Second-century writers such as Clement of Rome, Ignatius, and Hermes wrote, defining the pastoral office. Tertullian, Origen, Basil, Gregory of Nyssa, and John Chrysostom added instructions to pastors over the next two hundred years. By the fifth century the Church expanded across northern Europe and faced the challenge of Christianizing the barbarians. Pastors instructed their congregations to live out their Christian lives in compassion with one another in community, as an example to their unchristian neighbors. Pope Gregory the Great, in the sixth century, wrote a paper titled "Pastoral Care," in which he described the work of the pastor as offering moral and spiritual guidance to the church and also to the unchurched.[5]

During the Middle Ages pastoral care was often limited to dealing with the proper penance for committed sins. The Roman Church focused the energies of the clergy on administering the seven sacraments as the means to spiritual health. Although Francis of Assisi and Bernard of Clairvaux modeled both spiritual and physical ministry within the Church, this period of Church history was characterized by a lack of emphasis on pastoral care.

The Reformation brought a renewal of interest in pastoral care within the newly developing Protestant movement. Martin Luther strongly stressed the priesthood of all believers, which made pastoral care the responsibility of the entire Church. Two important books came out of the early sixteenth century: Zwingli's *The Shepherd* (1524) and Bucer's *On the True Care of Souls* (1538). John Calvin and John Knox both emphasized the importance of the pastor caring for the spiritual needs of the congregation.

Richard Baxter's book *The Reformed Pastor* (1656) became the most significant development of the seventeenth century. His development of Puritan pastoral care became the standard for ministers in the Reformed tradition for centuries after. This tradition emphasized the introspection of conscience and strict adherence to proper moral actions. Baxter himself divided pastoral care into seven functions: "converting the unconverted, giving advice to inquirers, building up the believers, shepherding the families in the parish, visiting the sick and dying, reproving the impenitent, and exercising discipline."[6]

John Wesley took the gospel out of church buildings and into the streets and fields of eighteenth-century England. He became convinced that the laity should fulfill a major role in providing pastoral care. This was important because Wesley's itinerant ministry did not allow him to do ongoing personal care with his converts. Through Wesley's Methodist small group or class meetings people received the support and encouragement needed to live as believers. D. Michael Henderson states in his book *John Wesley's Class Meeting: A Model for Making Disciples,* "Wesley . . . so mobilized the entire Methodist membership that nearly every member had some share in the ministry of the congregation."[7] Tom Albin summarizes Wesley's impact this way: "In fact you could say that the whole Wesley revival was really a revival of pastoral care and guidance."[8]

As Wesley's movement came to the New World, lay pastoral care became an important element in the expansion of the Church out to the frontiers of the newly created United States. Circuit riding preachers could only visit small communities periodically, so the task of care and encouragement fell upon the members of those tiny Methodist and Baptist congregations. As the nineteenth-century camp meeting movement swept across the expanding American landscape, newly evangelized believers learned to care for one another out of necessity, since there were not enough pastors to fill the church pulpit in every village and hamlet.

The twentieth century brought more formalized training for those entering ministry. Many potential ministers began attending college and even seminary before pastoring their first church. These schools of higher education taught courses on pastoral theology and homiletics to complement the study of theology, Bible, and Church history.

The beginning of the twentieth century marked the beginning of a new field of study: psychiatry. Sigmund Freud is generally considered the most significant early influence in this new discipline, which attempted to study the mind in the same way medicine studied the body. It was not long before those in ministry preparation were introduced to concepts of psychology and mental health. Clinical pastoral education became a part of most seminary programs by the 1950s. Carl Rogers's book *Client-Centered Therapy* instructed seminarians in the nondirective approach to counseling.

In the last quarter century Christian counselors have begun to make their mark in the counseling field. Writers such as Gary Collins, H. Norman Wright, and Archibald Hart have written books read by pastors and laypeople alike. Christian psychologists offer seminars in churches on subjects ranging from how to raise children and have a happy marriage to overcoming depression or addictions. Many Christian universities and seminaries now offer graduate degrees for people seeking to be Christian counselors. Today it is not uncommon for large churches to hire Christian or pastoral counselors as staff members to serve the needs of both church members and those in need from the surrounding communities.

Small groups were rediscovered after World War II by parachurch organizations such as InterVarsity Christian Fellowship, the Navigators, and Campus Crusade as they began ministry to college and university campuses. In the 1970s innovators such as Lyman Coleman and Bruce Larson reintroduced the concept of small groups back again to churches. Many churches now offer specialized small groups to provide support for people with a common concern, such as addiction or loss.

Lay-led pastoral care has become an essential part of ministry in many large churches today. There are more people in a church of thousands than a pastor and staff can possibly serve effectively. Lay care, either through small groups or specific ministries, overcomes the limiting factor of having enough paid staff to meet the needs of everyone in the church. One of the benefits of care by the laity is the sense of fulfillment when members utilize their God-given gifts and abilities.

▶ PASTORAL CARE IN THE TWENTY-FIRST CENTURY

In our opening story, Pastor Bill was overwhelmed by the task that awaited him as he began serving his first church. Perhaps it would be helpful to identify some of the terms connected with the pastoral role.

• *Pastoral ministry.* Everything a pastor does in connection with the church would be considered the ministry of the pastor.

This would include such diverse things as conducting board meetings, sermon preparation and delivery, promoting the missions program, leading a visitor to receive salvation, or driving a group of children to summer camp on the church van. Being a pastor is a lot like the farmer who steps out on the back porch each morning and realizes, in viewing the farm, there are fifty things he could do today, all of them urgent. Like the farmer, a pastor's ministry work is never done. Each pastor has some weekly routines, but there are enough unexpected challenges to keep the work from ever becoming dull or predictable.

• *Pastoral care.* Part of the task of ministry is pastoral care. Traditionally, pastoral care has included the activities of healing, compassion, sustaining, guiding, and reconciling people to one another and to God.

Thomas Oden, in his book *Classical Pastoral Care,* volume 1, *Becoming a Minister,* gives this definition:

> Pastoral Care is that branch of Christian theology that deals with care of persons by pastors. It is pastoral because it pertains to the offices, tasks, and duties of the pastor. It is care because it has charge of, and is deliberately attentive to the spiritual growth and destiny of persons. Pastoral care is analogous to a physician's care of the body. Since that particular sphere over which one exercises care is the psyche . . . pastoral care is also appropriately called the care of souls.[9]

The term *pastoral care* may imply that the pastor is the only one who should do this work. While care is an important responsibility for a pastor, pastoral care can also refer to the compassionate shepherding concern any Christian can give to another person.

Pastor and author Michael Slaughter is intent upon helping laypeople discover such a ministry. He writes, "The call of God is not only for those involved in professional ministry. God has created every human being with a divine purpose. The greatest thing we can do for another human being is to help each person discover God's call."[10] In fact, a layperson with the spiritual gift of pastor may be much more effective as a caregiver than a minister without that spiritual gift.

• *Pastoral counseling.* Within the larger sphere of pastoral care is the task of pastoral counseling. Howard Clinebell, in his landmark book *Basic Types of Pastoral Care and Counseling,* defines the term this way, "Pastoral counseling, one dimension of pastoral care, is the utilization of a variety of healing (therapeutic) methods to help people handle their problems and crises more growthfully and thus experience healing of their brokenness."[11]

Within this broad field of pastoral counseling there are now many specialties, such as supportive care, crisis care, bereavement care, marriage enrichment, and family enrichment, to name a few.

The skills and techniques of effective pastoral counseling are quite specific and will not be addressed in this book. However, it is useful to comment on how pervasive the practice is. It is natural for people to come to a pastor for advice and counsel on spiritual matters. But these days the pastor's study is often the first stop when there are marriage problems, family conflicts, personal depression, or important decisions. No one asks a minister if he or she is interested in doing counseling. It's assumed today that pastors counsel.

Pastoral counseling is usually done in a limited time frame, focusing on a specific solution to a need. One reason people turn to clergy is because their counsel is usually free. Also, ministers do not restrict themselves to daytime office hours and thus are generally available anytime there is a crisis. In addition, people may feel that a pastor has greater insight into the will of God than a layperson.

• *Pastoral psychotherapy.* This is a very specific form of pastoral counseling, focusing on long-term therapeutic work done by a pastoral counselor with extensive training in psychotherapy. Because it is so technical and requires training and experience, it is beyond the scope of most pastors.

▶ A Shepherd for the Present Age

Every age has to face a new set of circumstances that will influence the culture within and outside the Church. We have stepped over the boundary of one millennium and into a new one. And what we have discovered so far in this twenty-first century has been a mixed bag of peace and war, starvation and prosperity, safety and terrorism. The question on the minds of many in the Church is this: How can we "do church" in a way that can have a spiritual impact on the generation today?

More specifically for this book, how can we shepherd people who are facing the complexities of our stress-driven society? The words of a hymn written nearly two hundred fifty years ago by Charles Wesley keep coming back to my mind: "To serve the present age, / My calling to fulfill; / O may it all my pow'rs engage / To do my Master's will!" (from "A Charge to Keep I Have").

Serving the present age is different from serving the last one. Yet while society is rapidly changing and we're not always sure where that will lead us, basic human needs are the same.

Michael Slaughter writes, "America has been called the nation of strangers. One Gallup pole reported that four in ten Americans admit to frequent feelings of 'intense loneliness.' . . . By 2010 more than one in four householders will be single-parent homes."[12] Even though family conflicts abound, people are seeking authentic, loving relationships with people who care. There is an increased interest in spiritual reality, but people do not turn to the Church for the answers. With all our technological advancements, people have the same basic longings and desires that Jesus saw when he was here on earth.

The image of the pastor-shepherd serving in the twenty-first century is not an irrelevant one. People today are desperately looking for someone who will know their names and care about their hurts. The way you do that today may be somewhat different from someone pastoring a hundred years ago. Serving the present age means caring for people in meaningful, personal ways, using the same compassion and love Jesus showed during his ministry here on earth.

▶ PASTORS MAKE A DIFFERENCE

One of the early professional experiences that shaped my ministry took place during my seminary years as an associate pastor at College Church of the Nazarene in Olathe, Kansas.

The senior pastor, Paul Cunningham, received a phone call all pastors dread. A young couple and their beautiful little daughter were going away on a holiday trip to visit relatives. They were involved in a fatal accident on a Kansas highway.

As Paul and I rode down the road to the hospital we talked about the importance of a pastor being there when people need you. We entered the hospital room of the husband, Ron, with the news that his wife and little girl had not survived the crash. I observed how Pastor Paul seemed to know when it was appropriate to say words of encouragement and support, and when to simply stand at Ron's bedside as he wept and mourned the loss of his family. This was my first experience of walking with a man and his extended family through the planning of the funeral and the following months of grief work. I watched Ron as he found that his faith could help him through the toughest experiences life could throw at him.

Such moments are never easy for a pastor. You hurt with the family. There is also the responsibility of speaking a word from God at the funeral that will relate to the grieving loved ones and the larger church family. This can be a time of high stress and deep emotions. Yet, from that first experience of tragedy I learned that the pastor can make a difference. We stand humbly as undershepherds of that Great Shepherd, Jesus Christ, and at that moment become conduits or dispensers of God's grace. It is at once humbling and thrilling to be a pastor who cares for people in the name of Jesus.

▸ QUESTIONS FOR REFLECTION

▹ Why is it important to understand that pastoral care has been a part of the biblical and historical record of the Church and not simply an invention of the Church in the last one hundred years?

▹ Why do people turn first to a pastor for care and counsel rather than to someone outside a church setting? What advantages and disadvantages do pastors have over other healing professionals?

▹ What do you perceive to be the most difficult aspect of pastoral care for the minister personally and for the pastor's family?

▹ What are some of the unique challenges to providing pastoral care in the twenty-first century?

TWO

PROVIDING PASTORAL SOUL CARE

As Denise McDonald completed her first two months as a youth pastor, she gave herself a B grade. Her activities with the teens, although fun, had not produced the spiritual development she had hoped for when she arrived at Living Community Church.

Pastor Denise sat staring out the window, reflecting on her ministry, when the office door opened and a sophomore girl named Megan plopped herself down on the worn sofa across the room.

Megan was not from a church family but had been attending the youth activities regularly with her friend Kim. After some small talk about school and the weather, Megan revealed the real reason for her visit.

"My boyfriend has been pressuring me to do some things I just don't feel comfortable doing. He says that there really isn't any meaning in life beyond intimacy, so why not go ahead if we love each other. I've been watching some of the people in the youth group, especially Kim. She does seem to have something I don't have. When I ask her about it, she says it's because Jesus has come into her life. I don't know anything about this religious stuff, and it all kind of freaks me out. But I thought, you know, since you are a pastor and all that, that you might be able to help me out."

That afternoon Pastor Denise shared the good news of the gospel and Megan responded by faith to the call of Christ. At the end of their conversation Denise shared the importance of developing this new relationship with Jesus through prayer and Bible study. She set a time for Megan to come back in two days with Kim to begin the process of spiritual growth and development. As Denise thought later, maybe some of the spiritual seeds planted in the youth meetings had begun to take root after all. And there was the personal satisfaction of being a midwife at a spiritual birth.

Denise had to admit at that moment—nothing is more rewarding than helping the teens in her care find spiritual answers to their life questions.

▶ A DOCTOR FOR THE SOUL

John Frye, in his penetrating book *Jesus the Pastor*, tells of his experience working his way through seminary in a medical hospital.

One night an attractive woman came into the emergency room, her lip split open and eye swollen nearly shut, obviously as a result of a fight with someone. She began to relate an all-too-common tale of an abusive husband who struck her several times outside a bar. This woman wept openly, not so much from the physical wounds but in fear of what her husband in his drunken state might even now be doing to their children.

While John Frye helped calm the woman as the medical staff did what they could to stitch the cuts and reduce the swelling to her face, he realized that there was a deeper pain, radiating out from the spiritual part of her life, that could not be fixed with a bandage. As he watched the woman leave the hospital, a much more fundamental question began to form in his mind, "But who will doctor her soul?"[1]

▶ WHAT IS SOUL CARE?

In one sense soul care refers to everything a pastor does in ministry—from administering the sacraments and preaching, to visitation and administration. But across the centuries the term has been interpreted in a more restrictive manner.

Thomas Oden says, "In a narrow sense, the care of souls has come to refer to a more intensive part of that larger task, a personal ministry of conversation . . . the quiet sphere of one-on-one meeting with persons who look to pastors for interpersonal, moral, and spiritual guidance."[2] In his book *Care of Souls,* David Benner defines the task of soul care as "the support and restoration of the well-being of persons in their depth and totality, with particular concern for their inner life."[3]

Jesus demonstrated in the Gospels what it means to care for the total needs of people. His heart was filled with compassion for those who had suffered with physical diseases and handicaps. In just two chapters, beginning with Luke 4, Jesus cast out the unclean spirit from a man, healed Peter's mother-in-law of a high fever, helped some disciples catch fish, cured a man of leprosy, raised a paralytic, and called a despised tax collector named Levi to be one of his disciples. Not only did he have concern for individuals, but in Luke 8 he multiplied loaves and fish to a crowd of thousands who had not brought provisions when they came out to hear him teach. Jesus, on at least three occasions, raised dead people back to life again.

But there was something that would outlive handicaps, hunger, and even death. Jesus never promised that he would heal everyone who would come to him. The one thing he included in his universal invitation to everyone weighed down with burdens and concerns was, simply, rest for the soul.

He said, "Take my yoke upon you and learn from me, for I am gentle and humble in heart, and you will find rest for your souls" (Matt. 11:29). Because God created humans with the unique ability to make moral choices, he never forced people into a spiritual relationship. Jesus never tried to lure people into the Kingdom by trickery or insincere offers of cheap grace. Instead, he planted the seeds of the gospel through his teachings and allowed them to germinate in the hearts and minds of the listeners until they responded.

Jesus also revealed the ultimate value of our souls when he said in Matt. 16:26, "What good will it be for a man if he gains the whole world, yet forfeits his soul? Or what can a man give in exchange for his soul?" The message of John 3:16 is clear. God values people so much that his Son Jesus died on the Cross so that we could enjoy forgiveness and a spiritual relationship with God forever. If Jesus placed that value on the care of souls, it should take a place of high importance for anyone in ministry.

Benner cites William Clebsch and Charles Jaekle as suggesting that there have been four elements of soul care across the history of the Christian Church: healing, sustaining, reconciling, and guiding.

Healing means helping people toward wholeness, whether it is the physical, emotional, or spiritual healing of an individual. *Sustaining* involves helping people facing difficult circumstances survive and triumph, even when ultimate victory may seem improbable. *Reconciling* deals with the mending of broken relationships, whether these divisions are between individuals or groups within the church body. *Guiding* refers to leading people in making wise choices within the context of a growing spiritual maturity.[4]

▶ SOUL CARE FOR A NEW MILLENNIUM

During much of the twentieth century the idea of soul fell into disfavor in our modern world. One couldn't take a photograph or an X ray of a soul. A soul couldn't be jammed into a test tube or examined under an electron microscope. Social scientists took the position that the soul was an obsolete concept from the unenlightened past, not unlike the flat-earth theory in science.

With the cultural shift to a postmodern worldview, interest in the soul and the spiritual dimension is in vogue again. Moviegoers and television viewers are drawn to stories about psychics, or angelic and demonic manifestations that suggest a spiritual plane of reality waiting to be explored. People regularly consult mediums who claim the power to contact and communicate with the souls of dead loved ones. Many who at one time would have scoffed at the very idea of having a spiritual component now surf the Internet or call hotlines to learn more about their soul side. It is sad that many postmoderns believe in the spiritual and the supernatural but do not believe they will find the answers to their questions in Christianity.

For others, the mysteries of the spiritual world are simply too complex to understand. They hire personal trainers to build muscles and dietitians to plan a healthy eating regimen, but they would never think of consulting a pastor who could help them respond to the deep yearning to have an intimate, personal relationship with God.

Pastors could be likened to doctors of the soul—showing concern for the whole being with particular attention to the inner life of people. Many pastors develop an inferiority complex around other healing professionals, feeling that perhaps working with people's spiritual dimension is either less important or less scientific. Yet pastors have the opportunity to partner with other professionals to promote wholeness. They may encourage people to seek medical help when physical problems arise. Counselors and pastors can work hand in hand to assist people in finding mental and emotional wholeness. But pastors are trained and skilled to help people develop their spiritual lives under the direction of the Holy Spirit. For those doctors who work with the physical body, their effectiveness ends when the person dies. The pastor, on the other hand, has the opportunity to help prepare people to live on in relationship with God for eternity.

▸ THE CONTEXT OF SOUL CARE

Soul care takes place within a Christian community. While other religions emphasize individualism and solitary practices, the Bible stresses the importance of relationships.

A study of the passages where Paul uses the words "one another" reveals the importance of Christians effectively relating to others in the Body of Christ. It is a misconception to think that the only people who are responsible for soul care are the ordained ministers. One of the rediscovered themes of the Protestant Reformation was the priesthood of all believers. Paul, in Eph. 4, is clear that all the people of God are to do the works of ministry in the church. Any believer can provide soul care by encouraging, supporting, burden bearing, guiding, and developing accountability with another person. Whether in a church of ten or ten thousand, people need to feel a sense of belonging; that others know and care about their souls.

Pastors, as spiritual shepherds, do have a special role in the care of the people of the church. However, if the pastor is the only soul care provider, the church cannot grow beyond the number of people that a pastor is physically able to care for. Some pastors are unwilling to share in soul care ministries because they are afraid that others will not do as well. Others are unwilling to share the satisfaction of helping people with anyone else. This attitude is pure selfishness and has no place in pastoral ministry. The answer is not hiring more pastors in a church but developing more lay providers. Any pastor can multiply the ministry of the church by training laypeople to assist in giving care that provides wholeness, physically, mentally, socially, and spiritually. It is not enough for the pastor to be a caring person. A good shepherd will motivate others to help care for the needs of people and become a ministering congregation.

Many churches are developing effective programs where laypeople in the church provide soul care for one another. In a typical program, lay volunteers gather at the church one night each week to express care and concern for those in special need. Some make phone calls to those who have been ill or are facing serious problems. Others write notes of encouragement to people who may have been absent from the services. One group goes to visit in the homes of needy people or visitors to the church. Another group prays for each person or family receiving ministry from the church that evening. Such programs respond to the variety of needs within the congregation with both concern and spiritual support through prayer.

▶ THE CHARACTER OF CAREGIVERS

When they call a pastor, churches are understandably concerned that they get the right person for their congregation. But how do churches know they have selected the right person? Pastoral ministry is one profession where the character of the person may be every bit as important as the skills for ministry.

Back in the 1970s the Association of Theological Schools conducted a survey to discover what churches were seeking in a new pastor. Louis Bloede summarizes the results.

"Service without regard for acclaim" received the highest ranking. Ranked second was "personal integrity." The third highest factor had to do with Christian example, being "a person that people in the community can respect." Not until we get to the fourth place do we find mention of specific pastoral skills. This factor describes a person "who shows competence and responsibility by completing tasks, by being able to handle differences of opinions, and who senses the need to continue to grow in pastoral skills."[5]

Pastors responsible for the care of souls draw personal resources for ministry from the reservoir of their own spiritual relationship with God. Howard Rice writes, "But the principal tool of pastors is not a particular skill or technique; it is our very being. The principal tool for the work of pastoral ministry is one's own faith."[6]

Francis of Assisi was a well-to-do gentleman focused on his own personal needs when he came upon a beggar. As he looked at this unfortunate man, he was shocked to discover that the man's face was the face of Christ. It was that spiritual encounter with Jesus that changed the life direction of Francis. He began a ministry to the hungry, the poor, the sick, and the destitute around the village of Assisi, bringing light to the dark ages. The words of his familiar thirteenth-century prayer are appropriate for the twenty-first-century pastor.

> *Lord, make me an instrument of thy peace:*
> *Where there is hatred, let me sow love;*
> *Where there is injury, pardon;*
> *Where there is doubt, faith;*
> *Where there is despair, hope;*
> *Where there is darkness, light;*
> *Where there is sadness, joy.*
> *O divine Master, grant that I may not so much seek*
> *To be consoled as to console,*
> *To be understood as to understand,*
> *To be loved as to love;*
> *For it is in giving that we receive;*
> *It is in pardoning that we are pardoned;*
> *It is in dying that we are born to eternal life!*

People today have a deep hunger to experience something beyond their own ordinary existence. They are convinced there is the answer to this mystery of life, somewhere out there. They are not concerned about the color of the carpets or whether you sing from a hymnal or words projected on a screen. The fact that postmoderns hunger for spiritual fulfillment is really a sign of their hunger for God. This spiritual reality can only be found through an authentic spiritual relationship with Christ. Jesus' term "born again" from John 3 is really a spiritual awakening any person can experience.

▶ A SPIRITUAL GUIDE

For pastors, soul care can involve becoming a spiritual guide.

During the expansion of the United States in the second half of the nineteenth century, large wagon trains would join together to journey westward. Their dreams usually involved cheap land and new opportunities. Because there were few marked trails, the wagon train would hire a wagon master to give leadership to the group. This person's job was clear: to help the travelers arrive safely at their destination. A good guide understood how to work with people. He knew how to stay alive in the wilderness and had a good understanding of the trail. The wagon master often employed scouts who would ride ahead to find the best path to negotiate the next section of the trail. The leader of the wagon train had one advantage over the other travelers. He had traveled this trail before. He knew the dangers, the hardships ahead, and what was needed to survive the arduous journey. Without a wagon master it would have been difficult for the pioneers to arrive at their destination, or even survive.

Being a soul guide is a serious task. Fortunately for pastors and laypeople alike, providing soul care is not a purely human endeavor. Jesus promised the presence of the Holy Spirit within the life of every believer. "But the Counselor, the Holy Spirit, whom the Father will send in my name, will teach you all things and will remind you of everything I have said to you" (John 14:26). In addition, God extends his grace to his believers to aid in their growth and development. These "means of grace" promote maturity and development for Christians through the practice of spiritual disciplines.

Howard Rice mentions eight specific disciplines: (1) *Prayer,* which is basic to the Christian life. Pastors can provide many models for different personality types and temperaments. (2) *Reading Scripture* provides a way of hearing God's voice and receiving instructions for living. (3) *Meditation* is a way to focus on a word, concept, or scripture in silence and allow God to bring insights to one's mind. (4) *Feasting and fasting.* Fasting is denying something of value, food or activity, for a period of time to increase one's concentration in prayer. Feasting involves enjoying the good gifts of God with a heart of gratitude. (5) *Serving others* allows us to be the physical presence of Christ in the middle of someone's need. Whether we give food to the hungry or comfort to the hurting, we find that ministering to others brings blessings to our own lives. (6) *Worship and sacraments* usually come first to our minds when we think of the means of grace. When we gather together as the Body of Christ to acknowledge God's worth and regularly receive the sacrament of the Lord's Supper we experience oneness with Christ and fellow believers. (7) *Holy readings* allow us to connect with the great Christian writers of the past as well as contemporary spiritual authors. And (8) *Sabbath rest* provides a break from the hectic pace of our weekly schedule to renew the physical and spiritual dimensions of our lives. A pastor can guide the congregation to value these spiritual disciplines and experience the grace of God in a greater measure.[7]

▶ BECOMING A SPIRITUAL GUIDE

The whole subject of spiritual guidance or spiritual direction has been rediscovered by Protestants, largely through the writings of Roman Catholic writers of the past and present. Contemporary evangelical authors such as

Richard Foster, Dallas Willard, and Eugene Peterson now encourage pastors to not only seek a spiritual director for their own lives but also understand their responsibility to be spiritual directors to others. Peterson, in his book *Working the Angles: The Shape of Pastoral Integrity*, says that there are three "angles" of pastoral ministry every pastor needs to develop in order to survive in the parish: prayer, Scripture, and spiritual direction. When addressing the third angle he writes:

> Spiritual direction takes place when two people agree to give their full attention to what God is doing in one (or both) of their lives and seek to respond in faith. More often than not for pastors, these convergent and devout attentions are brief and unplanned; at other times they are planned and structured conversations. Whether planned or unplanned, three convictions underpin these meetings: (1) God is always doing something: an active grace is shaping this life into a mature salvation; (2) responding to God is not sheer guesswork; the Christian community has acquired wisdom through the centuries that provides guidance; (3) each soul is unique; no wisdom can simply be applied without discerning the particulars of this life, this situation.[8]

Rice uses the term *spiritual guidance* as the way a pastor comes alongside a person in the church who needs spiritual help for the journey.

> Spiritual guidance is the process of pointing people and groups, small or large, beyond the visible realities to the reality of God as the One without whom we cannot possibly understand our present situation. Guidance uses the insights and skills of spiritual direction and will use trained spiritual directors for referral. . . . This guidance takes place in the way a leader assists a person, a group, or a congregation to pay attention to the ways God is at work in their lives, individually and corporately. Spiritual guidance is less structured and formal than spiritual direction.[9]

There are times when a pastor will enter into a more formalized agreement with a person or small group to provide spiritual direction. The pastor may take on the role of teacher for the benefit of the instructed. However, the relationship can also be designed for the mutual growth and development of everyone involved. After all, a pastor needs to be accountable to people who can provide encouragement and affirmation. In some cases, such as working with someone of the opposite sex, the pastor may feel another person could be more effective in providing spiritual direction. A part of the pastor's role as a spiritual guide is to train other mature people to be guides and make sure those who desire spiritual direction receive it from someone. Spiritual guidance includes understanding the level of faith development among various members of the congregation. Pastors need to give special attention to those who have sinned or are falling away from the faith. The apostle Paul gives wise counsel to pastors and other church leaders in Gal. 6:1-2: "Brothers, if someone is caught in a sin, you who are spiritual should restore him gently. But watch yourself, or you also may be tempted. Carry each other's burdens, and in this way you will fulfill the law of Christ."

▶ QUALITIES OF A SPIRITUAL GUIDE

How can a pastor be an effective spiritual guide for the people of God? Some of the skills are similar to those of a good counselor. However, since spiritual issues are paramount here, there are unique qualifications for spiritual guidance.

A SENSITIVITY TO THE SPIRITUAL NEEDS OF OTHERS

Jesus had his spiritual antennae working when the Samaritan woman in John 4 came walking up to the well outside of Sychar. He recognized the woman needed more than a jar of well water. It wasn't simply a remedy for her unhappy home situation; this woman needed spiritual water that only Jesus could give.

Whether we are in our office or waiting in a checkout line at the supermarket, we need to look beyond the surface issues to the deeper spiritual issues in people's lives.

Recently a young man came by a pastor's house to do some electrical work. This pastor knew that the young man had been active in his local church in the past, so the pastor asked him how things were going spiritually. He hung his head and admitted that his colleagues at his previous place of work had been a bad influence. "I quit working there," he said, "but I'm still not where I need to be spiritually." As the two talked there in the basement, the young man admitted that, although he had confessed his sin, he had a hunger to know the joy he had experienced in the past. The pastor had the privilege of sharing with him some ways he could begin growing spiritually again. The Holy Spirit used an unplanned encounter to get this young believer back on track spiritually.

A WILLINGNESS TO PREPARE ONE'S OWN SOUL SPIRITUALLY

Paul reminds the Ephesians that "our struggle is not against flesh and blood, but against the rulers, against the authorities, against the powers of this dark world and against the spiritual forces of evil in the heavenly realms" (6:12). When pastors guide people spiritually, Satan and his forces inevitably show up, attempting to do anything to prevent spiritual progress. To do spiritual interventions requires that a pastor be prepared. Paul's advice is clear, "Therefore put on the full armor of God, so that when the day of evil comes, you may be able to stand your ground, and after you have done everything, to stand" (v. 13).

A pastor whose spiritual fuel tanks are constantly on empty cannot really be of much help to others.

AN ABILITY TO LISTEN WITH FULL FOCUS

What are the qualities necessary to be a good listener? Most skillful listeners have the ability to set aside everything distracting and concentrate on what the speaker has to say. Pastors who preach may think that talking is hard work. Actually, listening is much more difficult because it demands the focus of one's full attention, both on the words the other person is saying and the silent messages communicated by facial expressions and body language. Good listeners resist the temptation to be thinking of what to answer rather than staying engaged in the other person's communication.

Paying full attention to what someone is saying is one way of letting the other person know we value him or her as well as the message. Spiritual guides are also listening to the inner impressions of the Holy Spirit as he interprets even the deep feelings the person is not saying, so we can better understand what is communicated.

A RESISTANCE TO THE TEMPTATION TO CONTROL THE OTHER PERSON

It is easy to slip from being a spiritual guide to being a domineering parent. This is especially true if the pastor is older or has been in the faith longer.

Some pastors, in an attempt to guide, have created a dependency relationship so strong that the one being discipled is unable to make a decision alone. People in the church should never become dependent on the pastor, but on God. And there is the authority of Scripture to which all believers must submit. When a pastor gives spiritual guidance on a subject, the Scriptures can often provide an authoritative answer. But even in those situations, it is also important to be sensitive to what the Holy Spirit is saying to the person. Until the Spirit reveals truth to an individual, what a pastor may say does not carry much authority. Often when a pastor gives spiritual suggestions without undue pressure, the person is able to respond appropriately under the Holy Spirit's leadership.

AN ACQUAINTANCE WITH THE DISCIPLINES THAT MOST BENEFIT THE OTHER PERSON

A spiritual guide who understands and practices the spiritual disciplines will be able to lead people to experience their benefits. The means of grace are available to all believers who desire to mature in the faith. A wise pastor will try to have resources available or be able to suggest resources that would help those who would like to learn more about developing one or more of the spiritual disciplines.

A WILLINGNESS TO LOVINGLY CONFRONT AREAS OF CHANGE WITH THE HOLY SPIRIT'S GUIDANCE

The pastor, as shepherd, is responsible for the spiritual well-being of the sheep. The willingness of a member of the flock to listen to pastoral guidance is greatly affected by the confidence this person has in the character of the pastor.

It took courage for the prophet Nathan, after telling the story of a rich man who stole a poor neighbor's lamb, to point his bony finger at King David and say, "You are the man" who has stolen another man's wife. Confronting sin or areas of neglect is never easy. Pastors need to check their own motives and feelings to be sure this is God's timing and the proper place for such a confrontation. Hebrews tells us that no discipline is pleasant at the time. Some pastors, because of their nature, would rather avoid such conflict. However, to be a faithful shepherd means that sometimes a person needs to be confronted about wrongdoing, out of a heart motivated by deep, agape love for the person.

AN AWARENESS OF BEING AN AGENT OF GOD'S GRACE TO OTHERS

Ministers have the wonderful privilege, from time to time, of declaring or dispensing a word of God's grace to others. Some pastors have been so afraid, as Protestants, to in any way come off as claiming the power of forgiving sins that they have avoided proclaiming to others the forgiveness and freedom God has promised. True, Jesus himself said that no one could forgive sins but God alone. But believers have the privilege of declaring that what Jesus has provided for by his death on the Cross has been applied to this person.

Many people continue to live under the condemnation of past acts of sin, even after they have been forgiven by God. "God just couldn't forgive that," they say. If a person has honestly confessed a sin, the spiritual guide has the right and responsibility to announce, "On the authority of the Word of God, I declare that your sin has been forgiven in the name of Jesus Christ." Jesus made it very plain in John 8:36, "So if the Son sets you free, you will be free indeed." God's grace is not just freedom from the past but freedom to live a life of glorious freedom now. The Book of Galatians has been called the Magna Charta of Christian Liberty because it makes clear that we no longer live under the Law but under grace. And spiritual guides have the privilege of encouraging people to experience real freedom in Christ.

AN ENCOURAGER THAT GIVES FAITH TO MOVE AHEAD

In Acts 4:36 Luke introduces the reader to a man named Joseph who is much better known by his nickname. Some people are given nicknames like Shorty or Slim, because of physical characteristics. Joseph got his label because he liked to encourage people. Somebody probably said, "Let's call him Barnabas," which meant Son of Encouragement, and the name stuck. The Jerusalem church sent him up to Antioch and he did what came naturally—he encouraged the church. When Barnabas and Paul took their first missionary trip, Barnabas invited his cousin John Mark to go along. When Mark quit the trip and went home, Barnabas encouraged him to try again, even though it meant that Paul and Barnabas split up over the issue. It was the encouragement of Barnabas that helped John Mark become Paul's valuable coworker later, and the writer of the Gospel bearing his name.

Most people can look back to someone who gave a word of encouragement in a discouraging moment when it would have been easier to give up. While being an encourager is the most natural thing in the world for some, most people have to work at it. Yet this is an indispensable skill that anyone can master with the Holy Spirit's help. As an encourager you are the instrument of God who desires that all of his children make it victoriously. Your word can make a difference.

▸ THE PRIVILEGE OF BEING A SPIRITUAL GUIDE

The auction sale seemed to be the final memorial for this man of God. Both he and his wife passed away within too brief a period of time. Neither lived to be sixty. Life had ended too soon. God had called him more than thirty years ago to pastor a church in a small community of about two hundred in the northern United States. Until he suffered severe injuries in a car accident, he was the pastor not only of his own church but also of the whole community. This pastor served with the volunteer firemen, sat daily and drank coffee with the regulars at the local café, prayed at community functions, performed funerals for the unchurched, and did all the other things a pastor with a heart for the people of the town would do. His car accident and subsequent bout with cancer took his life and left a tremendous debt for the family to somehow pay. Then his wife died of cancer a short time later. The auction became the responsibility of one of the adult sons who lived there in the small community.

Item by item, the collection of the earthly goods that represented the life of this pastor and wife were auctioned away. As the community watched, something amazing began to happen. The prices the items were bringing were inflated. Some things sold for more than what they would be worth if they were new. Someone in the crowd was asked why the bids were going so high. He said, "For many of these people, this man had been their pastor even though they never set foot inside his church. It is their way of saying thank you to his family for his many years of ministry among us. They were saying, 'You cared for me as a person and this is one way I can help out.'"

What a wonderful tribute to a couple who dedicated their adult lives to caring for a small community of people and a local church, in a town that isn't much more than a tiny dot on a map. This pastoral couple understood the value of soul care. And whenever their names are mentioned in the region around this small village, people will remember their spiritual concern with a smile.

▶ QUESTIONS FOR REFLECTION

▷ Why is soul care a Christian function?

▷ Why is soul care best done within the context of a Christian community?

▷ What can people entering ministry today learn from Jesus' spiritual concern as shown in the Gospels?

▷ What are the most important qualities a pastor should demonstrate to be an effective spiritual guide?

THREE

UNLEASHING THE LAITY

Pete and Heather Johnson were exhausted—physically, mentally, and proba-bly spiritually. For a little over a year now they had been copastors of their first church in a bedroom community next to a large city. The church had been so excit-ed about the Johnsons coming and were generally positive about their copastor arrangement. It had been a grueling seventy-five-hour workweek for the pair. The climax came on a nonstop Sunday of leading the worship music, preaching, teach-ing Sunday School classes, making afternoon hospital calls, and each leading a small group in the evening. Heather was the one who first voiced the suspicion both had been sensing for some time.

"I think the real reason they like two pastors," Heather reflected, "is that they feel they have solved their labor problem. We do all the ministry while they stand back and watch. It's a pretty good deal for them, I'd say."

Pete thought for a moment before answering, "I've been hearing some grum-bling about people not feeling very involved anymore. And the new converts, they haven't really matured the way they should by this time. Mary and J. P. Jones are very talented, godly people, but they seem to just be going through the motions. I sense that they are starting to disconnect from the fellowship. Something is definitely wrong."

"I've noticed the same thing," Heather replied. "It seems like the harder we work, the less the church people do."

"It reminds me of playing basketball in college. I used to go over to the coach, exhausted, during a timeout. The band played and the crowd cheered, but they didn't contribute anything else. I often thought that if I could drag some of those people out of the stands and down on the playing floor where they could get involved, it could make the difference. That wasn't realistic, but you know what I mean."

They were silent for a few moments before Heather finally spoke. "Pete, do you think we have contributed to our own problem? We both sang in college choir, so we assumed we could do a better job with the music than they could. We both teach Sunday School classes because of our training, even though there are others who could teach."

"You're right, Heather!" Pete said. "We've taken on their jobs because we thought we could do it better. Sometimes we have felt satisfaction from doing the job well, but we have also robbed them of the joy of ministry. And besides, it has also

pushed us to the point of exhaustion. This may be the reason some people have seemed restless and unfulfilled around the church."

"You may be right about the problem. The question is: what do we do about it?"

▶ EVERY BELIEVER A MINISTER

In the last quarter century pastors have been awakening to the truth that for much of the Church's history it has operated on a wrong premise—that paid pastors were the only ones who could and should do ministry. In fact, every believer is called to be a minister. Elton Trueblood wrote these revolutionary words back in the 1950s:

> Whatever a person's ordinary vocation in the world, whether salesmanship or homemaking or farming, the ministry can be his other vocation and perhaps his truest vocation. Most vocations are mutually incompatible, but the ministry is compatible with all others, providing they are productive of human welfare.[1]

Lay ministry is essential to the church's health and its ability to express concern for others. The emphasis of this chapter will lay the foundation for the next chapter on lay pastoral care.

▶ THE NEW TESTAMENT ROLE

D. James Kennedy in the 1970s reminded the Church how Christians had misread Eph. 4:11-12, "It was he who gave some to be apostles, some to be prophets, some to be evangelists, and some to be pastors and teachers, to prepare God's people for works of service, so that the body of Christ may be built up."

It was never God's intention for those who had been called to fill the roles mentioned in verse 11 to be doing all the "works of service." The apostles, prophets, evangelists, and especially the pastors and teachers are instead charged with the responsibility of equipping and empowering "God's people for works of service, so that the body of Christ may be built up." For too long the ordained clergy were the ones "hired" to do the work of ministry, with the church looking on, waiting to be challenged to do part of the work. To use a military metaphor, imagine a general whose country is being invaded saying to the troops, "I am the professional and have been hired to fight the enemy. You have not been to military school, but I have. Watch me as I bravely go out to engage the enemy myself." That's absurd. If our country was being invaded, anyone who could do anything to help out would be called into action. With the forces of evil engaged against the Church, Paul exhorts everyone (not just pastors) in Eph. 6 to put on the full armor of God and take a stand.

In Acts 6 the Early Church faced up to the problem of too many needs and too few clergy. The twelve apostles did not have the time to oversee the daily food distribution to the widows as well as giving spiritual leadership to the growing community of believers. In a move that could only be inspired by God himself, the apostles appointed seven nonclergymen who were full of the Holy Spirit and wisdom to take charge of this daily ministry. And with that, lay ministry was born.

The apostle Peter in 1 Pet. 2:5 challenged the people of the Church to be "a holy priesthood, offering spiritual sacrifices acceptable to God through Jesus Christ." While Martin Luther made much of this concept of the priesthood of all believers, it took the Protestant Church nearly five hundred years to apply it to ministry. Bruce Larson says, "The best measure of a church is how many people walk out to be the royal priesthood on Monday and Tuesday and Wednesday. The basic product of the church is people in ministry."[2]

▶ WHY DOESN'T IT HAPPEN?

One would think that pastors would be thrilled with any help in doing ministry. Yet they are often the ones dragging their feet.

Some pastors view lay ministry as an intrusion into their own work domain. It means relinquishing control, and some see that as a clear threat. For others, it is an issue of quality. People who are not as well trained cannot be expected to do as good a job. And providing training can be hard work. Sometimes it is just easier to do it yourself. There is also the issue of affirmation. Some pastors thrive on the attention they receive for their work and do not want to share that with anyone else. Then there is the risk that if laypeople take on a ministry and fail, it may reflect negatively on the pastor's leadership of the church. Dale Galloway writes:

> The pastor must first change perspective and practice before lay ministry can flourish. Such change may be difficult because so many ministers have for years been steeped by their preparation and practice to believe real ministry has to be done by them. In this concept, laypersons were welcome to assist, but the ordained head of the church was the one who did real ministry.[3]

Laypeople also are hesitant to jump on board with lay ministry. Some feel they are inadequate to take on the responsibility for ministering to the needs of others. It may take on the form of a false humility—"Oh, I just couldn't do that." Or, people may look at the pastor's professional education and say,

"There's no way I can match that knowledge and experience." Fear of failing is another barrier. There is the false conception that pastors have all or at least most of the answers because they are more spiritual and have a direct connection to God. This is really a faith issue. The power to do any ministry comes from the Holy Spirit, not simply because one has training or a title. No one has all the answers. Everyone has fears and feelings of inadequacy from time to time. But believers are made adequate through Christ, who enables each one to do what he calls us to do by the Holy Spirit's power.

▶ DEFINING TERMS

Maybe one reason many struggle with the concept of lay ministry is found in the meaning of the term *ministry.* One layman, William Diehl, in his book *Ministry in Daily Life,* has found it useful to speak of four arenas of ministry: one's occupation, family, community, and church. He says, "As Christians, we have one calling, the universal calling to ministry. We can answer that call with simultaneous ministries in the four arenas cited above."[4] While this may seem to say that everything in life is ministry, Diehl says that anything destructive to the kingdom of God or to others is not ministry. "What protects or extends God's creation is ministry."[5] A simple way to define the term *ministry* would be: anything one does for others as a servant of God that is consistent with biblical principles.

Categorizing ministry is also a challenge. Bruce Larson identifies four kinds of ministry: (1) *material ministry,* involving giving money or material goods; (2) *spiritual ministry or evangelism,* leading to conversion and discipleship; (3) *healing ministry,* which leads to mental, physical, or emotional wholeness; and (4) *prophetic ministry,* which works to bring change within social structures or society as a whole.[6]

It is important not to limit ministry to those things that can be done in the context of a local church alone. For us to be salt and light to others, ministry needs to be extended to the world in which believers live and work most of the week besides Sunday.

What is driving this new emphasis on lay ministry? In part, it is because laypeople have demonstrated that they are capable of doing a wide variety of ministries, both inside and outside the church. There are many skills and tasks where laypeople are actually more qualified than their pastor. People today have much higher expectations of what the church must provide in a community. This may require a technical competence that may be far beyond the pastor's ability. For instance, a pastor's expertise and knowledge of computers may be much less than a high school student in the church. Why not give that high schooler an opportunity to utilize his or her skills in electronic technology in a way that can benefit the entire church. This can give a person a sense of belonging as he or she is contributing to the ongoing ministry of the church.

More and more churches are placing high expectations on those who join the church. For them, being a member is more than just showing up on Sunday. Involvement means finding a ministry and doing it. Laypeople have discovered that ministry provides an opportunity to make an eternal difference, and that in itself provides motivation and reward. Almost all ministries are in some way, directly or indirectly, acts of caring for others.

▶ MAKING DISCIPLES INTO MINISTERS

During the Vietnam War, the United States government was calling up young men and women by the thousands to serve in the military. Most who went to fight didn't go voluntarily. They were drafted. There were some who disagreed with the war or just didn't want to go where their lives were in danger. Some fled the country rather than serve. Many who were inducted begrudgingly served not out of a love for country but because they were forced to do so. The draft did not lift morale and often negatively affected productivity.

Some pastors today would like to institute a spiritual draft to get people to work in the church. If they could just force everyone to take on a job, the church labor shortage could be solved immediately. But since a draft wouldn't work, they try high-pressure recruiting tactics. When some people see the pastor or church recruiter coming down the church hall, they hide in the janitor's closet. Others leave for another church if the pressure gets too intense. There is a better way.

One excellent model is found at Frazer Memorial United Methodist Church in Montgomery, Alabama. George Hunter III reports that 83 percent of the 7,500 members of the church are involved in one of approximately two hundred ministries. One reason for the high involvement figure is the concept of volunteerism rather than recruiting. Each November the church distributes a "Ministry Menu" that lists the ministry opportunities for the following year. People can list their first or second choices on the menu. Once volunteers are connected to ministries, they are trained in January for a one-year responsibility. At the end of the year a person can volunteer to continue with that ministry or choose another one without feeling guilty or intimidated. If no one volunteers for a ministry, the leadership doesn't worry about it. Perhaps God is saying that the ministry is no longer needed. The primary responsibility of the staff is to train, coach, and facilitate those laypeople who are carrying out the ministry. People in the church frequently hear testimonies of laypeople who find great fulfillment in their ministry. But ministry is more than mere activity. Those in charge of lay ministry at Frazer Memorial look carefully at each purpose of each ministry. Will this activity meet a need and make disciples?[7]

Ed Mathison, pastor of Frazer Memorial, reports that in using the volunteer method, God makes the assignments to individuals. Laypeople themselves become very creative when taking on a responsibility to provide ministry. He says, "If you trust laypeople and they trust you, you can set them free to do unbelievable accomplishments for God. The caution is the control needs of the pastor. The challenge is to set laity free to think, create, and do great things for the King."[8]

▶ EQUIPPING THE WORKFORCE

Serving in the Kingdom begins with an understanding of our spiritual giftedness. When one becomes a believer, the Holy Spirit gives that person one or more spiritual gifts to help build the Church of Christ. The New Testament in Rom. 12, 1 Cor. 12, and Eph. 4 mentions a number of spiritual gifts given to the various members of a church. When people understand their unique gift mix, they have a better idea of where they can best serve in the church. Discovering spiritual gifts is a wonderful way to help people find ministries where they feel comfortable. There are a number of books and other resources available to help a church identify the spiritual gifts of its members.[9]

In addition to evaluating spiritual gifts there is an effective tool to assess the spiritual growth and maturity of the people in your congregation as they investigate ministry opportunities. David Slamp has written a ninety-six-item questionnaire to appraise a person's spiritual development in twelve areas of discipline: worship, personal devotion, giving, lay ministry, Bible knowledge, missions, fellowship, witnessing, attitude toward ministry, distinctive lifestyle, service, and social justice. This survey can help a pastor design a preaching and teaching program to help address some of the weaknesses within the congregation.[10]

Any layperson who is going to assume a new task in the church needs to be trained to do it effectively. Training is important, yet it is estimated that over 90 percent of laypeople receive no equipping to do ministry. By providing training for someone, the church is saying to that person, *You are important and the task is important enough for the church to invest time and energy to help you do it well.* Paul's challenge to pastors in Eph. 4:12 ("to prepare God's people for works of service") is very simple: train people to minister.

Training is best done in the context of the local church. Some churches do their equipping as a part of the Sunday morning adult education program. Others train during weeknight sessions, weekend seminars, once-a-month regional seminars, or concentrated one-month sessions. One church had a training program for lay leadership that required a commitment of at least twenty hours a week for over two years.

Classroom training may be very general, teaching material such as learning more about the Bible, or very specific instruction on how to share one's faith or care for needy people. One effective way to provide technical training for a task is to have the trainee observe, ask questions, and participate with a veteran on the job. Training also has a motivating element, catching from the mentor the anticipation of doing ministry in Jesus' name.

Jim Garlow cites Ken Van Wyke's study of churches that effectively train laypeople for ministry. "Surprisingly, [Van Wyke] found the one common ingredient that was always present in high function laity churches and always absent in low-functioning laity churches. It was a sense of excitement about doing Christ's work that flowed through the entire congregation."[11]

▶ THE MOTIVATION FACTOR

Back in the "clergy-dominated ministry" era, the way growing churches expanded ministries was to hire more staff to do the work. Today, as more churches have adopted the lay ministry approach, the strategy has changed. George Barna, in his book *The Habits of Highly Effective Churches,* reveals that these highly effective churches do not depend as heavily on paid staff. "Their objective is to facilitate as much ministry as humanly possible through the efforts of the congregation, with as few full-time, paid ministers as possible." Barna continues, "Highly effective churches are always suspicious of a growing payroll. While they understand that increased staff may facilitate productive ministry, they also recognize that increased reliance upon staff can quickly turn a movement of faith into a religious bureaucracy."[12]

How does the church keep volunteers continually involved in ministry? Here are some suggestions.

• *Set the bar high.* People need to know that the church is not simply a waiting room to rest in until the heavenly chariot carries them to heaven. People are not saved by good works, but they are saved in order to do good works. If people know that service is the norm, they will be more ready to accept their role as servants.

• *Tap underutilized resources.* People are retiring earlier, and many are discovering that sitting around watching television or playing shuffleboard all day gets boring. These people are looking for legitimate uses of their time that can make a difference. While some newly retired people may continue to have financial concerns and need to earn money, many are willing to voluntarily take on responsibilities that will challenge them mentally and spiritually. Most churches have people with free time who are just waiting to be asked.

• *Respect volunteers.* People who are willing to serve are a wonderful resource for a church. Pastors, especially, need to understand that lay ministers are in no way second-class citizens in the work of the Kingdom. Those who volunteer for ministry assignments are special people because they work out of a motive to serve God. They sacrifice time, energy, and sometimes their own personal finances to do ministry.

• *Provide the resources.* Most churches do not have enough budget money to give every ministry everything it desires to do the job. However, churches can show support to volunteer ministries within the church by providing some budget money to help them succeed. It is important to have accountability for the use of the church's money. But resourcing may go far beyond providing a budget. A volunteer ministry may need to use the church building, the church van, or office equipment to carry out its assignment. Churches show support when they do all they can to make a ministry succeed.

• *Work as a team.* People feel much better about volunteer work if they can see how they connect to the overall ministry of the church. The power of a team is much greater than simply the sum of the individual members. Pastors develop a team spirit when they include the heads of ministry teams regularly in staff meetings. Even if the church is not large enough to have paid staff, the unpaid volunteers can form the staff. Individual ministries in the church will also function better if the workers gather often for team meetings. A spirit of camaraderie and unity can be a powerful force for success when work teams get together.

• *Make workers feel important.* Find ways to say that volunteer ministry is greatly appreciated. Host recognition Sundays when you bring some of the workers in front of the congregation to acknowledge their efforts. One church used the newsletter to feature a lay worker of the month on the front cover with a large picture and brief description of his or her ministry. Give an annual dinner to honor those who serve in volunteer ministries.

Another way to show the significance of some important volunteer staff positions is to award a title and, if the church has space, provide an office. In doing this you elevate the person's responsibility in the eyes of the congregation as well as show the worker the importance of the job. Remember these volunteer staff workers with public recognition at Christmas and on their birthdays. Volunteers save the church a lot of money when one considers what would be paid if people had to be hired for the task. Don't take lay volunteers for granted. Little acts of thoughtfulness go a long way in helping workers feel they are noticed and appreciated.

• *Keep communicating.* Nothing builds team spirit more than helping the members of the team feel connected. "When people active in ministry do not know what is going on they lose their motivation for service and do not feel a part of the team," write Dennis E. Williams and Kenneth O. Gangel.[13]

Workers need to know what is happening within other ministries of the church so schedules don't conflict or compete. Good communication short-circuits rumors and misunderstandings in the church. People like the feeling that they know what's going on and aren't caught by surprises. Face-to-face meetings are best for communication, but sometimes that simply is not practical. Letters, phone calls, posters, announcements, ministry newsletters, and e-mail messages can be helpful substitutes to keep people informed. Effective communication is difficult at best. It is always better to err on the side of too much communication than risk the chance that someone may not get the message.

• *Let them do their job.* Don't assign people tasks and then stand looking over their shoulders, worried in case they make a mistake or do the job poorly. Alan Nelson writes, "When you make decisions over their heads, their sense of importance is diminished. Pulling rank is a common temptation for professionals because working with and through people takes more time and effort, but remember, you are developing people, not just programs."[14]

Pastors need to develop methods of accountability and evaluation for volunteers. However, if the pastor has done a good job of equipping the laity, the potential for ministry will be multiplied many times when the people of God are unleashed to do what the Spirit has gifted them to do. Laypeople can do many things better than the pastor, and their ministry frees the pastor to do those things specific to the role of shepherd of the flock.

WORKER RETENTION

One pastor at a new church discovered a serious problem. The church had gone through a building program, much of it done with volunteer help. One of the unintended victims of the program was the janitor who had to keep the church clean while the progress of the building program kept getting it dirty. He was a part-time worker with a full-time secular job, and the extra stress was too much. Not only did he quit the janitor's job when the project was completed, but he suffered spiritually for a two-year period after as well. All were working so hard getting the building done they failed to notice that one of their own had passed the point of burnout.

How can pastors keep people working without having casualties from frustration, discouragement, or exhaustion?

• *Define the job.* Misunderstanding what the job entails can create serious problems. What, exactly, is the church asking this person to do? Problems develop when the leader fails to express the expectations for the task, and the volunteer understands the job differently.

There are times when a formal job description should be worked out between the parties involved, spelling out the specifics of the task. Some tasks are so obvious that a simple verbal set of instructions are sufficient. Other times a person can be given a broad area of responsibility and allowed to develop a ministry that seems to fit the giftedness and personality of that individual. Whether formal or informal, a job description should describe the responsibilities, explain the chain of accountability, or define the committee involvement. In the building program mentioned above, the church should have clarified what the janitor was responsible to clean, rather than assuming he would take on all the extra workload.

• *Set a minimum time frame.* Frazer Memorial Church asks volunteers to make a one-year commitment. Some other churches elect members to the church board and other committees for two- or three-year terms of service. The length of time is not as important as the idea that there is an ending point. One hindrance to voluntary service is the fear of being stuck in an unsuitable or unfulfilling task until Jesus returns.

A limited time frame gives an individual a way out of a task with dignity. Leaving one job does not mean a volunteer is leaving the church or forsaking the faith. Sometimes people need a break or would like to try another ministry. Having a ministry time frame does not imply that people must abandon something they enjoy doing, unless there are specific stated terms of service. They can reenlist to do the same tasks where they feel comfortable serving the church.

• *Be available.* Pastors and ministry supervisors need to let volunteers know they are interested by being around the people as they do their work. In the business world it is called leadership by walking around. Whether it is before Sunday School starts or when people have gathered for a church workday, just being there to visit, encourage, and answer questions sends a message from the pastor to the people that they have not been forgotten. Let fellow workers know that the office door is open when they need to see their pastor.

• *Listen to suggestions.* Successful business companies have learned to reward those people on the assembly line who offer suggestions for improving productivity. They have come to realize that the people on the front line have the best understanding of how things ought to work. In the church those people who are actually doing a specific ministry may have a much better handle on how things function than the team leader or pastor. When suggestions from lay volunteers are implemented, they feel they have played a significant role in any successes that may result.

It is usually easier to keep someone working than to find a replacement. That is why retention is so important. But there are times when a person is unsuited for an assignment. When people recognize they are not right for a job, they usually want out. Rather than arguing, help those people find something else to do that suits their gifting, interests, and natural talents.

A more difficult challenge is working with those who don't want to step down. They may be doing damage to the Kingdom by driving people away. While some leaders immediately confront and remove the person, it is much better to seek the Holy Spirit's guidance for a win-win solution. What is the best way to save this person to the church without creating hard feelings? Pray and seek God's wisdom for a transition. But don't ignore the problem or things could get worse. Sometimes a church must go through a painful confrontation and even a temporary loss by removing someone who is doing harm so the church can ultimately move ahead.

SUPPORTING THE WORKFORCE

Many churches have found that in order to effectively use this lay workforce they need someone who would coordinate the efforts in a local church. In his book *Empowering Lay Volunteers,* Douglas W. Johnson suggests developing a coordinator of volunteers. Other churches have called this position director of lay ministry, director of lay development, or lay activities coordinator. "This is the individual who coordinates the increasing corps of persons who want to be a part of the church's frontline ministry. This person links volunteers and leadership into a working unit. The coordinator of volunteers provides the leaven for recruitment and the design for training—two very important needs for volunteers."[15]

While large churches may make this position a part of the paid staff, smaller churches may seek a volunteer to provide this leadership. A key to the success of such a position is a close working relationship with the pastor of the church. If the pastor is not convinced of the validity of lay ministry, or is unwilling to relinquish control and authority to a coordinator, the concept is doomed to failure.

The task of a volunteer coordinator is to match the needs of ministries in the church with laypeople who are gifted and interested in those ministries.

This person may be responsible for acquainting new members with their spiritual gifting and opportunities for service. The job description may also include training the laity for specific tasks. In churches where the coordination is voluntary, the responsibilities can be divided. One person may assume responsibility for initial contacts and assessment, while a second person takes charge of training and placing people with ministries. Another alternative is to form a committee for lay ministry that will oversee all aspects of volunteer work in the church, in cooperation with the pastor and staff. If it is possible, the coordinator should be a layperson working with other laypeople. The task of developing lay ministry may be the most important function of a local church that is going to reach its potential for the Kingdom.

Without a doubt, the pastor is the key person in the success of any lay ministry. Some pastors distrust the whole notion of the laity serving as ministers. They may be bound to old, traditional understandings separating clergy from laity. A few may even believe that allowing laypeople to serve somehow demeans their role as ordained pastors. Most pastors buy into the concept of lay ministry but are unclear how to implement it into the life of the church. Successful lay ministry begins when a pastor willingly shares the burdens and blessings of ministry with the people in the congregation. Somehow pastors need to understand the tremendous potential in releasing the laypeople of the church to do the work of ministry—not just on Sunday, but every day; not just in the church, but in the workplace, the home, the school, and the community.

▶ LAY MINISTRY IN ACTION

Jim Couchenour had been a successful businessman, working to develop a large construction company. But Jim was also a committed layman, working to make his local church effective. He served his denomination as chairman of the board of trustees at a Christian university, as well as giving leadership on many international boards. That would have been enough ministry commitment for some people, but not for Jim.

And then, in the late 1980s God began to burden him with the needs of a segment of his community. The only way to help these hurting people was forcing him to consider a very unorthodox, personal ministry to his hometown, Columbiana, Ohio.

It began one Tuesday evening when a woman called Jim to ask if he would go and find her husband at the local tavern. Goldie's Tap Room had the reputation of a place that sparked trouble for the community. Jim walked into this unfamiliar setting and heard the voice of the Holy Spirit speaking to him about the hurting people sitting at the bar. The next night he went back, not to preach, but to walk around showing the love of Jesus to anyone who wanted to talk. For the next seven months he went every Wednesday night and sat at the end of the bar with a diet soda while people talked to him about God and their personal needs. As he listened, he heard about problems he didn't even know existed in his small town.

The needs of the community weighed so heavily on his heart that he started a ministry center in 1988 called the Way Station. There Jim and other Christian laypeople began addressing the serious community needs of unemployment, drug dependency, sexual abuse, as well as programs for children and the need for some to learn English as a second language. The Way Station now has a large, attractive building that encompasses the distribution of food and clothing, manufacturing to provide jobs, and a gift shop that sells the merchandise. But Jim has not departed from his initial calling to hurting people in bars like Goldie's. He recently said that his dream is to have a godly presence every Friday and Saturday night in every bar throughout the area. Jim challenges laypeople to move from the sanctuary and into the streets of their communities where the needy people live.

The only way the Great Commission will finally be fulfilled is to unleash the vast untapped potential of lay ministry. The initiative for developing lay ministry and equipping laypeople to do ministry has been assigned to the pastor. Doing ministry is a form of caring. Some of these specific lay pastoral caring ministries are addressed more fully in the next chapter.

▶ QUESTIONS FOR REFLECTION

▷ Is there any difference between ministry done by the laity and ministry done by clergy? What is the basis of your answer?

▷ What are the greatest obstacles to lay ministry development in a local church?

▷ What is the pastor's responsibility in developing lay ministry in the local church?

▷ What are the advantages or disadvantages of a church appointing and developing a coordinator of volunteers or director of lay ministries?

FOUR

LAY-LED PASTORAL CARE

Ed Martinez recognized the knock on his office door. Maria delighted in doing things around the church and would stop by every week, asking what she could do. But she had already painted every Sunday School classroom and cleaned every surface in the whole church building. Ed was a little frustrated today. He had a sermon to work on, and there were now four people from the church who were in the hospital, actually four different hospitals. On top of all of that, he had another big concern—the weekend board retreat scheduled for Friday night and Saturday. With the retreat less than a day away, when was he going to get to his sick parishioners?

Maria knocked again, and as Ed opened his study door, the idea suddenly hit him as an inspiration. Why hadn't he thought of it before? "Maria, have you ever thought about doing caring ministry at the hospital? I know you took care of your mother when she was in bed after her broken hip."

"Oh, pastor," Maria said, "I've always felt a sense of reward when I have helped people who are sick and in need. If you think I could do it, I'd really enjoy it."

Certainly Maria could be as effective in visiting those four hospitalized people as he could, Ed thought. But what would the church members think? Would they feel that he was shirking his responsibilities? Was it worth the risk to let Maria do some of the hospital calling that week, and maybe other times in the future?

The following Tuesday Pastor Ed visited the two people who were still hospitalized. In both cases, before he had a chance to mention it, the hospitalized patients mentioned how they appreciated Maria stopping by to visit. One of them said, "Maria has a way of just lighting up a room when she enters. And her prayer for me was so meaningful. I really sensed that Jesus came and placed his hand on me as she lifted my need to the Father. She is such a compassionate person."

As Ed left the hospital his mind was already at work. Maybe Maria's willingness to paint and clean was really a search to find a meaningful way to serve others. It was obvious that she had a special knack for connecting and caring for people with hurts. Maybe there were others in the church who also enjoyed helping people this way. How could he involve them?

▶ WHO DOES PASTORAL CARE?

Is it possible for a pastor alone to provide adequate care for the people of the flock? This is a question pastors are increasingly asking.

Congregational members battle stress from their jobs, traffic, family expectations, congestion, and a host of other sources. Divorce, family conflict, crime, and substance abuse directly impact the families of even the most faithful church attenders. At the same time, the normal support systems people have used in the past may no longer be there for them. Family members live at opposite ends of the country. Community resources are often stretched because of budget constraints. Can the pastor step in to provide care for everyone in the church? With the other expectations the church places on the pastor's time, the answer is— probably not. George Hunter III writes in his book *Church for the Unchurched:*

> Most people in most churches do not, and cannot, get adequate on-going pastoral care from their pastor; crisis care yes, but ongoing care no. Christians need pastoral care when life is good, as well as when life is hard, but the pastor's expanded job description now makes it impossible for the pastor to be every member's personal chaplain. Few churches have, can afford, or can find enough ordained pastors and staff to go around. Every church, however, has enough people with appropriate abilities and spiritual gifts to "shepherd a flock" within the church membership. We are learning that many laypeople, with training, can do 90 percent of what an ordained pastor does.[1]

Hunter is not saying that pastors no longer need to give care to their people. Most pastors do their best to respond to crises and emergency care. But with all the other pastoral responsibilities, a pastor of a hundred people cannot have one-on-one contact with each person weekly or even monthly. Yet this regular pastoral care is important in developing spiritual maturity among church members. Many churches have dealt with the problem by unconsciously keeping their church small enough for the pastor to care for everyone in the church. The congregation members are happy if the pastor is there for them. But this philosophy flies in the face of the Great Commission to go and make new disciples. There is a better way—a New Testament way.

▶ THE PRIESTHOOD OF BELIEVERS

The apostle Peter wrote some encouraging words to a persecuted but growing community. "But you are a chosen people, a royal priesthood, a holy nation, a people belonging to God, that you may declare the praises of him who called you out of darkness into his wonderful light" (1 Pet. 2:9). Martin Luther understood the words *royal priesthood* to refer to all believers, not just the clergy. Howard Stone writes, "In the New Testament the terms *priesthood* or *priest* do not refer to the office of minister."[2] From Peter's era until today, every Christian is a priest in the Body of Christ. The biblical understanding of the role of priests was to mediate between God and people. At its best, pastoral care is representing Christ to a person and representing that person to Christ.

How does being a priest fit with the everyday task of being a carpenter, farmer, doctor, or secretary? Martin Luther understood that believers have a dual role while here on earth.

The first responsibility or calling is what he called one's station in life. "Luther included in this first type of vocation one's *occupation* (teacher, seamstress, poet, engineer, firefighter), one's *status* (single, husband, wife, child), or one's *place in life* (rich, poor, blind, sighted). . . . The second vocation or calling of every Christian is as a member of the priesthood of all believers."[3] The Bible does not support the idea that the laity simply sit and watch the pastor of the church do the ministry work. In fact, Eph. 4:12 clearly states that the pastor-teacher is to equip the saints for the work of ministry. No matter what believers do vocationally, they have a calling to be priests—conduits of God's forgiveness, grace, and healing to others.

Caring ministry is the privilege of every Christian.

▶ PREPARING THE CLERGY

Most pastors understand the concept of the priesthood of believers, at least in theory. But if that is true, why is there such a gap between the theory and practice of the laity providing the primary pastoral care?

While there are some laypeople who do not believe they can do quality care, or just don't want to be bothered, the greatest part of the problem rests more on the shoulders of clergy. Some pastors equate quality pastoral care with professional preparation. It's the "I can do it better" syndrome. While it is true that some crisis and psychological counseling requires a high level of skill development, laypeople can do many, if not most, types of regular pastoral care.

There are pastors who fear that if laypeople do most of the pastoral care, any failures will reflect personally on them in a negative way. Another concern of the clergy is that they would appear lazy or uncaring if they hand off ministry to others. Similarly, there is a real fear that releasing care to others would ultimately result in the loss of control. Many pastors truly enjoy the satisfaction that comes from their personal pastoral care efforts and are unwilling to share that fulfillment with others. However, other people who need care may be neglected because the pastor has not had time to get around to them.

▶ PREPARING LAY PASTORS

The face of twenty-first-century pastoral ministry will look much different from the past. Bill Easum writes of this changing paradigm, "The pastor's role is primarily to teach and equip laity for ministry in the world, not to perform ministry on behalf of the church. . . . The equipping pastor does very little ministry. Instead the equipping pastor steps aside and encourages the laity to be ministers of the congregation."[4] Since most clergy have been trained to be doers, equipping others to do ministry can be a real challenge.

Rick Warren tells how he and his wife, Kay, tried to do everything when they started Saddleback Church. After they had worked themselves to exhaustion they realized that things had to change. "As our church grew, I released one responsibility after another to lay ministers and to staff members. Today I only have two primary responsibilities: To *lead* and to *feed*—and even these responsibilities are now shared with six other pastors. . . . Why? Because I deeply believe the church was never meant to be a one-man superstar show!"[5]

Pastors need to take risks and encourage risk-taking among those who are doing pastoral care. Yes, things could go wrong, but doing nothing is a far worse alternative. Jesus sent out his disciples in ministry groups of two, long before these learners probably felt they were ready for the task. The two could encourage each other not to give up or be afraid. Bruce Larson writes, "Jesus shows us that an essential step in preparing people to minister is to encourage them to take risks, to go places where they may fail unless God intervenes."[6]

One of the most difficult steps for clergy is to release personal control. Jesus' disciples had this fear. One day John said to Jesus, "'Master, . . . we saw a man driving out demons in your name and we tried to stop him, because he is not one of us.' 'Do not stop him,' Jesus said, 'for whoever is not against you is for you'" (Luke 9:49-50). Many pastors are control freaks, afraid of anything they cannot script or direct. "And yet," as Larson observes, "if we don't release lay ministry from the control of the pastor and the staff, we end up with programs so small that a few people can run the whole thing. We miss the life-giving power of God, especially that which comes through lay people sharing in the ministry of pastoral care."[7]

Usually it is not difficult to release ministries or tasks we hate to do ourselves to others. Sharing ministry we enjoy or find fulfillment in doing may be a different matter. Pastors need to be honest with themselves at the motivational level. While not denying one's personal gifting and strengths, a pastor needs to decide whether a layperson could be strengthened by doing this ministry. Sometimes the ministry need is crucial or immediate and the pastor should respond. However, it is also important to train a layperson who will be able to respond to a similar need in the future. Jesus' disciples learned by watching their Master do ministry. It was not long before Jesus released the entire responsibility of caring for the Church to those he trained.

One of the indicators of a pastor's success is the degree to which the laity takes on the responsibility of ministry in the local church. Jesus demonstrated that the path to developing the skills of others is by personally becoming a servant. Stanley Menking challenges pastors this way, "The question of your willingness 'to wash feet' is not only a call for you to express your faith. It also stimulates the development of your faith. . . . Your spiritual development can be one of the benefits from seeking to help laity help others."[8] A pastor who models servanthood motivates the congregation to follow the same motivation.

WHAT MAKES A GOOD LAY CAREGIVER?

We live in a world full of hurting people. Remember Hal David and Burt Bacharach's popular 1970s song "What the World Needs Now Is Love"? Every Christian is under a divine mandate to share the love of Jesus with others. And yet there are those who have a special ability to express that love in personal, helping ways to people in need. Gary Collins writes in his book *How to Be a People Helper*, "In any helping relationship, the personality, values, attitudes, and beliefs of the helper are of primary importance."[9] There are several qualities needed to be an effective lay caregiver.

• *Empathy.* There is no quality more important than the ability to respond with feeling compassion to someone in need. Leroy Howe writes, "The word *empathy* suggests a capacity to know others' feelings and to feel them oneself, an acceptance of others with whatever feelings they exhibit, and an expression of the knowing and the feeling as a part of caring about and for them."[10]

A picture from a high school yearbook graphically illustrates the principle. The photographer captured a high jumper on the track team leaping up in the air and about to go over the high jump bar. But the attention of the viewer is drawn to the background of the picture. There are four of his teammates, each standing on one foot, with the other leg lifted up as if they were making the jump themselves. These four spectators probably did not realize they were trying to help their teammate by lifting a leg in the air. In their empathic response they were trying to help their friend over the bar.

It's not enough just to feel what the other person is feeling. People need to know that the caregiver is concerned about the situation. And yet, to be an effective people helper one must maintain an appropriate objectivity. A caregiver needs to be able to feel the pain while at the same time encouraging the hurting person toward a future better than the present moment. Empathy means caring, never trying to manipulate or control the other person. Instead, the helper's compassion provides the incentive the one being helped needs to move toward a solution to the problem.

• *Warmth.* Closely tied to empathy, warmth is the emotional connection a caring person conveys to another in need. It can be as overt as a smiling face or open, outstretched arms. Sometimes it is the subtle voice inflection or a look in the eye that says, "I really care about what happens to you."

Exuding warmth is such an inexact science. What may seem to be genuine expressions of concern to one person may come off as gushy and insincere phoniness to someone else. I had a friend who believed warmth was putting his face about eight inches from the other person's and looking him or her straight in the eye. While some may have caught his warmth, others found it to be disconcerting because he was invading their space. Warmth is best expressed by simply loving someone else the way Jesus would love that person.

• *Authenticity.* One of the less-known followers of Jesus, Nathanael, is only mentioned in John's Gospel. Some identify him with the disciple Bartholomew. Philip gives an insightful description of Nathanael to Jesus in John 1:47, "Here is a true Israelite, in whom there is nothing false." Being genuine or real means a caregiver lives consistently with what he or she says. Authentic people are not phony or deceptive but honest and sincere in their dealings with others.

Leroy Howe writes, "In shepherding terms, being genuine involves offering ourselves as finite, fallible, and fallen creatures, redeemed by God's grace and love, called and equipped to help others in the name of the One who continues to work redemptively on their and our behalf."[11] As helpers openly offer themselves in concern to others, hurting people find it easier to seek help. True authenticity means allowing others to see you as you really are, warts and all.

• *Ability to affirm.* No one in the twentieth century demonstrated better the meaning of affirmation and respect than Mother Teresa of Calcutta. She developed a ministry, reaching out to the very poorest class of humanity. She believed that the rejected untouchables who were left alone to die in the streets deserved the compassion and love of another human being. It was Mother Teresa's contention that every person was created in the image of God and deserved to be treated with dignity, despite a dirty, smelly, repulsive exterior. She was following the example of Jesus who went out of his way to treat lepers, prostitutes, and tax collectors with the same respect as the dignified religious leaders of Israel.

It is easy to make value judgments about a person based on appearance, social standing, actions, or attitudes. But effective caregivers have the ability to look beyond what the person is, to see what the person can become by the grace of God.

• *Encouragement.* People with needs are looking for someone to believe in them, encouraging them even when they may not believe in themselves.

My sixth grade teacher, Mr. Howard, was one of those great encouragers in my life. I remember feeling all through grade school that I was not a good student. That is, until the day Mr. Howard assigned me to the most advanced math group. Math was not my best subject, so I went up to his desk and told him he had made a big mistake. He said, "Bruce, you have the ability and I believe you can do it." It was one of those defining moments of my life. A few years back I found out that he was retired from teaching but still living in my hometown. After tracing down his phone number I called him up and told him my story. I concluded my phone conversation with these words, "One of the reasons I am a university professor today is that you told me as a sixth grader that you believed in me when I didn't believe in myself. Thank you for your encouragement."

Sometimes the difference between success and failure is the echo of the words, "I know you can do it," from the lips of an encouraging friend.

• *Involvement.* Simply feeling concern for another person is never enough. Caring people take action. We may misunderstand Jesus' story in Luke 10 about the victim of robbery who was left for dead along the road to Jericho. It is easy to judge the first two men who passed by as being uncaring and self-centered. They may have been shocked by the man's injuries but also torn by what to do. If the man on the ground was dead and they touched him, they would have been unable to serve in the Temple until they could undergo ceremonial cleansing. Rather than take the risk, they made their choice—don't get involved. It was a despised foreigner, a Samaritan, who finally stopped and saved the man's life.

Getting involved with someone else's need is risky business. People helpers take the risk of being rejected, misunderstood, and exploited in their attempt to help someone in need. Those who reach out to care are often torn by competing demands—which person to help and which to ignore. This can become an issue of priorities. It seems that there are always more needy people than there are resources to respond to the needs. But rather than doing nothing because the needs are too great, people helpers are willing to jump in and do something for someone.

• *Relational skills.* People helpers see needs as connected to the lives of real people. Collins says, "The helping relationship between the helper and the helpee is of great significance."[12] The best caregivers are able to develop warm, accepting relations with others. In fact, the power of the relationship may contribute more to the solution of a problem than any specific skills the helper may possess. A teacher may be able to influence a student far more through the conversations after class than by anything the instructor says in class. Helping often takes place between two equals, such as the relationship of two church friends. Other times the one needing help may seek out the guidance of a mentor or respected authority. The goal is not to simply have a relationship but to allow that relationship to be a factor in personal change or development.

▶ TYPES OF PASTORAL CARE

If Hunter's observation at the beginning of the chapter is true that 90 percent of the care an ordained minister does can be done by trained laypeople, then the varieties of caring lay ministry are nearly endless. Here are some categories of lay pastoral care.

• *Visitation.* Hunter contends, "In traditional churches virtually no one gets adequate, ongoing, 'regular,' week-by-week (or month-by-month, or season-by-season) pastoral care . . . Better-than-adequate crisis care depends upon a relationship that is established through regular pastoral care."[13] Laypeople who visit the members and friends of a local church can provide that needed regular pastoral care. Visitation counteracts the feeling of isolation that pervades our world. It is a way for God's love to become incarnational.

Visiting shut-ins is one specialized type of calling for lay caregivers. The elderly or those suffering from debilitating physical problems can feel that they have been forgotten by the church. These needy people may be in their homes or nursing care facilities. It is important to schedule regular visits to shut-ins designed to meet both the spiritual and personal needs of the individuals. Plan short visits to those who are recuperating and trying to regain strength. People who face chronic problems may enjoy a longer visit. In addition to scripture and prayer, these people may be lonely and want to visit about the activities of the church. Lay visitors need to listen and observe carefully both what the person is saying as well as the nonverbal messages. Is the person despondent or in need of special medical attention? The pastoral caregiver may pick up on special concerns that need to be addressed by other professionals. These lay visitors who call on shut-ins need to maintain a positive, uplifting spirit that fosters hope and encouragement.

• *Hospital care.* Most people are particularly appreciative of ministry when they are facing surgery or recovery from physical problems. In recent years, in an attempt to stem the increases in medical costs, people are spending less time in the hospital. Patients often show up just prior to surgery and are dismissed from the hospital as soon as possible the same day. This also makes the task of providing pastoral care more difficult because the patient is often hard to find in the hospital. One of the most important moments for hospital care is just before surgery when the patient may be apprehensive. The lay pastoral visitor may find that a brief portion from the Psalms and a prayer is just what the patient needs to face the unknown moments ahead.

A caregiver can also provide valuable ministry by staying with the family and friends of the patient who are waiting at the hospital for a serious surgery to be completed. Don't forget that once the surgery is over, the patient faces the challenges of recovery. Usually the most difficult time is two to three days following the surgery when the effects of the anesthetic and pain medicines have worn off. This becomes a wonderful opportunity for lay pastoral care, whether the person is still in the hospital or recuperating at home.

• *End-of-life comfort*. While many think that ministry to people who are dying or families after death is the exclusive responsibility of the ordained pastors, lay caregivers can play an important role as well. The pastoral staff and lay volunteers can partner together to be sure that a person facing death will have people from the church present as much as is practical. Some laypeople have more time than the pastor to give to those who are facing the reality of losing a loved one.

When death has occurred the family may receive a lot of support until after the funeral. The greatest need for care and comfort may come in the weeks and months after the loved one has died. The grieving family will go through the many emotions, such as depression, anger, and obsession with the lost loved one. They need people who can show their concern by being present and willing to listen. This is a wonderful opportunity for lay caregivers to begin a regular series of contacts by phone and in person with family members. Someone who has gone through a similar loss can be especially effective in understanding the hurts and frustrations of grief recovery. If there are several in the church who have lost loved ones, the lay pastoral care leaders could start a small group specifically designed to help those who are going through the grieving process. People recovering from loss will feel heightened emotions at the first anniversary of a loved one's death and beyond. A grief recovery group can give support to people at various stages of adjustment. Chapter 14 addresses this issue in much greater detail.

• *Counseling*. A common misconception today is that counseling can only be done by professionals. According to Collins, "Despite the many professionals in our stress-filled culture, most problems are handled by lay people, whether or not they feel qualified. Even if there could be a sufficient number of professional and pastoral counselors to handle everybody's needs, some people still would prefer to discuss their problems with a relative, neighbor, or friend."[14] Lay counselors don't charge fees, and some may feel more comfortable in sharing a problem with a familiar face from the congregation.

What makes a good lay counselor? Effective counselors have the ability to focus on the person they counsel by maintaining good eye contact, making proper verbal responses, and helping the person feel relaxed. They are able to lead the counselee to share the important details of his or her problem. Good lay counselors let people know that they are concerned. They are committed to help the counselee make the changes necessary to have a positive result, even if this means confronting difficult issues that can block progress. A church that wants to utilize laypeople for counseling needs to commit to train these workers.

An associate pastor of a large church ministering to five thousand people weekly said that their church begins caring lay ministry through small groups. Those needing specialized care are directed to need-focused small groups. For people needing individual attention, the church has trained lay counselors to help one-on-one. If people have needs that require professional help, the church maintains a list of psychologists and professional counselors for referral. Most of the personal counseling in this large church is done by laypeople.

• *Community care.* Many laypeople are finding unlimited opportunities for pastoral caring through compassionate ministry centers. Many of these centers minister to economically disadvantaged people who cannot afford to pay for medical, dental, or counseling services. Community care provides opportunities for both healing professionals and concerned lay caregivers to use their skills in voluntary service. In addition to the obvious ministries of feeding and clothing those in need, one longer term solution to the problem of poverty is job training.

People gain hope and self-confidence as they learn how to earn a living by doing meaningful work. Laypeople skilled in carpentry and cooking, carpet laying and computers can teach a trade while at the same time showing compassion. Job training can be empowering to those who seek to escape the grip of poverty.

• *Cross-cultural community care.* In certain communities the church has a unique opportunity to reach across cultural barriers. In North America, the large cities are becoming an increasing cultural melting pot as people from other world areas try to blend together in communities.

Collins states that when people come from another culture there usually is a five-stage personal reaction cycle in adjusting to the new setting. When the person first arrives, there is *enthusiastic acceptance* of this new culture. However, this initial euphoria is soon replaced by feelings of *doubt and reservation.* Perhaps the new setting is not as ideal as it first appeared. Frustrations begin to grow. Then the person goes through a time of *resentment and criticism* when it is easy to find fault with the people and structures of the new culture. It is difficult to be patient, as a people helper, during this period when criticism may reach intolerable levels. Most people do move on to the next phase of *adjustment* as they recognize that the critical attitudes are due to the differences in the new culture. The last stage is *accommodation and evaluation,* where the person feels a level of comfort by making connections to the people and customs of the new environment.[15]

Some lay caregivers may sense a deep inner concern for working with people cross-culturally. It is important to resist the notion that one's own culture is superior because it may be the only one the person really knows. Jesus showed how to respond with compassion toward people of other cultures by his conversation with the Samaritan woman in John 4. People who come from other places in the world bring valuable contributions to our society that make us better. Lay pastoral care can be a means of bridging the cultural gap.

▶ TRAINING THE LAITY FOR PASTORAL CARE

A pastor may choose to work with an individual to develop caregiving skills, but in most churches there will be several people who would respond to the opportunity for pastoral care training. When pastors spend time instructing others to be people helpers, they multiply the effectiveness of pastoral ministry to the church. There are several issues to consider when training laity for caring ministries.

OPEN VS. CLOSED CLASSES

Whenever a church begins a new ministry, the quality of the first group of trainees will largely determine the effectiveness of the program in the future. Churches have taken several approaches to find the right people for pastoral care training.

With the *open invitation* method an announcement is made to the entire congregation for anyone who is interested in receiving training. One of the problems with this approach is that the open invitation may attract people with serious personal problems who cannot give pastoral care, and in some cases, could actually do harm to others. It is possible to use an open invitation and weed out the unsuitable volunteers at a later time.

A second method is the *specific invitation* approach. The pastor and other leaders assess beforehand those people who have the spiritual gifts and natural abilities that are necessary to be effective caregivers. Then the pastor or lay leader may make the actual recruiting contacts for the program, or send a letter to those who have been selected. Other churches may select an *existing group* such as a group of deacons or an evangelism committee to be the first trainees for lay care.[16]

TRAINING CLASSES

Training can be done during the Sunday School hour or in training sessions during the week. Another approach is to do the major training during a weekend retreat with follow-up sessions once a month.

Jesus taught his disciples but also sent them out by twos to gain a practical, on-the-job understanding of the task. Training should include personal spiritual growth as well as skill development. It is important to have some hands-on experiences to supplement the classroom instruction. Hospital chaplains, nursing home administrators, and compassionate ministry centers normally welcome people who are gaining experience in order to serve effectively. Don't neglect to involve your trainees in community training experiences such as Red Cross CPR training. Explore formal educational opportunities in the area, such as local colleges and seminars that could help those interested in formal counseling training. The church could offer scholarship money for those who are committed to use their training for ministry. As a part of the training regimen, the church can incorporate advanced classes for those who would like to further sharpen their caring skills. Any equipping training should include periodic evaluation and feedback sessions designed to encourage and improve the person providing pastoral care.

COMMISSIONING LAY CAREGIVERS

From the earliest time in its history, the church has commissioned those who have been selected for specific ministries in the church. The Early Church in Acts 6 brought those set aside for lay service before the church. "They presented these men to the apostles, who prayed and laid their hands on them" (v. 6). Today those who enter full-time pastoral ministry are ordained by the church as a recognition of their calling. Those who provide lay pastoral care can also be formally commissioned at the end of their training.

A commissioning service gives a sense of God's blessing and anointing to those who are taking on this important role. This is also a message to the congregation that a layperson providing pastoral care represents the entire church body and has as much validity in providing ministry as an ordained clergy person. This commissioning could be for a specified period like a year or could be open-ended, as long as the person serves in a caring capacity. Stone includes a sample commissioning service in his book *The Caring Church: A Guide for Lay Pastoral Care* that could be adapted by a local congregation.

TRAINING RESOURCES

While there may be many excellent resources for lay pastoral care training, here are an organization and three books offered as examples.

Stephen Ministries: This is a transdenominational Christian education organization that provides high-quality training and resources to strengthen and expand lay ministry in congregations. They offer training in both the Stephen Series, a one-on-one lay ministry system, and the ChristCare Series, a small-group ministry system. Stephen Ministries provide a full range of ministry resources to equip laypeople for ministry. For further information, go to <www .stephenministries.org>.

How to Be a People Helper, by Gary R. Collins. I personally have used the earlier edition material for training in a local church.[17] There are twelve sessions with growth exercises and group interaction to be used with each chapter. Since Collins is a Christian psychologist, his material emphasizes lay counseling and does not focus on issues of pastoral care.

A Pastor in Every Pew: Equipping Laity for Pastoral Care, by Leroy Howe. This excellent book includes twenty chapters of information on developing specific lay ministries, as well as ten additional chapters at the end in the form of a training manual for equipping lay shepherds. The training manual has all the material needed to conduct lay ministry classes in a local church.

The Caring Church: A Guide for Lay Pastoral Care, by Howard W. Stone. This book is more brief, featuring eight training sessions. The material for teaching is excellent. He has also included A Service for Commissioning Lay Pastoral Carers in the appendix.

▸ LEADERSHIP FOR LAY PASTORAL CARE

A key to ongoing lay pastoral care is having strong leadership. If the congregation is going to take ownership of this ministry, it is important that the laity assume the leadership positions. The lay leader can serve as the liaison from the lay ministry structure to the pastor and staff of the church.

Stone raises the issue of responsibility. "First, how will people who are to be visited be assigned—by the pastor directly or by the lay leader, or sometimes one way and sometimes another? A second issue is accountability and feedback after lay pastoral care givers are assigned visits."[18] If the pastor is unwilling to release care opportunities to the laity, the whole idea of lay pastoral care will fail. However, if the pastor and lay leadership work as a team, the level of pastoral care will be much higher in the church.

▸ LAY MINISTRY CAUTIONS

As would be expected with anything having to do with human nature, there is a need for a few caveats when it comes to lay ministry

CONFIDENTIALITY

Rightly or wrongly, the church has developed a reputation of being a rumor mill, sharing gossip at the speed of light. For this reason many people are hesitant to share anything of a personal nature with someone else in the church.

Pastors are morally bound to the church's tradition of the seal of the confessional. This means that whatever is shared in a confidential setting is protected and cannot be divulged, even before a court of law. While legal protection may not extend to lay counseling in all legal jurisdictions, the congregation has the right to expect the same level of confidentiality from lay pastoral caregivers. What is shared in confidence during a lay care encounter should not be passed on without the permission of the person being helped.

There are two exceptions to the commitment to confidentiality: when a person threatens to do serious harm to himself or herself or to another person. A people helper needs to take steps to protect the person who is in perceived danger, even if it means breaking confidences. It can be helpful to let the person who is being counseled know at the beginning of a counseling session that it is a caregiver's responsibility to protect anyone whose life or safety is threatened. If there are laypeople who are interested in doing pastoral care but have a reputation for gossiping, it would be well to direct them to activities that have a low risk of being exposed to personal information.

It is always a good idea to know the restrictions of state and local governments regarding the use of laypeople in counseling. Some restrict the use of the term *counseling* when announcing the types of services that are offered by the church. Collins suggests, "It is wise to secure legal advice about whether lay persons in the local area could be sued for malpractice or for harming counselees through the giving of unsound advice or guidance."[19]

UNSUITABLE HELPERS

There are good people who for one reason or another should not be involved in pastoral care ministry. Menking says, "Of all the problems you will have to cope with in a lay ministry, none seems as difficult as handling the layperson who *should not join* the ministry or the one who is in the ministry but *ought to leave*."[20]

People who are gossipers, manipulative, or mentally unstable will not function well as people helpers. If you have an open invitation for anyone to participate in pastoral care, you run the risk of having unsuitable people volunteer. Some will quickly understand they don't fit in this ministry. While some will graciously withdraw, there are times when the only thing to do is ask the person to resign.

LAY WORKER BURNOUT

Helping people in need can sometimes be a tiring task. Some people in need will take all the time and energy one can give and then ask for more. Caregivers need support systems to maintain their energy and focus in ministry. They need someone to consult from time to time about problems and to be encouraged. If there are not too many caregivers in the church, the pastor may be able to be that encouraging person. However, this may also be part of the responsibility of the lay leader and leadership group.

It is good to plan periodic education and encouragement events to keep your caregivers motivated. This can provide an opportunity for developing people and counseling skills as well as helping to develop a team spirit among the pastoral care workers.

REFERRALS

Pastoral care workers need to gain a sense of their own personal skill and knowledge level in helping others. Chapter 8 will discuss the need to develop a referral network in the community. If pastors need to make referrals, there is an even greater need for lay workers to recognize the need to direct people to help they cannot provide. Lay pastoral caregivers can develop their own list of community resources they can call on when there is a need. Medical doctors make referrals all the time. It is not a sign of weakness but a realization that if we do not have all the skills necessary to aid a person, someone else may be able to help where we can't.

▶ THE WAY IT'S SUPPOSED TO WORK

Lay pastoral care is an old idea that has again come of age. Hunter illustrates the importance of the laity becoming involved in caring ministries by relating another story from Rick Warren at Saddleback Community Church. Pastor Warren received word that one of the charter members had suffered a heart attack and was at a local hospital emergency room. He responded by jumping into his car and rushing to the side of his church member. At the nurses' station he said, "I'm Pastor Rick, here to see Walt Stevens." The head nurse answered back with a question, "How many pastors does this church have? I'm sorry, you can't see him. Too many pastors have already seen him." Warren knew his way around the hospital and slipped around to the room after the nurse left. The patient saw his pastor and said, "Pastor Rick, what are you doing here? I must really be sick. Five lay pastors have already visited me." After a brief prayer Rick Warren left the room deeply moved. "This is the way God meant for the church to operate. God never meant it to be a one-man show . . . God works through the ministry of the laity and they have the right to know that God is working in their life."[21]

It's time for ordained ministers to unleash the laity to do caring ministries so the Body of Christ can truly experience the level of pastoral care the church and the people of the world need and should rightfully expect from the church.

▶ Questions for Reflection

▷ Why has the church come to expect that the job of pastoral care should be the exclusive domain of the ordained clergy?

▷ How much responsibility must a pastor assume to promote and provide opportunities for lay pastoral ministry in a local church?

▷ Are there areas of pastoral care that the ordained clergy should continue to maintain a maximum involvement?

▷ What concerns do you have in developing a lay pastoral care ministry in a local church?

FIVE

CARING THROUGH SMALL GROUPS

Casey and Donna Rodgers were excited about the potential of their first church in the small farming community that was now their home. Donna especially wanted their church to begin to look beyond the four walls to the many unchurched, hurting people living around them. But simply challenging people to reach out from the pulpit was not going to be enough. She and Casey would have to lead by example.

Donna was also making the personal adjustment of having an eighteen-month-old bundle of energy named Bradley who seemed to monopolize her time and energies. Even grocery shopping with Brad in the cart was sometimes an exhausting experience. She smiled as she watched another mother coming down the supermarket aisle toward her, while her toddler pulled cereal boxes off the shelves. Donna introduced herself and in no time the two mothers were laughing about the challenges of running grocery carts through the gauntlet of enticing boxes and cans their boys could grab. Tina confided that she felt so isolated from the world because of the demands of taking care of Toby. "If only I had another mother to talk to about child rearing. I'm a first-time mother and with our parents living five hours away, I sometimes feel so alone."

Donna thought quickly. "Tina, I know three other mothers with young children who have those same feelings sometimes. Would you be interested in meeting together at my house once a week for about an hour, say Tuesday mornings? We could bring our babies, sit on the floor, and let them play together a bit. I'd be happy to have a brief Bible study and we could pray for each other."

"I don't know much about the Bible. I haven't been to church since I was a little girl," Tina replied. "But I like the whole idea of having some adult conversation with other women who are facing the same challenges of being mothers. There's another gal down the street with a two-year-old girl whose husband just left her. I think she would be interested in a group like this. Do you want to start next week? If so, I'll invite her to come with me. She could really use some friends too."

By the time they exchanged phone numbers and said their good-byes in the supermarket parking lot, Donna was already planning the first meeting. The three mothers from the church would welcome this opportunity to be involved. A small group of mothers wasn't the way she had envisioned community outreach. But God had a plan and the whole thing came together so naturally. Thank you, God!

▶ A Divine Strategy

Have you ever wondered about Jesus' strategy during his very brief ministry here on earth? Many public relations experts today would say that Jesus did it all wrong. If they had been in charge, Jesus would have focused his energies on large events such as the feeding of the five thousand where his impact would be felt among the masses. They would have insisted he concentrate his ministry in the major population centers of the Roman Empire where he would gain name recognition. Jesus would have made several multinational tours showing that he was going to be the Savior of the whole world. After all, that's the way you get things started and promoted today.

But that certainly was not the way Jesus chose. Instead of huge crowds Jesus spent most of his time ministering to individuals and small gatherings of people. He seldom ventured far from the rural confines of the region of Galilee except for infrequent yearly trips to Jerusalem. The power centers of Rome and Athens were not even on his list of destination sites. Instead of trying to amass a large following, Jesus spent most of his time training a small group of twelve men to carry his message and do his ministry after he left the earth. The Master's philosophy seems to have been very simple—to grow big, you have to start small.

▶ A Biblical Foundation for Small Groups

Jesus knew what he was doing by focusing his energies to form this small group of disciples. Mark 3:14-15 says, "He appointed twelve—designating them apostles—that they might be with him and that he might send them out to preach and to have authority to drive out demons." Jesus was planning to take this diverse group with varied temperaments and mold them into a unified task force to impact the entire world with his message.

To accomplish this, the Master knew he would need to spend a lot of time together with these twelve men. Mark writes that Jesus was intentional, "that they might be with him" (v. 14). These men watched and listened as Jesus ministered and taught. They asked him about what he said and how he healed. And along the way they learned to care deeply for the other persons in the group.

It certainly wasn't a perfect collection of men. They bickered among themselves about the pecking order of their relative importance in the group. At times they lacked the basic faith their Master expected. And when Jesus needed their prayer support the most in the Garden of Gethsemane, they slept. Yet the night before Jesus was crucified he prayed in John 17, "I will remain in the world no longer, but they are still in the world, and I am coming to you. Holy Father, protect them by the power of your name—the name you gave me—so that they may be one as we are one" (v. 11). Jesus' prayer was answered. This small group of diverse individuals, through the power of the Holy Spirit, became the point persons for the expansion of the gospel throughout the known world.

▶ SMALL GROUPS IN THE EARLY CHURCH

The birth of the Church on the Day of Pentecost did not happen because of some slick organizational planning. The Holy Spirit infused a group of a hundred twenty individuals with such power that three thousand people responded to the message of Christ on the first day. Since there was no organizational plan in place, the tasks of nurturing new believers and evangelizing unbelievers evolved out of need. George Hunter III says, "The early church experienced two structures necessary and normative for the Messianic movement. They met as cells (or small groups) in 'house churches'; and the Christians of a city also met together in a common celebration or congregation."[1]

The first description of this primitive church functioning is found in Acts 2:42-47. They committed themselves to:
- Learn from the teaching of the apostles
- Enjoy the fellowship of the community of believers
- Remember Christ's death through the Communion meal
- Gather for times of prayer
- Focus on a common purpose
- Share their possessions with others in need
- Worship in celebration at the Temple
- Eat informally in each other's homes
- Offer thanksgiving and praise to God
- Earn the respect of the larger community, and
- Engage the lost with the gospel, resulting in conversions

The Jerusalem church seemed naturally to sense the truth that to grow bigger they had to also continue their focus on smaller groups of people by giving attention to the needs of individuals. By Acts 6 this local church had grown to the place that some widows who depended on the church for their daily food rations had fallen through the cracks and were being neglected. Fortunately, the church made the adjustments of personnel and resources to respond to this crisis because they were committed to caring for individuals.

▶ JOHN WESLEY'S "METHOD" FOR MINISTRY

It was at the beginning of the Industrial Revolution that John Wesley began his ministry to the masses of unchurched common people in eighteenth-century England. Wesley's own life had been dramatically changed by a personal experience of saving faith on Aldersgate Street. This conversion drove him to share his faith so that others could enjoy what he called "heart-felt religion." The Church of England at the time was spiritually lukewarm at best. It did not approve of Wesley's unorthodox methods of preaching to society's undesirables in the fields and streets. Since Wesley was a student of the New Testament he pored over the writings of the apostle Paul to find ways to develop disciples among the uneducated people he was reaching. Although he borrowed some from of the successes of such groups as the Moravians, the development of his approach to small groups was uniquely his own.

The centerpiece of Wesley's Methodist movement was the *society*, which would be comparable to the term *congregation* today. Society meetings focused on training and education so the people would understand the methods for living a godly life. In the beginning these society meetings were carefully scheduled so they would not conflict with the services of the Church of England, since it was Wesley's desire that they be loyal Anglicans.

John Wesley became convinced early on that the development of small groups would be the key to the success of the new movement. The primary small-group unit was the class meeting. Every Methodist was expected to be a part of a class. D. Michael Henderson writes, "The class meeting was the most influential instructional unit in Methodism and probably Wesley's greatest contribution to the technology of group experience."[2]

People who were sincerely seeking God were first invited to join a special small group, called the trial band, which focused on those who were investigating the faith. These people stayed with the trial band until they could be incorporated into the class meeting later. Tom Albin writes, "In the trial band, you find exactly the grace and power of the sincere seeker that one finds today in the 12-step groups. What does it take to be a part of AA? You have to say, I've got a problem and I need help from on high."[3] People who demonstrated faithfulness to the trial band were recommended to a class meeting after a few months.

Class meetings were a melting pot that brought together diverse people with a common purpose of experiencing personal faith. While in many of the Methodist activities men and women were separated, the class meetings were coeducational with many women taking leadership roles. People of different social backgrounds sat side by side in fellowship. Even those who were otherwise powerless in society could speak up when the class gathered. "At first, class meetings met in homes, shops, schoolrooms, attics and even coal-bins—wherever there was room for ten or twelve people to assemble. The chronicles of early Methodism record heroic tales of pious folk, committed to their class, who would undergo great harassment, walk long distances, endure hardship, and put up with bizarre settings in order to 'meet in class.'"[4]

Those who experienced the new birth could then join another small group called the band. This group focused on spiritual growth and discipleship in the context of confidentiality. While the class was open to everyone, the band was more homogeneous in makeup. Albin notes that the band meeting was also separated by gender and by marital status.[5] In this setting the new believer could learn how to live out the Christian life personally as a single man or a married woman among others of a similar status. Band meetings were smaller than class meetings, generally limited to four to eight people. This group of people felt free to ask probing questions of each other while expecting soul-searching, honest responses. The members of the band understood that Bible study, prayer, and accountability bound them together in the process of spiritual development.

The select band or company was at the top of the hierarchy of Methodist small groups. "The purpose of this group was to model or exemplify what Methodism was all about, especially the perfecting of the human spirit, and it was to provide a training experience in the doctrines and methods of Methodism," writes Henderson.[6]

Each of Wesley's small groups served a specific purpose. According to Albin, "The focus of the class meeting is on the mind, the band meeting focuses on the will, but the formational focus of the select society is the heart. The early Methodists would view the select society as equivalent to spiritual adulthood."[7] Wesley even developed a special small group, the Penitent Band, to help those who had fallen away from the faith and were now seeking to be restored to the fellowship.

There is no question that John Wesley understood the importance of infusing the New Testament spirit of *koinonia* from the primitive church into the life of a small group of people in an eighteenth-century context. That concept continues to be significant for the church in the twenty-first century.

▶ TWENTIETH-CENTURY DEVELOPMENTS

While the first half of the twentieth century did show some interest in small groups, especially the YMCA and Student Volunteer Movement, World War II became the turning point. Many military veterans came back from the war to enter college. In the late 1940s and early 1950s parachurch organizations such as InterVarsity Christian Fellowship, the Navigators, and Campus Crusade for Christ began making inroads on secular campuses to evangelize.

Small groups became one tool used by these groups to conserve and disciple converts.

While the church largely ignored the idea of small groups during the fifties, the sixties, and seventies brought about a change in strategy. Bruce Larson and Lyman Coleman reminded the church that small groups were an integral part of early Christianity and needed to be restored to a position of importance. Part of this renewed interest in small groups was a response to some voices in secular psychology who were stressing the need for interpersonal relationships as a path to mental health. Many small groups within the church during this period were influenced as much by pop psychology as the Bible.

Beginning in the 1980s the small-group movement moved to a more biblical foundation. Peter Wagner, Carl George, and others in the developing Church Growth Movement began to see the connection between the use of small groups and the corresponding growth of a local church.

▶ SMALL GROUPS TODAY

A new paradigm has emerged from the successes of small groups in the church. Worldwide, the best-known example is the Yoido Full Gospel Central Church in Seoul, Korea, pastored by Paul Yonggi Cho. Years ago the pastor became ill and, out of necessity, turned the day-by-day pastoral ministry functions over to the laity of the church. After Pastor Cho became well again, the church continued to function by providing for people through small groups. It is now considered to be the largest church in the history of Christianity with ministry to an estimated three-fourths of a million people. The secret to personal ministry in their church is the network of small groups where people are connected to a dozen or so others for caring and support.

Carl George, in his landmark book *Prepare Your Church for the Future,* coined a new term for cell-based churches—*metachurch.*[8] A metachurch is a church that is made up of small groups that function as the building blocks for growth. Just because a church has some small groups does not make it a metachurch. The term does not refer to churches of a certain size. A metachurch believes that structurally, small groups become the building stones for ministry, outreach, and care for the entire church. George writes, "My discovery, in short, is that the organizational principle of a Meta-Church allows the church to maintain quality, no matter how much numerical success it experiences."[9]

The development of the metachurch approach to doing church is truly revolutionary. As William Easum, in his book *Dancing with Dinosaurs,* boldly states, "The transition from the program-based congregation to the small group-based congregation is the most fundamental paradigm shift in the history of North American Christianity."[10]

Perhaps the best example of a metachurch in the United States during the latter part of the twentieth century was New Hope Community Church in Portland, Oregon. Under the leadership of the founding pastor, Dale Galloway, the church grew from its humble beginnings at a drive-in theater, to a church of small groups, ministering to a congregation in the thousands, through over six hundred small groups. For instance, the Tender Loving Care groups are designed to evangelize, disciple, and shepherd the members of the group. Eighty percent of the church members had never been in a church before coming to New Hope.

New Hope's small-group ministry is based on Acts 20:20, "You know that I have not hesitated to preach anything that would be helpful to you but have taught you publicly and from house to house."[11] Galloway writes, "I believe that no church with more than fifty members can be effective in pastoral care without enlisting and enabling lay people to do the daily work of that care." He contends that "the absolute necessity of small-group ministry within the church is a concept that must be understood and implemented by pastors and church leaders if we are ever to effectively equip the church for ministry in these last days."[12]

Pastor Rick Warren of Saddleback Valley Community Church in Orange County, California, has become a familiar name to pastors though his book *The Purpose-Driven Church*. For Warren, small groups are consistent with the church's five purposes of worship, evangelism, fellowship, discipleship, and service.

While not strictly defining itself as a metachurch, Saddleback has made a strong commitment to involving as many people as possible in a small group. They operate four types of groups for their people: community groups that focus on ministry to the group, care groups for people needing recovery or support, growth groups for discipleship, and mission groups that feature ministry opportunities.[13] In addition, Saddleback has created the Lighthouse Bible Study, small groups designed to engage seekers and those with doubts through a study of the Gospel of John.

Pastor Bill Hybels and the staff of Willow Creek Community Church in suburban Chicago have made a commitment to be a metachurch to meet the personal needs of one of the largest churches in the United States. Bill Donahue and Russ Robinson, who lead Willow Creek's small-group ministry, write, "Willow Creek has gone from being a church *with* small groups—that is, small groups being one of our programs—to being a church *of* small groups. Instead of ten to fifteen percent of the congregation connected into a small group, we have become a place where over 18,000 individuals are connected in 2,700 small groups."[14] Becoming a church of small groups has changed the way Willow Creek functions. Church growth expert George Hunter III observes, "The most strategic people in the whole system are not the paid staff, but the small group leaders. The staff's role changed from primarily doing ministry to primarily facilitating the ministries of the laity."[15] Willow Creek small groups are designed to create a personal sense of community in a large church. "What takes place in each little community—each group—must produce people fully devoted to Christ and his redemptive mission."[16]

It is a mistake to think that only large churches need to work to create a sense of community. In the smallest of churches people can stand off to the side, uninvolved, uncommitted, and unconnected to the life of the congregation. While small groups are not automatically the answer to the problems of the small congregation, they do provide a framework of compassion, accountability, and encouragement that fosters growing Christians.

▶ Ingredients of Effective Small Groups

Thirty years ago, people didn't ask too many questions about what went into the prepared food sold on grocery store shelves. The name on the front was enough to tell the customer that the package contained hot dogs, green beans, or breakfast cereal. Today, health-conscious people look at the list of ingredients on the side of the package to see if the contents will be nutritional to eat.

The makeup of a small group has also become very important to people. Getting a group of individuals together in a room could be a positive or negative experience, depending on what happens in the gathering. A small group that spends their time gossiping, complaining, or condemning can do great damage to the church and themselves. On the other hand, a small-group meeting can make a positive impact on those who attend.

What are the ingredients that make small groups helpful?

• *Fellowship.* Studies have shown that one of the most important reasons people stay with a particular church is that they have made meaningful friendships. If new people have not made a personal connection with six or seven others within the first few months, they will likely drop out. People all like to know that there are others in a group who can call them by name—people one can enjoy being with on a regular basis. Small groups provide the opportunity to feel a sense of community as people build relationships with each other.

• *Caring.* Knowing people inevitably leads to caring about them. When a person shares with the group that he or she is going for a job interview next week, the others will want to know how it went the next time they meet. You are much more concerned for people you know well. Jesus said in John 15:13, "Greater love has no one than this, that he lay down his life for his friends."

Sometimes a group member may be a caregiver—other times a care receiver. A few years back my wife went through chemotherapy to combat cancer. I have been a caregiver most of my adult life, but suddenly both of us found ourselves needing the care of others. Our small group prayed for us weekly, sent cards, and brought over food. One person loaned my wife a wig to wear while her hair grew back. We discovered, on the concerned faces and loving actions of those caring people, a representation of the love of Jesus embodied in human flesh.

• *Self-disclosure.* Many people harbor the fear that if people really knew them on the inside, they wouldn't be liked very well. As a result, it is easy construct an exterior shell that doesn't allow others to penetrate the image people want to project. At the same time we want intimacy. "Deep down, we all want people to know who we are—to care about our story, our pain, and our dreams."[17]

A line from a favorite wedding ceremony says this about marriage: "Marriage provides a oneness that is so close that we are loved in spite of what we are. It brings significance to life to be known and loved anyway." What is true about marriage is also true about relationships within a small group. Self-disclosure is really a demonstration of trust and acceptance. It makes it possible to show others their personal value as we are willing to share our failures, fears, and dreams in the safety of a caring community. Someone called it "sharing the gift of your need."

• *Speaking the truth.* What the small group says to an individual member can have a significant impact. Paul writes in Eph. 4:29, "Do not let any unwholesome talk come out of your mouths, but only what is helpful for building others up according to their needs." It goes to the motive of our speech, which he addresses earlier in the same chapter: *"speaking the truth in love"* (v. 15, italics added).

Truth speaking may take the form of positive encouragement. When people are listening to their inner voice of self-doubt, they need to hear the group say, "We believe in you. You are going to make it. We will stand with you to help you succeed." Other times, speaking the truth in love means to admonish or warn someone in the group. Paul instructs the church in Col. 1:28, "We proclaim him, admonishing and teaching everyone with all wisdom, so that we may present everyone perfect in Christ." Whenever truth is spoken, love must be the highest motive.

• *Accountability.* Every Jesus follower needs people who will ask, "Are you walking the walk—living the life you profess?" John Wesley's groups were instructed to ask very probing questions of each other, such as: What known sins have you committed since our last meeting? What temptations have you met with? Have you nothing you desire to keep secret?[18]

Sometimes we are hesitant to speak about issues in others' lives because we fear we will anger, hurt, or embarrass the other person. "But withholding truth robs people of opportunities for spiritual growth. Truth is the foundation of any authentic relationship."[19] Proverbs 27:6 says, "Wounds from a friend can be trusted, but an enemy multiplies kisses." Keeping people accountable is really an expression of love.

• *Worship.* Small-group gatherings provide a wonderful opportunity to encounter God. Some groups are formed specifically to study the Bible. There are printed materials written specifically for small-group study, or the group may choose to journey through a book of the Bible using an inductive method to Bible study. Roger Elrod suggests such an approach needs little reliance on reference works. "They can begin by *observing* the text, then *interpreting* their observations, and, finally *applying* the truth they discover. In inductive study we base our interpretations on observations made solely from the text in front of us."[20] Worship may also include group prayer, singing, and testimonies of God's grace at work. While worship may benefit the individuals of the group, the real purpose is to bring glory and honor to God.

▶ TYPES OF SMALL GROUPS

Carl George has developed a way to evaluate small groups by what they want to accomplish. He says, "Each one addresses four dimensions of ministry: loving (pastoral care), learning (Bible knowledge), deciding (internal administration), and doing (duties that serve those outside the group)."[21] All groups have a unique mix of these four dimensions that help achieve the purposes of that group. Care groups spend most of their energies loving one another, while study groups will spend more of their time learning. An usher's group emphasizes doing. A board committee may be a small group with a focus on deciding. Yet each of these groups will have elements of the other three dimensions as a part of their group dynamic. Some specific types of small groups are:

• *Mutual support groups.* Although they may go by different names, such as growth, support, or care groups, their purpose is to promote the spiritual development of the members through prayer, Bible study, and community building. These groups tend to focus on believers although some will encourage the members to bring in unsaved people. One technique that is often used is to include an empty chair in the circle as a reminder to invite a needy person to come to the next meeting.

• *Cell groups.* These are designed as the building blocks for churches that follow the metachurch model. Congregations are divided into cells by geography or interest. Cell groups may function much like mutual support groups. The cell group leader and assistant are responsible for personal contact and pastoral care within the group. Many churches are now using small groups to provide an evangelistic, discipling, and ministering structure for the entire church.[22]

• *CareRing groups.* Dr. David Slamp became concerned about an issue shared by many pastors, "How do we start small groups when we already have Sunday School classes?" While serving as director of small groups ministry at a large church with thousands of members, Slamp developed a program called Care-Rings, an approach that linked small groups and Sunday School classes together for greater effectiveness. He noticed that people who began attending a small group before they became involved in Sunday School would later join a class in addition to the small group. In addition, when new small groups were formed there was a ready pool of potential members in a Sunday School class. Slamp's CareRings also provided a built-in system of accountability, fellowship, caregiving, and practical application for the Scriptures, when the small groups were connected to classes. The Sunday School classes gave the small-group leaders an appropriate setting to share the values of small groups as well as an opportunity to recruit for their own CareRings.

Small groups within a Sunday School class give a needed sense of connectedness for those whose work schedules keep them from attending the class regularly. Slamp observes, "We can meet early in the morning, in the evening, in the middle of the afternoon—you name it. CareRings can accommodate those who can't make it to a class on Sunday mornings."[23] For pastors, it does not need to be a choice or either/or—Sunday School classes or small groups. The CareRing approach allows a church to take advantage of both tools to develop a web of relationships and spiritual growth. It can do better than either the Sunday School class or a small group could do alone.

• *Sunday School integration groups.* Such groups may meet on Sundays or during the week. They may utilize published material, discuss the pastor's sermon, or study books of the Bible. What makes a Sunday School class a small group has less to do with the subject of study and more with the way the class interacts and cares for one another.

• *Recovery groups.* Some groups tend to focus on overcoming a specific addiction, such as alcohol or pornography, while others respond to a personal issue like weight gain, divorce, or grief. Often church-related addiction groups use a combination of the 12-step formula with distinctly Christian activities, such as prayer and Bible study. They utilize the mutual support of others with similar needs, and encourage personal accountability. People may turn to recovery groups because they emphasize group support rather than formal counseling to overcome their specific problem. One of the premier church-based recovery programs is Celebrate Recovery, a biblically based, 12-step program for problems such as alcohol addiction, drug abuse, codependency, anger management, and other issues.[24]

• *Accountability groups.* The purpose of accountability groups is to encourage spiritual growth and discipleship. Wesley's select band would be an example. Accountability groups usually emphasize in-depth Bible study and other spiritual disciplines as well as personal responsibility and interpersonal concern.

• *Ministry groups.* Anytime a group of people unite together to perform a specific task, they can form a small group. Some groups are short-term, such as a missionary construction team. Others, such as greeters, Sunday School teachers, nursing home ministries, and church staff workers, may continue for years. While the focus is usually on a task, people who come together for work can also provide encouragement and support for each other.

• *Outreach groups.* Many churches and parachurch organizations such as Campus Crusade use group Bible studies as a way to engage pre-Christian people with the truths of the gospel. Saddleback Community's Lighthouse Bible Study is one example of church people using a small group to introduce their secular neighbors to the Word of God in the neutral environment of a home.

▶ THE SIZE OF SMALL GROUPS

How many people can one person leading a small group effectively care for? Jethro, Moses' father-in-law, observed that Moses was trying to deal with all the needs of all the people of Israel by himself. And he was exhausted trying. Jethro's solution was brilliant in its simplicity: "Select capable men from all the people—men who fear God, trustworthy men who hate dishonest gain—and appoint them as officials over thousands, hundreds, fifties and tens" (Exod. 18:21).

The principle here is simple: one person can personally deal effectively with a maximum of five to ten people. Overseers can give guidance to no more than ten leaders. Hospitals have found that nurses can only work efficiently with four patients who are ill. Nurses who must give primary care to seven or more sick patients cannot observe the slight changes in an individual that may spell the difference between recovery or death. Most successful small-group programs try to limit the size of a group to no more than twelve to sixteen people. When groups reach that size, leaders either divide them or create new groups.

Equipping small-group leaders to be effective is absolutely essential. Dale Galloway scheduled weekends of leader training three to four times a year in preparation for the development of new groups. Many churches train new group leaders with practical on-the-job experience by asking them to first serve as an assistant leader of an existing group before leading their own group.

▶ SMALL-GROUP STRUCTURE

It is important not only to train small-group leaders but also to create a structure to oversee and support those who lead. Without supervision and encouragement small-group leaders can feel isolated and forgotten. Utilizing the Jethro principle, supervisors or coaches can effectively work with between five and ten leaders.

Donahue and Robinson describe the Willow Creek coach's role as three-fold: (1) meeting with all their group leaders to develop leadership skills, (2) visiting the small groups to encourage and give suggestions, and (3) one-on-one time with each leader to encourage spiritual development. They write, "Coaches are primarily lovers of leaders. . . . A leader who is loved is a leader who will respond to correction or training."[25] Developing supervisor-coaches is one of the most significant factors in developing a successful small-group ministry in a local church. William Easum quotes Carl George in saying that "meta-math goes like this. If you can divide it by tens, it will carry tens of thousands; but if you divide it by hundreds, it will smother you with thousands."[26] A group of a dozen or so people who look after one another through concern and encouragement can provide 90 percent of the support an individual needs to survive and thrive as a Christian.

▶ SMALL GROUPS CAN MAKE A BIG DIFFERENCE

A century ago in the United States, people would sit on their front porches or steps and visit with neighbors who walked by on sidewalks or roads. Most people had at least some family members living nearby who could be counted on if a crisis arose. The church and school were centers of social activity for the community. Farmers helped each other out by gathering in crops or raising a barn when there was a need.

Today, we live in relative isolation. People ride shoulder to shoulder on subways and buses, trying hard not to even acknowledge one another. City violence has driven people from their front steps into the safety of their houses. Many people would be hard-pressed to give even the names of the neighbors on either side of their dwelling. When we enter a bank or at a government office, our identity is a number typed into a computer or read off a card with a scanning machine. People desperately want to know that there is someone else out there who cares about them. They want a sense of community, even if they can't give it a name.

Many churches have discovered that the New Testament concept of believers meeting together in homes is suddenly relevant for the twenty-first century. Yet, not every church applauds the idea as helpful. Some churches are unwilling to change from methods of their past. Others fear that groups meeting outside the church could sow seeds of discontent and cause church splits. If people segregate themselves away from others, they could develop cliques and hurt church unity. There are pastors that are hesitant to release any pastoral care because they feel they have been called to do all the shepherding themselves. And some pastors see small-group ministry as just one more program they must run on their already overloaded schedule.

It is unfair and unrealistic to believe that developing a small-group ministry will solve all the problems a local church faces. In fact, a successful small-group program could create a whole new set of problems that come when a church experiences growth. There is no question that small groups that study the Scriptures, pray, love one another, and minister to others will make a difference in the lives of the individuals who participate and in their local church. As Donahue and Robinson note, "A church built on small groups will become a community that can reach a wider community. This is God's will for his people. This is our privilege as leaders. This is worth giving ourselves to—one life at a time."[27]

▶ QUESTIONS FOR REFLECTION

　▷ What is your rationale for the need for small groups as a part of a local church?

　▷ What would be the biggest obstacles to implementing a small-group ministry in a church of seventy-five to a hundred in attendance or in a church with three hundred attendees?

　▷ What would be the characteristics you would look for in selecting people to be small-group leaders? Coaches of small-group leaders?

UNIT 2

PASTORAL CARE ROLES

PASTORAL CARE AS SHEPHERDING

Joe Franklin had been at his first assignment as associate pastor of music and worship for three weeks when Roberta stopped by his office. Joe had become acquainted with her because she played the piano for the church services. It was obvious from her demeanor that she was very upset and wanted to talk. After a moment Roberta began to share with Joe her concern for the family that lived next to her. They had been in an accident and their four-year-old girl, Amy, had broken her arm and suffered a concussion. Roberta had taken care of the youngster several times and had become very attached because she had no grandchildren of her own. "I feel like they are family to me," Roberta said. "Amy could have been killed, and as far as I know, they don't know the Lord. What can we do to help them?"

Being so new in his first church job, Joe had not faced a ministry situation quite like this, but Roberta had sought his help. After they prayed together for Amy and the family, they began to discuss what could be done. It became obvious that Roberta wanted to hand off the responsibility to Joe since she didn't feel qualified to help out. But Joe recognized the concern and compassion Roberta had for the family. He finally said, "Why don't we work together to help this family?"

Roberta was at first apprehensive that Joe would ask her to become involved in what she thought was a pastor's work, but she agreed to try. Joe met her at the hospital and Roberta was overjoyed at discovering that Amy was not as seriously injured as the early reports indicated. During the next few days Roberta visited with Amy and her parents around the hospital bed. Then, when Amy went home, Roberta volunteered to stay with her while her mother worked. Six weeks later in the morning worship service Joe was surprised to see Roberta leading Amy and her family to seats near the front of the sanctuary. As they were all leaving after the service, Roberta whispered to Pastor Joe, "Thank you for helping me realize that I could do something to minister to Amy and her parents. I had always thought that only pastors could do this stuff. If you know of any other people that need personal attention like this, let me know."

▶ A SHEPHERD IN CENTURY TWENTY-ONE?

As a boy growing up in the church, I knew that around the middle of November the Sunday School teachers would begin recruiting people in our class for the annual Christmas program. We had mixed feelings about this. Everyone knew that at the end of the program we would each get a bag filled with hard candy, chocolates, and nuts. The bad part was the realization that we would have to perform in the program for our goodies. Some were asked to sing while others memorized poems. One element of every year's program was a reenactment of Luke's account of the first Christmas. The sought-after roles of Mary, Joseph, and the angel Gabriel always went to the bright and talented kids. Finally, after all the other parts were assigned, the leftover kids were named to the role at the very bottom of the dramatic pecking order—the shepherds.

Everyone knew that you didn't need to be very bright to play the role of a shepherd. Shepherds were usually herded on to the platform at the proper moment by a teacher from a room off to the side. Someone labored hard to make Mary and Joseph's costumes. Shepherds were relegated to wearing people's faded, oversized old bathrobes. The stars of the performance spoke lines. Shepherds either stood or knelt in front of the manger with eyes fixed on some girl's donated baby doll with one arm missing. Who in his or her right mind would want to be stuck with the role of shepherd?

My idea of being a shepherd also suffered because of the images I saw growing up. I especially remember a picture that hung in my junior boys classroom. It showed Jesus holding a lamb in his arms while he led a flock of sheep. He looked very effeminate, with long, brown, wavy locks and a full-length, flowing robe made from material that glistened like silk and looked like it would not last a day working in a field. We sang "I Want to Be like Jesus," but I hoped Jesus didn't ask me to look and dress like that. And then as a fourteen-year-old boy, he called me to be a minister. I said yes to becoming a pastor, but I might not have if I had known that the calling included being a shepherd to God's people.

▶ OLD TESTAMENT SHEPHERDING IMAGES

Two of the most revered leaders in Israel's history spent significant time as shepherds. Moses, while living in the palace of Pharaoh, was exposed to the best leadership training Egypt could provide at that time. Yet he learned the practical skills of caring, nurture, and desert survival while tending his father-in-law's sheep in the remote, arid land of Midian.

Moses' many years of practical experience as a shepherd in the desert came in very handy when God called him back to Egypt to lead Israel through similar surroundings.

When God wanted a new king to succeed Saul, he sent Samuel to the house of Jesse in the village of Bethlehem. After God had rejected the older, taller, stronger sons, Samuel asked Jesse if he had any other boys. Jesse's youngest son, David, was out in the field tending the family flock of sheep. God was not looking at the outward appearance the new king would exhibit. He was looking at the heart. Only one who would be willing to risk his own life to protect the sheep against a lion and a bear would be brave enough to unite the nation. Only one who would be willing to humbly serve sheep could be entrusted with the responsibility of leading the nation of Israel. According to Ps. 78:70-72, God "chose David his servant and took him from the sheep pens; from tending the sheep he brought him to be the shepherd of his people Jacob, of Israel his inheritance. And David shepherded them with integrity of heart; with skillful hands he led them." At his inauguration the people of Israel challenged David, "And the LORD your God said to you, 'You will shepherd my people Israel, and you will become their ruler'" (1 Chron. 11:2).

David was a man after God's own heart. His tenure as king was known as Israel's Golden Age. Even though his life was later marred by sinful failure, the Jewish people considered David, the former shepherd boy, the greatest king to ever rule Israel.

During the time of the prophets, the term *shepherd* was frequently used to describe the ideal kings of the Old Testament. The prophets challenged the kings to rule with faithfulness over God's people. There was no higher calling than to care for the people of the nation with compassion and integrity.

William Barclay, in his Daily Study Bible Series, describes the equipment of a shepherd in biblical times. Almost every shepherd had an animal-skinned bag with his food, which he called a *scrip;* his *sling,* which could be used to protect the sheep; a *staff,* which was a short club to ward off intruders; and a *rod,* that familiar long stick with a crook at one end that could be used to rescue a sheep in an emergency. During the time when the Bible was being written, sheep were raised, not so much for food as to provide fleece that could be made into wool. Because sheep were kept for a long time, the shepherd often named his sheep and talked to them in a singsong voice that the sheep could recognize.[1]

People have made Ps. 23 one of their favorite passages of Scripture because of the comforting images of God as a Shepherd of his sheep. These are wonderful characteristics for pastoral ministry today.

• *Feeding.* Verse 2 says, "He makes me lie down in green pastures, he leads me beside quiet waters." One of the major responsibilities of any shepherd is to be sure that the sheep have plenty of food and water. Any pastor worthy of the name will preach and teach the Word of God so the flock will grow spiritually. "But solid food is for the mature, who by constant use have trained themselves to distinguish good from evil" (Heb. 5:14)

• *Restoring.* Verse 3 says, "He restores my soul." Spiritual shepherds pick up sheep that have fallen. They encourage those who are depressed and discouraged. They give those who are weary an opportunity to rest. Pastor-shepherds are sensitive to the personal needs of the sheep, knowing when to encourage and when to challenge people to move ahead.

• *Protecting.* Verse 4 says, "Your rod and your staff, they comfort me." Pastors show great concern for the well-being of the flock. Satan is at work to destroy people, and the shepherd utilizes the full arsenal of spiritual weapons to keep each person from falling away from the faith. David Wiersbe says, "Along with teaching what is right, we must make the sheep aware of what is wrong to prevent them from falling prey to purveyors of non-Christian religions."[2]

• *Healing.* Verse 5 says, "You anoint my head with oil; my cup overflows." A pastor, when anointing a person with oil, symbolically brings the presence of the Holy Spirit to bear upon his or her physical and emotional wounds. Think about James 5:15, "And the prayer offered in faith will make the sick person well; the Lord will raise him up." It is a privilege for any shepherd to be a healing instrument of God's presence wherever there are hurts.

• *Nurturing.* Isaiah 40:11 says, "He tends his flock like a shepherd: He gathers the lambs in his arms and carries them close to his heart; he gently leads those that have young." While not a part of Ps. 23, this verse provides an additional image of shepherding compassion, motivated by a heart of love. Sheep are unique beings, with individual needs. While a corporation may be concerned about the bottom line of profit, pastors are in the people business. Although the Church is made up of individuals formed into one Body of Christ, each person within the Body has different gifts and talents. Jesus said in Luke 15 that a single sheep had value because, if one was lost, a shepherd began an all-out search to recover that sheep.

▶ New Testament Shepherding Images

Jesus develops some interesting images of himself in the "I am" passages in John's Gospel. He says of himself, I am . . . "the bread of life" (6:35), "the light of the world" (8:12), "the gate for the sheep" (10:7), "the resurrection and the life" (11:25), "the way and the truth and the life" (14:6), and "the true vine" (15:1). All of these descriptions are unique to the divinity of Jesus. However, there is one figure of speech that has application for pastors today: Jesus boldly identifies himself in John 10:11 as "the good shepherd."

In fact, John 10:1-18 gives us a detailed description from the lips of Jesus, describing himself as the model for those who will pastor in his name.

Here are some New Testament additions to shepherding qualities in the Psalms and elsewhere.

• *Knowing.* John 10:3 says, "He calls his own sheep by name." Nothing is more valuable than to know a person's name. A name speaks to a person's core identity. People have a basic need to be known by someone else. Obviously, in a very large church, the pastor cannot know everyone by name. But it is the pastor's responsibility as a shepherd, to be sure that someone knows and cares for each individual personally.

• *Leading.* John 10:3-4 says, "He . . . leads them out. . . . He goes out ahead of them." Shepherds lead sheep. They don't let the sheep simply wander aimlessly about. Just as shepherds give direction to the flock for food and shelter, the pastor of a church gives leadership for the nurture, growth, and development of the congregation. Pastors lead from the front, never driving the flock. Leading the church requires modeling, not pressuring or manipulating.

• *Vulnerability.* John 10:14 says, "I know my sheep and my sheep know me." A pastor needs to be transparent enough so that the congregation can begin to know the personal character of their leader. The ability to lead a congregation begins with a pastor earning the trust of the followers. People are slow to have confidence in a shepherd they do not know. It takes courage for a pastor to allow the people to see how the grace of God is personally at work in his or her life. Yet, only when they understand the inner character of their pastor will they see their leader as someone they can follow.

• *Serving the flock.* John 10:11 says, "The good shepherd lays down his life for the sheep." Jesus said in the next verse that hired hands are not real shepherds because they run away when the going gets tough. Shepherds realize the personal value of the sheep and will do almost anything for the good of the flock. The goal of the real pastor is not personal achievement but ultimately is to hear the voice of God saying, "Well done, good and faithful servant." Jesus did not come to be served, but to serve and give his life for the sheep.

• *Welcoming.* John 10:16 says, "I have other sheep that are not of this sheep pen. I must bring them also." Jesus' invitation went beyond the Jewish disciples who listened. He was welcoming the Gentile world that would be impacted in a few short years by the growing Church. Shepherds resist the notion that the sheepfold is off-limits to outsiders who would like to come in. It is too easy to stress unity and community to the point that people don't want to invite anyone else into the holy huddle they have created. Pastors have a passion for reaching to the unsaved of the community, as well as reaching across cultures to anyone who will hear the voice of God and respond to the wonderful invitation to come and be a part of God's flock.

• *Cooperating.* John 10:16 says, "There shall be one flock and one shepherd." A pastor must realize that the church he or she pastors is only a small part of the much larger universal Church of Jesus Christ. The kingdom of God is much bigger than one church or even one denomination. Shepherds work to bring unity to the Body of Christ, locally and universally. Sometimes pastors may be called upon to help out people who will never be a part of their local congregation. It is enough to know that God views his flock as one, and his shepherds are called to care for all his people.

There are two other shepherding qualities found elsewhere in the New Testament:

• *Equipping.* Hebrews 13:20-21 says, "May the God of peace, who through the blood of the eternal covenant brought back from the dead our Lord Jesus, that great Shepherd of the sheep, equip you with everything good for doing his will." Pastor-shepherds are the instruments the Great Shepherd uses to equip the flock to carry out the work God has given the Church, according to Eph. 4:11-16.

• *Modeling.* 1 Peter 5:2-3 says, "Be shepherds of God's flock . . . not lording it over those entrusted to you, but being examples to the flock." This is one place the shepherd/sheep metaphor breaks down. In church life, the shepherd is not a different species from the sheep. The pastor-shepherd is a sheep as well. Paul himself demonstrated how pastors model the lifestyle of faith when he said, "Follow my example, as I follow the example of Christ" (1 Cor. 11:1).

Using Jesus as the model for pastoral shepherding can be a bit overwhelming at first glance. Can anyone following the call of Christ hope to fulfill all the characteristics listed above in the way Jesus lived them out? Probably not. Some things will come naturally while other aspects will require more effort. Perhaps because the Jesus model was so daunting, the Church in the last half century has gone in search of a different model for ministry.

▸ Using the Wrong Model

In his insightful book *Escape from Church, Inc.: The Return of the Pastor-Shepherd,* E. Glenn Wagner states the problem very clearly: "During the past few decades we in the church have been busy creating, not communities, but corporations—and there is a vast difference!"[3]

He goes on to contrast the corporate emphases (programs, products, money, numbers, organization, management, and bottom line) with what should be the church's emphases (community-building, relationships, ministry, intimacy, compassion, mentoring, and encouragement). Wagner then asks, "Where did we go astray? How did we end up tying ourselves to a model that sees the church more as a corporation than as a community of faith? When did we start training CEOs rather than pastors?"[4]

Part of the problem has developed out of a sincere spiritual desire to see the local church grow and become an effective force in the world. Many pastors have bought into the idea that there is much to learn about running the church from the leadership gurus of the secular world. If the church would only become more organized and structured for success, it could not help but grow. There are principles of leadership that business leaders can teach us in ministry. Careful strategizing and planning have a place in the church. But is using the CEO model the best way to learn about shepherding?

Obviously, the most important person in implementing and leading the corporate model in the church is the chief executive officer, the pastor. However, for many in pastoral ministry this CEO model has not brought a sense of fulfillment. The number of pastors leaving their positions because of burnout and disillusionment is on the increase. Joseph Stowell, former president of Moody Bible Institute, says, "Perhaps we have taken more the corporate model of leadership and imposed that into pastoral ministry, as if Jack Welch [former head of General Electric] were the premium pastor in America. That, I think, is creating deep levels of frustration for pastors in America today. They can't live up to that standard."[5]

Many pastors are frustrated in ministry because they feel that running an organization was not what God called them to do. Now, there is nothing wrong with having an organizational structure so the church can utilize its limited resources efficiently. Like it or not, administration is a necessary part of the pastoral role. But fundamentally a church is a community of people, not a corporation answering to its shareholders. People do not want to think of themselves as a name on a membership list or a worker bee busy in the hive. They want to feel like they belong to a family of believers where somebody knows their name and cares what happens in their lives. Whether church members are called a family or a flock, they all need a shepherd who will make sure that each person feels cared for and needed.

▶ Avoiding the Model Altogether

Some pastors have moved away from the shepherding motif, saying that it is a carryover from a simpler age long ago. People today are too sophisticated and busy to want someone to shepherd them. Actually, the opposite is true.

As a culture we have moved away from a sense of community where people knew their neighbors and helped each other out. Family members are often separated thousands of miles from each other. People work in offices and other workspaces, isolated by cubicles and dividers, laboring in their own private environment. At home, people surf cyberspace in search of some type of virtual connectedness. Sociologist Linda Wilcox writes of her concern in this area, "The Stanford Institute for Quantitative Study of Society found that one in seven on-line users is in danger of losing contact with 'real human beings.' Researchers at Carnegie Mellon examined Net users in Pittsburgh over two years and found that frequent users were more likely to become depressed."[6]

In the separation and loneliness of our present world, people are desperate for some sense of community. But even the reality shows on television that try to explore the inner human feelings of the participants fail in helping people really connect with others.

Perhaps the concept of shepherding is too uncool for twenty-first-century people. Glenn Wagner says he thinks "many Westerners reject the shepherd model because they consider it primitive, outdated, and unsophisticated."[7] These people are searching for a new, cutting-edge approach to care that no one has ever thought of before. However, the biblical truths about people are not dated or faddish but timeless in their scope. Shepherding still works because people need someone who will know them and care for them.

There are pastors who reject the shepherding model because they believe it limits the growth potential of the church. This is true if one believes that the pastor must do all of the shepherding. A pastor who does all the shepherding work in a local church will not be able to effectively minister to more than about a hundred people. However, the Bible never says that the pastor is to do all the caregiving in a church. Chapter 4 clearly develops the case for lay pastoral care or shepherding. Ephesians 4:11-12, the only Bible passage to use the word *pastor,* informs us that they are to "prepare God's people for works of service."

▶ SHEPHERDING IS A MINDSET

How does a pastor of a larger congregation function as a shepherd when the needs of the people are far beyond the scope of what any one person can possibly do to meet them? The answer is twofold.

First, the pastor has the overall responsibility for seeing that each person of the flock receives personal care. For example, a farmer who operates a large dairy farm may not personally milk and feed each cow in the herd. A good farmer will be responsible for making sure, through the workers on the farm, that each cow is milked, fed, and cared for. Pastor-shepherds work to create and maintain a strong sense of community in the church so each member feels needed and connected.

Second, while pastors can't do all the work of shepherding, they must maintain the heart of a shepherd. Jesus looked down on Jerusalem and wept because the people there were lost, like sheep that didn't have a shepherd. It goes without saying that to be a shepherd you have to walk with the sheep and have a concern for their needs.

There is a tension for a pastor between being a shepherd or servant, while at the same time assuming the necessary role as leader of the church. The pastor could spend all his or her available time taking individual parishioners to the doctor's office or grocery store and neglect the necessary work of sermon preparation to feed the entire flock. What about a pastor's responsibility to take care of himself or herself and spend time with family? Pastor Leith Anderson, in a *Leadership* magazine interview on the pastor's twin tasks of serving and leading, shares three personal guidelines:

> 1. *Serve the greater number rather than the greatest need.* If you can serve 100 people or one person who seems to have a greater need, as a rule, you serve the greater number. 2. *Give priority to the basics.* For pastors [that means] next week's sermon and prayer and going to the board and staff meetings and having regular family time and having available margins for an unanticipated crisis. 3. *Be aware of your limitations.* Sometimes we think, *I'm a servant to everybody, therefore I have to serve anyone who asks,* when you may in fact do more damage than good by trying to serve beyond your competence.[8]

▶ SHEPHERDING IS HARD WORK

Pastors hear the same lame joke over and over from people who think they are being clever: "Pastoring has to be a great job. After all, you only have to work one hour a week." The truth is, being the pastor of a church is a full-time job, even for those who need to be bivocational in order to provide for their financial needs. And the work is exhausting.

A recent study of Protestant clergy in America indicated that the average full-time pastor works forty-six hours a week and spends nearly nine hours of that doing pastoral care. The only category that took more time (fifteen hours a week) was preaching and worship, which included preparation time.[9] Other surveys list the pastor's average work schedule at over sixty hours weekly. The modern shepherds of God's flock certainly feel the emotional exhaustion that comes from helping people.

In Luke 8 Jesus was on his way to heal the daughter of Jairus when suddenly he stopped and asked who touched him. At one level it was an absurd question because there were people everywhere pushing and jostling to see the Master. Verse 46 says, "But Jesus said, 'Someone touched me; I know that power has gone out from me.'"

When people are in need, they take emotional energy from the one giving help. Spiritual shepherds go through the day being touched by people and freely dispensing that emotional energy. Over a period of time the very act of serving others, especially in difficult circumstances, can deplete a pastor's emotional and physical resources to the point of exhaustion.

Shepherding is hard because caring for people can be painful. Pastors can give their best to help a person who will misunderstand the intent and turn against the pastor by biting the helping hand. A pastor can invest time and emotional energy in an individual only to have that person leave for another church that seems to be offering a "better deal." Glenn Wagner observes, "Not all sheep are loving, not all sheep bring us joy. Some nip at our heels and ram us when our backs are turned, not just once but year after year."[10] Personally, I have found that the deepest wounds, the most painful hurts as a pastor, came not from the outside world, but from the people of the congregation during the process of trying to shepherd them. Perhaps the hurt is greater because, while pastors expect Satan's attacks, they are unprepared when God's people rip into them when they come to their people as vulnerable shepherds, with open hands.

Shepherding in the twenty-first century is especially hard because our culture is not oriented toward receiving our help. The values of privacy, independence, and pluralism are sacred in the minds of people. Wilcox comments, "It is not uncommon for us, thanks to CNN, to know more about what's happening on the other side of the planet than what's happening on the other side of the fence."[11] But the more people believe they can function without needing anyone else, the lonelier they feel in those quiet moments when they are alone and in need.

Postmoderns long for community and connectedness with others. Church futurist Leonard Sweet says in his book *Post-Modern Pilgrims* that the power of connection is a healing power. "Healing connections are here, there, and everywhere for the picking if the church can help post-moderns understand what it means to be connected—connected to one another, connected to creation, even connected to the church itself."[12]

What is the pastor's role in all of this? Sweet says:

> Three-quarters of all pastors see themselves as gifted at either teaching or preaching. Yet Jesus' ministry had three components: preaching,

teaching, and healing. If moral and spiritual transformation is to occur communally as well as individually, pastors will need to upgrade their healing role and hone their healing skills to at least the same levels as preaching and teaching.[13]

One of the primary avenues for pastors to bring healing is by being a shepherd to people.

▶ SHEEP NEED A SHEPHERD

As Jesus looked at the Galilean crowds in Matt. 9:36, his concern was that "they were harassed and helpless, *like sheep without a shepherd*" (italics added). Sheep are strange animals. They seem to be void of any natural ability to defend themselves from attack. Sheep lack the horns of a ram, the teeth of a wolf, the claws of a bear, the speed of a cheetah, or the cunning of a fox. They need a shepherd for protection from outside danger.

Sometimes they need protection from themselves. Sheep have a tendency to wander off. In their focused desire to search for food, they can lose track of where they are and soon be lost. Isaiah 53:6 refers to this tendency. "We all, like sheep, have gone astray, each of us has turned to his own way." Shepherds need to be constantly alert to sheep that may be straying too far from the rest of the flock. They are not always discerning in what they eat. The shepherd has to make sure the sheep graze in good pastures and do not eat any noxious weeds. Isn't it amazing, the similarities between sheep and church members? Perhaps that is why God chose the title of *pastor* or *shepherd* for those who are given the responsibility of leading the flock.

Although it has its share of pain and disappointments, the role of pastor can also be very fulfilling. Shepherds function as spiritual midwives when new lambs are born.

One pastor remembers a young high school couple that began attending his first church at the invitation of one of the church members. During one service this pastor had the strong impression that this couple would make a decision for Christ if he would present the gospel. After the minister argued with God that he had another sermon planned, he changed the sermon and, sure enough, this young man and woman responded to the invitation. What an exciting moment for the pastor and for this couple. The pastor watched them grow as the friend who first invited the couple to church began to disciple them. Soon this young man responded to God's call to enter pastoral ministry. Between graduation from college and entering seminary this couple, now married, came back to their home church to serve in local youth ministry. Later, the young man graduated from seminary and the pastor moved to another church.

After serving in his first formal pastoral position of a rural congregation in another state, the young pastor received a call to pastor the church where they were saved and were called to the ministry. The older pastor-mentor was later called back to celebrate this couple's ten-year anniversary of service to that church. It was obvious to him that God was at work in the life of this couple, moving them from the point of their salvation, through the process of pastoral training, to the place where this man was now the shepherd of that same congregation where he began his spiritual journey. There was a sense of real satisfaction in the heart of the pastor-mentor as well. Not only had his ministry there seen sheep being born, but there were now new shepherds serving Christ's church. His ministry was being reproduced and multiplied.

▶ PRESENT-DAY SHEPHERDING

Our world is becoming increasingly impersonal. Try calling a corporation or business. A phone message gives a series of options designed to direct the customer to a department for a needed response. However, the options may not exactly fit the situation. The customer may need to talk to a real person, but instead is sent from option to option and finally encouraged to leave a voice mail with the promise that someone will get back to the customer later.

Imagine a church voice mail message like this. "We really care about you and your need. Press 1 if you are a member, or press 2 for all others. If you need spiritual guidance, press the star button. If you need financial counseling, press the pound button now. If you are feeling anxious, depressed, or lonely, press 7 to hear an inspiring thought from the pastor. To discuss family problems, press 9 for our youth pastor. For an emergency, go directly to the church office between the hours of 9 A.M. and 4 P.M. Tuesday through Thursday. For all other concerns, press 4 and leave a message, including your name and a brief description of the problem. Remember, your personal needs are our top priority."

What people really want in a time of need is the face-to-face contact of a real person, listening in real time, someone who can respond in a helpful manner—someone like a pastor-shepherd. In a day when other professions have abandoned making house calls, the pastor has a unique opportunity to make personal contact with people in their homes or at work. Pastor-shepherds don't normally need a special appointment or invitation. It is most natural for pastors to help people in the settings where they feel most comfortable.

However, the context of ministry has changed radically in the last hundred years. Pastors in the beginning of the twentieth century related to their church families in a very different way. There were fewer single-parent families then. Most women did not work outside the home. Extended family members often lived close by. Wage earners traveled a shorter distance to work. Evenings were free of television and most of the other forms of entertainment familiar today. Neighbors visited across the back fence and helped each other as needs arose. And a visit from the pastor in the home was generally welcome and even expected on a regular basis.

Times have changed. There are several reasons pastors make fewer house calls today. For one thing, there are fewer people in the home during daytime hours. Between both parents working, and the kids involved in sports and music lessons, a pastor may find it hard to find anyone around the house during the daylight hours. Also, when people do come home they value their personal time. After the pressures of the job and a long commute, they want uninterrupted personal space. For many, personal time is more valuable than money. Privacy is also an important issue. Because people fear crime and intrusion they may live in gated communities or private apartment buildings designed for protection from outside intrusions. Pastors have to be more persistent and creative to be able to spend time personally shepherding people.

It is natural to connect the words *pastor* and *parish* in terms of pastoral calling. Thomas Oden defines the parish as the "geographical area to which the pastor is accountable on behalf of the apostolic mission. Leaving one's own house, one's own secure and controlled surroundings, is therefore essential to the definition of a visit."[14] Being a pastor means going both to the church members and to the larger community with the purpose of encouraging spiritual growth and personal well-being.

▶ WHY VISITATION TODAY?

Jesus, the Good Shepherd, spent a major part of his ministry on earth in contact with individuals where they lived. He visited in the homes of people like Mary and Martha, Matthew, and Simon, the Leper. Other times he encountered people in the marketplace, along the seashore, at a community well, or at a tax booth. Jesus tried to reach out to people from the various segments of society, such as Sadducees, Pharisees, Zealots, Herodians, and even Romans. Wherever people were, Jesus was likely to make it a point to engage them in conversation in order to bring help.

Spending time with sheep is still an essential part of being a shepherd. E-mail and voice mail, while helpful, do not substitute for face-to-face, personal contact with the people of the congregation. When God wanted to communicate his love to the human race, he did not simply send a book or a series of preachers. The Incarnation is all about God coming down to earth personally in the form of a person—Jesus Christ. That's what pastoral care is all about—putting a human face and voice to the love of God for an individual. People receive messages all day long by television and other electronic media that they are only one of a nameless mass of humanity. What they desperately crave is someone who will say to them, "I know your name and I care about you."

Shepherds spend enough time with sheep so they know their parishioners by name and the sheep recognize their shepherd's voice. In a large congregation the shepherding may be more effectively done by a lay shepherd who takes the responsibility for a small group of sheep. Who does the shepherding is not nearly as important as the fact that every sheep is receiving some personal care from the church. While the pastor of a larger church may not know every parishioner by name, he or she has the responsibility to make sure that none of the sheep are left out or forgotten.

Pastoral visitation is important because it purposely seeks out people who are in need of spiritual counsel and guidance. Effective pastors don't simply hang out a shingle or hand out business cards saying, "I'm here if you want to make an appointment." Part of being a shepherd is taking the initiative to go where there is a need even before the person may be ready to request help. Visitation, be it lay or pastoral, makes a strong statement to the congregation that people are important.

▶ WHO NEEDS A VISIT?

While churches need to be certain that no one is neglected, there are certain contacts that must take priority. Obviously, people facing a crisis, grief, or serious conflict need immediate attention. The same goes for people in the hospital. These issues will be covered in detail later in the book. But what about those who have good health and have been fortunate to avoid major problems in life? Do these people need shepherding?

George Hunter III says, "Regular pastoral care (much more than crisis care) is an important producer of a people who share their faith. Most Christians who share their faith and invite others to Christ and the Church are themselves in regular spiritual conversation and prayer with a significant other who serves as their pastor."[15] While lay pastoral care can be effective in providing those regular contacts, the pastor also needs to make regular, nonemergency contacts with members of the congregation.

To be effective in pastoral contact, the minister needs to be creative. Instead of stopping by unannounced at homes in the evening, hoping to find people at home, try to make appointments. Busy pastors also make use of breakfast or lunchtimes to visit with people over some food. Many people would welcome the pastor stopping by their place of employment for a brief conversation. This also gives the pastor insight into the real-life setting where people spend most of their time. Take advantage of unscheduled moments when a person may stop by the church or the pastor crosses paths with a member at the shopping mall. God may have planned that encounter to provide ministry for the person's need.

Pastors can find opportunities for pastoral calling during the daytime hours with those who are not at work or those who work evenings or the late shift. People in nursing homes and other care facilities face special challenges of loneliness and boredom. When the pastor or some other person from the church stops by to call regularly, it is a reminder that God has not forgotten about them either. Nursing home ministry can be a wonderful opportunity to love the unlovely in the name of Jesus.

▶ LISTENING TO YOUR HEART

One last word to shepherds: listen to your heart. One who carries the responsibility of spiritually leading the flock needs to be sensitive to the needs of individuals. Some needs are obvious because they are vocalized or expressed in other ways. Other needs come to the surface only after probing or making oneself approachable. The Holy Spirit has a way of letting a pastor know when someone specific is in need of special care.

In Acts 8 Philip sensed God's leading to go to a remote desert location. He acted in obedience and had the opportunity to minister to a government official from Ethiopia. When someone's name or a situation continues to come to mind, it may be God's way of saying, that person needs special attention. By responding to those inner promptings pastors can develop an increased sensitivity to the Spirit's leading in personal ministry. Shepherding is an act of the heart, prompted by God, to care for his sheep.

▶ QUESTIONS FOR REFLECTION

▷ In what ways do you feel that shepherding is compatible with ministry in the twenty-first century?

▷ What aspects of shepherding do you find appealing as you minister or anticipate ministry?

▷ What aspects of shepherding cause you concern or anxiety? How can you respond to those difficult shepherding tasks?

▷ Why is it important to involve laypeople in shepherding ministries?

SEVEN

PASTORAL CARE AS COUNSELING

Tina Short had been hired by the Central City church to be their pastor, for her preaching ability as much as anything else. She had been a high school speech teacher when God began directing her toward the pastorate. And after her ministerial training was over, standing in the pulpit on Sunday mornings had become her greatest joy. It was her recent series from the Psalms that had begun to change her ministry. As she spoke of God's concern for problems such as depression, loneliness, and anger, people began coming out of the proverbial woodwork wanting to talk to her. Preaching to a crowd about a problem was easy compared with trying to help someone who was dealing with that problem in real life.

And it took so much of her time. With all of the other responsibilities of pastoring and shepherding her flock, Tina was becoming frustrated with the increased counseling load. She also wasn't convinced she was helping some of the people who were coming to her. Some seemed just to like the personal attention she gave to them in the counseling sessions. Others didn't follow through on what they agreed they should do. With her limited counseling training Tina felt she needed guidance in being an effective people helper. How could her one-on-one time with people really bring about the life changes these people desired?

▶ WHY PASTORAL COUNSELING?

Most people responding to a call to pastoral ministry do not think initially about counseling as part of the responsibility. However, in the first pastoral assignment the realization usually sets in: counseling is something that can't be avoided. As seminary professor and psychologist James Hamilton writes, "No minister can avoid counseling unless he locks himself in his study."[1]

With all the responsibilities of pastoral ministry, few pastors have opportunity to prepare themselves adequately to match the training of those in the professional counseling field. Yet this does not seem to matter to the parishioners and others who come to the pastor seeking help. Hamilton continues:

> A pastor is not a psychologist, yet he is called upon for psychological counseling. He is not a vocational counselor, but he is sought for help in this area. He is not an educational counselor, but often youth come to him with problems concerning their courses of study. Neither is he a psychiatrist; nevertheless he is sometimes confronted with the deep seeded problems of persons needing psychiatric care and must, therefore, be

99

aware of the manifestations of these problems in order to make intelligent referrals. However, he must above all else, know how to counsel persons with religious problems, and so should become as proficient in this area as possible.[2]

The question is not "if" a pastor will counsel, but "how well" will the pastor fulfill the responsibility.

Counseling goes to the very heart of the meaning of pastoral ministry. Thomas Oden makes this clear. "*Therapeia* in the Greek means a helping, serving, healing relationship. A *therapon* (from which our term 'therapist' comes) is one who helps, serves, and heals. The Latin translation for *therapon* is *ministerium,* from which our word 'minister' (helper, servant) comes. . . . The pastoral office has from its beginnings been thought of literally as a therapeutic relationship."[3]

How does one distinguish pastoral counseling from other functions of pastoral care? David Benner, in his book *Strategic Pastoral Counseling,* defines pastoral counseling as "a helping relationship where, through a series of structured contacts, the counselor seeks to alleviate distress and promote growth in the one seeking help. Such counseling aims to help the person think, feel, and behave differently, and it does this through dialogue within a relationship."[4] Psychologist Gary Collins explains that pastoral counseling "is a more specialized part of pastoral care that involves helping individuals, families, or groups as they cope with the pressures and crises of life. Pastoral counseling uses a variety of healing methods to help people deal with problems in ways that are consistent with biblical teaching."[5] It is this spiritual dimension that separates pastoral counseling from all other types of counseling, even Christian counseling done outside the context of the church. Pastors are legitimately concerned more with the spiritual growth and development of the individual. It is the pastor's unique religious preparation and training that makes this area of spiritual counsel so valuable to the members of a congregation.

There are many reasons why people turn first to their pastor when they need counsel. First, the pastor is usually known by the person seeking help. That means there is already a level of rapport established. The counselee has observed the pastor in the pulpit or ministering to a family and feels that the minister is someone who can be trusted. Second, the pastor may already know the counselee through contacts at church. This can save the time needed to gather personal and family information necessary to better understand the counseling situation. Third, the pastor is generally more available for counseling at short notice. One does not need to wait several weeks for an appointment. Another factor in seeking pastoral counsel is that normally the pastor does not charge for the sessions. Often people will not seek help for some problems because they do not feel they have the money available for a private counselor. Perhaps the most significant reason people seek a pastor for counseling is the spiritual understanding a minister brings to the situation. This is obviously true if the problem is a spiritual one. These people come believing that they need God's help in facing a problem, and the person best suited to help them is their pastor.

▶ JESUS, THE WONDERFUL COUNSELOR

One of the traditions of Christmas enjoyed around the world is the presentation of Handel's *Messiah*. But when he interpreted Isa. 9:6, he got it wrong. The choir sings, "And he shall be called Wonderful, [pause] Counselor, the mighty God." Although the Messiah could be called *wonderful*, that wasn't Isaiah's intention. Jesus is the *Wonderful Counselor*. (The old spiritual "Glory Hallelujah" got it right: "I call Jesus the Wonderful Counselor . . . glory hallelujah.")

When it comes to pastoral counseling models, there was simply no one better than Jesus to help people with needs. Here are a few of his counseling characteristics:

• *Jesus showed great compassion to people.* In Mark 8:2 he made this statement of concern, "I feel compassion for these people; they have already been with me for three days and have nothing to eat."

• *Jesus accepted people where they were.* It was not uncommon for Jesus to have dinner with despised people like tax collectors. In fact, he invited one, Matthew, to be one of the twelve disciples.

• *Jesus gave people hope and encouragement.* To a group of discouraged disciples in the Upper Room Jesus said, "In this world you will have trouble. But take heart! I have overcome the world" (John 16:33).

• *Jesus addressed real needs.* Nicodemus approached Jesus with some religious questions, but the real need was a personal relationship with God. Jesus patiently taught him the meaning of being born again.

• *Jesus emphasized right behavior.* The woman caught in the act of adultery in John 8 did not receive a lecture on her moral failure, but rather a word of forgiveness and a challenge to follow a new life.

• *Jesus also urged people to accept responsibility.* To the man by the pool in John 5 Jesus asked, "Do you want to get well?" (v. 6). If you are sick, people take care of you. Healing meant the man would need to assume responsibility for himself. Jesus told him, "Get up! Pick up your mat and walk" (v. 8).

• *Jesus gave people worth.* Lepers were the social outcasts of the nation, shunned by family and friends. No one felt more rejection than a leper. Yet Jesus approached them and healed them and restored them to the community.

The list could go on. Jesus was a master at seeing needs and helping people. In Jesus we understand the meaning of the title Wonderful Counselor.

▶ Guiding Principles for Pastoral Counseling

It is impossible in a single chapter to begin to cover all that needs to be said about pastoral counseling. There are many good books dealing with approaches and techniques for effective counseling. This chapter will instead address some of the foundational principles for counseling in a pastoral context:

Equip yourself to be able to help others.

A person preparing for the pastorate may feel that a large amount of education is necessary to be an effective counselor. While it would be wonderful for every pastor to have a doctoral degree in counseling, there are other areas— such as theology, biblical studies, church history, preaching, and leadership— that can't be neglected in the preparation process. Some ministry students may have an opportunity to obtain advanced training in counseling, and counseling may be of special interest to a pastor. However, most ministers will be lifelong learners, reading books and attending conferences to sharpen the pastoral counseling skills. It is important to understand that advanced study is only one component in effective counseling. A pastor who is a good listener and cares about people can be successful in helping people.

Know your limitations.

You may have good people skills and a knack for sensing needs but be unfamiliar with people who are facing severe psychological problems. A mechanic may know how to change spark plugs and rotate tires but be completely lost when it comes to an automobile's computer systems. When auto issues come up that are beyond the skill level of the family mechanic, the only course of action is to have someone with sophisticated training work on that engine. It is essential for the pastor to know his or her competencies and be willing to seek help for the person who needs additional guidance. There will be times, however, when the person seeking help either has no resources or refuses to be referred to anyone else. If this is the case, the minister can try to help to the limits of his or her pastoral counseling ability.

Recognize that the counselee is made in God's image and has value.

There are times when the counselee's problem or personality or personal appearance can be offensive to the pastor. It is easy to think, *I don't want to deal with this person.* Jesus, on the other hand, seemed to take delight in responding to prostitutes, tax collectors, lepers, and others that most of the Jewish population rejected. Perhaps it was because he understood that the value of a person was worth the whole world. It may help, when confronted by a person that may be personally repugnant, to remind oneself that this is a person for whom Christ died. As a pastor, I am Jesus' representative, sent to be of help. A pastor's unspoken attitude of acceptance may be the crucial first step in helping that person to wholeness.

Seek first to help the person to wholeness in Christ, and then to find a solution to the problem.

One of the things that separate pastoral counseling from other types of counseling is the emphasis on a right relationship with God as the foundation for problem solving. Many of the problems presented to a pastor have a specific spiritual component. Never apologize for being a spiritual leader. Most people come to a pastor because they expect spiritual guidance. If someone is totally resistant to the use of prayer and biblical principles, a pastor may find it difficult to be of help. Pastors need to recognize that giving spiritual guidance requires both skill and sensitivity to the Holy Spirit's leading in the counselee's life.

Remember that a person has the right to accept or reject help.

The old adage, *You can lead a horse to water, but you can't make him drink,* certainly applies to counseling. A pastor can offer help but can't force a person to take it. One dimension of being created in the image of God is a person's ability to make moral choices. Jesus understood this when he encountered the rich young man in Mark 10. When this man inquired about eternal life, Jesus told him the requirements. The final stipulation of giving all his earthly goods was just too much. Sadly, the young man walked away because the cost was more than he was willing to pay. Jesus did not run after him with a compromise offer. The young man made his choice. Pastors need to understand that some people do not want to be helped or are unwilling to accept the conditions they will be required to take to remedy the situation.

Remember that both the pastor and the counselee must work together toward a solution.

Some people want the pastor to give all the answers and even take the actions needed to resolve a problem. When the pastor takes the responsibility for mapping out a plan of action, he or she runs the risk of taking the blame if it doesn't work out to the counselee's satisfaction. On the other hand, a pastor who is too nondirective may come across as uncaring and detached. Counseling is a cooperative venture as the pastor reflects, offers suggestions, supports, and encourages the counselee in moving toward an agreed-upon solution.

Embrace your role as a spiritual guide.

Since pastoral counseling has a uniquely spiritual dimension, the pastor is the natural person to guide the counselee along this path. William Willimon says, "A guide is one who knows something—perhaps not everything—but something. . . . The guide is expected to lead and to advise. The guide has no power to force those who seek guidance to accept the guide's leading and advice, but the guide has a responsibility to guide."[6] The specialized ministerial training, the collection of past pastoral experiences, and the knowledge of the parishioner all assist the pastor in giving guidance. Any shepherd who refuses or neglects to be a spiritual guide to those under his or her care is shirking a major responsibility.

But guidance is not limited only to those in trouble. Perhaps those who have grown spiritually cold or complacent are in even greater need of a guide. Willimon reports hearing the great preacher George Buttrick say, "It takes a very special pastor to visit that person who has just been promoted at the bank, or the person whose child has just been accepted at Harvard University. The skillful pastor knows the spiritual peril that lies in what the world considers good news, or health, or success."[7] Spiritual guidance is one of the responsibilities that make pastors unique among people helpers.

Utilize the spiritual resources of the church.

There is a wealth of supportive material readily available to the pastor in the context of the church community. The Bible itself provides a rich resource for instruction, encouragement, and spiritual guidance in a counseling session as well as for assignments between visits. A pastor can give guidance in the use of prayer for direction and spiritual strengthening. Many churches have prayer groups or prayer chains that will intercede for specific needs, even if they are anonymous. Often there are Christian books, tapes, and other helps designed to help the counselee through a specific problem. Counselees may gain special understanding from talking to a person from the church that has faced a similar situation. Some churches have support groups to bring together several people who are dealing with a common problem. These groups provide insight and encouragement in a loving, spiritual context.

▶ PASTORAL COUNSELING SKILLS

Pastors, regardless of their level of training, will find basic people skills helpful in their counseling. In fact, some people who have no formal counseling training are excellent in counseling simply because they have learned to relate to others by utilizing these skills. Anyone can develop these qualities that make counselors successful people helpers.

• *Listening.* This skill seems to be so obvious, so simple, but it is really hard work. One problem counselors face is that the brain can process information so much faster than a person can speak. There is a natural temptation to let one's mind wander and think about other things, while at the same time trying to catch what the counselee is saying. Listening is more than just hearing words. Really listening involves watching the subtle body movements, catching voice inflections, and trying to understand what isn't being spoken. It means focusing the mind on the words, interpreting their meaning with your heart, and responding back to the speaker with signals that you understand what is being said. These can be hand gestures and head nods, or verbal encouragement such as, "and then what happened" or "tell me more about how you felt."

• *Being present.* The counselee needs to have the feeling that the pastor's attention is focused on the problem at hand. It is easy to be distracted by people walking by, noises outside, what the person has already said, or even what to respond. For that reason it is good to try to either move away from behind a desk or move distracting work material away from one's line of vision. Being present lets the counselee know that the counselor is focusing undivided attention on the issue at hand. Collins describes it as, "Looking at the counselee as he or she speaks, but without either staring or letting your eyes wander around the room."[8] People feel comforted when they know that the counselor has set everything aside to give help. Benner talks of counseling as "structured being-with" a person. "To unpack this, I would suggest, first, that counseling involves being as a priority over doing; second, that in counseling this being takes the form of being-with; and, third, that in counseling this being-with is structured."[9]

• *Empathy.* This is the counselor's attempt to understand what the counselee is thinking and feeling. Many people confuse empathy with sympathy, which expresses pity and concern while looking on. A counselor with empathy tries to view and interpret the situation from the other person's point of view. Jesus showed empathy in John 11 when he stood beside Martha outside the grave of her brother, Lazarus, and wept with her. Pastors need to be careful not to say, "I know exactly how you feel." It is impossible to fully know the feelings of another individual, even if one has experienced a similar situation. However, con sitive counselors will work hard to try to put themselves in the mind and emotions of the counselee and ask themselves, "How would I respond if I were this person and facing this situation?"

• *Being real.* The counselee wants to have the sense that the pastor is a real, genuine person and not wearing a mask. This is sometimes difficult because people develop unrealistic expectations of a pastor as being superhuman. The pastor needs to convey to the counselee that he or she is understanding, sensitive, vulnerable, and sincere. A pastor's willingness to be genuine with the counselee will help that person to feel free to share the most personal concerns.

• *Acceptance.* It is a common belief among those outside the church that pastors are narrow-minded and judgmental, evaluating people's worthiness for heaven. This certainly was not Jesus' approach. When the woman of Samaria in John 4 came to the well and saw Jesus, a Jew, sitting there, she was not expecting acceptance. As her story of marriage failures began to unfold, Jesus never gave the impression that he approved of her lifestyle. The Master did express his concern for her and his acceptance of her as a person of worth and value. Verse 39 sums up the result of Jesus' acceptance, "Many of the Samaritans from that town believed in him because of the woman's testimony, 'He told me everything I ever did.'"

Jesus had a wonderful way of making sinners feel loved and accepted by eating with them, even though they may not have felt themselves worthy of such attention. Jesus had the ability to see people's potential if they would receive his help. It is easy to judge people on what they have done rather than on what they can become by the saving grace of God. The wonderful message of the gospel is that God accepts us as sinners and changes us by grace into his saints. Pastors can be messengers of reconciliation by displaying an attitude of acceptance toward those whose actions or appearance may not always be acceptable. Gary Collins defines this as warmth. "This word implies caring, respecting, or possessing a sincere, non-smothering concern for the counselee regardless of his or her actions or attitudes."[10] This acceptance grows out of a Christian heart of agape love that expresses the love of Jesus to people in need.

▶ CAUTIONS FOR PASTORAL COUNSELORS

Armed with key foundational principles and honed people skills, the pastor must also be cautious when it comes to the role of counselor. Here are a few recommendations.

Don't use pastoral counseling as the source for developing human relationships.

Pastoring can be a lonely job. People look to the pastor as a leader but not necessarily as a close friend. In the counseling situation, some of the barriers created by the pastoral role are broken down, and it is easier to get to know a person at a deeper level. Some pastors enjoy the closeness, friendship, and intimacy of the sessions and may prolong the counseling longer than is necessary. While there may be nothing wrong with the developing friendship, one should not use the counseling sessions for personal fulfillment or satisfaction.

Don't take on the responsibility for the counselee's thoughts and actions.

Some people who come for counseling really want the pastor to make the decisions for their lives. *Transference,* as Collins describes it, is "the tendency of some individuals to transfer feelings about a person in the past to a person in the present."[11] A woman who comes to her male pastor with concerns about her marriage may see in him the listening, sympathetic, caring person her husband is not. Or, an insecure young man may be unable to make an important decision and say, "Oh pastor, you are so much wiser than I am. You tell me what I should do." Making choices for others is fraught with danger. If the counselor's choice does not prove to be the right one, the counselee may be slow to accept any responsibility for the failure. As pastors counsel they need to constantly ask themselves if the counselee is trying to use manipulation for his or her own purposes. Don't be backed into a corner by the counselee's unwillingness to make a decision. Counselors may make suggestions or options, but let the final choice be the counselee's.

Don't use the counseling sessions to gratify personal needs.

Willimon explains, "The pastor wants to be an effective and helpful counselor. So, out of the pastor's need to be an all-powerful savior in this situation, the pastor becomes the messiah, the person who takes inappropriate and unrealistic responsibility for the counselee's problem."[12]

Sometimes the problem of the counselee may be similar to one the counselor is facing. Psychologists use the term *countertransference* to describe the counselor's temptation to work on his or her own problems in the counseling session. Collins writes, "When the counseling session becomes a place for solving your own problems, counselees are not likely to be helped, and you could be tempted to make statements or act in ways that would be regretted later."[13] A pastor may develop romantic feelings toward the counselee that make it impossible to separate the needs of the counselee from the counselor's own personal desires. Psychologist Archibald Hart puts it this way, "Countertransference occurs when a pastor responds to the client with inappropriate feelings of affection."[14]

For this reason a pastor needs to set personal boundaries before counseling begins in order to provide protection within the context of trying to help people. Pastors need to know themselves, understand their limitations, and refer people to other helping professionals when necessary, so they do not hurt others and do damage to their ministry.

Resist the role of a parent or dictator to the flock.

There have been some pastors who have distorted their understanding of the shepherding role to include making all important decisions for individuals of the flock. They focus on words such as *submission* and *authority* as the basis for directing other people's lives. Other pastors have the personality of a rescuer, trying to save people from the consequences of their own decisions. A pastor does have the role of being a spiritual guide but should not bear the responsibility for telling people what they need to do. God is their Father, not the pastor.

Don't become sexually involved with the counselee.

In the open, sharing atmosphere of a counseling session it is easy for the counselor to let down his or her guard. Emotional intimacy on a nonsexual level can quickly switch to sexual intimacy if one is not careful. The counselor may ask questions of a sexual nature that are beyond what is appropriate or necessary, simply for personal gratification. The counselee may make overtures by gestures or words. Sometimes a hug or a touch in this private, emotionally charged atmosphere is enough to cause the counselor to abandon restraint. The cost of such a misjudgment is immense: loss of position, reputation, respect, and even marriage and family. There are several cases where a state has taken legal action against a pastor who has used a position of authority and power to seduce a counselee. When temptation is strong, the only recourse is to flee. H. B. London writes, "God's enabling grace is far greater than the enemy's temptations. Appeal to Christ's atoning sacrifice provides a way of escape for holding hallowed the most treasured of all relationships—with Him—as well as the priceless ones on this earth."[15]

Avoid taking sides in a dispute.

Sometimes it is a difficult task for a pastor to remain neutral in a conflict between family members or people in the church. This is especially hard if one person is not a Christian or has done things that are against the pastor's moral convictions. It is sometimes difficult to determine who is right when you understand that people often play creatively or selectively with the truth. Individuals may tell only what they believe will help their argument. People say and do what makes sense to them, even though it may make no sense to those on the other side of the dispute or to the counselor. The pastor that takes a side becomes an adversary for the person taking the other side and often alienates that person. This makes it more difficult to work redemptively toward a solution all can accept. If it is possible, it is good for the pastor to be available to everyone in a dispute to be able to minister to each one in the future.

Maintain the confidentiality of the counseling relationship.

People need to have the sense that what is said within the counseling room will never be shared with anyone. When individuals share their concerns or confess their guilt in private, the pastor acts as a representative of God. Pastors, in their priestly role, can take such an opportunity of confession to announce God's promise of forgiveness to the individual. Such private confession should never be later heard in any public setting. Some ministers have even gone to jail for contempt of court, rather than reveal to a court judge what a person had confessed in counseling. The sanctity of the confessional is a sacred responsibility of every pastor. A pastor that shares a confidence, even as a thinly veiled sermon illustration, may prevent that counselee from ever sharing any private information again with you or any other clergyperson. Other people in the church may become hesitant to share anything personal for fear it could end up in a future sermon.

The only two exceptions to the confidentiality principle are: one, if the counselee has threatened to do bodily harm to himself or herself, such as suicide; or two, if the counselee threatens to do serious bodily harm to someone else. In many states, pastors and other helping professionals such as teachers, doctors, and nurses are required by law to report evidence or even suspicion of child abuse. The reasoning is clear. Children, and others such as senior adults or disabled people, may be incapable of defending themselves from such abuse.

It is helpful to share these exceptions, when appropriate, with the counselee even before the formal counseling process begins. When a pastor feels that personal information needs be shared with someone else, it is good to get the counselee's permission first. If the counselee does not give permission, the pastor should at least warn the individual that he or she feels compelled to report information, even without permission.

Do not counsel above your training and abilities.

Pastors are much like general practitioners in the medical profession. They are required to do a number of tasks, such as preaching, teaching, leading, managing, financing, and counseling. It is possible to earn a Ph.D. in every one of those fields. A few pastors may do the work to become an expert in one area, but most sharpen their skills to at least be proficient in each area of responsibility. For instance, a person who developed a brain tumor requiring delicate surgery probably wouldn't ask a family doctor to do the cutting. Family practitioners work hard in their training to develop a broad understanding of the way the body functions. But most patients, if they need someone to cut around the delicate tissues of the brain, will opt for the very best brain surgeon they can find.

Most pastors do not have counseling training beyond taking a course or two and perhaps reading a few books on the subject. This may serve the congregation well for most of the ordinary problems people face. Like physicians, pastors need to take an oath that says, *First of all, do no harm.* There are certain psychiatric problems that are far beyond the skill level of most pastors. It is possible to do harm rather than good when trying to work with some serious psychological illnesses without adequate training. One of the important pastoral skills discussed later in this book is the ability to recognize personal limitations and make referrals. Family doctors make good use of specialists by making referrals whenever necessary. Pastors need to do the same.

▶ COMPETENT TO COUNSEL

It is impossible to have a thorough discussion on the subject of pastoral counseling in one chapter. There are many fine books on the market to enhance a pastor's understanding of counseling. Begin with materials that are Christian in orientation and written from a pastoral perspective. I personally favor a short-term approach to pastoral counseling. It fits the limited time allotment most pastors have available for counseling. The short-term counseling model also fits the pastor's skill level, given the limited experience and training most have in counseling. Make it a goal to become the best counselor possible with the skills you are developing. If formal class work is not an option, try to attend a seminar or talk to experienced pastors.

Most importantly, remember that pastors who counsel become a tool of the Holy Spirit. Some people who come to a pastor for guidance will never seek help from anyone else. A pastor may humbly enter a person's life as a representative of Jesus, the Wonderful Counselor. God sends the Holy Spirit to illuminate the thoughts, enlighten the understanding, and inspire the words of any true servant of Jesus. As the pastor seeks the Spirit's help in the counseling session he will give insights that would seem impossible in any other setting. Jesus promised, "But the Counselor, the Holy Spirit, whom the Father will send in my name, will teach you all things and will remind you of everything I have said to you" (John 14:26). He also sends his power to enable counselees to make changes they would not even attempt on their own. The Spirit gives comfort to those whose hearts are breaking, hope to those who have all but given up, love for those who desire revenge, and courage for those who are afraid. When pastors counsel, they have the resources of heaven at their disposal. A piece of marble on my desk has a picture of an eagle and this quote from Isa. 40:29-31:

> *He gives strength to the weary*
> *and increases the power of the weak.*
> *Even youths grow tired and weary,*
> *and young men stumble and fall;*
> *but those who hope in the LORD*
> *will renew their strength.*
> *They will soar on wings like eagles;*
> *they will run and not grow weary,*
> *they will walk and not be faint.*

What a great reminder to every person in ministry. Pastors preach, care, and counsel under the direction of the God. And this all-powerful God knows all things. He has the power to either change the situation or empower the pastor to meet the situation.

▶ QUESTIONS FOR REFLECTION

▷ How does a pastor overcome the feeling of inadequacy when there are other professionals in the community who have more training and experience in helping people through counseling?

▷ What are some advantages pastors have over other counseling professionals in counseling people of the congregation?

▷ What are the three cautions regarding pastoral counseling that concern you most, and why are these concerns for you?

▷ How does a pastor determine how much time should be spent counseling when there are so many other time demands in the workweek?

EIGHT

PASTORAL CARE AS COLLABORATION

Pastor Frank Lawson was about to finish his work at the church late on Friday afternoon when there was a knock on the door of his office. A woman stood there holding a child about six months old wrapped in a blanket. Frank had never seen her before at church. He did notice that she was dressed very poorly, with no warm coat to withstand the wintry weather outside.

The young woman, Jane, told a familiar story. Her husband had abandoned her and her baby, and she couldn't work with such a small child to care for. She had been evicted from her small one-room apartment because she didn't have the money to pay the rent. The baby needed medication for a cold, but she didn't have the money. In fact, neither of them had eaten that day because all the money was gone. She had family in a town about two hundred miles away but they didn't have any extra money to send her either. Jane said with a pleading voice, "If you could just give us $100 we could get something to eat and buy a bus ticket home where at least I could have a roof over our heads and some food to eat . . . I don't know where else to turn."

Frank's mind filled with questions as the woman talked. He asked himself why she had waited until 4:30 on Friday afternoon to ask for help when all the welfare agencies were closed for the weekend. Was this a legitimate need or was she trying to run a scam? How many churches had she already visited that afternoon with the same story? But then, what if this was really the truth and they were in desperate straits? What if this was his daughter alone and in need in a faraway city? What do you do in a case like this?

The church kept about $50 in petty cash locked in another office for emergencies, but it wasn't enough for her need. Frank could go to an ATM machine and draw out another $50 of his own money. But, was that the right thing to do? He remembered the community resource notebook he had put together when he moved to town and pulled it from the shelf. The one resource he thought of for needs like this was the local Salvation Army. Many of the churches of the community, including theirs, contributed monthly to a fund administered by the Salvation Army to help people who were in need. The United Way supplied extra money for special circumstances. A Salvation Army captain had told Frank to call should he have anyone with a need.

Frank went next door to get his wife, and they drove the young woman with the baby down to the Community Center. Captain Bowers made a few calls himself, and after determining that the woman's needs were real, made arrangements to

*get the woman to her home. They found her a warm coat, boots, and even a nice
insulated blanket for the baby. After they had fed the two, Frank and his wife put
Jane and the baby on the bus. She said, "I don't know how I can ever thank you."
That night Frank realized that, with the suspicions in his mind, he might have sent
Jane and her baby away without any help if there had not been other resources in
the community to call upon for assistance.*

▶ WORKING TOGETHER

No one understands collaboration better than the Salvation Army. Since
its founding in 1865 by William Booth, it has expanded from London to many
areas of the world. From their beginning they have emphasized biblical evangelism and social betterment. Their mission is twofold: "to preach the gospel of Jesus Christ and to meet human needs in His name without discrimination."[1]

The Salvation Army's commitment to meeting the needs of hurting people has led them to connect with others who share common concerns. From
community leaders who volunteer to ring bells in front of Christmas kettles, to
corporations who donate their products for emergency responses, the army
draws from many resources beyond their own people. How could this religious
community possibly meet all the needs they see, from disaster relief and ref-
ugee aid, to hunger and homelessness, by drawing exclusively from the resources of their own people? The Salvation Army has developed a sterling reputation for financial integrity coupled with an encompassing compassion for
needy people. From this trust they are able to recruit others to help them meet
people's needs. Is everyone who helps the Salvation Army a Christian? No, but
the army has found areas of common concern where people with different
views can collaborate to work together.

▶ BRIDGING TO THE COMMUNITY

Across the ages there have been those in the church that have promoted a
fortress mentality—those within the church hiding away from the problems
and negative influences of the world. It is easier to turn away from the ugly social issues and hurting people rather than confronting them with answers.

Other churches have tried to measure effectiveness by developing ministries that will make them appear successful to other churches—having the
biggest building or the largest attendance in town. And yet, as Robert Lewis
observes, "A successful church often remains a stranger to its very own community."[2] The majority of the resources and energy in some of these churches are
invested in maintaining the image rather than bridging to the community with
a helping hand.

But the overall picture is not a bleak one. Many churches are building bridges to help their local communities. While there are critics who say that the Church in the North America benefits far more from tax breaks than it gives back to the community, a recent study reveals that the opposite is true. Ram Cnaan, professor of social work at the University of Pennsylvania, studied the impact of three hundred local congregations upon their communities.[3] He found that the monthly value of a congregation's community services averaged $15,307 per month based on the value of building use and the labor of volunteers.

In commenting about the study Marshall Shelly says, "The most significant finding is that nearly all the congregations in the study provided some form of social and community service, most commonly for children, the elderly, the poor, and the homeless."[4] Many congregations underestimated the impact they were having in their community. Cnaan says about congregations, "I found that things they thought are *not* social programs really *are* social programs. Congregations use other words: ministries, women's groups, auxiliary groups—they have endless names. In the congregation's mind, 'social services' were big projects in collaboration with the government. For us, a social service is something done in a consistent manner to help the needy."[5] If churches were to suddenly withdraw from community programs, most homeless shelters, soup kitchens, addiction support programs, and after-school children's programs would soon disappear.

Churches have a wonderful opportunity to collaborate with community leaders to provide services to their neighbors. Churches can address neighborhood concerns by providing children's summer and after-school programs, teen athletic and cultural enrichment programs, and senior adult health and activity programs. There are usually people in the neighborhood who need food, clothing, housing, or utilities assistance. The church can also make available personal and group counseling for those who cannot find help elsewhere. I have heard Robert Schuller, pastor of the Crystal Cathedral in Garden Grove, California, say, "Find a hurt and heal it. Find a need and fill it."

Every church has unique gifts, interests, and abilities that emerge from the members, the building, and the resources. Also, every community is unique in its needs. It is easy to try to copy what some other church has successfully done in another location. But God may want your church to build different bridges that will meet concerns that no one else has tried to solve. Robert Lewis writes, "Jesus Christ was a daring bridge builder of another kind. Against his overwhelming odds, he imagined a bridge of unprecedented spiritual influence—one that could span a chasm roaring with skepticism, indifference, hostility, even persecution."[6] In his Sermon on the Mount he challenged his followers to be "the salt of the earth"[7] and "the light of the world"[8] to show the importance of making a difference to the culture all around them.

Collaboration means the church takes the first step of offering its resources and energies to the community as a loving expression of concern and compassion. Service is one way the entire church can express pastoral care to the neighborhood.

Because pastors are not specialists in all the serious problems people bring into the church office, they are faced with a difficult choice. Is it best to try to help the person even though the pastor lacks the resources or skills to help the situation, or should the pastor try to find others who would be better suited to deal with the issue? There are times when a pastor tries to provide some help because there simply isn't anyone else available or the one seeking help is unwilling to be referred to someone else. Usually, however, a person with a serious concern is willing to go to anyone who can help solve the problem. While the previous chapter addressed how the pastor responds to a need by counsel, this chapter will discuss how the needs of individuals can best be met by others. Most pastors who take seriously their responsibility to care for their flock try to put the well-being of the hurting person first when deciding whether or not to refer.

▶ The Right Time to Refer

One of my nonclergy colleagues was in a discussion about the pastor's role in counseling and helping others. He said, "Pastoral counseling is easy—refer, refer, refer." In his joking manner he was voicing a common misconception that pastors simply pass off all the problems they don't want to handle themselves. In that sense he was wrong. Most pastors don't try to avoid unpleasant issues that face their parishioners. Part of being a shepherd is dealing compassionately with those who are hurting. But in another sense he was right. Though pastoral counseling is never easy, the generalist role of the pastor discussed in the last chapter naturally leads to referring some people with needs to others who can provide better assistance.

A pastor should consider a referral when the presenting problem is more complex than one's training and experience to deal with the issue. Imagine planning to pilot a small plane and discovering that the engine is not running smoothly. The teenage boy who does odd jobs around the airport says, "I've watched a few mechanics and I think I might be able to correct the problem." Would a pilot trust someone who has a lot of confidence but no training to diagnose and repair an aircraft? One might let an unskilled fifteen-year-old replace the windshield wiper blades on a car, but most pilots would want the confidence that an airplane engine has been tuned by a professional to perfect running condition when the wheels lift off the runway.

There may be personal reasons for a pastor to make a referral. Every pastor brings to the counseling setting the many life experiences, good or bad, that shape his or her personal life. For instance, a pastor who experienced the childhood physical abuse of a parent may find it too difficult to be objective if the subject is addressed in a counseling session. It is possible for a pastor to feel a personality conflict or a strong negative reaction that clouds the ability to view this parishioner with objectivity. Sometimes the pastor just feels that someone else would do a better job working with this problem. However, pastors shouldn't discount their effectiveness too quickly. William Oglesby Jr. correctly observes, "There are those ministers who are too quick to refer, failing to realize the potentiality of their own relationship to the parishioner."[9] Having someone they know and trust can be a powerful tool for healing in the mind of a needy person.

Another legitimate reason to refer is the lack of time. Because the pastor has many tasks in the church, counseling needs to be fit in with the other responsibilities. When a serious need arises, the pastor may not have time to do more than a quick assessment of the problem before finding someone who has the time and skills to do the proper follow-up. Some issues may be within the competence level of the pastor, but the other demands of ministry do not leave enough time to invest in working with this specific problem. Everyone in ministry must come to grips with the most effective use of his or her allotted time. Even before needs arise, a wise pastor will set boundaries on the amount of time that will be given to counsel during a week so that there will be enough time for the other ministerial responsibilities to the whole congregation.

There may be times when counseling could put the pastor, other church members, or the church itself in jeopardy. A parishioner may need to share intimate details that, if the pastor knew, might make it difficult for the pastor to have the same level of respect. Sometimes people feel they need to go to another church because the minister knows too many embarrassing details of their lives. It may also be best to refer when facing an issue that may have legal or liability ramifications for the pastor or the church.

It is almost always necessary to ask for outside assistance when a person is suicidal or homicidal. Human lives may depend upon the pastor taking the right course of action when a person threatens such drastic action. Anytime the counselee even hints of doing harm to himself or herself or anyone else, the words must be taken seriously. Often these people need to be taken to a hospital or other place of safety for their personal protection. Whenever others are in danger, the police should be notified to provide protection. This is the one time when it is proper to break the oath of silence in order to protect the well-being of those who are in danger. Situations like domestic conflict can quickly erupt into violence. A pastor is far better off to seek assistance before the counselee carries out threats than to live with the regret of not acting quickly enough to prevent a tragedy.

If a pastor suspects that someone has a serious physical disorder, don't hesitate to refer the person to a medical doctor for a checkup. A woman in one of my pastorates went through a sudden change in emotional outlook. Instead of her usual optimistic outlook she had become depressed and was feeling physically lethargic. At my urging she went to see her family doctor, who discovered a serious thyroid problem. She underwent the treatment and was soon feeling her normal self again.

People with severe mental or emotional disturbances need to be referred to competent professionals. Generally people with paranoid concerns, compulsive behavior, the disoriented, severely depressed, or those who are out of touch with reality need the help of a psychologist. Some psychological problems may require a psychiatrist (a medical doctor specializing in mental or emotional behavior) who can prescribe medication to aid in recovery. It is sad that some Christian people attach a stigma to anyone who uses medicine to correct a mental disease. Actually, using properly administered drugs to correct a chemical imbalance in the brain is similar to a diabetic taking a drug to correct a glucose imbalance. Psychologist Jim Pettitt says, "Pastors without a graduate degree in a specific counseling area should refrain from dealing with psychological pathology, leaving such counseling to trained and licensed professionals."[10]

Sexual counseling with people of either sex is clearly outside the expertise of the average pastoral counselor and should be referred to others more skillful. David Switzer says we should also refer when "we are sexually attracted to the person to the degree that our attention to him or her as a distressed human being is consistently (or very frequently) disrupted and our disciplined helping responses (the facilitative condition) are compromised."[11] The untrained pastor is ill-equipped to address such issues and should admit that openly to the counselee up front. It is far better to refer than to try to walk the fine line between trying to help and being caught up in fascination and sexual attraction, which could lead to incalculable tragedy.

It is important to understand that referral does not mean abandonment. Even though a pastor may refer a person to a specialist, he or she continues to show interest and help the person in any way possible. It is important to provide both spiritual nurture to the church member and collaborative connection to the professional who continues to work with the parishioner. Switzer uses the term *transferal* rather than *referral.* "In such instances we're not merely making recommendations and seeking to elicit the others' cooperation in *their* taking the initiative to follow through on whatever action is appropriate. In transferal, we continue to work actively with and for a person with primary responsibility until she or he is in personal contact with the professional or agency or hospital that then assumes such responsibility."[12] Sometimes this means making periodic contacts with the referral agency to check on the parishioner's progress. The agency may have suggestions for the pastor to do follow-up work with the individual at a later date. In the truest sense, referral is a collaborative exercise.

▶ FINDING THE RIGHT RESOURCES

A pastor moving to a new church should begin building a referral file of professional individuals in private practice, community agencies, and religious organizations that can form a collaboration network of resources for a church. One effective way to begin this process is to build relationships by meeting with those who could potentially be used for referrals. Usually doctors, counselors, and other helpers welcome the opportunity to present their services to a pastor because referrals are the way they expand their practice. When building a referral file, list the name of the agency or organization, a phone number, the name of a contact person, the cost of services, and any additional information that would be helpful in making a referral later. If pastoring in a smaller town, the radius of the referral network may need to be expanded to other adjoining communities that offer needed services. Pastors should not overlook the resources of other churches in your area. Churches often combine to provide cooperative help that they might not be able to do individually. When leaving a church, consider passing on the referral information as a gift for the next pastor.

A pastor has the responsibility to know the individuals to whom he or she might make a referral. Does this person have a good reputation in the community? Do other pastors use this person? What experience and training does the person possess? Are there accrediting agencies or professional organizations that have approved this person's skills? What is this individual's philosophy of applying his or her skills? What is this person's personal faith? If the person is not a Christian, what is his or her approach in working with people of faith? You should not make a referral to anyone who will tear down or discourage the belief system of a church member.

Community resources fall into one of three general categories: private practice, community agencies, and religious organizations.

PRIVATE PRACTICE

Psychologists and professional counselors may be connected to community or religious agencies, but many function independently with their own offices. A licensed psychologist's training includes a doctor's degree, as well as hundreds of hours of supervised counseling to complete the licensure process required by the state. In most cases, counselors must have at least a master's degree in counseling as well as the state required supervised counseling to be licensed. A special category of professional counseling is pastoral counseling. Although those advertising as pastoral counselors normally have graduate training in both theology and counseling, this field is not as carefully regulated. The term may indicate a religious orientation but does not mean the counselor has had pastoral experience or adequate counseling training. It is especially important to investigate both the credentials and the training of those using the title *pastoral counselor.*

Psychologists or counselors may be Christian but will vary in their approach and philosophy. Pastoral counselors may be more comfortable using Scripture and prayer than Christian psychologists. The personality of the client may fit better with one counselor than another. You will discover that some counselors are more effective than others. Talk with other pastors, visit with the counselor, and then develop a list of two or three you feel most comfortable using for referral counseling.

Psychiatrists are medical doctors and can prescribe medication for mental disorders. They tend to deal with the more serious problems of psychosis, mental retardation, brain injury, depression, anxiety, or other psychological problems that may require hospitalization. While in the past many within the religious community viewed psychiatry with great mistrust, this attitude has changed. Oglesby states, "Aided by groups whose purpose it has been to bring representatives of each discipline together in face-to-face dialogue, there has emerged a more responsible understanding on the part of both as to the concerns and responsibilities of the other."[13] Some psychiatrists may do counseling, although it is often to determine the use and effectiveness of medication. The cost of using a psychiatrist is usually higher than an equal time with a psychologist or counselor.

Medical doctors can also be a wonderful referral source for a parishioner's well-being. Often the pastor may be the first one to observe an individual's need for some type of medical attention. Howard Clinebell writes:

> It is important for pastors to build working relationships with one or more physicians in the community. A counselee who has not had a physical check-up recently should be strongly encouraged to do so if the pastor has any suspicion that the person may need medical attention. If there is the

slightest suspicion that neurological, endocrine, or other medical problems may be lurking behind or complicating psychological or interpersonal conflicts, the pastor should *insist* that the person consult a doctor.[14]

It is helpful to know a physician well enough to be able to discuss your pastoral concerns personally and get the parishioner in to see the doctor as soon as practical.

Should pastors make referrals only to Christian doctors or counselors? The short answer is no. There may be Christian professionals in the community who are competent, but there will be specialized physical problems where the only person who can help may not be a Christian. Generally, it is best to refer to the helper who has the greatest skill and experience as long as it would not be a detriment or compromise a parishioner's spiritual foundation. One way to insure this is to talk to the professional about the concerns and seek assurance that this person will be cooperative.

COMMUNITY AGENCIES

In most larger communities there are private organizations that address many of the most common needs people face. Some agencies, such as the Red Cross, have a broad focus, dealing with such diverse issues as collecting donated blood and responding to community crises, such as floods or tornadoes. Other agencies address a single issue, such as cancer, abuse, or AIDS. Support for most of these agencies comes from private donations and community-wide appeals, such as the United Way. Many local agencies are part of national or international organizations that can provide additional support and networking opportunities. Much of their labor force comes from volunteers who believe strongly in addressing the concerns of the agency.

Local, state, and federal governmental agencies are also concerned with the welfare of the community. A pastor needs to know what services these agencies can provide for people needing help. The best way to be informed is to interview the agency director to know how that agency functions.

Often people who come to you for help do not know what assistance is available to them. Are there fees involved? How does one qualify for services? You can become their advocate by investigating and representing the person to the appropriate agencies.

RELIGIOUS ORGANIZATIONS

In addition to the Salvation Army, which provides a broad range of ongoing and crisis services, there are other church-based local ministries in many communities. Jesus spoke often about the needs of the poor who were found everywhere he went. Christian people have historically responded to the human needs of hunger, clothing, and shelter. But sometimes it is difficult for a single church to provide for the many needs in their responsibility area. In many communities churches have banded together to form social ministry organizations to combine their resources and protect against duplication. Often, a local ministerial group may serve as the catalyst, bringing together both churches and organizations needed to address specific community needs.

Other Christian organizations focus their energies on a single social issue, such as abortion or crisis pregnancy. Because they represent a variety of churches they may draw some of their support directly from the budgets of those supporting churches. By collaborating together, Christians can provide such services as after-school child care, low-cost medical clinics, youth tutoring, job placement, and classes on financial management or parenting. One local church may provide a support group and invite members of other churches to participate. Another church may open their facility to a Boy Scout troop made up of youngsters from several congregations. A third church may operate a clothing and food distribution center with other churches contributing supplies. By joining together in cooperative programs, the churches present a united Christian front to the community that reflects the Spirit of Jesus in a forceful way.

▶ Challenges of Connecting People with Resources

At first glance, making a referral may appear to be as easy as making a phone call. But there are some challenges for a pastor.

First, it is sometimes difficult to know exactly what type of help the person may need. For example, if the person's depression has a physical source, then someone with a medical degree is the logical source of help. But if the depression seems to be coming from unresolved personal issues, a counselor is a better choice. And what does a pastor do if the person seems to be dealing with both physical and psychological issues? A pastor needs to make an assessment for referral based upon what seems to be the best first step toward wholeness, realizing that there may need to be other referrals for this person in the future.

A second challenge facing pastors, especially in more remote locations, is finding the resources the parishioner really needs. It may take several phone calls to other communities in order to find the person or agency that can really help this person with his or her problem. If the source of help is some distance away, the individual may be weighing whether it is worth the cost of time and money to get help. Sometimes people will settle for less then the best help simply because the best is just too inconvenient.

A third concern for the pastor is the individual who does not have the financial resources to obtain help. The United States does not currently offer a universal medical plan for all its citizens. This means that often the people with the greatest needs do not have proper health coverage. Professional specialists generally do not work for nothing. They have spent time and much money to gain their skills. They have many overhead costs and rightfully feel they should be properly reimbursed. While hospitals in the United States are legally bound to give emergency treatment to anyone who shows up on their doorstep, they are not required to provide an elective surgery simply because a patient wants it. Pastors may need to speak to hospitals, doctors, and other helping agencies to elicit the help for a needy person. Medical people will, on occasion, donate their time and resources to work with someone who has a specialized need. Governmental agencies sometimes step in to provide some assistance for destitute people with needs. As pastor, you can become an advocate, presenting a human face to a medical or mental concern.

But this may also be a time when the church demonstrates Christian concern and intercedes by providing financial aid. In the parable of the sheep and goats in Matt. 25 the righteous ask the King in verse 39, "When did we see you sick or in prison and go to visit you?" The answer Jesus gave in the next verse showed the importance of human intervention, "I tell you the truth, whatever you did for one of the least of these brothers of mine, you did for me" (v. 40).

The fourth challenge facing pastors is this: referral is all but impossible if the needy individual is unwilling to see or talk to anyone else but the pastor. There can be many reasons for this reluctance. The person may not want to go through the process of starting over with another counselor. There can be a mistrust of anyone who does not share the same values as the pastor. The minister can get the feeling that if he or she does not help this individual, no one else will. People who refuse to follow through on a referral have made a decision about the problem—it will be solved only if the resources and helpers fit their approval. Frankly, there will be people a pastor cannot help because they are, for whatever reason, unwilling to seek the help they need. A pastor who has offered the best help available and been turned down, must then release the individual and not feel responsible for the choices that have been made.

This can lead to a fifth challenge. A pastor can develop a messiah complex—no one can help this person like I can. When this feeling comes, a pastor needs to personally ask this question, "What personal needs am I trying to satisfy in helping this other person?" Switzer says, "When we find ourselves beginning to feel this way, it's usually a sign that referral is *definitely* called for."[15]

▶ Principles of Referral

Let the person know early about the possibility of referral. Clinebell says, "Persons who have mustered their courage to come to their pastor expecting help, usually feel some degree of rejection if it becomes necessary to refer them."[16] If you can explain as early as possible why more specialized help is needed, the parishioner has time to begin to get used to the idea.

Make the reasons for referral clear. The reason may be a lack of skill or experience with the problem at hand. Referral may be the best course of action because the helping agency has had much success in working with this specialized issue. According to Randy Christian, "We increase the likelihood of a successful referral by answering all legitimate questions straightforwardly and giving counselees time to think about the referral."[17] When making a referral, explain the approximate cost and any other expectations required for the services of the referral agency.

Refer to a person rather than an agency. Often the person needing help feels afraid or intimidated going to an impersonal organization for help. But if the pastor knows that the contact person's name is Mary Long, it will be easier to send the counselee directly to the right person for help. Asking for Mary Long may get the needy person to the source of help much faster than going through secretaries and receptionists whose job it is to filter phone calls. When creating a resource file of referrals for future use, make note of the names of the people most likely to give the assistance needed.

When possible let the counselee make the contact. This can be empowering, giving people the feeling that they have some control and ownership of what takes place in the helping process. If there is more than one possible source of referral assistance, give the counselee the information about each resource and let the individual choose the one he or she prefers. Sometimes a pastor may make the initial contact with the agency or individual, explaining the situation, but it will be the counselee's responsibility to make the appointment.

Help to prepare the counselee for the best possible result from the referral. The parishioner may have unrealistic expectations of what the referral agency can do or how long the process should last. When possible, the pastor should help the individual come to a realistic understanding of what to expect. If the person's expectations are low, the pastor's role may be to create a sense of hope and optimism that there is a light at the end of the tunnel. It is important to help the person commit to follow through on the appointments and the homework assignments.

Let the parishioner know you will continue to give support and encouragement. A periodic phone call or an inquiry when seeing the person privately at church will communicate pastoral concern with their progress. It is not necessary to pry into the very personal aspects of counseling or treatment. Just knowing that the pastor is still interested can be very comforting as the parishioner continues work toward wholeness. As shepherd, the pastor continues to provide spiritual support the church member will need to deal with the problem.

Assure the counselee that the pastor/parishioner relationship will not change. Many members fear that once the pastor knows of their personal problems and treatment, this relationship will change forever. Some will feel that going to another church is the only option. However, the pastor's attitude of acceptance and concern can alleviate this feeling of anxiety. Walking with them in their hour of need can make the pastor/parishioner bond even more significant than before.

Check with the referral agency or individual periodically. Ask how the person is progressing. See if there is anything you can do to help the person continue work on a solution to the problem. If issues of confidentiality prevent the professional from divulging too much personal information, you can ask your parishioner to sign a release of information document to allow the agency to share pertinent information with you. Because most helping agencies depend on referrals to stay in business, they are usually anxious to work with local pastors as fellow professionals who are concerned with the well-being of their client.

▶ BEING A COLLABORATOR

When moving to a new church a pastor has a wonderful opportunity to do an objective assessment of the church and its potential role in the community. Periodically throughout the pastor's tenure at that church, those same issues should be revisited and reassessed.

What are the needs within the community that are not being addressed by any other church? These needs could range from inadequate day care and used clothing, to grief support groups and help for unwed mothers. Are there human resources within the church that could be used to address these needs? Could the church's buildings or property be used in some way for reaching out into the community to help people? Are these concerns best addressed by the local church alone or is collaboration with other churches or agencies a better option? Who are those helpers in the community that might form the best referral network? Get acquainted with them. Ask them about their requirements and fees for services. Let them know that you would be available as a clergyperson to assist them should they need assistance. There may be many collaborative partners in the community who are simply waiting to be asked. The ministry of a local church can certainly be strengthened by utilizing those resources.

▶ Questions for Reflection

▷ Why do you think pastors are sometimes hesitant to collaborate with others in the community to help solve a need?

▷ Where would you turn to refer a person who comes to you threatening to commit suicide?

▷ How would you approach getting help for a man threatening to kill his spouse because of her unfaithfulness to him?

▷ Are there any community agencies you would hesitate to support or use for referrals and why would you reject them?

NINE

PASTORAL CARE AND
THE MEANS OF GRACE

When Pastor Michelle Jennings finally had an opportunity to meet the mystery church visitor, it was through a chance encounter at the local convenience store and gas station. Michelle had watched this woman for several Sundays enter the service ten minutes after the worship began and then leave before the final benediction. No one in the small congregation knew the identity of this dark-haired, slender woman with sad eyes who looked to be in her mid-twenties. When twice the ushers asked her to fill out a visitor's card, she shook her head and walked away. Michelle told the ushers after the second rejection, "Let her come in peace and respect her privacy. When she is ready to identify herself, she will."

And that was what made the meeting at the convenience store so special. Michelle had gone to the back of the store to pick up some milk when the mystery woman suddenly appeared. She stuck out her hand, introduced herself as Donna Franz, and asked if they could talk. There were three small tables with umbrellas outside the store and quickly Michelle carried two soft drinks out to where Donna was waiting.

For the next hour Donna told her story, at first hesitantly, then with a sense of relief. She had grown up on a small farm as a part of a churchgoing family. After high school Donna took a job as a secretary at a local business and was enjoying her new freedom, even though she lived at home. She met a man named Jason at work when he came in to sell her company some copy machines. He was seven years older and did not hold to any of the values she had been taught as a child. Since her parents objected to their dating, she and Jason ran off to a large city and got married. Donna let her parents know what had happened, but Jason insisted that they cut all ties to her family. The couple moved several times before finally settling in their present location, twelve hundred miles from her hometown.

Donna told how three years ago she gave birth to a girl they named Kaitlin. From the beginning there were health concerns. Five months ago the doctors found a fast-growing mass in the baby's brain and Kaitlin died a week later.

Donna said, "Jason wouldn't let me call my parents. He said we could handle this alone. Then, three weeks after Kaitlin's death, Jason told me he couldn't stand my crying and all the pressure. He packed his suitcase, told me I could have all of our furniture, and then just left."

Michelle reached for some paper napkins off the condiment shelf next to the table. Donna wiped away her tears and continued. "I started coming to your church a few weeks ago to somehow connect to something of the past that could bring some security and stability. I just couldn't bring myself to talk to anyone. Something happened to me as I sat in your church week after week. Some of the songs you sang brought back memories from my past. I began to have a sense of God's presence as you read scriptures. Although you didn't know it, the prayers the church prayed seemed to be designed specifically for me. But to me, probably the most important thing in the service was your weekly sermon, especially the one on the prodigal son last Sunday. You reminded me that God loved me and understood my pain. When you said that it was never too late to return to Father's House I began my journey back to God. I've begun reading again the Bible I brought from home. And I've started praying, really asking the Heavenly Father for strength and help. You said you were going to serve Communion next Sunday. For the first time in many years, I'm looking forward to participating."

Michelle took Donna's hands and offered to pray for healing for her. When she finished they rejoiced for a few minutes together, even though it was obvious that Donna was still suffering. Then Donna said, "I forgot to tell you, I called my parents last night and we talked for over an hour. They have invited me to move back home for a time and I've decided to do that. My dad's coming in his pickup in two weeks to take me and my things back to the farm until I can get settled in my own place somewhere near home. Pastor, you need to know that this would never have happened except for you, and your accepting congregation, who gave me time to start healing as I attended your services. Thank you!"

▶ PASTORAL CARE TAKES MANY FORMS

Pastors hold a unique place among caregivers because of our responsibility to care for souls. William Willimon says, "Pastors care for people *in the name of Jesus.* The shepherd is responsible not only to the flock, but also to God for the flock. We worry not only about the health and happiness of our people, but about their salvation as well."[1] It is common to associate pastoral care with formal counseling or other intentional works of ministry directed to help an individual. What is less obvious is the pastoral care provided indirectly through the means of grace.

In his excellent book *Pastoral Care and the Means of Grace,* Ralph Underwood says, "The means of grace are ways to encounter the God of transcendence, order, and freedom—ways that are explicitly set aside, designated, and tried-and-true. Such means of grace impose no limit on God—God gives God's grace in countless ways. Yet, over the generations the people of God have come to affirm particular ways of waiting for God, ways not to be neglected."[2] Underwood goes on to mention faith activities, such as prayer, Scripture, reconciliation, and the sacraments as specific means of grace.

Underwood singles out John Wesley as "representative of those who endeavor to combine high appreciation for the means of grace and an emphasis on radical transformation."[3] Throughout his ministry Wesley encouraged his people "to seek God's grace through the various outward signs, words, and actions that God has ordained as 'ordinary' channels for conveying saving grace to humanity."[4]

Apparently, before the Reformation the Western church had limited the means of receiving grace to the seven sacraments of the church. Theologian Randy Maddox writes:

> Wesley was convinced of the effective communication of God's grace through the sacraments of baptism and Eucharist, and through means like liturgy and formal prayers that had come to be emphasized in Anglicanism. . . . Indeed, one of the central features of the Methodist revival was Wesley's expectation that his people would avail themselves of *both* the traditional means of grace present in Anglican worship and such distinctive means as class meetings, love feasts, and covenant renewal services.[5]

Wesley understood the need for people to respond to the means of grace by faith. He condemned those who desired the end result of grace without availing themselves of the means of grace—for example, "those who expect growth in faith and holiness without regular participation in the means through which God has chosen to convey grace."[6]

Providing pastoral care by the means of grace is a difficult concept for some to grasp. For one reason, it is hard to measure. Pastors can count the number of hours in counseling sessions held or the number of cans of soup handed out at a ministry center. However, it is hard to measure the effectiveness of a sermon or a prayer in the lives of specific individuals. In fact, most pastors have at some time been guilty of almost apologizing for saying to someone in need, "I will pray for you," as though praying is a last-ditch substitute when there is nothing more tangible to be done. It is easy to support that attitude by quoting James 2:17, "In the same way, faith by itself, if it is not accompanied by action, is dead." But the opposite is also true: Action, if not accompanied by faith, is also dead. And it is sometimes easier to perform the action than to appropriate the faith. God's grace can bring results that could never be accomplished by individual activities alone.

Another disconcerting aspect for some is centered in the very concept of grace. Grace is God's benevolent response to our need. While we may participate by providing ways God can dispense his grace, in one sense the actual dispensing is out of our hands. God acts in sovereign ways that humans cannot always program or predict, to do his will in people's lives. And yet, God can and does use various human activities as avenues through which his grace is released.

Peter and John met a lame man as they were walking to the Temple in Acts 3. The man was begging for money as his solution to the physical limitations he daily faced. The easiest course of action for Peter and John was to open their purses and drop a little money in front of the beggar. Fortunately, they didn't have any money with them, so they had to depend on God to graciously act on behalf of this man. Peter said to this lame man, "Silver or gold I do not have, but what I have I give you. In the name of Jesus Christ of Nazareth, walk."[7] Peter may have spoken the words, but he had no power to heal. It was the grace of God that enabled the lame man to leap to his feet and walk into the Temple court with the two apostles.

The means of grace implies a divine-human partnership. The grace element obviously is God's initiative. He provides for us daily what we neither deserve nor merit by our own goodness. But some of the means by which grace can come to us are found in the activities of the Church. In other words, humans cannot provide the grace, but the Church can provide the means—the activities that God can use to dispense his grace. Willimon writes, "One of the greatest gifts we have to offer persons who struggle through life is the Body of Christ, that people whom Jesus has formed as his presence in the world."[8]

While God's grace can come to us in many forms, for many purposes, the focus of this chapter will center on specific activities or practices that will allow God's grace to flow to people in need of pastoral care.

▶ WORSHIP AS PASTORAL CARE

If pastoral care has been historically understood as the care of souls, then worship is a natural setting for such care to take place. Pastors who lead worship are emphasizing, in Willimon's words, "the *priestly* dimension of pastoral care."[9] It is interesting that with the great advances in counseling skills and medicines to correct almost any emotional malady, many people still turn first to the pastor and the church when serious problems arise. Perhaps it is an indication that prevenient grace is at work to draw them to a place where real answers can still be found.

Darius Salter says that the pastor has a specific task, "to make sure that all people understand that God is approachable. All laity and clergy have the right to issue an invitation to approach God. It is the responsibility of the priest to proclaim this invitation in public."[10] The pastor has overall leadership responsibility for everything that takes place when the flock gathers to worship together. It is a privilege to lead the congregation to experience the living, speaking God, who is available and anxious to meet all who will call upon his name.

Worship is an ideal setting for people to experience the grace of God. After all, whenever the Church gathers, the people of God bring their needs and concerns with them into the service. In that moment when worship begins, those present cease to be simply a group of individuals in a room. Individuals become one unit: the Church, the "called out ones," the Body of Christ, the fellowship of believers. Worship dispels the idea that we are isolated and alone. Our attention shifts from a self-focus to an awareness of others in this gathered community of faith. "In worship it is no longer just 'me and God' facing the world; it is 'God and us.'"[11] Paul conveys this compassionate communal concern when he writes, "Carry each other's burdens, and in this way you will fulfill the law of Christ."[12]

But this caring for one another is sometimes difficult when our culture says, "Remain private and don't let anyone know what you are really feeling." Too many people are like the woman in Mark 5 who suffers desperate hurts but would rather touch Jesus' garment secretly than openly confess her need in front of others. It is interesting that Jesus gently forced her out of the shadows to identify herself in front of the crowd. Willimon says, "An important pastoral role is helping pain go public, encouraging the public processing of pain. We do this in our leadership of worship when we urge the congregation to engage in public confession and forgiveness; when we receive the monetary offering; when we, through various acts of worship, urge people to lay their lives upon the altar of God to be blessed, broken and given to the world as the Body of Christ."[13] There are some issues that are best revealed in a smaller context, such as a small group or Sunday School class. But the principle is clear: burdens are easier to carry when they are shared with God in the context of other caring believers.

The Church, from its earliest days, has understood that gathering together in worship is an important means of God's grace. James gives these words of instruction to the Church:

> Is any one of you in trouble? He should pray. Is anyone happy? Let him sing songs of praise. Is any one of you sick? He should call the elders of the church to pray over him and anoint him with oil in the name of the Lord. And the prayer offered in faith will make the sick person well; the Lord will raise him up. If he has sinned, he will be forgiven. Therefore confess your sins to each other and pray for each other so that you may be healed. The prayer of a righteous man is powerful and effective (*James 5:13-15*).

Notice that sharing problems or sickness or joy should be done in the context of the gathered believers in worship. James is very clear when he says that public confession and prayer are means by which we can experience the healing grace of God. Sometimes confession and healing take place in front of the entire congregation while other times it may be in a smaller group gathered for a time of specific prayer. An important element, whatever the context, is a willingness to share our personal lives with each other in caring and compassion. God can work when even two or three people come together and invite him to be present with them.

Whenever God's people gather in worship we should anticipate God's working in our midst. The truth is, many people come to church carrying the problems and burdens of the previous weeks. They feel discouraged and hopeless rather than optimistic and hopeful. These people may not be expecting anything to change as the result of their coming. Paul Anderson says, "Worship breaks into that circle by requiring people to do something—something positive and hopeful—to give glory to God."[14] Praise is a powerful antidote to discouragement. David wrote these words when he was facing a difficult situation, "Glorify the LORD with me; let us exalt his name together. I sought the LORD, and he answered me; he delivered me from all my fears" (Ps. 34:3-4).[15] Creating that sense of hope in the presence of God should be a natural result of true worship. When God makes his presence known in the midst of the singing, scriptures, prayers, and preaching, the effect can be transforming in the hearts of the worshiping people. Howard Rice says:

> It is unnecessary to create an artificial mood or to pump people up into feeling good. The stuff of transformation resides in the power of the gospel proclaimed with fidelity to its message and careful application to the lives of those present. . . . Worship creates space in people's hearts and souls so the transforming power can reach them.[16]

In the divine-human encounter of worship God dispenses his grace in ways people can't even anticipate. There is no way that a pastor can know of the deep hurts that lurk behind the smiling faces of those who sit in the pews. If we knew, we might be overwhelmed and discouraged. How can pastors possibly address all those needs that are so serious and urgent? And yet, as Paul Anderson writes, "Jesus, the 'Wonderful Counselor,' knows better than I how to get through to people. He sends the Paraclete, the Helper, to come alongside people. So although I don't schedule counseling appointments on Sunday, God often does—right during the worship service.[17]

▶ Preaching as Pastoral Care

Over four hundred years before Paul began his itinerant preaching missions, the Greek poet Euripides said, "The tongue is mightier than the blade."

Paul found himself doing battle in Greece on two fronts: one, a set of religious dogmas held by the Jews, and two, the philosophical outlook of the Greek culture that dominated the Roman world of his time. In 1 Cor. 1 he sums up for his readers in Corinth the issue facing the church, "For the message of the cross is foolishness to those who are perishing, but to us who are being saved it is the power of God" (v. 18). He continues his argument in verses 21-25:

> For since in the wisdom of God the world through its wisdom did not know him, God was pleased through the foolishness of what was preached to save those who believe. Jews demand miraculous signs and Greeks look for wisdom, but we preach Christ crucified: a stumbling block to Jews and foolishness to Gentiles, but to those whom God has called, both Jews and Greeks, Christ the power of God and the wisdom of God. For the foolishness of God is wiser than man's wisdom, and the weakness of God is stronger than man's strength.

Paul is stating that Christ's kingdom will be built, his Church will be established, not by vast armies but by speaking words. He refers to God's plan for victory as "the foolishness of what was preached" (v. 21). The answer was not in simply saying words. The Greek philosophers had tried that for centuries. The power of the words were found in the specific message, "We preach Christ crucified" (v. 23) as the power for victory. It worked in the Roman world, and it works in the twenty-first century world as well.

The use of words continues to be one of the most powerful tools available to provide help and hope for people in need. Willimon puts it this way, "The world belongs to those who can describe the world truthfully, those who are able to name rightfully what is going on among us. Thus, the pastor works with words faithfully to describe the world as God's world, the sphere of the activity of the Holy Spirit, that beloved but troubled realm for which Jesus died."[18] It is a great challenge to do what John Stott refers to as, "preaching between two worlds"—taking the truths written in an ancient world and making them relevant words for our contemporary world. "Our basic struggle, on a Sunday morning, revolves around the questions: Who gets to name the world? Who is authorized to tell the story of what is going on among us? This is why I believe that our preaching is primary, even to our care."[19]

Is it presumptuous for us to think that change can come about merely because we speak words? Perhaps it is, if preachers are simply making speeches based upon personal opinion or outlook. But if preaching is the proclamation of the master story, the good news that Jesus was crucified, died, and then rose from the grave in victory—the mere telling of the story has life-changing power.

In fact, after Peter and John administered God's grace to the lame man on the Temple steps in Acts 3 they were hauled in before the Sanhedrin. Peter stood fearlessly before this Jewish court and proclaimed the crucifixion and resurrection of Jesus without apology. These Jewish leaders were alarmed that two men they saw as unschooled and ordinary could have such power with words. The Sanhedrin thought they could silence Peter and John with a warning that they were not to preach about Jesus anymore. "But Peter and John replied, 'Judge for yourselves whether it is right in God's sight to obey you rather than God. For we cannot help speaking about what we have seen and heard.' After further threats they let them go. They could not decide how to punish them, because all the people were praising God for what had happened" (Acts 4:19-21).

For preaching to become a means of grace, Scripture needs to work its way into the hurts and concerns of the preacher. Thomas Oden says, "The preacher must first enter deeply into his own feeling process and experience if he is to drive home a point profoundly in the hearts of others. Luther spoke candidly of getting in touch with his anger as an emotive exercise that stimulated and improved his preaching."[20] Indeed, Jesus' ministry was characterized by his deep concern for the hurting people around him. He seemed to have a way of looking into the hearts of his listeners and sensing their concerns. One can sense his deep, compassionate understanding of people's pain in his words, "Come to me, all you who are weary and burdened, and I will give you rest. Take my yoke upon you and learn from me, for I am gentle and humble in heart, and you will find rest for your souls. For my yoke is easy and my burden is light" (Matt. 11:28-30).

Pastors must also preach out of the context of their own pain. John Piper writes, "God has ordained that our preaching become deeper and more winsome as we are broken, humbled, and made low, and desperately dependent on grace by the trials in our lives. . . . God aims to break us of all pretenses to self-sufficiency, and make us lowly and childlike in our dependence on God. This is the kind of preacher to whom the suffering come."[21] Piper contends that when we preach from our weakness people can see Christ and understand that they are truly loved. Also, our own suffering as preachers forces us to the Scriptures for a word of hope for the congregation.[22]

I heard John Piper speak in a college chapel service about the personal pain of watching his teenage son leave home and live the life of a prodigal for a time, estranged from his family. Any parent who heard the sermon knew that Piper could understand the anxiety and suffering involved in raising children.

Pastoral care in preaching begins when we share with others the comfort we have received from God through our own hardships. Paul describes it this way in 2 Cor. 1:3-4: "Praise be to the God and Father of our Lord Jesus Christ, the Father of compassion and the God of all comfort, who comforts us in all our troubles, so that we can comfort those in any trouble with the comfort we ourselves have received from God." It is sometimes hard to accept the fact that personal suffering can be used to help others. But that is what Paul says in verses 6 through 7: "If we are distressed, it is for your comfort and salvation; if we are comforted, it is for your comfort, which produces in you patient endurance of the same sufferings we suffer. And our hope for you is firm, because we know that just as you share in our sufferings, so also you share in our comfort." To allow others to experience the grace of God, preachers need to be willing to be vulnerable and honest about God's working in our own lives.

Also, shepherds must be willing to permit our parishioners to provide comfort for us when we need it. This is not a sign of weakness, but strength, as we abandon the myth of pastoral invincibility. When the pastor is vulnerable and open to receiving care and comfort from others, the congregation will find it easier to seek comfort from the pastor when they need it.

Building relationships within the congregation will make the preacher's sermons more effective in providing pastoral care. Donald Capps refers to the late Henri Nouwen's book *Creative Ministry* as addressing this need for relationships with the congregation. "Nouwen says that preaching needs to reflect the insights the pastor gains from involvement in the lives of parishioners. . . . Through words, preachers effect a dialogue between their own life experiences and those of listeners."[23] Nouwen also emphasizes the importance of the pastor's availability by putting "the full range of his life-experiences—his experiences in prayer, in conversation and in his lonely hours—at the disposal of those who ask him to be their preacher."[24] This is not easy because in making ourselves available we truly open ourselves up for others to personally inspect our lives and have access to our time and energies.

How can preaching best become a tool for pastoral care to people in the new millennium? Perhaps the place to begin is by learning to ask questions. More specifically, pastors need to be listening for the questions people in the broader cultural context are asking today. What are the questions in the minds of those in the congregation when they hear the words of the text?

Listeners before the postmodern age were interested in having every factual question answered. They were looking for evidences and arguments to somehow convince them of the truths they were seeking to discover. People of the postmodern era are not as concerned about factual answers. In fact, they are accustomed to living with ambiguities, with facts that don't always harmonize. Pastor Michael Slaughter writes, "Preachers who engage the 21st century culture will affirm the mystery and paradox of the gospel. . . . The Church was born in paradox. Jesus was both fully God and fully human. . . . God is one yet exists in three persons."[25] Postmoderns are asking questions. Which god of the many gods should I follow? How can I experience this God of the Bible? Can knowing this God make a difference as I face problems in my life?

Effective preaching today often involves telling stories. Dan Kimball, in his book *The Emerging Church,* says, "Tell the grand wonderful story, over and over again. We cannot assume that people know the whole thing. We must constantly paint the big picture of the Bible story and tell it in as many ways as possible through our preaching."[26]

There has been a great increase in interest in the use of narrative passages over the last fifteen to twenty years. Edward Wimberly writes about the importance of storytelling in pastoral care. "Storytelling is not normally associated with pastoral counseling, yet for more than a decade telling stories and using metaphors in counseling has been on the rise. These stories help us learn from Jesus how to feel about ourselves, our relationships, and our ministry."[27] Narratives, especially the parables of Jesus, can be very effective in helping people who seek change in their lives. "Parabolic stories are told in such a way that the person's view of the world is undermined and he or she is ready to accept another way of looking at things."[28] People today are attracted to stories where they can identify with one or more of the characters as they struggle with life.

How does the Bible story or character address the life issues that are common to living today? Slaughter says, "Postmoderns don't care about the Bible's infallibility as much as its integrity and moral value. They are not looking for theological comparisons but for spiritual connection and life relevance. The 21st century communicator will act as a guide helping the postmodern seeker find the integrity of the eternal wisdom revealed in the biblical text without compromising biblical truth."[29]

Preaching today promises many great opportunities for God's grace to be applied to people seeking a God they can know and experience. This God cares for them and their real-life problems.

▶ SCRIPTURE AS PASTORAL CARE

The Bible is one of the most valuable tools pastors can use to help needy people discover God's plan and will for their lives. Scripture is what Ralph Underwood calls "the substance of pastoral care."[30] Paul instructs his young pastor, Timothy, on the proper use of God's Word, "All Scripture is God-breathed and is useful for teaching, rebuking, correcting and training in righteousness, so that the man of God may be thoroughly equipped for every good work" (2 Tim. 3:16-17). There is the obvious connection between the scripture and preaching, but pastors must never neglect the private use of the Bible as a means of grace.

Throughout the Old Testament, and especially in the Psalms, the people of God are encouraged to think and meditate on God's Word. The first song in Israel's Psalter compliments the wise follower of God. "But his delight is in the law of the LORD, and on his law he meditates day and night" (Ps. 1:2). In the 119th psalm, the psalmist offers several prayers regarding his attitude toward Scripture: "I have hidden your word in my heart that I might not sin against you" (v. 11). "Oh, how I love your law! I meditate on it all day long" (v. 97). "Direct my footsteps according to your word; let no sin rule over me" (v. 133). There is great value in studying, meditating, and praying the Scriptures as a means of God's grace.

One of the older, traditional approaches to Scripture returning to use today is the *lectio divina,* or divine reading. There are four dimensions to the process: "(1) *lectio,* reading and listening to the text; (2) *meditatio,* reflecting on the Word; (3) *oratio,* praying for the Word to touch the heart; and (4) *contemplation,* encountering the silence too deep for words."[31] The *lectio divina* is not simply a technique but a way to approach Scripture involving both prayer and exegesis for divine illumination. This approach could be taught to those who desire to meet God in his Word.

While there is little discussion among pastors about the importance of the Bible, they do sometimes disagree about how Scripture is used. Caricatures abound of well-meaning Christians who figuratively use the Bible to hit people over the head in condemnation, or jam the Word down people's throats before they are ready to receive it. Salter writes that "some people in every congregation feel that life has dealt them a bad blow. They perceive that God is the inflicter of their misfortune. They desperately need the God of hope."[32] While Scripture conveys hope, God's Word cannot be ground up and sprinkled over a situation like pixie dust, designed to make everything nice and happy. "On the contrary, biblical words may be even more painful than joyful when first heard. Nevertheless, they move us toward reality in Christ."[33] The Bible must first of all work in the life of the pastor. "Understanding of the Bible sensitizes pastors, teaches them what to look for in others and themselves, and prepares them to attend to God's presence, even in the least likely nooks and crannies of people's lives."[34] We believe the Bible provides the antidote for sin, and thus, it is the ultimate hope for everyone.

How can pastors use Scripture in pastoral care as the *authoritative* Word of God, without being *authoritarian*? Edward Wimberly contrasts the two approaches. "Authoritarian uses of Scripture seek to make children of counselees and to frustrate the growth of persons toward their full possibilities as human beings. Authoritative uses of Scripture aim to appropriate those dimensions of Scripture that support the empowering of humans to become full and responsible participants in life."[35] The Bible does have authority because, although humans penned the words, the ultimate source is the Creator-Redeemer God. Apart from the Son of God, Jesus Christ, the Bible is the most complete revelation we have of who God is and what he desires of us. So how do we use the Bible as a means of God's grace?

Donald Capps, in his book *Biblical Approaches to Pastoral Counseling,* suggests three effective uses of the Bible in pastoral care:

• The first is the use of the Bible as an instrument of *diagnosis.* Wimberly describes this as the dynamic approach, where "Bible passages are chosen for their relevance to the psychological dynamics in the life of the counselee."[36] Often people are asked to give their favorite Bible story or Bible verse. They may see themselves in the story identified as one of the characters or claiming the promise of a favorite verse. A pastor can explore with individuals why a passage of scripture is important to them and where they see themselves in the passage.

• A second use of the Bible is *instructional.* Capps explains this approach, "Sometimes this involves helping parishioners understand the intended meaning of a particular biblical text that they have misunderstood or distorted, such as biblical passages on marriage and divorce. Other times, this means introducing a biblical text or reference that relates to the counselee's problem."[37]

Scripture has the authority to influence moral behavior. I remember dealing with a person who was proposing to do something that was totally inconsistent with the teachings of the Bible. By opening to a few passages of scripture this person came to understand that this plan of his could not possibly be God's will because it contradicted the plain, clear teachings of the Bible.

• A third use of the Bible is *hope-giving comfort.* When people are facing serious crises, handling debilitating physical illnesses, or dealing with the aftermath of ongoing bereavement, pastors need to remember that these people often want to hear a word from God. It is common for hurting people to turn to the Psalms for words of comfort. Some look to Paul's writings that offer hope, even in difficult circumstances. People may find encouragement and ongoing support by memorizing hope-giving passages. Those scriptures will remain within the mind so individuals can draw strength whenever that verse enters their conscious awareness.

Both Capps and Wimberly encourage people to use the great narrative passages of the Bible. Wimberly says, "Identification with particular Bible stories and characters is often related to the drawing power of the Bible story and the character itself. . . . Biblical stories often contain an invitation to the reader to adopt the perspective, feelings, and attitudes of the characters as a way to influence the life of the reader and the hearer."[38]

The beauty of the great biblical narratives is this: although the characters may have lived from two to four thousand years ago, human nature and human predicaments have not changed at all. These were real people, living with real families, facing real problems and having to make tough decisions. While not every biblical character was heroic, not every person made right choices, the Bible reveals ways in which God interacted and intervened with grace and mercy to those who sought him by faith. The Bible is ultimately a story of hope—God has made salvation available for all humans, even though no one deserves it. In that, the Bible is a means of grace. Don't be afraid to use it in pastoral conversations.

▶ PRAYER AS PASTORAL CARE

While prayer is a vital part a pastor's own personal spiritual journey, prayer as a means of grace is often understood only in the context of the larger community of faith. But prayer may begin in private as a pastor intercedes for the needs of the flock before God. It then moves into more public areas, such hospitals and homes when the pastor prays with individuals. The pastor's most obvious public prayer role is leading the congregation in prayers within the worship experience. Martin Luther emphasized the importance of public prayer when he said, "A Christian congregation should never gather together without the preaching of God's Word and prayer, no matter briefly."[39]

Public prayer is not an opportunity for the pastor to float a cleverly crafted set of phrases in front of the worshipers, designed to impress the human hearers. Pastors need to pray with a sense of humility because they are leading their flock to the very throne room of God. Salter writes, "The priestly prayer is to ask God to take planned words for corporate worship and use them beyond our intentions to bring word, event, and setting together in ways we have not even imagined. Thus the minister must confess that human wisdom is inadequate and planning is myopic."[40]

Through public prayer people come to an awareness that what may have been common space is now sacred space. This is especially important when the church worships in a rented facility such as a school or office building that may be used for other activities during the week. But even people gathering in a worshipful church sanctuary need to be reminded that they have come for an encounter with God. Whenever the people of God join together in public prayer they need to be aware of a divine presence in their midst.

Moses experienced this on an ordinary day of tending sheep in the Midian desert. Suddenly a bush burst into flames but didn't burn up. When Moses went over to investigate, the voice of God spoke from the bush. "Do not come any closer . . . Take off your sandals, for the place where you are standing is holy ground" (Exod. 3:5). Common sand became holy ground. Anyplace, no matter how common, becomes a sacred space when God reveals himself to his people in prayer. The act of prayer itself is God's gift of grace to his people. He graciously invites us to come boldly before him in prayer with our worship and our requests. In addition, Jesus, our elder Brother, is interceding for us when we can't put into words the deep yearnings of our hearts.

Corporate prayer also stimulates private prayer. Howard Rice says, "Public prayer is a means of grace that strengthens, stretches, and prepares believers for private prayer. Without public prayer, private prayers frequently become narrowly self-centered. . . . The discipline of public prayer calls the congregation beyond itself and serves as a check upon individual laziness and forgetfulness."[41] Jesus' disciples one day observed him praying, and when he had finished they requested, "Lord, teach us to pray, just as John taught his disciples" (Luke 11:1). Jesus proceeded to teach his followers a prayer, commonly called the Lord's Prayer. Jesus intended the prayer to be a model for his disciples when they prayed in private. In the pastoral prayer the pastor also models for the congregation the form and general content to use when they pray individually.

When I was a pastor, one of the most significant components of the worship service was the pastoral prayer. It was the moment I assumed my pastoral-priestly role as the shepherd interceding to the Father for the flock under my care. Because this was the time when I publicly interceded for the congregation, I did not relinquish this role to anyone else, even staff members or visiting pastors. Since I was the representative of the people of God, my role was to voice what the congregation as a whole would pray.

Usually the pastoral prayer time began with an invitation for all who would like to come forward and kneel at the altar with any personal request they would like to present to God in prayer. While I did not write out my prayer verbatim, I did have an outline I tried to follow in prayer. Usually the order began with adoration and thanksgiving, often with a brief scripture of praise. Next came prayers on behalf of the congregation, leading them in confessing sins and shortcomings. Then I prayed for specific needs of the congregation that I had previously noted in my prayer outline. The prayer concluded either acknowledging the Trinity or with the phrase, "in Jesus' name, Amen."

While this model worked well with my understanding of the priestly role, each pastor needs to thoughtfully and creatively develop effective ways to represent the flock before the Heavenly Father.

Willimon says, "The pastor's ministry of public prayer will be based in great part on the pastor's own prayer life, the pastor's continual practice of the presence of God in prayer."[42] It also provides an opportunity for the pastor to instruct the congregation on the importance of individual prayer throughout the week.

Worship becomes personal when the pastor gives the congregation the opportunity to represent their personal needs publicly, either by standing, or moving forward for prayer. God's grace is at work in specific needs that are represented at the altar. Grace is also present as members of the congregation who know of the individual's need come alongside and lay hands on the person praying, showing concern and support. People may experience physical healing, make spiritual decisions, and mend broken relationships. Some experience their secret prayers answered that were never voiced aloud.

Neil Wiseman suggests an interesting variation. A pastor he knows invites visitors and needy people from the congregation to meet him at the front of the sanctuary at the end of the service. He listens to each individual's need and then offers a personal prayer. This pastor then gives a New Testament to every visitor. The people who come forward are impacted by this pastor's willingness to show personal care for their needs.[43]

The benediction is often ignored completely or dismissed as merely an official way of ending a service. Other pastors have begun to see its significance in the worship service. Personally, the benediction took on new meaning for me after worshiping in several services with college chaplain and author Richard Allan Farmer. Farmer emphasizes the benediction as a blessing from God proclaimed to the congregation by the pastor.

While there are several scriptural blessings, such as Jude 24-25, I prefer an extemporaneous benediction. A pastor can begin by asking the congregation to stand to receive this blessing from God. Since the pastor is addressing the people of God, he or she should assure them that God will be with them, that his grace will be at work in their lives. When it is appropriate, interject a positive element of the sermon into the blessing. The congregation is going into the world to be the Church scattered. Remind them that they go with the power and blessing of the Holy Spirit. It is certainly appropriate to lift both hands toward the congregation throughout the blessing, indicating that God's grace is being extended to them.

One pastor reported receiving one of those dreaded calls in the middle of the night. One of the young men in the church had been in an accident and was taken by ambulance, unconscious and in critical condition, to the local hospital. This pastor went to be with the family and together they prayed that God would spare his life. Over the next several days the church joined the family in intercessory prayer, both publicly and privately.

Then one day the injured man suddenly opened his eyes and was awake, conscious again of his family standing by. As the pastor and family were rejoicing, the doctor came into the room and said to the mother, "It was nothing we did. This was Mom power."

"No," she replied, "this was God power."

The family and the pastor knew that in response to their prayers, God had chosen to bring healing to this young man. Prayer was the means by which God's grace was dispensed.

▶ THE SACRAMENTS AS PASTORAL CARE

COMMUNION

When it came to the means of grace, John Wesley never gave a list of those that were most important in his mind. However, Maddox recounts that "he clearly had a particular appreciation for the contribution of the Lord's Supper to this end. He referred to it as the 'grand channel' whereby the grace of the Spirit is conveyed to human souls, and identified partaking communion as the first step in working out our salvation."[44] For Wesley, "the Lord's Supper was truly a *sacrament* that conveys to believers the gracious gift of Christ."[45]

A pastor has the wonderful privilege of inviting the church to gather at Christ's table and eat with him and with others of the Body of Believers. Willimon uses the imagery of Paul offering food to fellow passengers who have been stuck in a storm for fourteen days (Acts 27). Paul "takes bread, blesses bread, breaks bread, and gives bread to those on board. In this familiar fourfold action—this eucharistic gesture of taking, blessing, breaking, and giving bread —Paul feeds the frightened multitudes in much the same way Jesus fed the multitudes before him."[46]

Whether this was a real Communion meal or not, it is a reminder to us that something unique and special takes place in the breaking of the bread. It is one means by which grace comes to us. "The gifts of God—bread and wine— are transformed as signs of Christ's real presence among us. The church—ordinary people of flesh and blood—is changed into the Body of Christ. . . . A meal of only bread and wine becomes a stunning victory banquet for God's triumphant kingdom."[47]

At the Communion table we find Jesus uniting all who gather there into one body. And yet, sincere believers often draw the line here, excluding those who are not of their particular faith community. A gathering of church leaders from various church bodies were looking for ways to be able to cooperate together for effective ministry as the Body of Christ. As the meeting progressed, everyone was feeling good about the spirit of unity among the various denominations represented. That is, until someone suggested that it would be appropriate to share a Communion meal before they all left. Several leaders said they were forbidden by their church polity to participate in the Eucharist with certain other representatives, and the whole idea was finally dropped.

I personally experienced the opposite response at a four-day pastors' prayer summit in the mountains of Idaho. Over fifty ministers from over a dozen denominations gathered for a time of intense prayer for personal needs and to call upon God for spiritual revival in the region. Each evening the activities concluded with Communion. The group had come as pastors from diverse backgrounds: Wesleyans and Calvinists, mainliners and evangelicals, charismatics and fundamentalists. But when the participants came to the table, suddenly we were one—fellow ministers of the gospel of Jesus Christ. In those evenings while we were partaking of the Lord's Supper, those pastors were becoming the answer to Jesus' prayer for the church in the Upper Room, "that all of them may be one, Father, just as you are in me and I am in you" (John 17:21).

The Lord's Supper has powerful implications for pastoral care. The most obvious is the dramatic life-change that comes when one truly receives salvation by faith through Jesus Christ. As we taste the physical representations of Jesus' body and blood, we are reminded that God has forgiven us and we are now experiencing spiritual life. Pastor David Hansen describes the effect of the Eucharist, "People are freed for new life—new life with God and new life with each other. The Table is a feast. It is a celebration of our life together founded on God's work in Christ. We gather as a community broken by our sin and leave as a community healed by God's forgiveness."[48]

In Communion the Church remembers the willingness of Christ, the Son of God, to lay down his life for sinful humanity. It is difficult to look at Christ's sacrifice without responding with the full consecration of our gifts and abilities for Christ's use in the world. Paul writes in Rom. 12:1, "Therefore, I urge you, brothers, in view of God's mercy, to offer your bodies as living sacrifices, holy and pleasing to God—this is your spiritual act of worship." The Lord's Supper should provide the motivation for all believers to take their places as "living sacrifices," the hands and feet of Jesus, serving others as he would serve. Maddox says, "In the Lord's Supper we do not merely accept *gracious* forgiveness from Christ as Priest, we renew our *responsive* allegiance to Christ as King."[49]

In John Wesley's day the Lord's Supper had become for many a way of certifying one's moral conduct and good standing in the church rather than a means to receive God's grace. The issue of worthiness kept many sensitive people from coming to the table out of a fear of the wrath of God. Wesley believed that God offered both converting grace and saving grace through the Lord's Supper. But this created a problem. Should those who feel the need to receive the saving grace of God be encouraged to come to the table instead of being excluded as being unworthy?

"Wesley began to do precisely this, offering an 'open table' for which the only initial requirement of the recipient was a desire to receive God's grace to live in faithful response, not some prior fitness or assurance."[50] Wesley taught that in order for such grace to be effective, one would have to respond to it. Thus, the pastor took on the role of encouraging individuals to respond to the opportunities for grace, especially through the Lord's Supper. Communion offers those who are being awakened to spiritual things, the opportunity to receive grace, prevenient grace, that can draw them to salvation. This understanding makes the Lord's Supper an important means of grace to all who sincerely desire to receive it.

There are several methods for serving Communion in the worship service. Smaller congregations may prefer coming to an altar and partaking of the elements while kneeling. The time needed to serve everyone while kneeling may make this approach difficult for larger churches. Also, some sanctuaries do not have altars available for people to kneel. A variation of this approach that is gaining acceptance is to serve the elements by intinction, meaning to dip. The communicants move to the front of the sanctuary or to designated serving stations where they first receive the bread, often torn from a larger loaf. The bread is then dipped in the wine and either eaten immediately or when the person returns to his or her seat. Other churches customarily distribute first the bread, divided into small pieces and served on plates. Then they pass trays with small individual cups containing the juice. Often these cups are disposable. Other Communion serving sets have single trays that contain places for both bread and wine cups. Some churches purchase small individualized containers that have both elements sealed separately. Their advantage is that the elements are sanitary and cannot be spilled before use. The Communion elements can be distributed when the congregation enters the sanctuary or just prior to the partaking of the Lord's Supper. While some congregations may use only one approach to serving, others find it beneficial to vary the serving methods to bring freshness to the Eucharist.

The Communion meal can provide a connection to members of the local Body of Believers who could not attend the church service. Underwood writes, "If the blessing in the Eucharist unites the community that has voiced reconciliation and peace to one another, then the Eucharist taken from the sanctuary to the marginalized and vulnerable who cannot attend worship, binds them and makes them one with the worshiping community. . . . In some churches when the Eucharist is celebrated those who are to receive the sacrament after the service in homes and institutions are included specifically in the prayers of intercession."[51] A pastor serving Communion in a hospital, convalescent center, or home is taking a tangible symbol of God's grace to those who need it most. Often the eyes of shut-in people suddenly become alert as the pastor hands them the elements and speak those words of encouragement and hope connected with this sacrament.

BAPTISM

Baptism, the other sacrament for most Protestants, is also a means of grace. As such, Ralph Underwood argues that "baptism is the foundation or 'preface' of pastoral care. This initiation rite represents the foundational reality of the Christian faith and life, and consequently it represents the basis of pastoral care as an expression of Christian living and service."[52] It is a tangible, physical ritual signifying that a person has become a part of a community of believers, the Church.

There is powerful symbolism when one is lowered under the water, depicting death to the old life of sin, and is lifted again out of the water, testifying to the new life in Christ. These are elements of tomb and womb—death and fresh life. Death is confirmed in the question asked in some rituals today, "Do you reject Satan and all his works and all his empty promises?" The candidates reply, "I do." Paul uses this death and life imagery in Gal. 2:20, "I have been crucified with Christ and I no longer live, but Christ lives in me. The life I live in the body, I live by faith in the Son of God, who loved me and gave himself for me."

Baptism testifies to the grace that comes through the divine presence in the life of the believer. Throughout its history the Church has held that baptism is more than cosmetic. It must reflect the radical, behavioral change in the life of the believer. The fourth-century bishop Gregory of Nyssa wrote, "If the 'birth from above' is a refashioning of man's nature, we must ask what change is made to bring the grace of regeneration to perfection. . . . If the life after initiation (baptism) is of the same quality as the uninitiated life, then, though it may be a bold thing to say, I say it without flinching; in the case of such people the water is merely water, for the gift of the Holy Spirit in no way shows itself in what takes place."[53]

Baptism provides many implications for pastoral care. One is found in the renunciation of the evil practices of the past. I remember one young man who somehow wandered into the church where I was pastoring. As the church reached out to him it was obvious that there was a longing for a life more ful-filling than what he was currently experiencing. Among his many personal vices, he earned extra money by selling drugs to people at the factory where he worked. One day he finally took that important step of receiving Jesus Christ as his Lord and Savior. Life for him took a 180-degree turnabout. He forsook all of the sinful practices that had promised him so much but produced so lit-tle. What he couldn't change by his own willpower, God enabled him to change by divine grace.

This man's baptism became an opportunity for him to profess his faith to the community. Both his church friends and his work buddies could see that he was transformed into a new and different person than he was in the past. In this way, his baptism became a means for other unbelievers to be touched by the drawing power of God's grace.

Since baptism takes place publicly in the context of the faith community, it also has a positive impact on the church. Believers who watch often relive their own personal baptismal experiences. The Body of Believers are strengthened by a new resolve to be faithful to the baptismal promises. Baptism is a reminder to everyone who watches that there are others who need to know Christ's life-changing salvation in their lives. Evangelism should be a natural result of bap-tism, in the life of both the baptismal candidate and the witnessing church.

▶ GOD USES MANY MEANS

This chapter is not intended as an exhaustive discussion of the various means by which God's grace is extended to people. God administers his grace through such things as Christian music, small groups, Sunday School classes, church camps, fellowship dinners, men's ministries, accountability partners, va-cation Bible school, devotional books, women's Bible studies, service to others, large stadium events, and one-on-one conversations over coffee. The list is nearly endless. Perhaps the more important question is this: Is the church ef-fectively using the various means of grace to lead people to salvation and into a developing, growing relationship with Christ?

▶ QUESTIONS FOR REFLECTION

▷ Why should a pastor be concerned about the means of grace in providing pas-toral care?

▷ What are some ways you see worship assisting in pastoral care?

▷ How can the use of prayer and Scripture help an individual who is dealing with a serious physical problem, such as cancer?

UNIT 3

PASTORAL PRESENCE

TEN

THE PASTOR'S PRESENCE
IN RESOLVING CONFLICT

This was the last thing Pastor Ricky Lopez expected to happen in the parking lot after a church service. Two of his church members got into a discussion that escalated to shouts, and then shoves. If some other men from the church had not intervened when the coats came off, the congregation would have witnessed an actual fight on the pavement right behind the church. By the time the pastor got outside, the excitement was over and both men were gone.

Ricky remembered conversations with Joe and T. J. three months earlier. These two, who had been acquaintances since childhood, decided to go into a lawn-care business together. Both men were recent but fervent converts to the faith. Because they were both Christians, they told the pastor, the business was guaranteed to succeed. T. J. had most of the start-up money and Joe supplied the lawn maintenance expertise. What neither of them possessed was an understanding of how to manage a small business.

The problems began small. Joe was upset with T. J.'s spill of gasoline on a lawn that caused them to lose a business account. Some customers were being billed twice, and T. J. felt like Joe should pay more attention to the finances if they were going to make it.

Pastor Ricky was sitting down to Sunday dinner when T. J. called on the phone. For the next forty-five minutes the pastor listened as T. J. vented his frustration about his partner. Joe was to take all the previous week's receipts to the bank for deposit, so they could each draw a salary and pay some bills. Instead, Joe left the envelope in his pickup while he ran into a convenience store to pick up some milk for his new baby. When he came out three minutes later the envelope with the cash and checks was gone.

"When I confronted him about the problem," T. J. explained, "Joe got really defensive. He said that it was a theft and there was nothing we could do to get the money back. How do I know that Joe didn't pocket the money himself? This business partnership is just not working out. I may have to take him to court to get back the money that is missing due to his carelessness. Will you stand with me on this one, Pastor?"

Ricky had no sooner punched the off button on the phone when it began ringing again. It was Joe's turn. The partnership that looked so promising was not working out very well. T. J. didn't have a clue about lawn maintenance, and it was

149

creating problems for the clientele Joe had built up with his careful work. Joe was getting calls from irate customers who were taking their business elsewhere.

"I'm working as hard as I can," Joe complained, "trying to keep everyone happy. But T. J. wants me to be an accountant as well, keeping records and billing for the work we've done. And now he's accusing me of either losing the money or stealing it. I can't help it that the money was stolen from my pickup." Joe ended the conversation by pleading, "Pastor, you need to help me tell T. J. that if he doesn't get off my back, I'm quitting this partnership. Will you do that for me?"

▶ WHY CAN'T WE JUST GET ALONG?

An arrest on the streets of a large American city is not usually cause for more than just a passing glance by passersby. But one incident on March 3, 1991, would change the complexion of Los Angeles for years to come. Rodney King, an African-American, was stopped by police while driving his car. Although King had a history of combativeness, the police officers—three white and one Latino—went too far by repeatedly kicking and beating him with batons until he was finally subdued.

The incident might still have gone unnoticed except for a bystander with a camera who videotaped the event. News broadcasts showed the highlights of the beating over and over to viewers around the globe. The policemen who beat King were later acquitted of charges of using excessive force, by a jury that did not include one African-American. When the news of the verdict hit the streets of Los Angeles, rioting broke out all over the city, resulting in the deaths of fifty people and a billion dollars in damages. At the height of the conflict, Rodney King stepped in front of the television cameras and pled with the rioters to stop. His words form a question that should be asked whenever conflict breaks out: "Can we all just get along?"

Among the most familiar teachings of Jesus are a series of short statements in Matt. 5 called the Beatitudes. These brief descriptions combine to form a composite sketch of Jesus' ideal Kingdom person. Notice, one of these characteristics addresses the issue of conflict, "Blessed are the peacemakers, for they will be called sons of God."[1] Jesus may have been reflecting on the words of David in Ps. 34:14, "Turn from evil and do good; seek peace and pursue it."

But it would be naive to think that if Christians in the Church were simply spiritual or Spirit-filled, there would never be conflicts between individuals. The truth is that churches are made up of people with human failings, opposing viewpoints, and very fallible judgments. Conflict often short-circuits the process of care between people, fellow members of the Body of Christ, because they cannot get past their differences to see their common concerns. I have never forgotten a short poem Chuck Swindoll quoted on his radio broadcast many years ago:

> *To dwell above with folks we love,*
> *Oh yes, that will be glory.*
> *To dwell below with folks we know,*
> *Well, that's a different story.*

From the earliest days of the Church in the Book of Acts, conflict has been a catalyst for growth. In the early chapters Peter and John differed with the Sanhedrin over the right to preach Jesus as the Christ. These two men continued to proclaim the good news in spite of the objections of others. Chapter 6 tells about the Church's conflict between the local Jewish widows and the Hellenistic widows over the daily distribution of food. The apostles did not have the time to devote to this problem and appointed people to address this concern. This was the first example of laypeople being assigned to lead a church ministry.

The apostle Paul was no stranger to conflict. Even before his conversion, when he was still known as Saul, he was in conflict with the church in Damascus over their belief that Jesus was the Messiah. This led to Saul's traveling to the city to stamp out those people of the Way. While he traveled along the road, driven by his conflict, he came face-to-face with Jesus and was converted. Later, Saul (now Paul) and Barnabas confronted Peter and the Jerusalem church over the requirement that Gentile converts must live under Jewish law. The Council at Jerusalem in Acts 15 settled the dispute and set the stage for the growth of Christianity to the Gentile people around the world. Even Paul and Barnabas had a strong disagreement over taking John Mark as they planned for their second missionary journey. Because they could not come to terms about a solution, Paul chose Silas and Barnabas took Mark on separate missionary teams. In each of these cases, the conflict forced people to make changes and opened the possibility for the Church to further expand its ministry base.

Not all conflict in the Church is positive. One study investigating the impact of conflict in churches on pastors reported that 10 percent of pastors said that they gave more than 40 percent of their time to managing conflict. An additional 26 percent of pastors said that between 20 and 40 percent of their workweek was spent dealing with conflict issues in their church. This means that a third of pastors spent the equivalent of an entire day every week of the year on conflict resolution.[2]

Conflict can exact a far greater toll in churches than wasted time. Disagreements can bring hard feelings, misunderstandings, feuds, gossip, and emotional attacks. People withdraw from leadership, undermine church programs, withhold their financial support, or actually leave a church when they are at odds with others.

Since some conflict is inevitable because we are humans interacting together, how we deal with these differences becomes all-important. Hugh Halverstadt writes, "Christian understandings of God's love mean much more than interpersonal respectfulness, but parties' respectful behavior in a conflict is a necessary way of approximating God's love."[3]

What transforms a potentially destructive conflict into a constructive, growth-producing experience for individuals and the church? Professor David Kale notes two theological concepts as foundational: *transformation* and *community*. He writes, "Our goal is conflict transformation where God is allowed to work through the conflict to bring new life into the church, providing it with power and resources it did not previously have for achieving His commission."[4] On the concept of community Kale says, "For transformation conflict to occur, members put the good of the church ahead of their own personal needs and interests. When members are willing to do this, the transforming power of God will often meet their deep personal needs in ways they never anticipated."[5]

Our discussion of conflict will first address interpersonal differences between two or more people who are part of a church, then move to conflicts that involve broader issues within the Church as a community.

▶ "To Dwell Below with Folks We Know"

One of David's Song of Ascents begins this way, "How good and pleasant it is when brothers live together in unity!"[6] It sounds great, doesn't it? But relationships can move from "good and pleasant" to "bad and ugly" when selfishness or misunderstanding is added to the mix. Sometimes serious conflict can even erupt between two people who hold good and valid, yet opposing, viewpoints. Good people may differ in what they value as important or in the result they desire.

In the absence of Paul, its founding pastor, the new church in Corinth struggled with settling disagreements between members. Some were using the local court system to settle legal disputes between individual believers. Paul strongly urged them not to sue one another. L. Randolph Lowry, a Christian lawyer, writes, "In a judicial resolution there will always be a winner and a loser when the verdict is read. But Paul contends that the Christian loses in this kind of dispute resolution, regardless of the verdict. This loss may be economic or emotional; it may also be the loss of one's reputation or ministry."[7]

Paul's reasoning was very clear: Christians should never air their dirty laundry before unbelievers and then ask the ungodly to rule on their dispute. There may be times when a court can be used to decide on a fine point of civil law. However, it was Paul's opinion that the cases were trivial and made these litigant members the laughingstock of the neighborhood. If a decision had to be reached, create a court within the church with Christian judges to make the decision. But there is a deeper issue here. Paul asks, "Why not rather be wronged? Why not rather be cheated?" (1 Cor. 6:7). It takes a spiritually mature person to say, "I don't have to be right all the time. I can even be victimized, if necessary, for the good of the Kingdom."

How does a Christian deal with a conflict involving a brother or sister in Christ? The Gospel writer Matthew was concerned with the way the young church he pastored dealt with interpersonal conflict. He related to his readers, and to us, the instructions of Jesus on the subject.

> If your brother sins against you, go and show him his fault, just between the two of you. If he listens to you, you have won your brother over. But if he will not listen, take one or two others along, so that "every matter may be established by the testimony of two or three witnesses." If he refuses to listen to them, tell it to the church; and if he refuses to listen even to the church, treat him as you would a pagan or a tax collector *(18: 15-17)*.

The passage seems to indicate that this process of reconciliation was already well established by the time Matthew wrote these words of Jesus'. The word "sins" used in verse 15 is very general in nature and could be interpreted as any missing of the mark that could lead to misunderstanding. There is a four-step process in the text for working out differences between individuals in the church.

1. Personal conversation (v. 15)

Many Christians feel that if they have been wronged by another believer, the best thing to do is to try to ignore it. This may be true if you can forgive and forget it immediately. But what if the hurt will not go away? William Barclay says, "The worst thing that we can do about a wrong is to brood about it. That is fatal. It can poison the whole mind and life, until we can think of nothing else but our sense of personal injury."[8]

Some people feel free to tell others, even their pastor, about their hurt. Yet they fail to let the person who injured them know about their feelings. The source of many interpersonal conflicts is a misunderstanding of the words or actions by the other party. People do and say things that make sense to them, although it may be misinterpreted by those who observe. Most of the time there is a complex combination of information and ideas running through our brains that help us make a decision. There is no way that a person listening to us can be privy to even a small percentage of the influencing thoughts that run through our minds.

Jesus said that a private, personal conversation with the other person is the best venue to begin discussing misinterpretations, slights, or hurts that can grow out of proportion if left unchecked.

Some time ago I became frustrated by the actions of one my colleagues at the university where I teach. It seemed to me that the best way to register my complaint was to write the president an e-mail message and send a copy of the letter to the offending colleague. The next day my friend wrote me a reply to my letter. "I got a copy of your e-mail yesterday," he wrote. "Why in the world didn't you talk to me first, before you sent a letter to the president?"

I didn't have an answer for him. It made me think about how I would have felt if he had done the same thing to me. Instead of thinking the process through, I had been more concerned about expressing my frustration to someone who could do something about it. With the Holy Spirit's thumb in my back, I apologized by e-mail to my colleague for my thoughtlessness and insensitivity. Later that day I saw him walking across campus and apologized again in person. My friend did the right thing by confronting me with my "sin" against him. Had he not cared enough to deal with the problem, our relationship could have been damaged and I would not have known why.

Jesus says in verse 15, "If he listens to you, you have won your brother over." This doesn't mean you have convinced your brother that you are right. You and your brother may never fully agree on the issue. Some conflict grows from personality differences. Keith Huttenlocker writes, "Whether it is between church members or between the pastor and church members, personality-centered conflict has its basis in prescriptive expectations. Someone is unwilling to allow another to be different."[9] We are usually less tolerant of those with whom we have personality conflicts. Even if you are never best friends with the brother or sister who has wronged you, you can come to an understanding of resolution. And with that understanding of resolution, the relationship is restored. This is the most important goal of all interpersonal conflict.

2. Small-group resolution (v. 16)

If the conflict with the brother or sister is not resolved at the personal level, Jesus instructs us to "take one or two others along, so that every matter may be established by the testimony of two or three witnesses."[10] The message here is very clear: don't give up on the process of resolution if the first encounter was not successful. The purpose of involving "one or two others" is not to shift the weight of argument to your side. For that reason, it is helpful that both people be agreeable to the other individuals who are brought into the process. By involving others with wisdom and sensitivity to come into the discussion, all parties can work together to bring reconciliation. These people can bring a needed objectivity into the debate. It is easy to see the speck in the other person's eye and be blind to the log in our own.

If a pastor is helping to negotiate this process, it may be best to have all parties involved meet in a neutral location such as the church office. It is important that the pastor, as shepherd, show equal concern for everyone. In the opening vignette, both T. J. and Joe were expecting Pastor Lopez to side with their personal position. Pastor Lopez would be wise to invite two people from the church who have some business understanding and personal knowledge of both sides to help sort out the issues. The resolution at this level often involves a compromise agreeable to both parties, even though it may not be the solution either side personally desires.

3. A public discussion (v. 17a)

The goal of any conflict is to find resolution as quickly as possible with as few others involved as necessary. But if the differences cannot be resolved in the presence of a small group of helpers, Jesus gives the instruction to take the next step. "If he refuses to listen to them, tell it to the church."[11] This is a serious move because it involves an exposure of the conflict to a larger group of people. This may result in fueling emotions, distorting the facts, and forcing fellow church members to choose sides. Before taking this step all parties should be encouraged to pray and seek the guidance of the Holy Spirit for wisdom.

In T. J. and Joe's case, the conflict involves some financial information about their business that they may not want available for public knowledge. And there is always the danger of gossip among people who do not have all the facts.

Bringing the issue before the church does not necessarily imply the entire church membership. Most churches have some type of representative board that does spiritual planning and conducts business on behalf of the congregation. This may be the best venue for the church to thoroughly consider the merits of the conflict. Another option is for the governing board to appoint a smaller committee to address the conflict. Depending on the content of the dispute, the board may have its meeting open to the public or hear the issue in executive session with only board members and invited participants present. The church board's responsibility at this stage is to listen to the accounts of the dispute from all parties, including the neutral witnesses from the previous stage. If the purpose is to resolve the conflict, the board may give advice, but the issue would not be resolved until all the people involved agreed to a resolution.

4. The church's decision (v. 17b)

There are some conflicts that may not be resolved, even after the church board has tried to bring about a solution to the problem. At this final stage, Lowry says, "The two sides admit their inability to resolve the conflict and 'tell it to the church.' In a sense, the church, or its leadership, becomes the arbitrator who must make a wise decision regarding a particular behavior and the nature of the fellowship."[12] If there are no moral issues involved, the church may decide not to take sides or make a ruling in the matter. Paul and Barnabas felt that their differences were serious enough to go their separate ways in ministry, even though Paul later spoke highly of John Mark's usefulness to the Kingdom. Conflict does not mean that one person has to be a villain. The church may simply decide to back away from choosing sides.

However, when a conflict has stemmed from serious, publicly known sin, the church may have the responsibility to call for repentance and restitution. A good principle to remember is that while most private sins require private confession, public sin, or sin that affects the public, needs a public acknowledgment of wrongdoing.

Some years ago a personal acquaintance was involved in working with a nationally known evangelical leader who was accused of immoral behavior with a woman. This man was brought in front of the church he attended, and he shamefully admitted his sin. To the leader's credit, after he confessed his wrongdoing he submitted himself to the church for a plan of restoration. The church contacted several ministers to develop a comprehensive process of accountability and counsel to rebuild this man's spiritual relationship with God and the community of believers. At the conclusion of this process the church held a service of restoration that allowed this man to again serve the church. This church became an instrument of God's grace and mercy extended to an individual. Without the vital role of the local church in requiring this man to accept responsibility for his actions, he would have forfeited the possibility of returning to ministry in the future.

There are times when a person brought before the church for sinful behavior refuses to acknowledge the sin and repent. Or, the church may be hesitant to confront overt sin in a person who is in leadership. Paul wrote to the church in Corinth[13] asking them to address the immoral behavior of a member who had sexual relations with his father's wife. The whole church knew about it but had chosen to ignore the wrongness of the situation. Paul's concern was that by tolerating publicly known immoral behavior among those who should have known better, they were giving permission for others to yield to temptation. Paul's instructions were difficult, but clear: "You must not associate with anyone who calls himself a brother but is sexually immoral or greedy, an idolater or a slanderer, a drunkard or a swindler."[14] Paul is not saying that the church should shun ungodly people who need to know the life-changing presence of Jesus. But, one who claims to be a Christian is held to a different, higher standard. The Church must always handle such issues in a spirit of compassion, with the goal of restoring this person to a walk of faith.

Lowry believes that a process utilizing churches to work out disputes can be effective today. He says there are several options: One is avoiding or ignoring the problem, if the issues of the conflict are not worth fighting over. A second option is negotiating a settlement by the parties talking together and compromising toward an agreeable result. A third is mediation where a third party facilitates moving those in conflict to find a resolution. A fourth option, arbitration, gives the third party the power to make a decision. Lowry observes that the four options correspond to the four steps found in Matt. 18.[15]

▶ "JEALOUSY AND QUARRELING AMONG YOU"[16]

Every believer has probably asked the question at one time or another, If the Church really is the Bride of Christ, why is it that she is so susceptible to conflict within the ranks? Don't forget, the local church is made up of individuals, each coming from a unique background and having a unique perspective of an issue. There are those who develop a selfish expectation of what a church ought to be doing, based on their own personal needs or desires. Their mantra is: *Give me . . . Give me. I need . . . I need.* Some value traditions and history. Others like innovation and cutting-edge planning. Sincere people can have honest differences and still love God supremely. Conflict develops when one side attaches spiritual value to a nonspiritual difference of opinion. In other words, painting the walls blue rather than green is not a spiritual issue, even if a person on one side of an argument tries to make a point spiritual: God likes blue, because when looking up to the heavens, the skies are blue.

LACK OF COMMUNICATION

There are several causes of conflict in a local church. One of the most common is miscommunication or the lack of communication. I had the opportunity one Sunday evening to drop in on a church I had formerly pastored. It was a holiday weekend and I thought the crowd might be down some. However, I was unprepared for the empty parking lot when I drove up. My watch told me that the starting time was only ten minutes away. After checking every door to see if at least one was unlocked, I began to walk back to my car. Someone came out from one of the locked doors and informed me that the service had been canceled because of the holiday. I laughed about it as I drove away. There was no way I could have known about the change. But what about a current member who had been out of town for two weeks and showed up for the service. Since there were no announcements about the cancellation on the church door, a member could be very upset about not being informed.

When the church fails to communicate the facts of an issue clearly to everyone, it is easy for rumors and misinformation to spread like wildfire. Remember the Sago mining disaster in West Virginia? Word got out that twelve of the thirteen trapped miners were alive, and even the media reported the joyful news. Unfortunately the rumor was false; only one miner left the mine alive.

And knowing just the facts may not solve the conflict. Several people may witness the same accident, but they disagree on exactly what took place. Listeners can hear the same speech and draw different conclusions about what was said. Even Sergeant Joe Friday's oft-repeated statement on the old *Dragnet* television show—"Just the facts, ma'am"—turns out to be wrong. (What he actually said was, "All we want are the facts.")

What each person sees or hears is filtered through a complex series of experiences from the past, and what comes out is a perspective that helps the person make sense of this new issue. Using all the church's savings to purchase a church van may be regarded as a careless use of funds to a person who lived during the Great Depression of the 1930s in America. Times could get tough again. This person may believe that you need to hold some money back for a rainy day. Younger people might look at the same savings account and believe strongly that any money the church has should be used right now, not left sitting in a bank somewhere. Who is right? It all depends on your perspective, which may grow out of your past.

CULTURAL DIFFERENCES

It is easy for conflict to develop amid a climate of cultural stresses or changes. A church in a city near where I live had dwindled down to just a few older faithful members. There was very little hope of this church surviving. In recent days a young pastor of a different denomination began the process of planting a new church in the very same neighborhood of this dying church. The older, dying church congregation made an offer to the young pastor: "You can have our building if you will let us become a part of your church." But what might seem a blessing on the surface could become a detriment to this church plant. Why has the older church failed to reach new people in the recent past? It could be that they drove off anyone who tried to bring about positive change to reach the community. For some people in that church, the possibility of change might be just too painful to comprehend. There are churches that choose to die rather than face up to the need for change. The conflicts over change can be heated and hurtful.

POWER ISSUES

Many church conflicts can be boiled down to an issue of power. Factions in the church may struggle to gain control of church governance. There are churches that have existed for years under the tyranny of one family or even one individual who makes all the decisions in the church. David Kale observes, "Power struggles between the pastor and the board or other influential members have the capacity to do great damage to the church's effectiveness and future. Some cases result in the pastor or the church members—and sometimes both—leaving the church, seriously disrupting the church's ability to achieve its mission."[17]

It is natural, in any group of humans, for some people to exert greater influence than others. Throughout the Bible God has raised up leaders who have used power and influence to get things done. That is not necessarily an abuse of power. Without leadership a church will tend to be inert and not do anything. Some people view all power as corrupting, but that is a naive understanding of the way humans interact. Power develops into conflict when people perceive that abuse has taken place for some type of personal gain. And the only way for such conflict to be resolved is to develop an atmosphere of trust. In a free society the citizens voluntarily give limited power to government officials such as police to provide security for the good of all. Likewise, without that sense of trust, the church will operate with suspicion, rather than have a sense of confidence in the other members of the Body.

FINANCES

In marriages a major source of conflict is the issue of finances, and that is true of many churches too. If there were unlimited financial resources in the church, few people would worry about spending. However, there are few, if any, churches that have more money than they could possibly use. And for that reason, heated conflicts develop over the distribution of limited resources to accomplish the greatest good. Churches can get in serious trouble when they are careless in accounting for the money they receive and disburse. Whenever congregational members become suspicious of how money is spent or how financial decisions are made, their first response is to quit giving. One pastor carried the church's checkbook with him everywhere he went, personally writing checks as he deemed necessary. While few people actually accused the pastor of financial misdealing, no one knew where the money went. Eventually people began leaving this church because of their lack of trust in the management of the church's finances.

People also get upset over how the money in church is spent. Most members are passionate about their favorite area of ministry and want an adequate budget so that program can grow and develop. But should the church be more concerned about the comfort of its members, or in trying to reach the un-churched? Actually, the church budget is a clear reflection of what a church believes to be important. A local church that claims to be evangelistic but spends little of the budget in reaching the lost is making a strong statement about its values.

Budget conflicts usually come from two sources. One arises out of a conflicting philosophy over the best way to accomplish the church's purposes. Can we reach the most unsaved people by a vacation Bible school, a citywide youth event, or an extended revival meeting in the church? Good people may strongly differ over strategy and methodology.

Second, conflicts can also develop when the church lacks the basic resources to do much more than keep the doors open. There are older churches in economically depressed communities with wonderful histories that can barely scrape together enough money to pay the utilities and the pastor's support. They have eliminated ministries from the budget that they formerly funded, and this creates a sense of frustration and even desperation.

CORE VALUES

More serious conflicts can erupt over the issues of core values. There are congregations in perpetual conflict over worship styles, social activism, community responsibility, passion for evangelism, and other local issues. Even more painful are the conflicts within denominations over such issues as gay rights, abortion, and homosexual clergy. Such conflicts are so emotionally charged that they threaten to split these church bodies into splinters. Kale says, "For those involved, church fights are not about incidentals but rather about the core values on which the church is based. And that is exactly why they often turn so nasty."[18] These churches may agonize over whether to leave the denominational connectedness and traditions of the past over a single divisive issue. The question boils down to this: Since you can't lay down your life for every contentious issue, what are the hills you are willing to die on? When do you say with Luther, "Here I stand. I can do no other"? When it comes to the core beliefs of a church, there are people who are willing to fight to the death, as a mother bear defending her cubs, because they believe if you lose here, you have lost it all.

▶ "Live at Peace with Each Other"[19]

It is important to understand that conflict is not always a negative force in a church. As we said earlier, it can bring about positive change. William Willimon says, "In conflict, a group is energized. As an old pastor once told me, 'You can put out a fire easier than you can raise the dead!' Where there is absolutely no dissatisfaction, no vision of anything better, no pain, there is little chance of action."[20] Conflict can be the basis of growth and change. However, it can also be the source of pain and hurt, disillusionment, and destruction. Paul told Titus to remind the church "to slander no one, to be peaceable and considerate, and to show true humility toward all men" (Titus 3:2). How people respond to differences will determine whether the end result is negative or positive. Here are ten steps to use in responding to church conflict.

1. Gather as much information on the issue as possible.

Willimon says, "This initial step is a relatively nonthreatening gesture toward the parties of the conflict whereby one is only seeking better understanding of what is at stake."[21] It is easy to have a skewed view of the problem when only one side of the argument has been heard. Without trying to be Sherlock Holmes, attempt to gather as much factual, objective information as possible about the conflicting subject. This fact-finding stage can actually provide a cooling off period where the participants have a little time to reflect on the issue.

2. Try to gain understanding about the people involved.

If you do not know the principal participants in the conflict, it helps to find out about their history in past conflicts. There are some people who have an inner compulsion to stir up trouble. They actually enjoy the adrenaline rush that comes in a conflict. Other people who are labeled as troublemakers may simply have a different viewpoint from the majority and a boldness to state their perspective.

Also, people may respond differently than predicted in special situations. One man I pastored could deal with most issues in a level-headed manner except when it came to his son. Inwardly, the man was frustrated and embarrassed by his teenager's unpredictable behavior. Yet, he felt he had to defend his son's actions, even when they were obviously wrong. Most people have areas of life, blind spots where emotions rule over logic. A grandmother lived in an inner-city neighborhood that was controlled by a drug-selling gang. She got fed up with the way these young mobsters were terrorizing her neighborhood. One evening she couldn't take it any longer, got out her pistol, and shot one of the boys who had climbed up to sit on her front porch. In her fear and anger she perceived danger, even though there was not an immediate threat. Resolving conflict often begins by understanding the motives and perspectives of those involved. Remember, people respond in ways that make sense to them.

3. Keep focused on the primary issue at hand.

Often the problem that is first presented is not the real issue. Parents who come complaining to a teacher that their fourth grader was not given a special part in the Christmas pageant may really be concerned that the boy is not accepted by the rest of the class. A mother may complain to the pastor that her little daughter was not invited to a birthday party with the rest of her Sunday School class, and the family is threatening to leave the church. But what is the real problem here? The issue may really be a conflict with the choir director over the mother's desire to sing a solo.

It is easy, in the midst of resolving one conflict, for people to see this as an opportunity to air all of their grievances with people and programs in the church. This becomes frustrating to the other participants of the original conflict who wonder, *What does this have to do with our conflict?* When helping people resolve a conflict, it is important to continually bring the discussion back to the issue at hand and not become bogged down with other problems. It can be done by saying something like, "Let me remind all of you why we are here today."

4. Work at good communication between the parties involved.

Any communication has four components: a sender, a receiver, a medium, and a message. But communication can become confused in the midst of conflict. The sender may be yelling. The receiver is so busy thinking of a response, he or she is not listening. The medium is a collage of facial expressions, gestures, and sounds that come across confusing. The message may be more intimidation or emotional appeal than information. Keith Huttenlocker says that good communication is strategic because it promotes dialogue, de-escalates tension, and strives to solve problems, not prosecute people.[22]

Dialogue must be open; with no hidden messages that cloud the process. The term *dialogue* implies that everyone has a chance to express thoughts with the goal of making one's position understood. When people begin to talk face-to-face, the tension drops because they lessen the distortion and exaggeration that may be a part of their argument. Dialogue focuses on the solution that can come in the future. Even God communicates to us to bring about change. Isaiah wrote, "'Come now, let us reason together,' says the LORD. 'Though your sins are like scarlet, they shall be as white as snow.'"[23] Huttenlocker concludes,

"There are few conflicts in the church that cannot be resolved when those involved master good communication skills. When we can use communication to make it part of the solution instead of part of the problem, all relationships in the church acquire greater authenticity and deeper intimacy."[24]

5. Help people to treat each other fairly in the conflict.

Many writers on the subject of conflict in the church emphasize the need for people to fight fair. Kale describes fair fighting as an honest expression of one's feelings and thoughts, as well as taking ownership for those ideas and being accountable for what is said. It also means addressing the issues rather than attacking people.[25] Mediators need to protect the integrity of the discussion by refusing to allow anyone to become a verbal bully. Good communication does not permit poor behavior, such as name calling, judging people's motives, demeaning other people, or trying to produce guilt. Not only are such tactics unfair, but they undermine the standards of Christian conduct outlined in the New Testament.

6. Work to heal and strengthen relationships.

Recently two descendents of Alexander Hamilton and Aaron Burr reenacted the famous duel between these early American political leaders. Burr and Hamilton were both brilliant political strategists who stood at opposite poles in their beliefs of how the new nation should be governed. As often happens in conflicts, the combination of jealousy and hard feelings over political attacks forced Burr to challenge Hamilton to a duel with pistols in order to save his honor. In a moment of time Hamilton lay mortally wounded and Aaron Burr, the vice president of the United States at that time, effectively ended his political career. Tragically, the blazing guns solved nothing, but a face-to-face discussion might have helped sooth the discord.

One very effective way to handle conflict is to emphasize the importance of the relationship over the importance of the issues in the dispute. One of the problems in the ongoing Israeli-Palestinian conflict is that instead of talking and trying to get to know each other, both sides have erected physical and psychological walls of separation. A church is a community of faith made up of people in relation to one another. In the past, church members used to remind themselves of their spiritual family connections by calling each other brother and sister. Today, even with our differences, we are still held together in relationships by the glue of agape love.

How can the Church build on those relationships within the Body of Christ to solve conflict? It begins by accepting one another as valuable even though there may be differences. But it goes beyond that to genuine caring and support when anyone is in need. "'All for one and one for all' is nowhere more applicable than within the church. Wherever commitment is demonstrated, community is strengthened."[26] Church relationships are stronger when we live together with integrity, which generates respect. I remember buying a used car from a salesman who attended my church. The man was not the stereotypical, fast-talking, tire-kicking, wheeler-dealer. Yet, he was the top used car salesman for that dealership, primarily because people knew he was honest. I once asked him to give me the best deal he could, and when he told me the price, I bought the car on the spot without any bargaining. His word was good enough for me. Credibility is a major quality people look for when forming their opinions about people in the church. As members value their relationship with others in the church, they tend to overlook or settle their differences more easily.

7. Find points of common concern or mutual agreement.

Too often conflict focuses on the negative—the disagreements that separate people. Churches have split and members have gone their separate ways over things as trivial as having a kitchen inside a church building. One of the oldest members of my home church recently died. As I reflected on his life I remembered that he held the lifelong position that people should not eat in the church. This issue could have been significant enough for his family to leave the church. But the church family valued his presence in the Body, and he decided that being a part of that church was important to him. So, the conflict became a nonissue. When the church had a fellowship supper, he didn't come and they didn't expect a hot dish from his family either. He and the church had too many valuable things in common to let this peripheral issue separate them and spoil over fifty years of fellowship.

8. Don't be too quick to get an agreement on an issue if it's not resolved.

There are some who will go to any length to avoid open conflict in a church. If you ask them whether they were hurt by an incident, they'll say no even though they were deeply wounded. They may answer, "Whatever you want," when they are asked an opinion, while secretly harboring resentment for what has happened. These people may feel bullied into agreeing to a decision that is not their own. When the voice vote is taken in a meeting and one person, with head down, says nothing, it is obvious that it is not a unanimous decision. Sometimes it is helpful to wait on a decision so people come to peace in their own minds. Forcing a person into an agreement may in the long run have a far more detrimental effect than simply waiting for the person to come around to the decision. However, a church can be hindered by one person who is dragging his or her feet.

9. Work toward a win-win solution if possible.

One reason people dislike conflict is that they think of results in terms of winners and losers. Or, worse yet, they think of both sides as losing. In the Burr-Hamilton duel, both lost. Burr lost his political future while Hamilton lost his life. A better way to resolve conflict is to allow the loser to "save face" so the blow of defeat is somehow softened. However, the best solution is to find a win-win answer where both sides feel they have gained something. If a one-car family has two teenage drivers who both want the use of the car on Friday night, one solution is to say that since there is conflict neither teen will drive—a lose-lose result where everyone is disappointed. But both drivers could win if one gets the car this Friday and the other next week. Or, perhaps they could ride together to an event. Developing a win-win strategy involves both sides revealing what they really want and what areas they would be willing to compromise. People feel they have succeeded if something is accomplished from the conflict. However, when the contested issue involves a serious moral principle, such as the case of incest mentioned in 1 Cor. 5, there may be little room for compromise.

10. Covenant to abide by the decision of the group if possible.

In 1 Cor. 6 Paul addresses the problem of church members settling conflicts in a civil court. Paul sarcastically states in verse 5, "I say this to shame you. Is it possible that there is nobody among you wise enough to judge a dispute between believers?" His point is unmistakable: Christians should be able to work out their differences in the context of a church. The secret to the resolution is an agreement by all concerned to abide by the church's decision. The rationale is rooted in the belief that the Body of Christ represents a caring community who desires the best for each of its members. The church values the biblical concepts of mercy, grace, love, acceptance, and forgiveness. Since we all fail at times to perform as well as we would like, the church should be the one place where everyone can come for help. Paul wrote to the Ephesians, "Submit to one another out of reverence for Christ" (5:21). Conflicts can be more easily resolved when each person desires Christ's way over his or her own way.

▶ LIVING IN HARMONY

What is the answer to Rodney King's question, "Can we all just get along?" If we believe that Christians are humans with flaws, then the answer is probably "No, not all the time." While all who are part of the Church claim to be united in the love of Jesus, there is a wide variety of personal tastes and ideas, likes and dislikes. Sometimes living together in this community of faith is an adventure. The Hebrew writer addresses this issue with some good advice: "Make every effort to live in peace with all men and to be holy; without holiness no one will see the Lord" (12:14). Learning to resolve conflict with the brothers and sisters who are part of the Body of Christ is one way to live out the life of the indwelling Holy Spirit within each believer.

▶ QUESTIONS FOR REFLECTION

▷ What is the pastor's role in implementing the Matt. 18 process to bring a peaceful resolution in a conflict between two Christians?

▷ Are there things a church can do to minimize conflict from developing?

▷ What are the risks and rewards for a pastor who takes on the role of peacemaker in a serious church conflict?

ELEVEN

THE PASTOR'S PRESENCE IN CRISIS

Pastor Jane Farmer had developed a dread of those late-night phone calls over her short ministerial career. Usually people did not call you at midnight with good news. That kind of information could wait until morning. But a crisis could not be delayed very long. The ringing phone yanked her out of sleep into a groggy state of consciousness. She glanced at the nightstand. Her alarm clock said 1:47 A.M. Jane groaned as she reached for the noisy telephone. It was Frank Walker, panic in his voice, trying to relate that there was another crisis involving their teenage son, Jason. Could she come over and help them?

Forty minutes later Jane walked into the front room of the Walker home to find Frank and his wife, Brenda, sitting on the sofa in a state of shock. Frank's mother and Brenda's brother were already there to offer support. Pastor Jane began to gather bits and pieces of the events of the past eighteen hours as these parents shared the details of their concern. Jason had gotten into an argument yesterday morning with his mother over his perception that his parents were trying to control and ruin his life. He stomped out of the house, saying he was going over to his friend Brian's house, where at least they wouldn't hassle him all day. Brenda and Frank didn't worry too much when he didn't show up at suppertime. He would often stay away for six or eight hours as a way to get his folks to worry about him. But they became concerned when he didn't come home by his 12:30 curfew. Frank discovered that Brenda's car was missing from the garage. They called Brian's house and found that Brian was missing as well.

With Pastor Jane's help they did a thorough search of Jason's room. His duffle bag and backpack were gone, as well as clothing and a portable music player. The screen had been removed from Jason's bedroom window. Then Brenda checked her purse. Her credit card and money were gone. It seemed obvious that Jason had crawled into the house, taken what he needed, and disappeared with the car. Frank said they had no choice but to contact the police and report these boys as runaways.

Now nearly two weeks have passed. The car was found abandoned about four hundred miles away in a large city, the engine destroyed. Brenda's credit card was used a couple of times the first three days, but since then there has been no activity. Pastor Jane has come by the house every day along with people from the church, but there is no resolution in sight. Frank and Brenda wish that they could at least get a phone call that Jason is alive and OK. They lean heavily on their church friends, and especially their pastor, for support. Brenda's comment sums up their feelings, "If only Jason would contact us and let us know he is alive, the worst of this crisis would then be over."

▶ CRISES: EVERYBODY HAS THEM, NOBODY WANTS THEM

The dictionary defines *crisis* as a crucial time or a turning point in the life of a person. Psychologist Gary Collins states, "A crisis is any event or series of circumstances that threatens a person's well-being and interferes with his or her routines of daily living. Crises are stressful because they disrupt our lives, often have long-lasting implications, and force us to find ways of coping that we may not have tried before."[1] Swilhard and Richardson give this explanation of the origin of a crisis, "It is precipitated by some event that upsets spiritual and emotional equilibrium. Basically it is the disequilibrium produced by a perceived threat or adjustment that we find difficult to handle."[2]

Many writers on the subject describe two types of crises. The first and most common type is a *developmental* crisis. These are times of change that come in the normal development of a person's growth. Howard Clinebell says, "These stressful experiences are the occasions of crises for an individual to the extent that they pose problems for which her or his previous coping abilities are inadequate. Each developmental stage and crisis is the occasion for a variety of caring and counseling opportunities."[3] Some of these would include birth, going to kindergarten, adolescence, leaving home, entering an occupation, getting married, having children, retirement, and facing one's own death. These may be joyous or difficult occasions, but they always require extra effort or stress for the person going through the experience of change.

The second type of crisis is *accidental* or *situational*. These might be an unexpected car accident, a loss of job, the discovery of cancer, a divorce, a fire; the list goes on and on. These are less predictable and have greater impact. Such crises can create difficulty for a person at any age. Howard Stone says, "They are the emotional trials and dysfunctions which result from unusual circumstances."[4] Because accidental crises usually come on suddenly, they almost always demand an immediate response.

While some may think that experiencing a crisis is the result of living in a contemporary society, even the ancient people of the Bible faced crisis moments. Think of Abraham, looking down on his promised son Isaac, as he was about to offer him as a sacrifice; surely this was a crucial moment. When David volunteered to accept Goliath's challenge of a fight to the death, he was facing one of the toughest crises of his young life. A great crisis moment in Jesus' life came when he knelt in the garden and surrendered to the eternal plan of dying for humankind. This moment was so intense that blood vessels burst on his forehead and mingled with the sweat that dripped to the ground. A young Jewish man named Saul was knocked to the ground while journeying to Damascus and then confronted by the appearance of the risen Christ. That crisis became the turning point for the man who would later become Paul, the apostle to the Gentiles.

In centuries past, people who faced crises tended to look to their immediate or extended family for support and direction. Today, in our mobile society, family members are scattered across countries and even around the globe. With family so distant, people often feel isolated and alone, with no one to turn to for help. For this reason the church, and pastors specifically, are the first ones called when a crisis strikes.

"Helping those in crisis can be a very important phase of one's ministry," writes Norm Wright. "Two of the tasks of the church's ministry are to equip all members to better handle their own crises and to equip them to help other people in crisis."[5] Haddon Robinson calls this the "halo effect" in ministry—the high regard church members may have for their pastor and the importance of the pastor in helping them face a crisis. This trust and confidence develops as a pastor is involved with individuals and families through crisis experiences. While a minister may be given the title pastor upon arriving at a church, it is not until a pastor sits with people in hospital waiting rooms or sees families through times of conflict that they begin to say with meaning, "This is my pastor."

One of the reasons people turn so often to the church or a pastor is the deeply held belief that people of faith can somehow bring hope to seemingly hopeless situations. While attending a small Christian college I had the privilege of hearing the world-renowned psychiatrist, Dr. Viktor Frankl. Frankl was imprisoned in a Nazi prison camp during World War II, simply because he was Jewish. Once there, he noticed that when individual prisoners lost hope, they quickly died. He later observed, "Woe to him who saw no more sense in his life, no aim, no purpose . . . He was soon lost."[6] However, for those who could find some purpose for living, something to focus on beyond the present crisis, the chances of survival increased dramatically. Frankl himself said that when the days became difficult because of hard labor and lack of food he had to seek something hopeful for a mental focus. He would often picture himself after the war was over, standing in a comfortable auditorium, lecturing on the psychology of the Nazi death camp.

▶ THE SOURCE OF A CRISIS

Where did this crisis come from? Most people raise this question in their minds when a crisis, especially an accidental or situational one, intersects nor mal living. Some have bought into the idea that we are mere puppets on a string and God, the playwright, scripts everything that happens to us, both good and evil. The problem with this position is that not only does it ignore God-given free will, but also it makes God the author of evil. While we may not fully understand God's providence, we know his character. It would be inconsistent with God's nature for him to design and plan the rape or murder of an individual. On the other hand, God has not taken a hands-off policy in dealing with humans here on earth. He is intimately concerned and involved with his love, mercy, and grace.

From a biblical perspective, there are three possible sources of a crisis.

1. Divine origin

There can be moments of crisis in our lives that come from the plan of God for us as individuals. One of the most obvious examples is the crisis moment of salvation. God does not want anyone to perish, but rather desires that everyone experience pardon for sin and a personal relationship with Him. It is a crisis, for in that moment life is radically changed and we become children of the Heavenly Father. Yet, God does not force us into this relationship against our will. We respond to his gracious offer by faith. God also may lead at other crisis moments by revealing his will for our lives in a marriage partner, a career calling, or a move to a new location.

This is why Christians should seek to know and understand God's will or direction in those important decisions of life. Sometimes God's directives are very clear. Sometimes God expects us to make wise decisions based upon our understanding of the truth revealed in the Bible. It is wonderful to be able to look back later and see that God has ordered our steps in a crisis situation, even though we may not have fully understood it at that time. At significant moments of decision in my pastoral career God has revealed his will to me in some way through the leadership of the Holy Spirit. There were crisis moments when I sensed I should stay. Other times I felt led to move to a new assignment, even though it meant moving farther away from family and friends.

2. Natural origin

We live in a created world that is ruled by certain natural laws. Recently a childhood friend reminded me of a time when I was about seven years old. Our family was visiting her family for Sunday dinner and we were out climbing a tree in the front yard. As I was going up the tree I put all my weight on a branch and it broke. The law of gravity pulled me back to terra firma and I landed on my back, struggling to breathe with the wind knocked out of me. God could have suspended the law of gravity for a few seconds, but my friend sitting in the tree above might have floated off the tree into space. We depend upon these natural forces such as gravity to be always consistent.

Many crises develop because we live in this natural creation of God. Hitting one's thumb with a hammer has an inevitable result—pain. While no one likes pain, it can also have a positive effect. Without functioning nerve endings in the hand, we might lay our hand on a hot stove and suffer a severe burn without being unaware of it. Pain serves as an effective warning device, telling us that something is wrong.

Some people want to charge God with the responsibility of a car accident when the real culprit may be human error or malfunctioning equipment. Could God have prevented the accident? Yes. And sometimes he does. We may not be aware of the times when the delay of a stoplight may have prevented an accident that could have happened later. And yet God does not always stop accidents. There are occurrences in nature, such as floods, earthquakes, hurricanes, droughts, and fires, that are a natural part of the global weather patterns. Insurance companies sometimes label these "acts of God" to avoid paying for damages. Even these are a part of living in the natural world around us.

We must also recognize that the natural creation of God's world has been corrupted by the Fall. Humans have not yet totally conquered the diseases of cancer, AIDS, and some other infectious diseases that take the lives of millions each year around the globe. It is not always easy to explain why God has intervened to bring deliverance from cancer for one close friend, while another good friend is in the final days of life, due to a rare form of cancer. While we live on this planet we will continually deal with the pain of natural crises while we look forward to heaven where these concerns will be in the past.

3. Sinful origin

It is a fact that many crises come as a result of sin. Dr. Frankl suffered the result of an ungodly political system that imprisoned and killed millions of people, simply because they were different from the majority. Across the centuries of church history, beginning with Stephen in the Book of Acts, martyrs have been asked to lay down their lives rather than deny the faith. In recent times African, Asian, and Arab Christians have died in the crossfire of religious wars or individual persecution.

For most people, the crises caused by sin are much more personal. Some face crises as a result of being victims of crimes they did not commit. There is the elderly woman who lost her small life savings because someone swindled her out of her meager investments. Consider the young girl who was molested by an uncle for five years and now cannot trust any man. Or, there is the husband who lost his wife and child in a car accident caused by a drunk driver. These people suffer because of the sins of others. But sin in our own lives can cause a crisis. A wife who indulges in an extramarital affair and ends up losing her marriage and the custody of her child needs to accept responsibility for her actions.

Pastors and lay counselors may need to help people understand the origin of the crisis they face. Howard Stone maintains that "all crises are religious at their core; they involve ultimate issues with which one must come to terms if one's life is to be fulfilling. The minister's counseling is in its final and basic concern spiritual."[7]

▶ The Development of a Crisis

It's helpful to understand how most crises typically unfold and expand.

• *A precipitating event.* While it is true that developmental crises such as adolescence or senility gradually occur over a period of time, the origin of most situational or accidental crises can usually be traced to a single event. This event may be a positive one. A wedding usually is a very happy occasion. However, it can precipitate a situational crisis as two people, coming from very diverse parentage and family beliefs, begin to build a life together. Sometimes a person's expectations for the future can be changed in a moment. A relative of mine married a talented and physically strong young man who had the opportunity to play in the National Football League as a lineman. He was looking forward to having a successful career playing the game he loved. But a single play in the course of one game changed his future. He seriously injured his knee while blocking his opponent. His recovery has sidelined him for such a length of time that he may not ever be able to return to his team to fulfill his dream. Whenever an event changes the equilibrium of your life in a significant way, you have the beginning of what counseling authorities call an emotionally hazardous event. Wright says, "A hazardous event is some occurrence that starts a chain reaction of events culminating in a crisis."[8]

• *An appraisal of the situation.* Every person has a unique viewpoint of the crisis event. Say a man named Bill suddenly dies. His wife may view the loss as the end of intimate companionship and economic support. A sister may see this death as the end of a lifelong family tie that can never be replaced. A business associate may think of finding someone to fill Bill's position in the company. Although different, each view is legitimate for that person in the common crisis. Stone says, "The importance of the loss to the bereaved person, for example, determines to a great extent whether or not a crisis will develop."[9]

• *An upsetting reaction.* While people may face several upsetting events in the course of a week, there must be something more to set off a crisis. A person may have an idea rejected at a meeting or hear from the doctor about the need to have a minor surgery and shrug it off as one of the daily ups and downs of life. However, if my job is in jeopardy, I may be worrying that my ideas are not welcome, or in the time I'm off work for surgery the company may hire someone else. Sickness or depression can also lower our ability to deal with an issue without becoming stressed out. There are some events that by their very nature are upsetting—the death of a family member, facing a divorce, the loss of a job—that naturally will precipitate a crisis. Other times the upsetting event is seemingly insignificant, "the straw that broke the camel's back," after a series of serious events that the person has handled without difficulty.

• *An uncertain response.* People ask questions such as, "What am I supposed to do about this event?" "What resources do I have?" "What friends do I call?" "How am I going to cope?" It is not uncommon for people to feel the emotions of worry, anxiety, and anger when their world seems to have caved in around them. They often are convinced that life will never be normal again. It is easy to assign guilt, either to oneself or to others: *If only . . . I had done this. If only . . . she had not done that.*

• *A crisis exists.* When a person cannot manage the situation alone, the crisis has begun. Norman Wright gives four indications that an individual is in a state of crisis.

1. *Symptoms of stress.* These include depression, anxiety, and headaches.

2. *A feeling of panic or defeat.* The person has either tried everything and nothing works or is unable to try anything to find a solution. Many turn to drugs and alcohol or retreat into excessive sleep.

3. *A focus on relief,* at any cost. This person is not able to handle things rationally and may exhibit some rather bizarre behavior.

4. *A time of lowered efficiency.* Some people in a crisis can function normally, but their effectiveness may be lowered to only 60 percent of what they could do under less stressful circumstances.[10]

▶ PEOPLE IN THE MIDST OF A CRISIS

When a pastor is put in the position of helping in a crisis, the primary focus is on the people and not the problem. The stress has left them overwhelmed and often unable to cope. They may want to become dependent on the pastor for all decisions, not wanting to be left alone. Or, they may reject any attempt from anyone help out for fear that they may lose their independence. Even the validity of one's personal faith can become an issue. A crisis may cause a person to spend every waking moment reading the Bible or pray ing. Other people may wonder if God really cares since they feel all alone in the struggle.

Some who observe a person in crisis may conclude that the person is mentally ill. Howard Stone observes:

> It is important to stress that conflict and unhappiness are not necessarily synonymous with mental illness. . . . It must be noted, however, that although persons in crisis are not necessarily mentally ill, they may experience very strong emotional reactions such as anxiety, depression, tension, panic, a personal and social sense of confusion and chaos, feelings of loss, helplessness, hopelessness, or disorganization, etc.[11]

The stresses that bring on a crisis are cumulative within a brief timeframe. Thomas H. Holmes and R. H. Rahe, professors of psychiatry at the University of Washington, developed a scale to determine the impact of stress from common life experiences. Called the Social Readjustment Rating Scale[12] Holmes and Rahe assigned a point value to the impact of stress connected with common experiences in life. The highest point value, 100, is given for the death of a spouse. Halfway down the scale, marriage ranked a 50. Forty-three experiences were evaluated, with vacation and Christmas among the lowest stressors with 13 and 12 respectively. According to the study 50 percent of people who accumulated a stress score of between 150 and 200 within one year became sick. The rate of sickness rose to over 80 percent for those with a score of over 300. This scale can alert pastors and lay caregivers to individuals who have faced clusters of life changes and are in danger of cumulative stress overloads.

The more coping mechanisms and support a person has, the less severe the crisis will be and the quicker the person will return to normal life. According to Stone, "A crisis will occur only when the person's early attempts at coping with the threat fail. Where traditional coping fails, disruption from the appraised threat remains and in fact increases."[13] As a helper, an effective approach may be to actually list some of the things an individual can do to cope or deal with the situation.

Going through a crisis can change a person's values and outlook on life. A person may learn from the way people gathered around and helped them, that it is not good to go through life as a loner, isolated from others. It is not unusual, for instance, for someone who has overcome cancer to become a crusader for cancer prevention by joining the local unit of the American Cancer Society and participating in fund-raising activities. A crisis can also have a negative impact. Frank lost his wife to death suddenly and unexpectedly. Although Frank had helped other people in their crisis moments, when his crisis hit, he had great difficulty coping. He developed a deep anger and resentment toward

God for not doing something to spare his wife. Frank was a man who was always in control of situations, and now he had to deal with issues that were largely outside his control. A couple of years later he married a woman he had known most of his life, but that did not bring the satisfaction he so desperately sought and he quickly divorced her. He tried professional counseling, but that didn't help either. This man who had at one time served God faithfully, now has abandoned his former faith and values in a vain search to find the happiness that seems to be eluding him. Some people who go through a major crisis do not come out on the other side the same as they were before.

Stone believes that one of the most significant concepts in crisis intervention is what he calls "heightened psychological accessibility." When people are in crisis they are "less defensive and more vulnerable to change than they are in non-crisis periods."[14] People are willing to listen to suggestions and attempt new approaches because they realize that what they have been doing is not working for them.

This is especially true when it comes to spiritual matters. A man came to the office to talk about the stresses in his life brought on by his recent divorce. Although he had been raised in a Christian home and had been attending a church of a different denomination, he did not have a personal relationship with Christ. I had spoken to this man months earlier and he seemed at that time to be totally unresponsive to the gospel. However, in the midst of the greatest stress-producing crisis of his life, this man confessed his sins and received Christ by faith. Often, people are most receptive to the gospel while in the hospital or in a pastor's office discussing their crisis. Most people in crisis moments do not have foxhole conversions that are quickly forgotten once the crisis is over. A crisis provides the opening the Holy Spirit uses to allow grace to bring about lasting change.

Working through a crisis can help make a person a stronger person or the crisis can destroy the person from the inside. This is the bitter or better consequence. The Bible character Joseph is a wonderful example of one benefiting from adversity. From what the Scriptures reveal about him, he becomes one of the most Christlike persons in the Old Testament. Talk about facing crises! Joseph's Holmes-Rahe score would have gone off the chart. His brothers sold him into slavery as a teenager. The wife of the man who bought him as a servant falsely accused him of sexual assault. He languished in prison, all but forgotten, until Pharaoh made him second in command in all of Egypt. Finally after saving his family from starvation by bringing them to Egypt, his brothers had to face their own misdeeds. After their father, Jacob, died they pled on their faces before Joseph for mercy. In one of the most powerful statements of forgiveness in all of Scripture, Joseph told his brothers, "You intended to harm me, but God intended it for good to accomplish what is now being done, the saving of many lives" (Gen. 50:20).

Many would say that Joseph had every right to be bitter for what his brothers had done. Instead he allowed his crises to shape him, by the grace of God, into one of the most admired men in all of Egypt. There are few great Christians whose lives have not been tempered in some way by fires of adversity to become resilient, strong, trusting people of faith. This is what the writer of the Book of Hebrews meant when he wrote, "No discipline seems pleasant at the time, but painful. Later on, however, it produces a harvest of righteousness and peace for those who have been trained by it" (12:11).

▶ THE PATTERN OF A CRISIS

Although each crisis is unique, all crises tend to follow a rather predictable pattern. Norm Wright has developed a crisis sequence made up of four phases that most people follow while going through a life-changing event.[15]

1. The impact

Phase one is usually very brief, from a few hours to a few days. When a major crisis comes, the person knows it. In fact, most people can think of little else. There is numbness and shock as the reality of the event begins to sink in. In this phase it is hard to think clearly. The person is struggling to decide whether to face the situation or try to escape. If the crisis is the death of a loved one, the individual will look at pictures and reminisce about the past. He or she may have feelings of guilt over things that were done poorly or left undone. People can even feel guilt if they have been spared pain or difficulties that a loved one had to face. Help comes when a person can accept his or her personal feelings as normal.

2. Withdrawal and confusion

Phase two is usually accompanied by a drop in the emotional level. This phase is longer, measured in days and weeks. Wright says, "When this occurs, there is usually a worn-out feeling or depression. The person has no more feeling to experience."[16] Yet it is common to express feelings of anger, resentment, and even rage.

One of my most vivid memories of conducting a funeral is of a mother who had received poor medical care in the hospital. A widow in her early forties, she had left behind several children. Because the family had no church home, the funeral director asked me to conduct a brief service in a small cemetery chapel. As I delivered the brief homily I asked a rhetorical question,

"What do we do at a time like this?" I was getting ready to give the answer, "We turn to Jesus," when the oldest son, probably thirteen, blurted out, "We sue those blankity-blank doctors, that's what we do!" The teenager's response was a normal one, given his deep loss and uncertain future.

Stressed people who share their feelings with friends at this stage may shock and offend. When they see how people respond to their feelings, they may take the opposite response and try to repress their emotions. But God is never shocked. He understands and accepts us with our feelings. It is at this phase that the person may need the most physical contact with friends, and yet these important contacts may begin to drop off as time goes by. Wright makes a wonderful suggestion. Following the funeral, one minister "writes the name of the family on his desk calendar every three months for the next two years to remind him to continue to reach out and minister to them over that period of time."[17]

This is also a phase of confusion. A woman dealing with chemotherapy may avoid going out in public rather than handling her loss of hair by wearing a wig. A man dealing with the loss of a job may offer all kinds of excuses why he should not go out and apply for another job. Often the person wants to replace what was lost by marrying a new spouse or selling the house and moving to a new area as an attempt to quickly regain a sense of normalcy. The problem is that the person has not yet fully released the emotions of the past loss. It is not uncommon for a person who makes drastic changes at this time later regrets the decision.

3. The adjustment

Phase three takes longer to experience. Things are starting to turn for the better. Depression is not as constant. Hope and positive emotions slowly begin to grow. Life begins to take on new meaning after climbing out of the pit of despair. The person can begin to solve problems. Wright says, "He fluctuates and will have down times. He still needs someone to be close or available."[18] It is possible to begin to introduce spiritual insights because the person is now able to look deeper within.

4. Reconstruction-reconciliation

Phase four can begin because there is a new sense of hope and confidence. Often the anger and bitterness of the past has been replaced with a new optimism. There will be times of sadness, especially on anniversaries or special events that remind one of the past, but these tend to be momentary. While life may never be the same as before the crisis, the person can sense an anticipation of a new future that incorporates the changes that have come.

▶ INTERVENING IN A CRISIS

If you are going to fill the role of helper in a really serious crisis, there are several effective steps to take. These are general guidelines and may need to be adjusted to meet an individual situation.

1. *Respond immediately.*

When you are notified about a possible crisis, you need to assess immediately the seriousness of the situation. There are people who love to create mountains out of molehills. Some like the pastor's presence because it can add importance to an insignificant situation. However, if people are facing a severe crisis, such as a serious car accident or an accidental drowning of a child, the quicker the response, the better. While the power of prayer over the phone is not questioned, it is much more important that the pastor or someone from the church be personally present, if at all possible. A helper may need to leave the dinner table or get out of bed in the middle of the night to be with a family in an emergency waiting room. Arriving twelve hours later may be too late and the family may think that the pastor doesn't really care about them. It's insensitive to try to schedule a counseling session two weeks later for a person who is threatening suicide. Generally speaking, the more severe the crisis, the more urgent the response time.

People in crisis have a vivid memory of those first moments. They will forever remember the pastor's presence at their moment of need. Not long ago, we received a beautiful bouquet of flowers from a family we had ministered to more than twenty years earlier. Their son had nearly died and had gone through a long period of recuperation. The note with the flowers simply said, "Thank you for being there with our family when we needed you." The whole church ministered to this family through the crisis. Yet the symbol of the church's concern was focused on the pastor.

2. *Assess the situation.*

The pastor coming into a crisis situation needs to find out what has happened or is happening. People may be in a state of panic or shock and it becomes difficult to discover the facts. There are some who like to blow up an insignificant event into a major drama. A three-year-old cat that has climbed up a tree and won't come down is not in the same category as a three-year-old child that has been seriously injured by a car. A couple having a disagreement over whether to buy a red or black sofa may be able to come into the office next week to iron out their differences. People under stress may not have all their facts straight or may have only part of the information. Pastors need to function like an emergency telephone operator who makes a quick assessment to determine what should be the first response of help. If there is any doubt, respond with greater help than is needed rather than discover later that you didn't give serious consideration to the crisis.

3. Bring calm to the situation.

Sometimes this means coming into the setting and simply being present for a few minutes. We are prone to want to talk too quickly in a tense situation. Job's companions were very helpful at first, sitting with their friend while he suffered. They made their big mistake when they opened their mouths. Often a touch on a shoulder or hand can have a greater calming influence than any speech we can give. A person in crisis may not even hear our words, but he or she can feel our presence as we grasp his or her hands. Someone has called touch "the language of crisis." When you do speak, your first words should be reassuring.

4. Establish rapport.

If the person in crisis is an active part of the church or is well known to the pastor, this may not be necessary. But often pastors and other helpers are called in to help in a crisis of a stranger because no one else is available. The halo effect a pastor enjoys with the church may mean nothing here. I have found it helpful to introduce myself as soon as I enter the crisis location. Beginning with the one who seems to be in charge or the one who is the focus of the attention, I then work my way around, introducing myself to the others who have gathered. A pastor can gather a lot of information, both verbal and nonverbal, with the people in the room. If the crisis setting is a hospital, it is good to identify yourself to the nurses and doctors as well.

5. Be a good listener.

It is a mistake to try to give prescriptive answers in the initial moments of a crisis. Use the good attending techniques of eye contact, leaning forward to indicate your interest, reflecting back what the person is saying for clarification, and perhaps getting the person a glass of water. If it is appropriate, hold the person's hand as a point of connection as the person talks.

Stone suggests, "It is important not to allow yourself to be distracted by outside noises, interruptions, and phone calls, or by inner distractions such as thinking about all the things you have to do that day. Your parishioners will generally be aware if you are distracted, and as a result they will not reveal as much about themselves."[19]

6. Determine what immediate action must be taken.

Some medical crises require a quick response. Stroke and heart attack victims who get immediate attention have a much higher chance of recovery. Is it necessary to call for an ambulance, or are medical personnel already on their way to give help? Can the person be driven by car to a hospital or doctor's office? Should the police be called in a domestic dispute that threatens to become violent? Do we need a lawyer right now? Are there family members that should be contacted about the crisis? Other people at the scene of the crisis may be able to assist with the right response.

If death is imminent, the family may be faced with decisions that need to be made quickly. Should the person be put on life support or left on such systems? What about organ donations? Does the person have a living will? Is there anyone who has the legal authority to authorize surgery for a patient who is a minor? These questions may not have obvious answers.

People involved in the crisis may not be thinking clearly about such decisions, or they would rather avoid them altogether. Whenever it is feasible, encourage the person in the crisis to make these decisions. However, there are times when the pastor or helper may need to give support and even assistance in the decision making process. Gary Gulbranson gives this advice, "In helping a family deal with doctors, funeral directors and lawyers, remember: If these professionals are not making sense to us, they almost certainly are not making sense to the crisis victim, who is normally too intimidated to ask many questions. So, we need to ask questions on the victim's behalf and help interpret the technical language, procedures, and decisions."[20]

Don't be afraid to call upon the resources of others in the church. You might need someone to do emergency babysitting or help find temporary housing for family members arriving from out of town. Sometimes a cake or a salad and some sandwiches can allow the people in crisis to focus on other more important issues. People in the Body of Christ are usually more than ready to help in an emergency when they are asked.

7. Help the person set goals for the future.

As you talk about the crisis, begin to focus on what could be done to make the future preferable to the present situation. If the person cannot think ahead with any optimism, the pastor may make some suggestions to see if the individual finds them of interest. Make sure that there are several alternatives so it does not appear as though you are trying to determine the future for him or her. Distant goals may be too much for a person in crisis to even fathom. People in crisis may need to consider short, attainable goals and then later build on their earlier successes. It is important for people in crisis to take ownership of their future goals. Ask them questions about the advantages and disadvantages of pursuing these goals. Without a dream, it is hard to press ahead to the future with any confidence.

8. Develop a plan of action to move toward the goal.

Remember the old adage: "The journey of a thousand miles begins with a single step." Too often the future looks so daunting that people never get started on the journey. Ask the person, "What is the first step you can take to begin moving to achieve your goal?"

George came to my office, desperate for help. He was separated from his wife, and she wanted to divorce him. During the course of counseling George came to faith in Jesus Christ as his personal Savior. After he began his walk with the Lord, he said that he would like to see his marriage restored. His wife was not a Christian and knew nothing about the changes that had taken place in his life. In the course of discussing a strategy, George decided he would invite his wife out to dinner and tell her about the transformation. Something must have happened at that dinner because she came to church the following Sunday and soon after received Christ into her life. Within days of her conversion they reconciled and began raising their son and daughter in their now Christian home. Recently I ran into this couple by chance in a restaurant and we had a moment to review what had happened in their lives. As they showed pictures of their grandchildren, I reflected on how a crisis that threatened to destroy their marriage nearly twenty years earlier had given them a future that they had not dreamed possible at the time. And it all began when George asked his estranged wife to dinner to share his testimony.

9. Evaluate the person's support system.

Too often the factors that have brought the individual to a point of crisis are difficult to change or overcome without help. A family who faces the crisis of bankruptcy may need to seek help from a financial counselor in order to keep them from repeating the same financial mistakes again. Many who have overcome addictions are able to remain sober only because of a support group to whom they are accountable. Support comes in many forms. One family with a young son facing a severe illness found support in people who would come by and read children's books. A church rallied around a senior adult who needed medical treatment by driving the person to a regional hospital weekly, a ninety-mile trip. Individuals in crisis with no support network will find it much more difficult when dealing with the recovery process. Sometimes the pastor must try to put together a support team where none exists naturally.

10. Help with acceptance.

A man who has lost an arm in an accident will never have that fully functioning arm again, no matter how much he may wish or pray. Modern science has made marvelous technological strides in developing prosthetic arms that can enable people to perform functions that were thought impossible a generation ago. But an artificial arm is not going to be the same as the arm the man had when he was born. Part of overcoming the trauma of such an injury is finally coming to terms with the fact that life from now on will need to be lived with one natural arm and one artificial arm. Gary Collins writes, "Acceptance, like healing, takes time. Often it involves a painful, conscious thinking about the situation, an expression of feelings, a readjustment of one's lifestyle, a building of new relationships, and a planning for the future."[21] Acceptance is realizing life will be different than it was. A woman whose husband is killed at war may later meet another man and marry again. Life can be happy and fulfilling again, but it will not be the same. When people accept what is, not what might have been, they can move on.

11. Foster a sense of hope.

People who have been beaten down by a crisis may feel that nothing will ever change. Before they can believe in themselves, they need to have an understanding that someone else believes in them. We can use even a small measure of success as the basis for showing people that they can succeed. Another way to encourage a person is to emphasize that the two of you are working together as a team. You assume the role of giving encouragement and support. Wright states, "You are developing a team effort in planning and evaluating the situation. Self-reliance comes from the counselee's being involved in the planning."[22] Once people start to gain confidence, they begin to believe that they can succeed on their own.

12. Commit to follow up.

Most experts in grief counseling suggest that a pastor plan for follow-up while the idea is fresh. After the death of a spouse or a child, the survivor should be contacted by phone or a visit every three months for the next year and at least twice the following year. After performing a wedding, schedule at least two postmarital counseling contacts within the first year of marriage. Plan for future follow-up with people by writing dates on a calendar. Some people who have faced crises may simply need a word of encouragement when you see them at church or around the community. Follow-up lets people know that they have not been forgotten and reminds them of the grace God has shown throughout their crisis.

▶ CRISIS INTERVENTION IS A MINISTRY

It is natural for pastors to become involved in the crises that affect those in the congregation. After all, it is usually the pastor who gets the first call. But giving crisis care need not be limited to clergy and professional medical and mental health workers. Many churches are training lay crisis care workers as a part of their lay pastoral care team. Stone writes, "Crisis intervention, whether undertaken by members of the congregation or the minister, or both, is a specialized form of ministry aimed at encountering and caring for those in crisis."[23] What a wonderful way to be agents of God's love, healing, and compassion to those in time of desperate need.

▶ QUESTIONS FOR REFLECTION

▷ What would you say to someone who is convinced that a crisis such as colon cancer, which is of natural origin, is really sent by God?

▷ Why is it that people in the early stages of a serious crisis find it so difficult to make decisions or perform tasks that would be easy for them at another time?

▷ How should a pastor respond to a parishioner who is in the midst of a serious crisis but refuses help from the pastor or anyone else in the church, preferring to deal with the situation alone?

TWELVE

THE PASTOR'S PRESENCE
IN CELEBRATION

*Ed White had not given much thought to what was involved in doing wed-
dings in his first church. In the back of his mind he was aware that pastors married
and buried people. He just was not that in tune to the process of marrying. Even his
own wedding was largely the product of his wife, Dawn, and his mother-in-law.
Although Ed just did what he was told, he had to admit that the ceremony had
been meaningful and beautiful.*

*Through the stresses of schooling Dawn had been a foundation of strength for
him. And now, five years and two children later, he had come to the realization
that his marriage was the most important thing in his life, aside from his relationship with God. The success of the marriage must have been the grace of God alone
because he had little preparation. Dawn's parents were wonderful Christians, but
his family background was a mess. His mom and dad had split up before he was
three and his mother made three other attempts at marriage by the time he finished
high school. It was only the church he started attending as a teen and his new-
found faith that kept him from falling off the deep end. Although the pastor of the
small church he attended was a wonderful person, he did little to help Ed and
Dawn as they approached their wedding. Dawn, with wisdom and patience, had
borne the greatest share of the responsibility in getting their marriage started right.*

*When Todd and Heidi came to him saying that they were thinking of getting
married, Ed began to panic. How could he help this couple start their marriage on
the right track? He didn't have much to offer from his childhood, watching one after
another of his mother's marriages crash and burn. Dawn's folks, on the other hand,
had made their marriage strong by their commitment and devotion to each other.
After his wedding Ed made up his mind that he wanted a marriage like his in-
laws', even though he didn't fully know how to go about it. But how could he communicate the things he had learned, and was still learning about marriage, to Todd
and Heidi? What responsibility did he have to this couple to prepare them for the
wedding and the experience of marriage?*

*It seemed quite obvious to Pastor Ed that he needed more resources to do an
adequate job of preparation. First, he gave a call to one of his college professors to
ask for any materials that would be helpful. Next, he checked out some online book-
sellers to see what print and video resources were available. The next week, when
the local pastors of the small community met for their monthly coffee, Ed asked*

185

them how they were doing premarital preparation. None of the pastors were really satisfied with their present approach. By the end of the morning they all agreed that to prepare couples in the community for marriage they would work together to put on a twice yearly, combined series of marriage preparation classes. They covenanted together that none of them would perform a wedding without a premarital counseling certificate signed by one of the local pastors. Ed was put in charge of designing the format and gathering the resources for the community program.

Pastor Ed had become convinced that he would need to have personal contact with a couple in addition to the community program. How could he make those sessions meaningful? Then he thought of Dawn. She could be of great help in guiding the couple through the wedding plans. And, together they could talk about what they had learned during their five-year marriage. In fact, he decided that he would ask Dawn to be the wedding coordinator for the church, channeling her artistic and creative abilities to help couples in planning for this most important day of their lives. Ed was already feeling better about Todd and Heidi's wedding six months in the future.

▶ THE WEDDING IS A CELEBRATION

One of the highest moments in the life of a couple is that day they stand before a minister, a congregation, and most importantly, God, to pledge their love to each other and accept the uniting bond of marriage. That date will forever be remembered, marked on the calendar as their anniversary date—a date celebrating their commitment to each other. Jesus understood how important this celebration was when he attended the wedding in Cana recorded in John 2. For this couple, probably poor peasants in the village, this would be the biggest moment in their lives. The families probably scraped together as much money as they could to show the proper hospitality to the guests. And to run out of wine at a moment like this would be a shame they would never be able to overcome. Jesus turned the water into wine, not because of his mother's request but to help the newlyweds begin their life together on a positive note.

Wedding celebrations become wonderful opportunities for pastoral ministry. The late Dr. W. A. Criswell said, "The arrangement for the beautiful occasion opens the door for the pastor into the very heart of all the people involved. He is a wise pastor who takes advantage of the providence to counsel the couple in Christian homemaking and to encouraging the parties to make Christ and his church the center of their lives."[1]

Centering the marriage on Christ may seem obvious for those who are part of the church. However, pastors are often asked to perform weddings for people who do not attend the services but have chosen the church, perhaps because of its location or its beauty. This can also be an opportunity to help the unchurched couple see the need of God in their home as they begin married life together. David Wiersbe cautions, "But couples from outside the church family are often more interested in a wedding than a marriage. Therefore, our church wedding planning brochure states clearly that our investment is in a lifelong marriage and not in a one-day event."[2]

▶ MARRIAGE IS A COMMITMENT

There is good reason for pastors to take seriously their responsibility to make the wedding a spiritual service and prepare people to live in permanent union together. "In the 1930s, one out of seven marriages ended in divorce. In the 1960s it was one out of four. Of the 2.4 million couples who will get married this year in the United States, it is predicted that at least fifty percent will not survive."[3] Too many people accept the prevailing sentiment that if a marriage doesn't work out, one can always find another mate. Commitment takes a backseat to personal happiness. When problems arise, and they inevitably will, it is easier to bail out than to work it out.

If people think that the divorce issue is only a serious problem for those outside the church, they are deceiving themselves. Christian researcher George Barna, in a 1996 survey, discovered that the percentage of born-again Christians who had been married and admitted to being divorced (27%) was higher than the percentage of non-Christians who had been married and then divorced (23%).[4] Too often couples go through the wedding ceremony and then just hope for the best.

Because divorce has been accepted as an inevitable consequence of society's shifting values, the common understanding of what makes up a family has changed. Wright says, "Only 25 percent of the households are 'traditional' anymore—two parents with children. There are as many single-person households as there are traditional." He does see a ray of hope for marriage due to the fact that the age for first marriages has risen considerably higher than it had been. "The divorce rate for our country has leveled off and, because of the delay of age in marriage, the rate may actually drop."[5]

One of the problems with the decline of traditional marriage is that there are fewer role models of successful marriage. People's understandings of marriage are most influenced by the marriages they observed growing up, particularly their own family if their parents were together. Sadly, too many approach their wedding without ever actually observing a good marriage in action. Pastor Ed White, in the opening vignette, is an example, being raised with a poor model of marriage. Fortunately, his wife's parents provided for him a positive contrast by their healthy marriage.

Pastors can move decisively against the cultural trends and help couples develop permanent, fulfilling marriages. Even people without good marriage role models can learn how to live together in harmony with God's help. Young men and women who are anxiously anticipating marriage are more often more highly motivated to learn how to have a good marriage than a husband and wife who have lived together in conflict for many years. People who have never experienced married life together cannot fully anticipate the kinds of issues that lie ahead. However, good premarital preparation can provide them with techniques for handling the challenges. It can prevent people from falling into some of the pitfalls that doom marriages to failure.

In the Garden of Eden God presided over the first wedding ceremony uniting Adam and Eve, and by his blessing indicated to humankind that this union had both physical and spiritual dimensions. While God continues to be present at each wedding, the minister becomes the agent of God, uniting and blessing the couple in marriage. Pastors must take seriously their role as God's representative in the wedding process. While pastors cannot guarantee that the ceremonies they conduct will all be permanent unions, they can do their best to clarify the significance the Creator places on the pledges made before the altar. When pastors say these words of Jesus to a couple, "Therefore what God has joined together, let man not separate,"[6] they are reminding them that God signs the marriage certificate even before the minister.

Because the divorce rate has been increasing, even among church members, some church leaders have been promoting the concept of covenant marriage. The idea behind this movement is to encourage people to renew their marriages and strengthen their families through a stronger commitment by declaring that they have chosen their mate for life wisely. A covenant marriage limits somewhat the grounds that can be used for divorce—in most cases only abuse, abandonment, or adultery. A couple choosing a covenant marriage is required to complete a premarital counseling program. If problems arise in the marriage, they are required to have counseling and a two-year waiting period before filing for a divorce. Those who are already married can choose to upgrade to a covenant marriage. Studies in the United States have shown that the two largest factors causing poverty are divorce and children born out of wedlock. In response to this concern, several states have enacted laws that allow couples to choose covenant marriage vows as a way of pledging their moral commitment to a permanent bond. Early indications seem to show that people entering a covenant marriage have a far lower divorce rate.[7]

▶ Is Premarital Preparation Necessary?

In Western culture, the process of courtship leading to marriage is very interesting. Couples start dating, spending a lot of time talking and having fun together, and finally developing a relationship. But courtship is not real life. The individuals are trying to put their best foot forward, to make their best impression, in order to convince the other person of their desirability and value. The title of Oscar Hammerstein's song from the musical *The King and I* expressed this sentiment well: "Getting to Know You."

But, the dating relationship can be deceiving. "Consequently," psychologist James Dobson says, "the bride and groom enter into marriage with an array of private assumptions about how life will be lived after the wedding. Major conflicts occur a few weeks later when they discover that they differ radically on what each partner considers to be the nonnegotiable issues."[8] The premarital preparation process allows the pastor to openly explore with the couple some of the possible conflicts that could arise after the wedding is over. The entire engagement period should be characterized by discovering as much as possible about the thoughts, dreams, and values of the prospective mate. All this prepares one better for marriage. The wedding ceremony I have used for many years has these lines. "Marriage provides a oneness that is so close that we are loved in spite of what we are. It brings significance to life to be known and loved anyway."

The counselor and author Norman Wright gave the following advice on the radio program *Focus on the Family* regarding the issues of premarital counseling: "Couples should not announce their engagement or select a wedding date until at least half of the counseling sessions are completed. That way they can gracefully go their separate ways if unresolved conflicts and problems emerge."[9] Premarital counseling can either help affirm a couple's choice to be married or prevent the disaster of marriage where there are serious issues of incompatibility.

▶ The Focus of Premarital Counseling

When a couple comes to the pastor announcing their interest in marriage, one of the responsibilities the pastor must assume is an assessment of their readiness to be married. There is excitement surrounding the idea of engagement. In one church there were two or three young women in the singles group that became engaged about the same time. This seemed to set off a flurry of interest among some of the other singles, to quickly find a potential mate and not be left behind. As a result, at least one person made a premature decision, quickly got married, and saw that marriage fail within months.

It's easy to get caught up by the physical attractiveness of a dating partner without thinking through what it would be like having to live together for a lifetime. A couple may come to a pastor with the news of an unexpected pregnancy and assume they "have to get married." But if their chance of success in marriage is marginal at best, there can be even greater problems ahead if they get married. Two wrong actions do not equal a right action.

Loneliness is not always a good motivation for marriage. The Bible does say, "It is not good for the man to be alone" (Gen. 2:18). But, there are some things worse than being alone. Incompatibility in marriage can make a person long for the solitude of loneliness again. A pastor, when first meeting with a couple, needs to be clear that part of the counseling process will be assessing their chances for success in marriage. If there is strong reason to believe that this marriage is likely to fail, the pastor reserves the right not to marry the couple, even if the wedding date is set and the invitations have been mailed. In addition, this couple needs to know that either or both of them can withdraw from the counseling or postpone the wedding if they have serious misgivings about this marriage.

Another very practical aspect of premarital preparation is a discussion of the details of the wedding service. As pastor you need to clear the date on the church calendar as well as discuss the location of the wedding service and reception. It is helpful to write down the names of those who will be participating, how many guests are expected, the music for the ceremony, and any other details that are necessary. Put this wedding information in a file that can be quickly referenced, and save it until after the ceremony is over.

TESTING RESOURCES

There are two excellent testing aids to assist in premarital counseling. One is the Taylor-Johnson Temperament Analysis (T-JTA).[10] The T-JTA assists the counselor in understanding the individual and his or her relationships to others by measuring temperament and personality patterns. There is also a crisscross scale that allows the counselor to help both persons to evaluate their perception of the other individual. This gives the counselor insight into how each person views and interacts with the potential mate. A minister must take a training course to qualify to administer and work with the T-JTA. I have found this test to be very useful in premarital counseling.

A second premarital counseling tool is PREPARE II—Premarital Personal and Relationship Evaluation.[11] This assessment, now used by over a million couples, focuses on six goals for marriage. This tool evaluates the couple's relationships, communication skills, techniques for conflict resolution, financial concerns, extended family relationships, and goal setting. PREPARE II has been very effective in predicting marital success. It is now possible for couples to take the test online and have the graded results sent to the pastor. This material has become very popular with pastors because it focuses exclusively on the marital relationship. Pastors must take a day-long training session to be qualified to use PREPARE II. Both T-JTA and PREPARE II are very effective in helping the couple understand both themselves and their future mate.

MARITAL ROLES

One common source of conflict in marriage is the misunderstanding of marital roles. The husband and wife may enter marriage with their own individual preconceived idea of what they are supposed to do and what their partner's role is in the marriage. The man may strongly believe that it is the wife's responsibility to do all the cooking because that is what his mother did best. The new wife, on the other hand, may have been raised in a home where the husband took on the role of chef. One of my sister-in-laws is excellent at housecleaning but absolutely hates dealing with the cooking chores. The marital stereotypes just don't apply to all people. Because individuals are trying to present their best side while dating, the issue of who does what in the marriage may not come up, that is, unless the pastor raises the issue in counseling.

Misunderstandings can extend even to the differences between morning people and night people. Some people wake up in the morning bright-eyed and full of energy, while others find the morning sun a serious intrusion. These differences in people's biological clocks can become a source of serious conflict. It is helpful to find out about a future mate's sleep and waking pattern. A night owl does not necessarily have to marry another night person to be happy. The real question is, what adjustments can be made so a person's individuality can be honored without developing resentment and conflict? It is important for the couple to work out their own understanding of their roles in the marriage and home. There is no right set of expectations other than what the couple decides will work best for them.

FAMILY BACKGROUND

The family backgrounds of both individuals need to be thoroughly explored in premarital counseling. A person does not only marry a mate but the mate's family as well. Where will the newly married couple spend holidays? How well does the mate get along with parents and future in-laws? Is there a tendency for a family member to be intrusive or domineering? Ask questions such as: "How were feelings of love and tenderness expressed in your home? How would you like feelings of warmth and tenderness shown to you in public and in your home?"[12] People tend to have the same expectations after they are married that they experienced in their family growing up. Or, perhaps a person wants the spouse to respond the opposite of a parent because of irritating or hurtful memories in the past. Even the sickness or injury of a parent growing up can change the expectation of what is normal behavior in the eye of the person about to be married. The pastor can guide the couple to establish a middle ground so they can develop their own life as a family. It is so helpful to address larger family issues before the marriage takes place. In counseling, the pastor can encourage each person to work diligently to develop a strong relationship with the future in-laws.

COMMUNICATION SKILLS

A key issue in determining the future success of the marital relationship is developing strong communication skills. As Les and Leslie Parrott write, "In a recent poll, almost all (97 percent) who rate their communication with their partner as excellent are happily married, compared to only 56 percent who rate their communication as poor."[13] They go on to say that certain types of communicating are ineffective:

- *Placating,* which means saying "yes" or "whatever you want" all the time instead of speaking truthfully.
- *Blaming,* which always criticizes by using broad generalizations, such as "you always . . ." or "you never . . ." to cover their own inadequacies.
- *Computing,* meaning that the person functions impersonally and without emotion, always being right and never admitting mistakes.
- The *distracting* person wants to avoid any stress in communication by changing the subject to turn the conversation to safer ground.

Good communication centers around three terms that also characterize good counseling skills: *warmth, genuineness,* and *empathy.*[14] A pastor can approach the issue by asking questions like: "What does your future partner do or say to encourage communication between the two of you? How could you improve your personal communication to your partner?"

HANDLING CONFLICT

Couples need to be prepared to deal with disagreements that will naturally arise in a marriage. You could begin with questions such as: "How were conflicts handled in your home as you were growing up? How would you like to handle disagreements in your family?" Conflict is normal and to be expected. But understanding how to fight fair is important so the individuals do not create long-term hurts. Fights can develop over sex, money, children, and even where to go on vacation. Learning to fight fair begins with addressing the conflict without attacking the other person. Good conflicts don't leave lasting scars because the individuals don't blame or shut the other out. It can be a time to air honest differences and arrive at a compromise. Sometimes couples may even have to agree to disagree. Make a commitment to resolve differences quickly. The Bible admonishes, "'In your anger do not sin': Do not let the sun go down while you are still angry" (Eph. 4:26). Someone gave this a contemporary twist: "Don't pillow your head until you clear the air." Learn to argue about things that are really important and let some things slide that don't really matter in the larger scheme of things.

SPIRITUAL NEEDS

Pastors often find that this time before marriage provides an excellent opportunity to address spiritual needs. Even strong Christians want to know what they can do to make sure that their home is Christ-honoring. For those whose faith is not as evident, the counseling sessions can provide a platform for confronting spiritual needs. People at moments of change are much more open to making spiritual decisions. Couples have the opportunity to establish patterns of family and corporate worship at the beginning of their marriage that can strengthen their life together. Sociologist Andrew Greeley surveyed married people and found that the happiest couples are those who value prayer as a part of their life together. "Couples who frequently pray . . . also report considerably higher sexual satisfaction and more sexual ecstasy!"[15]

PRAYER

Praying together is not always easy. Time schedules and even conflict differences can work against a couple's prayer life. But when together in prayer a couple develops intimacy with God, they open themselves to a heightened intimacy with each other. A variation of the familiar saying is really true, "The couple that prays together, stays together."

▶ COMMITMENT TO PREMARITAL PREPARATION

I remember when, as a young pastor, I became aware of the need to become more effective as a premarital counselor. I tried to work with couples before their weddings, but there was little good material available at that time for a pastor to use. This need came to clear focus when a middle-aged widow came with the news that she was going to get married. I met with this couple and tried to prepare them for marriage but felt very uneasy about their chances for marital success. When I married them I tried to comfort myself with the understanding that, after all, this was really their decision. The marriage lasted less then three months before they separated and divorced. Was there anything a pastor could do in situations like this one, to prevent divorces and prepare people for marriage?

At about this time H. Norman Wright wrote a landmark book for pastors, *Premarital Counseling.*[16] In this book Wright laid out the content of a premarital counseling program with five sessions. He also advocated using the Taylor-Johnson Temperament Analysis as an effective counseling tool. These resources have helped countless pastors develop their own premarital counseling programs to better equip couples for marriage. Today, there are many excellent materials available to help a pastor provide quality premarital counseling.

• *Resources.* It takes planning and commitment to develop an effective premarital preparation plan for your church. One of the best references for creating a comprehensive pastoral program is Wright's *Premarital Counseling Handbook.* The book provides content suggestions to develop four to six sessions of counseling. It is also helpful to provide reading resources for the couple to use between sessions. One of the best is Les and Leslie Parrott's book *Saving Your Marriage Before It Starts: Seven Questions to Ask Before (and After) You Marry.*[17] There are two workbooks with the same title available—one for men and another for women. The book and workbooks provide a wonderful source for discussion in the counseling sessions. Test material such as PREPARE II can provide supplementary help for counseling couples. Pastors may also recommend additional reading and video resources on subjects such as finances, communication, or human sexuality in marriage.

• *United efforts.* In some communities, several churches have united together to produce a single premarital counseling program for any engaged couple from the area. Pastor Ed made that suggestion in the opening vignette. To be married in any of the participating churches of the community, the couple would need to produce a certificate showing that they had completed the program. By combining resources, the churches are able to offer a comprehensive series of classes. As a result, these communities have seen the understanding and quality of marriages elevated because couples have been more adequately prepared. Some states have passed laws requiring premarital counseling as a condition for obtaining a marriage license.

• *Fees.* Any discussion of counseling must include the issue of fees. A couple receiving premarital counseling from a professional counselor might expect to pay $300 or more. However, a pastor who is paid a salary by the church should avoid assigning a fee to parishioners for premarital counseling services. It is appropriate for a church to charge a counseling fee to cover the cost of materials, including books, printed materials, and tests needed for the program. While some couples are hesitant to go out and buy books just because the counselor suggests it, they will pay the necessary fees for the required counseling and the materials are then provided as a part of the fee. Another idea is to have the church develop a lending library that would make the needed materials available to all couples preparing for marriage.

• *Wedding policy.* One of the best ways to establish the significance of marriage preparation in a local church is to develop an official church wedding policy, adopted by the church board or other ruling body. This policy should include the requirement of premarital counseling for any couple who desire to be married in the church. It is helpful to state the number of premarital counseling sessions required as well as any fees for counseling materials. The couple should also be aware of any church restrictions, such as the use of alcohol and tobacco, as well as any additional charges for the use of the building, personnel such as a sound person, and equipment for the wedding itself. It might be helpful to include in the wording of the policy that the pastor reserves the right to refuse to marry a couple that would not cooperate in premarital counseling or, in the judgment of the pastor, showed little chance of permanence in marriage. Simply attending the counseling sessions would not guarantee a church wedding.

Performing a wedding for unchurched people can be an opportunity for ministry and evangelism. In setting policy the board should balance the cost to the church of hosting a wedding with the goodwill and outreach potential of having community people entering the church building. A carefully crafted wedding policy will minimize the possibility of misunderstanding. It is important to present a written copy of the church's wedding policy when a couple inquires about a wedding, or at the first premarital counseling session.

• *Legalities.* Because a wedding has both spiritual and legal significance, a pastor presiding at a wedding signs legal documents so the marriage can be recognized by local, state, or national governments. Marriage license forms vary from one area to another, and it is the pastor's responsibility to carefully follow the requirements of the law. Some jurisdictions require the minister to register before performing any weddings. Some localities may ask for witnesses to sign the wedding license, while others require the signatures of the bride and groom. If the license is not properly filled out and returned to the right government office, the legality of the wedding may be in question. The church and the pastor should also keep a permanent record of the wedding. Courts have recognized the legal standing of the church's record of a wedding to establish the validity of the marriage if other documentation has been lost.

▶ Getting Ready for the Wedding

For most married people, the wedding service is one of the major highlights of life. It marks a major life transition where two people pledge to live together under the mutual commitment and bond of love for as long as they both live on this earth. Because this is such a high moment, often accompanied with great pageantry, it is common to have a rehearsal, usually the day before the wedding.

The pastor who presides over the wedding is normally in charge of the rehearsal. Some churches have a wedding coordinator who works with the couple to plan the details of the wedding day. This person assists the pastor in rehearsing the parts of the service. The details of the wedding service are normally discussed as a part of one of the premarital counseling sessions. It is the pastor's responsibility to insure that the plans of the couple, discussed with the pastor, be carried in the wedding service. This begins by taking careful notes and diagrams of the locations where people would stand. It is helpful to assure the couple beforehand that you, as pastor, will protect the integrity of their planning through the rehearsal. If the couple needs to make any changes, all they would need to do is talk to the pastor who is directing the rehearsal. Most rehearsals go quickly and smoothly if the pastor gives leadership to the rehearsal and confidently follows through on the wedding plans the couple has made.

To start the rehearsal the pastor should gather the participants together and give a personal introduction, welcoming everyone to the church or other location. It helps set a spiritual tone for the rehearsal by reminding the participants that the wedding is a service of worship and then offering a prayer asking God's blessing, even on the practice. After prayer the bride and groom should introduce their families and wedding party members if everyone is not acquainted. The pastor can then give a brief explanation of the various elements of the wedding and ask if there are any preliminary questions.

Much of the rehearsal is helping the participants know where they are to stand and when they are to move. In most traditional weddings the bride and her attendants stand to the left of center as one faces the front of the church, while the groom and male attendants are on the right. If these locations are established by prior planning, have the participants begin by moving to where they will stand during the service, then practice moving to those places. Go through all the elements of the service at least once so everyone can understand how the service flows and where people move at each portion of the ceremony. Simple wedding ceremonies may need only a single review of the service, while complex weddings involving many people may require a second walk-through. If the wedding is to be outside, try to duplicate the conditions of the wedding during the rehearsal out-of-doors. Small children can be delightful walking down the aisle, but because of their short attention span, it is usually better to have them be seated with someone in the congregation when they are done with their part. At the close of the rehearsal ask if there are any other questions before reminding them the time they are to be at their places for the wedding. A good rehearsal gives a sense of confidence that everyone understands his or her role in the service.

▶ THE WEDDING CELEBRATION

Amid the fragrant flowers, lighted candles, and beautiful music in the church it is easy to forget the sacredness of the moment. David Larsen reminds us, "The wedding itself is not primarily a performance or a spectacle of opulence. It is first and foremost a service for the worship of God in which family and friends gather joyfully around the wedded couple and commend them to God in their journey through life together as husband and wife."[18] While the bride and groom may be the focus of everyone's eyes, God is the focus of our attention.

• *Order of service.* While some religious traditions may have unique variations of the wedding, this is a typical order of service (with additions, changes in order, and adaptations for local customs and individual preferences): Music prelude; seating of parents and grandparents; the processional; greetings and betrothal (giving of the bride, questions to bride and groom); special music; Scripture reading; homily; wedding vows and exchange of rings; prayer; unity candle; pronouncement of man and wife; benediction; presentation of couple; and recessional.

• *Sermon.* Some traditions have a prescribed ritual without a homily. Others encourage an individualized wedding sermon to be a part of the service. There is certainly nothing in Scripture either prohibiting or encouraging a wedding homily. "Wedding sermons should have some definite characteristics, including (1) brevity; (2) a theology that clearly represents God's design for marriage; (3) suitability for the occasion, formal or informal; and (4) an appropriate target, on the couple or on the congregation."[19] This sermon is not the occasion for the typical three points and a poem. Five to seven minutes, optimistically focusing on a scriptural truth, should be sufficient. While you may direct the focus of the sermon toward the wedding couple, married couples in the congregation often join hands and apply the words of the service in a reaffirmation of their own wedding pledges.

• *Photography.* The bride and groom usually want this special moment recorded for history. Today this may mean both a photographer and a videographer so all the sights and sounds of the wedding can be recalled in the future. A general principle should apply to all who record the event: Do nothing that will in any way detract from the sacredness of this service of worship. Pictures can be taken from the side or rear of the sanctuary without lights or flash that will turn the attention from the wedding. The old custom of the groom not seeing the bride before the wedding is no longer valid for many people. Couples now have their wedding photos taken before the ceremony instead of waiting until the wedding is over. It eliminates the guests having to wait at the reception for the wedding party to arrive. Also, everyone looks fresher, with their hairdos in place, before the wedding. Usually the photographer then has ample time to take all the scheduled pictures without having anyone feeling rushed.

• *Pastoral preparation.* As pastor, make sure you know exactly what you are to do and say during the service. Many pastors print out a full manuscript of everything that will be said during the ceremony. I learned an embarrassing lesson when I mistakenly forgot to erase a name from another wedding I had earlier penciled into the book I was using at the time. After the ceremony the groom said to me, "Pastor, thanks for performing our wedding, but who was that 'Jane' you mentioned in the middle of the ceremony." Today it is easy to have the basic ceremony in the computer. Before the rehearsal, go through the ceremony adding all the extra aspects of the service and typing in the proper names of the people wherever they are used. Put the manuscript in a notebook and keep that in front of you as you conduct the wedding.

• *Music.* Wedding music is an important part of most weddings. As pastor, you can spare embarrassment by taking the time before the service to review the text of the music to determine if the words are appropriate as a part of a worship service. Couples sometimes select a song because it had a romantic connection to their courtship, without considering the meaning of all the lyrics. One way to deal with the issue is to include a statement in the wedding policy that the pastor will review all music before the wedding.

• *Special elements.* A couple may see elements of other weddings they want to include in their own ceremony. Some people like to use a unity candle in the service. This may have great symbolic meaning to the couple as they take two separate lighted candles representing their separate lives, and together light a third candle symbolizing their two lives that are coming together as one. Other couples demonstrate their servant spirit to each other by alternately washing each other's feet.

• *Communion.* Serving Communion to the wedding couple after prayer has become a common practice at weddings. However, Larsen believes that serving Communion to only the wedding couple "seriously violates Protestant principles. Far better would be a Communion service for believers in the wedding party in a chapel or parlor of the church before the wedding proper."[20] Another option would be to serve everyone in the congregation as a part of the wedding service of worship.

• *Follow-up.* A pastor should plan to follow up on the premarital counseling with a one-year checkup with the couple around their first anniversary. This session can build upon the rapport the pastor established before the wedding. It can be an opportunity to address any issues that have arisen during their first year together as well as a moment to celebrate this first milestone in their marriage.

▶ CELEBRATING THE SACRAMENTS

While the theological foundations for the use of the sacraments in pastoral care were addressed in chapter 9, additional material is included in this chapter to make their use a celebration for the church.

CELEBRATING COMMUNION

For Christians, the greatest significance of God's Son coming to earth is not found in his teachings and miracles. It is rather his actions that take center stage, his demonstrating love for us by willingly dying on the Cross for our sins. Jesus initiated a ceremony by offering bread and wine to his disciples so we can be constantly reminded of his sacrificial death and victorious resurrection. The sacrament of the Lord's Supper is a celebration of Jesus providing for us what we could never provide for ourselves.

There is a hunger today to find meaning in the power of symbols. Psychologist Rollo May argues that the loss of symbols constitutes one of our culture's chief difficulties. "Without signs or symbols in *this world* to show us another world or a means of coping with the trials and strains of this world, we have nowhere to turn but to despair and absurdity."[21] Fortunately, some today are now beginning to rediscover the rich power of symbols. One indication of this is the increased interest in and practice of Communion as an important part of the worship service.

My denomination makes Communion available to all who have repented and received salvation by faith, whether or not they are members of the local church. It is a celebration of the fellowship we enjoy as members of the family of the twice-born. Whenever we share this meal together we celebrate the forgiveness and new life provided by his death on the Cross and his resurrection on the third day. The Eucharist is also a foretaste of his coming a second time to receive his Bride—the Church. "The Lord's Supper is a feast celebrating life. It looks forward to the day when men and women shall come from the east and west and from the north and south and sit at the table in the kingdom of God."[22]

One way to increase the anticipation and celebration of the Lord's Supper is by creativity and variety. Jeffrey Arthurs suggests one such example of a creative variation: Place a bread-baking machine in the back of the sanctuary with the timer set so that the bread will be completed just before the end of the service. "As you preach on the body of Christ and how we are 'one loaf,' or how our prayers are a sweet aroma to God, the smell of the bread permeates the room. After the message, use that loaf for the Communion bread."[23] For those who are unable to be in the worship service for physical reasons, taking the Lord's Supper to the home allows shut-ins to celebrate with the rest of the faith community.

CELEBRATION OF BAPTISM

The sacrament of baptism is foundational for us because Jesus, the sinless Son of God, was himself baptized as he identified with sinful humanity. "Jesus used the word 'baptism' in referring to His own passion (Matt. 20:22) and instituted baptism in the context of His death and resurrection (Matt. 28:18-20)."[24] For the Early Church, baptism became an important rite of initiation into the Christian faith. In the beginning baptisms were conducted only on Easter Sunday morning but in later times expanded to other times of the year. "Baptism is a celebration of God's grace, not of human achievement. . . . It always points beyond itself to celebrate God's grace and covenant faithfulness. . . . It is a communal action of the gathered congregation, which represents the church in all times and places."[25]

The methodologies of this sacrament vary greatly according tradition and available resources. There are three modes of baptism recognized by Christian churches: sprinkling, pouring, and immersion.

Infants are always baptized by sprinkling or pouring water over the forehead. In our day we find immersion baptisms held in many locations, such as church baptisteries, lakes, rivers, and swimming pools. Some believe that baptisms should be performed in moving water. If you baptize by immersion in a swift-moving river or creek, always lower the head toward the source of the flowing water. Modesty is always a concern when immersing people in the water. While some churches use old choir robes or specially constructed baptismal robes, casual dark clothing with a swimming suit worn beneath is certainly appropriate. If the baptism will be in a church's baptistery the temperature of the water should be comfortable, near body temperature. Instruct people to use one hand to hold their nose and use their other hand to hold the wrist. Then place your top hand on top of their hands while supporting their body with your other hand on their back before immersing them. When baptizing someone who is large in an outdoor setting, try to move to deeper than the normal waist-deep water because a submerged body is lighter and easier to handle.

For baptism to have real significance, a pastor should take time to instruct the participants on the significance of the act and review the pledges of the ritual. Whether the service is held in the sanctuary or out-of-doors, there should be a sense of reverence throughout the service. If this is a separate service from the Sunday worship service, begin with singing appropriate hymns or choruses that speak of salvation and our faith. Include scriptures, especially the Gospel references to Jesus' baptism, Paul's instructions in Rom. 6:1-11, and other passages that reference commitment.

Most denominations have a ritual the pastor reads to the candidates. The ceremony usually requires a response from the candidates. Just before each person is baptized, ask the candidate to give a testimony of conversion and personal faith. As the person is lowered into the water, the pastor makes a statement such as: "[Full name], because of your confession of faith and your obedience to the Bible's command, I baptize you in the name of the Father, and of the Son, and of the Holy Spirit."

The person is lowered slowly until completely submerged and then slowly lifted out of the water until in an upright position again. "The more slowly and smoothly this act is performed, the more likely it will be perceived as worshipful."[26] Because people can lose their balance after coming up out of the water, the pastor or another person should steady them with a hand until they are ready to move away from the pastor or out of the baptistery or lake.

Some churches have made baptism an opportunity for preevangelism by printing up formal invitations for the baptismal service. Each candidate can hand out the invitations to unsaved friends and relatives to come as the person witnesses to personal faith. This can be a powerful testimony to those who have seen the person's lifestyle changes after conversion. Other ways to make this service meaningful would include taking pictures of the baptism for the candidates and providing certificates to document the event. Also, consider serving Communion to the congregation as a part of the baptismal worship service.

One of the most memorable baptismal events I have witnessed took place on a June Sunday morning at Willow Creek Community Church in the Chicago area. Although the actual immersion baptism would take place outdoors in the pond in front of the church that afternoon, the Sunday morning service focused on this special event. Approximately one hundred fifty people came forward, each accompanied by someone who was instrumental in this person's coming to faith. Each person nailed a slip of paper, listing some sins of his or her past, to an eight foot wooden cross before being sprinkled with water by one of four pastors on the platform. As I watched the candidates young and old come forward, I was struck by the powerful witness this must be making to unsaved people who were in the service that Sunday. While baptism is a high moment of celebration, both for the one who has received Christ as Savior and the community of faith that witnesses the testimony, it is also an opportunity to declare to unbelievers that Jesus is Lord.

▶ OTHER CELEBRATIONS

CELEBRATING NEWBORN CHILDREN

One of the special days for new parents is the first Sunday a new child is brought to church. The parents and grandparents beam with pride as they proudly display this infant who is new to the family and the church. When visiting the new parents and baby at the hospital, I request that the couple tell an usher the first time the baby is at church. On that Sunday the usher would notify me, and I would ask the parents to come forward to show the baby to the congregation. Usually I would hold the baby myself and congratulate the parents. This introduction can be the beginning of a bond that is forged between this infant and the congregation that pledges to care for the child in the future. "This often satisfies the need of the non-Christian parents who want their infant recognized by the church but may be unwilling to carry out pledges of the dedication/baptism ceremony."[27] To make the baby's first Sunday a memorable one, the church could give a small gift to the parents as a keepsake to remember this celebration moment.

My own denomination allows for the rite of either infant baptism or infant dedication. There is not space here to debate the merits of each position. Historical references to infant baptism can be found in church history as early as the third century. The early Eastern Church had a rite on the eighth day of birth where the parents brought the child to the church, gave it a name, and received a blessing. My own personal pastoral preference has been infant dedication, although I have baptized children if that is the preference of the parents. The soul of an innocent child is protected by the prevenient grace of God, and dedication provides a later opportunity for the person to declare personal faith through believer baptism. Both infant rituals of baptism and dedication can be significant moments of celebration in the life of the church.

Although infant dedication is really a pledge made by parents, a child receives the grace of God by being raised in the Christian faith and taken to church. In my tradition, the rite requires that the parents take responsibility for personally guiding the child's understanding of God by use of the Scriptures, protecting the child from ungodly influences, as well as insuring that the child is faithfully brought to the church. When parents dedicate their child, they acknowledge the fact that this child is not theirs, but God's. The church community also has a part in raising the child. The pastor can include a pledge that the congregation accept their responsibility in teaching the child and supporting the parents. "The ceremony is an expression of thanks to God for the gift of the child and is an act of obedience to God's Word (Luke 2:22-24)."[28]

A dedication ritual ought to include a pronouncement of a blessing upon the child, such as Jesus gave in Mark 10:16. Some pastors prefer to hold the small child, while other pastors place their hands on the infant while he or she is held by one of the parents. Hymns, special music, and responsive readings can add to the significance of the ceremony of celebration. Isaiah 54:13 is a wonderful promise to use at the conclusion of the blessing. As Bruce Petersen writes:

> The ceremony of dedication and blessing can be a special means of bonding two parents and their infant to their God. It also creates a unique relationship between you as pastor and this family. The dedication or baptism of an infant can be made a deeply spiritual moment, remembered forever, if pastors will prepare the participants for its sacredness.[29]

CELEBRATION OF MARRIAGE AND FAMILY

Some churches regularly celebrate the institution of marriage with opportunities for couples to renew their wedding vows. One church has a wedding renewal service on the first Sunday of every year. A church may invite all married couples to the front of the sanctuary where together husbands and wives join hands to pledge their continued love and faithfulness to each other. Other couples may wish to renew their vows in a private setting. This can be especially effective if the couple has been separated or has experienced marital discord and then has decided to rekindle their relationship together. Renewing wedding vows can be part of a special milestone, such as a silver or golden wedding anniversary.

When my wife and I celebrated our twenty-fifth anniversary, our church made it a special occasion. My wife put on her wedding dress and our daughter wore one of the bridesmaid's dresses. We renewed our vows and the whole church turned out for a reception.

Significant wedding anniversaries provide an opportunity for the church to join with family members in honoring a couple's commitment to each other.

Anniversary celebrations speak positively to the permanence of marriage in a culture that has made divorce the easy way out when times are tough.

CONGREGATIONAL CELEBRATION

When the people of God gather on Sunday, the act of worship is a celebration of Jesus' death on the Cross and resurrection from the grave. Believers need to be reminded that our salvation and life together as the Body of Christ is only possible because God has extended his grace to our lives. Churches especially enjoy celebrating the seasons of Christmas and Easter with unique services and special music. In addition, there are those milestones in the life of the church, like a mortgage burning or the dedication of a new building, when the congregation takes time to rejoice in what God has helped them to attain.

One of the most sacred moments for those entering ministry is the service of ordination. Whether the local church or a denomination ordains a person to special Christian service, this day will never be forgotten by the ordained minister. By this ceremony the church is affirming that the minister has demonstrated the gifts and graces for ministry. The church also acknowledges the call of God on this person's life for a lifetime of service.

MILESTONE CELEBRATIONS

The people of God often take opportunity to celebrate important moments of individual achievement. Many churches take time to honor high school and college graduates with recognition services or special receptions. These become significant moments of passage for young people into a new phase of life. Retirement parties celebrate the value of hard, diligent work over a lifetime. While some mark the end of vocational employment, it is also appropriate to recognize people who have given long years of service in the local church. Even those significant life achievements, such as a ninetieth or one hundredth birthday, provide a wonderful opportunity to honor someone's life and achievement. Milestone celebrations remind the church that individual achievement is also a corporate victory, worthy of rejoicing.

We are privileged as Christians to receive so many blessings from God. As pastors we should sometimes take on the role of drum major, leading the parade of celebration. The church needs those festive moments when we joyously come together to rejoice—and have a party.

▶ QUESTIONS FOR REFLECTION

  ▷ What are the responsibilities a pastor assumes when consenting to counsel a couple before marriage?

▷ How can a pastor insure that the wedding is a service of worship rather than simply a ceremony or performance?

▷ What can a pastor do to make Communion a meaningful part of a worship service?

▷ When the pastor has an instruction session before baptism, what issues should be discussed?

THIRTEEN

THE PASTOR'S PRESENCE
IN HUMAN SUFFERING

How could a healthy husband and father come down with such a debilitating disease, Pastor Dennis Chang wondered as he drove across town? Ken Fong had become the most influential lay leader in the church. For several years he worked tirelessly with the teens as well as handling the responsibility of worship leader with his wife, Kim. Pastor Dennis remembered when Ken began complaining about feeling tired along with having painful muscle cramping. Kim at first suggested and then insisted that Ken go see a doctor. No one was prepared for the diagnosis: amyotrophic lateral sclerosis, ALS, a degenerative nerve disorder commonly referred to as Lou Gehrig's Disease. The family learned that ALS affects the nerve fibers in the spine that control the voluntary movement of the muscles.

The word about Ken Fong's disease spread quickly through the congregation. People asked what they could do to help Ken and the family. Ken himself was committed to functioning in as normal a fashion as possible. But as time went by, one by one, he had to drop the tasks he so enjoyed doing around the church. Fortunately, Ken's insurance business was able to function with little interruption because Kim was able to do the computer work from home. Ken's mind remained alert, but the extremities of his body were beginning to atrophy because of disuse.

Pastor Dennis was faithful in visiting the Fong family weekly, trying to be as encouraging as possible in a situation that seemed hopeless. Yes, Dennis believed in the healing power of the Holy Spirit to bring strength back to Ken's lifeless limbs. As pastor he anointed Ken, and the church prayed, but it didn't seem like God was going to answer their prayers that way. He had often looked into the eyes of Kim as she sat next to her husband's bed. Sometimes he saw fear, other times weariness. She needed comfort and strength too, for the extra responsibilities that rested heavily upon her shoulders.

It seemed so unfair, Dennis thought as he drove. There was that guy, Bill, who worked on his car. Talk about a vile fellow. He drank heavily, psychologically abused his wife and kids, and cursed God with every sentence he spoke. Then last week, after a drunken binge, Bill drove off an embankment and walked away from the accident without a scratch, while the car went up in flames. Ken, on the other hand, had lived a clean, healthy life, serving God, working in the church—and he ends up with Lou Gehrig's Disease. Dennis was also reminded of the fact that he was a year younger than Ken. Just because he was a pastor did not make him immune to some debilitating disease like ALS. He wondered what it was really like, lying in a bed as Ken did, knowing you would never get up again under your own strength.

He slowed the car down a bit because it was only about a mile from the Fong home. Dennis really didn't have a clue about what to say to Ken and Kim. He turned the radio off and began to pray, silently at first, then out loud, "O God, how can I be of comfort to these precious friends who desperately need to hear a word from you today? Help me know what to say and when to be quiet. May I be Jesus to these people today." Pastor Dennis Chang turned off the key, walked up the sidewalk, and rang the doorbell.

▶ A BIBLICAL CONTEXT FOR COMFORT

During the Christmas season we hear the timeless sounds of Handel's *Messiah* reminding us again of Isaiah's words, "Comfort ye, comfort ye my people, saith your God."[1] We sing the familiar words of the eighteenth-century English carol, "O tidings of comfort and joy, comfort and joy."[2] The word *comfort* and its variants are found nearly eighty times in the Bible. Many references speak of God's reassuring presence, such as the often quoted verse from Ps. 23: "Your rod and your staff, they comfort me" (v. 4).

When Jesus came as the Good Shepherd, he made it a point to provide personal comfort to those in distress. John in the second chapter of his Gospel tells of a young couple who faced a social disaster at their wedding when their wine ran out, and Jesus provided comfort by turning water into wine. Later in chapter 4, in the same town of Cana, he met a governmental official whose boy was deathly ill some distance away in Capernaum. By a word Jesus brought comfort to the concerned father and healing to his sick son. Elsewhere in the Gospel of John, Jesus comforted an invalid who had waited for thirty-eight years to be healed.[3] He stepped between an angry mob bent on stoning, and a woman accused of adultery, finally telling her, "Then neither do I condemn you. . . . Go now and leave your life of sin."[4]

Nowhere was the extent of Jesus' compassion more evident than when he stood beside Mary and Martha, weeping as he stared at the tomb of his friend Lazarus. Even those nearby who watched could see that Jesus felt for his friend. The comfort the two sisters felt from Jesus' presence and concern turned to joy as Jesus commanded Lazarus to come out of the grave.[5]

Jesus comforted his mother while he was dying on the Cross by asking John to watch over her.[6] And could the disciples ever forget huddling together in fear behind locked doors that first Easter Sunday evening? Jesus suddenly appeared in the room and said those words of comfort, "Peace be with you! As the Father has sent me, I am sending you."[7] Perhaps they remembered the words of assurance he had given them the previous Thursday evening around the Passover table. Jesus had said that, although he was leaving them, the Father would send them a *Paraclete:* a counselor, a supporter, an advocate, a helper who would stand alongside with comfort.

No book in the New Testament deals with the subject of comfort more thoroughly than 2 Corinthians, especially chapter 1, verses 3-7. Murray Harris writes, "The paragraph embodies the chief emphasis of chapters 1—7: 'comfort in the midst of affliction'. The *paraklesis* ('comfort') root occurs no fewer than ten times in vv. 3-7, the *thlipsis* ('trouble,' 'affliction') root three times, and the *thema* ('suffering') root four times."[8] Paul is saying that God is the source of comfort for all types of distress. Since by his grace we have all received his comfort for our lives, we should be a conduit of God's comfort to those around us who are in need of it. For those in ministry, providing comfort is not so much a duty to perform as it is a privilege to participate as God's representative, dispensing his grace.

▶ THE PROBLEM OF SUFFERING

No one providing pastoral care can really be effective without coming to grips with the presence of evil and suffering in a world created and ruled by a good and loving God. This tension is not usually one that ministers talk about, but it arises out of questions that parishioners ask their pastor in their time of need.

"Why am I suffering from this painful disease if I am a Christian and God says he loves me?" "If God can heal my child, why doesn't he?" "How could God allow my husband to be killed by that drunk driver?" "What have I done to deserve being in this situation?" "Is this God who is punishing me?"

These issues are not insignificant or peripheral. In fact they are at the very core of our faith. Philip Yancey voices the frustration and disillusionment many feel in the title of his book *Disappointment with God.*[9] It is easy to question God and even move to the position of abandoning the faith when pain and suffering get up close and personal. David Switzer agrees that suffering has been and is a universal concern. "These are issues which people struggle with in the Bible, and these are the same questions that are being posed many thousands of times every day in hospitals, and homes and nursing homes and emergency rooms and other places."[10] Coming to terms with the issue of pain and suffering calls for careful Bible study and theological reflection.

THEODICY: SPEAKING OF GOD'S GOODNESS AMID EVIL

Anyone who has attempted to bring comfort to someone facing serious pain has wondered: *What do I say to this person who is suffering?* Thomas Oden writes, "Theodicy means to speak justly of God amid the awesome fact of suffering. Its task is to vindicate the divine attributes, especially justice, mercy, and love in relation to the continuing existence of evil. It wishes to speak about God *(theos)* with justice *(dikē)* precisely at those points at which the divine purpose seems most implausible and questionable, namely, amid suffering."[11]

The basis of theodicy is the fact that there is a God. If there isn't, the whole debate is meaningless. But if God does exist, if he is personal, loving, all-powerful, then we have to deal with the tension of suffering and evil existing in the world he created and controls. Oden raises three premature, inadequate solutions that should be rejected. First, you can pretend that evil and suffering does not really exist, or pretend that it has no power to demoralize. Two, it is possible to be so overwhelmed with evil and suffering around you that you question whether God is personally concerned with people. Three, God is concerned about evil, and struggles for good, but doesn't have the power to fully combat suffering and evil today.[12]

On a spring day in the year 2000, my wife came to my office after visiting her doctor. I was unprepared for the news she gave me. The doctor's diagnosis was unmistakable: she had non-Hodgkin's lymphoma, a malignant disease that develops in the lymphatic system of the body. The very word *cancer* strikes terror in the hearts of most patients. For us, it marked the beginning of about six months of intense treatment including chemotherapy and other drugs.

Of course, we requested prayer for our need. Our local church and campus community, as well as friends around the globe, joined in praying for her recovery. In the midst of this process, before we knew the final outcome of treatment, I began to reflect personally on this issue of pain and disease. I knew of other Christians facing similar forms of cancer who had been healed of the disease. As a pastor I had watched other wonderful Christians with great faith who wasted away as the effects of cancer took their toll until they died. I finally had come to the conclusion that just because my wife was a faithful Christian was no guarantee that God was somehow obligated to remove the cancer threat.

What did it mean to face such a disease as cancer as a Christian? It became clear from the experience that no matter what happened, God was with us. The words of Isaiah took on special meaning, "When you pass through the waters, I will be with you; and when you pass through the rivers, they will not sweep over you. When you walk through the fire, you will not be burned; the flames will not set you ablaze. For I am the LORD, your God, the Holy One of Israel, your Savior" (Isa. 43:2-3).

We are never alone. God walks with us, even though the final ultimate victory over our suffering may be in eternity rather than in our present existence here on earth. Our present culture has bought into the idea that we must avoid pain at all cost. People fight, with every resource at their disposal, the natural process of aging. Today we want to avoid anything that might possibly inconvenience our lifestyle of pursuing personal happiness.

William Willimon tells of an experience early in his ministry, entering a hospital room shortly after the birth of a child to a couple in his church. The doctor entered with the news that "there were problems with the birth." This doctor was trying to explain that the child had Down syndrome and, although there were only minor and correctible respiratory problems they should "consider letting nature take its course, and then in a few days there shouldn't be a problem." The couple was confused and wondered why the corrective surgery was not the first thing to be done.

"You must understand that studies show that parents who keep these children have a high incidence of marital distress and separation. Is it fair for you to bring this sort of suffering upon your other two children?" the doctor asked.

The mother replied that their children had every advantage they could have in the world. None of them had any experience in what suffering was like. She concluded, "I don't know if God's hand is in this or not, but I could certainly see why it would make sense for a child like this to be born into a family like ours. Our children will do just fine. When you think about it, this is a really great opportunity."

The doctor, confused, turned to Willimon and said, "Reverend, I hope that you can talk some reason into them."[13]

The apostle Paul never bought into the idea that avoiding suffering is the chief goal of one's life. In fact, he says just the opposite. "For just as the suffering of Christ flow over into our lives, so also through Christ our comfort overflows. If we are distressed, it is for your comfort and salvation; if we are comforted, it is for your comfort, which produces in you patient endurance of the same sufferings we suffer" (2 Cor. 1:5-6). In Paul's view, suffering with faithfulness could be a means of encouraging others to live with endurance.

GOD DOES NOT CAUSE SUFFERING

It is important to understand that God does not will or cause suffering even though he may permit it to happen as the result of our fallen world. It is not uncommon to hear some well-meaning person say to a couple who has lost a young child to disease or accident something like: "Well, God must have wanted little Mary to sing in his angel choir in heaven." No! God does not rip a child out of a home to fill a vacant choir slot. He is there weeping with this family, just as Jesus wept with Mary and Martha. God created this world to be a place of goodness. Sin corrupted both humanity and the environment from its original intention. And, although suffering and evil are not the creation of God, he is at work to bring good out of every situation, whether it be immediate good or ultimate good.

In an attempt to try to make sense out of heartbreak or pain, some people want to see the event as a part of a specific purpose God desires to accomplish. They think that if they could only identify that purpose, they would get God's message and things would make sense. To that Yancey responds this way: "Maybe God *isn't trying to tell us anything specific* each time we hurt. . . . Half the time we know why we get sick: too little exercise, a poor diet, contact with a germ. Do we really expect God to go around protecting us whenever we encounter something dangerous?"[14] C. S. Lewis adds to this discussion in his book *The Problem of Pain,* "We want not so much a father in heaven as a grandfather in heaven—whose plan for the universe was such that it might be said at the end of each day, 'A good time was had by all.'"[15] There are some things that happen that will never make sense to us because God did not cause them to enter our lives. Rather than listening for God's message, it would be better to look for signs of his presence.

God created humankind with the privilege of free will. That was essential to God's desire for us to be able to enjoy a relationship with him. Yet, with the privilege of choosing this good relationship was the risk that man would choose the wrong. God, with the infinite capacity to love and know us, knew that there was no other way for us to enjoy this relationship with our Creator without granting us the privilege of free will. Because people have this ability to choose, they must take responsibility for the choices they make. A person may choose to abuse illegal drugs, but there may be a price to pay in poor health.

But a person's choice may have an effect far beyond himself or herself. For instance, a man or woman may say, "It is my choice to get drunk and it's nobody's business but my own." Yet, a person near my home chose to get drunk, got in the car and drove down the wrong lane on a divided highway, hitting an oncoming car and killing three innocent teenage boys. Very few choices are made in total isolation. Someone may think he or she can commit suicide without affecting anyone else. However, whether a family member or a friend, a fellow worker or a neighbor, someone will be impacted by such a selfish act.

It might seem that evil is winning the war. But God's power is not limited by the sin and suffering of this world. Oden writes, "Even though God permits the free will to act irresponsibly (otherwise how could it be free?) and to live with the tragic social-historical consequences of those choices, nonetheless God does not simply stand by forever and watch history deteriorate."[16]

SUFFERING AS TEACHER

Is there any reason then for God to allow suffering? There are times when suffering can be a wonderful teacher. A parent can tell a small child not to touch a hot stove, but often the child doesn't believe until he or she touches it and experiences the pain. Suffering, especially the kind that comes about as a result of our bad choices, can be an effective teacher. Hebrews 12:6 reminds us, "The Lord disciplines those he loves."

Suffering can also make us more compassionate toward others who are facing similar situations. Often, those with the greatest sensitivity to the needs of others are people who have suffered much themselves. Suffering also has the capacity to force us to our knees in prayer. When things are going well, there is a real tendency for us to become self-sufficient. We can handle things ourselves, thank you. But when suffering enters our lives and we can't immediately solve the problem ourselves, we turn to God as our source. When God has our attention, there is no limit to what we can learn from his voice. This can be the blessing of suffering for us. An anonymous Confederate soldier captured the meaning of this truth well when he wrote:

> *I asked God for strength that I might achieve;*
> *I was made weak that I might learn humbly to obey.*
> *I asked for help that I might do greater things;*
> *I was given infirmity that I might do better things.*
> *I asked for riches that I might be happy;*
> *I was given poverty that I might be wise.*
> *I asked for power that I might have the praise of men;*
> *I was given weakness that I might feel the need of God.*
> *I asked for all things that I might enjoy my life;*
> *I was given life that I might enjoy all things.*
> *I got nothing that I asked for, but everything I had hoped for.*
> *I am among men most richly blessed.*[17]

▶ THE PASTOR'S CHALLENGE OF COMFORTING

It would seem that providing pastoral comfort would be a natural part of any person's role in ministry. Actually, visiting and caring for the sick has its own set of concerns for most pastors. Part of this stems from the fact that we are humans with our own experiences from the past that shape our ministry. Henri Nouwen reminds his readers in his book *The Wounded Healer*, that all who are in ministry have a fundamental woundedness that can be a source of strength and healing when working with others.[18] This begins with an honest appraisal of what we bring with us to the needy situation.

Michael Kirkindoll suggests that a pastor's woundedness involves at least three areas of life. The first is "the wounds of our childhood and our past."[19] Our past life experiences shape the way we respond in the present moment. When I was in seminary my wife had a serious car accident that left her unconscious for eleven days with multiple injuries. It took six weeks of recuperation in the hospital and some of the injuries continue to affect her to the present. Later as pastor, whenever I found myself ministering to someone with head trauma or broken bones, I would go back to relive my own experience as a husband caring for his wife. On the other hand, a pastor may fear working with sick people because of a parent that was chronically ill. It is important to explore why we may be hesitant to minister in particular situations.

Second, Kirkindoll states that those in ministry "are particularly at risk for being wounded by the unreasonable expectations of ministry."[20] Most pastors, at one time or another, have had parishioners who were really upset because the pastor had not been by to see them while they were in the hospital. The problem was that they or others forgot to notify the pastor or the church of the hospitalization. Some people love to play the game How Long Will It Take for the Pastor to Find Out About My Need. It is nearly impossible for a pastor to win that game! With the many tasks that are a part of most pastors' job descriptions, there is just not enough hours in the week to do everything that every member thinks is important.

A third area of concern usually comes later in ministry through "the wounds of a lack of self-awareness."[21] It is possible to become so professional that we lose the capacity or desire to really care for people. Giving comfort or healing can exact a toll on us in terms of time and emotional energy.

CARING OUT OF YOUR OWN STRENGTH

Luke, who was himself a physician, reports an incident where Jesus was on his way to heal the dying daughter of Jairus, a synagogue ruler. As he walked, the crowds pushed against him, but he stopped. A woman with a physical need reached out to him with hope that in that touch she would be healed. Jesus asked, "Who touched me?" (Luke 8:45). But no one would own up to it, for everyone was touching him. Then he made an interesting comment, "Someone touched me; I know that power has gone out from me" (v. 46).

Jesus clarified what most helpers understand: you invest your own strength and energy when caring for others. The danger in ministry is to hold back that personal investment of oneself. Sometimes it's because we have little energy left to give. Or, it may be that we are protecting ourselves from the hurts of our wounded past. Kirkindoll says, "If you pretend that you do not feel the pain and suffering of your parishioners, you soon fail to feel your own pain or even your legitimate concern for yourself and your family. The inability of a pastor to mourn, either privately or publicly, the loss and pain of caring for [her] flock leads to emotional depression and spiritual deadness, robbing the pastor, her family, and her church of the spiritual vitality and involvement that they have a right to want and to expect."[22]

SETTINGS THAT ARE OFTEN UNCOMFORTABLE

Another challenge facing the pastor is the location where we bring comfort. It's often a hospital, a place in which it can be an uncomfortable environment to minister, with its strange smells, sterile rooms, lack of privacy and quiet. Medical doctors and nurses can come across as monarchs of their own kingdom, with their own policies and procedures that seem strange and disconcerting to the pastor. Some hospital personnel may seem to have little regard for the importance of the spiritual dimension of a patient's life. In this setting we may feel a bit intimidated because we are out of our natural element.

It is also tempting to feel inadequate in a hospital setting. We don't have medical procedures to perform. Switzer writes:

> We say a few things, ask a few questions, listen a bit, read the Bible, pray, all this often interrupted by others doing their own task at the moment or even asking us to step out of the room while they do it. They seem to know what they're doing and why; we who are representing the church are not always so sure about what we are doing and why we are doing it and how it's particularly helpful to the person in this situation.[23]

DIFFICULT QUESTIONS

Patients often ask questions that we find it difficult to answer on the spot. Preaching sermons on difficult issues is not as much of a problem. Pastors have time to study and do research during the week, so on Sunday we come into the pulpit with well-thought-out comments on the scripture passage. However, people seldom give a pastor time to prepare for the questions they ask from a sickbed. "Did I do something wrong so that God has sent me this disease?" "What is it like to die?" "Do Christians go directly to heaven, or do we rest in the ground until the resurrection?" "Do you think God will send my dad to hell because he never went to church, even though he was a good person?" What makes it especially difficult to answer some questions is trying to understand the real, unspoken questions behind the verbalized ones.

Pastors need to resist the temptation to rush in to a sufferer's life with the goal of fixing that person's problem rather than ministering to the person's need. Eugene Peterson states, "Nothing, in the long run, does more to demean the person who suffers than to condescendingly busy oneself in fixing him or her up, and nothing can provide more meaning to suffering than a resolute and quiet faithfulness in taking the suffering seriously and offering a companionship through the time of waiting for the morning."[24]

People in pastoral ministry tend to view words as tools of healing. We think that if we could just say the right thing, the situation could be resolved. Yet, there are times in ministry when there just isn't anything that needs to be said, not even a scripture to be read or a prayer to be prayed at that moment. Simply being with the person is enough, a ministry of presence.

SETTING ASIDE ONE'S OWN FEELINGS

Another challenge in providing ministry to those who are sick is seeing the terrible devastation certain diseases bring to the body. It is disconcerting to look down upon the body that was once strong, healthy, young, and athletic but is now a skinny 105 pounds of skin and bones because of AIDS or cancer. How painful to watch a parent gently care for a four-year-old who is losing a battle with leukemia. Pastors are all too aware of our own mortality in moments like that. It can be frightening because, except for the grace of God, we could be lying in that bed. And we may feel some guilt because we have been fortunate to avoid the sickness that the person lying there did not deserve to have either.

How do we respond as pastors to people we don't like very well? While ideally everyone in the church will treat the pastor with respect and love, reality may be somewhat different. The person suffering may have spread vicious gossip about our ministry that is both unfair and untrue. Or, it might be a board member who has been critical and difficult to work with in committee meetings. Or this scenario: A man will take his family and leave the church in a huff over some perceived failure of your work as a pastor or you as a person. Then a relative will call with the news that this person is in the hospital and needs a pastor to visit him. "If we are responsible, we are responsive. Remember that agape love, caring, doesn't require that we like the persons involved."[25]

This is the time to set personal feelings aside in order to minister as a representative of Jesus Christ. This may provide an opportunity to practice forgiveness and experience the healing of that relationship. It may mean that we must be willing to take the first step of reconciliation. If there is strong resistance to your presence, you could explore other options such as asking another clergy or layperson to go in your place. But we should not overlook the therapeutic benefit that could come, even to us, if we are willing to brave the initial uncomfortable moments and move toward the long-term goal of relational healing.

There is always a question of physical risk when visiting people with infectious diseases. Some years back, as the disease of AIDS began to spread and medical personnel did not know fully what constituted an unsafe risk, people with disease were often kept in isolation. It was not unlike the practice of dealing with leprosy in Jesus' day. If you contracted leprosy, you were isolated from family and the community. Yet Jesus, time and again, disregarded the social restrictions in order to bring healing to lepers and people with other diseases.

Although we know much more today about safety in having contact with communicable diseases, some pastors are hesitant to visit people who may put them at risk, no matter how small. Oden writes, "Even though we expect a minister to use prudent discretion in such instances, there is an unwritten rule in curacy that wherever pastoral services are genuinely needed, the pastor will make a good faith effort to be there. Particularly when urgently needed, the minister has no more 'right' than a fireman or a combat soldier to avoid the arena of immediate risk-laden need, even if it involves bodily peril, provided reasonable protections and safety measures are exercised."[26]

In each of us there is a natural tendency to shield oneself from the pain that others are suffering. If we are honest, we can sometimes identify with the religious officials in the parable of the Good Samaritan who walked on the other side of the road rather than risking involvement. It can be easier to back away or even avoid some uncomfortable situations, rather than engaging the situation of one who is hurting. Yet, to bring comfort means we must be willing to come alongside those that are hurting and actually identify with them in their suffering. Galatians 6:2 says it well, "Carry each other's burdens, and in this way you will fulfill the law of Christ."

▶ COMFORT WITHIN THE COMMUNITY

The importance of the Christian community is one of the ancient values that the Church is rediscovering as we move into the twenty-first century. That community is the local church, the Body of Believers that meet at Twelfth Avenue and Vine Street or Highway 17 and County Road 9 every Sunday for worship and fellowship. The church is coming to a fresh understanding of the truth that the Early Church appreciated: we really do need each other.

A church can play a large role in comforting when the entire community is allowed to help carry the suffering of one of its members. A century ago the community where people lived was much more interdependent. If a person got sick, the neighbors took turns nursing the person back to health while providing food and other help for the family. People did not normally die alone. The family, friends, and neighbors gathered around the deathbed in support. But as families have scattered to live great distances from one another, suffering became more individualized. Today, people go to medical clinics where they take a number and are seen by a medical person who does not even know their names without looking at the medical chart. In hospitals the large wards have long been replaced by semiprivate, and even more preferable, private rooms where the patient can suffer alone in isolation. The only person to see the patient is the nurse who comes in every few hours to change the water pitcher. Family and personal problems are handled in private counseling sessions, so know one else needs to be aware of the emotional pain and suffering.

In the midst of our society's increased emphasis on the right to privacy, the Church needs to move back once again to being a community of caring believers. And leading the move from the front should be the pastors of the flock. Eugene Peterson states, "Pastoral work cannot adequately function if it is limited to private comfort and individual consolation. The neighbors must be brought into the room; the congregation must gather so that the sufferers come to realize that the pain they cannot resign themselves to is understood by others."[27]

Paul, writing to the church in Corinth, likened the local church to a body. In his metaphor the body is completely interdependent. We need the various parts of the body to supply for us what we can't supply for ourselves as individuals. Then he makes an interesting observation, "If one part suffers, every part suffers with it" (1 Cor. 12:26). Have you ever had a bad toothache? Now, an individual tooth is not absolutely vital to the functioning of the human body. After all, a dentist can pull a single tooth that is giving a person trouble and then throw it away. But, if we have a tooth that is throbbing with pain because a piece of meat is stuck there, we can't think of anything else. And a tooth cannot fix itself. It sends signals out to the rest of the body that something is wrong, but the brain must recognize the source of pain and organize the body to solve the problem. It can be as simple as the brain commanding the hand to get a toothpick to remove the foreign object. One part of the body helps another part to relieve the pain. Willimon observes, "An important pastoral role is helping pain to go public, encouraging the public processing of pain."[28]

THE ENTIRE BODY OF CHRIST HELPING

This process of comforting and healing is done on many fronts. It is not the sole domain of the pastor. Laypeople need to be involved as the Body comforts one another from within. Bringing comfort to the Body of Christ is not an exclusively public activity. Often hurts are first revealed in a private setting before they move toward the public community. As Peterson explains it, "Pastoral work among the suffering wears a path between home and sanctuary— listens to the poured out, individualized grief and brings it into the sanctuary where it becomes part of the common grief, is placed at the foot of the cross and subjected to the powers of salvation that are diagrammed in all theologies of atonement."[29] Some issues are so private that to protect individuals from the gossip of others, the issues must remain confidential. However, the community of faith can support and encourage without knowing the exact nature or all the details of the hurt. People can pray one for another with the understanding that the Spirit can interpret the needs and the requests from a general petition on the part of the congregation.

Visiting and comforting other members of the community of faith is a tangible expression of our love for God. In one of Jesus' final parables in Matt. 25 he speaks of the reward the Son of Man will give for comforting one another. "'I was sick and you looked after me, I was in prison and you came to visit me.' . . . 'Lord, . . . when did we see you sick or in prison and go to visit you?' . . . 'I tell you the truth, whatever you did for one of the least of these brothers of mine, you did for me'" (vv. 36, 39-40). When we serve others we are actually serving Christ. "If we visit Christ in visiting the sick, we not only *serve* Christ, but we may find Christ for ourselves in our relationship with and ministrations to the sick and suffering. It becomes a means of grace for us."[30] And in visiting the sick, the church becomes the hands and feet of Christ, demonstrating to others how much God cares for them. Comforting service can become an effective evangelistic witness to those outside the community who know little about Jesus except for what they see Christians doing for others.

HEALING AND THE CONFESSION OF SIN

Confessing one's faults or sins to another person, whether that person is a pastor, a fellow Christian, or to God himself, can be a significant part of spiritual healing. "Whatever the nature of the confession, you, as the representative of God, are being asked for the reassurance that prayers for forgiveness are being heard and answered by God."[31] There can be a connection between guilt and illnesses that may at first seem unrelated. Such things as bitterness and unresolved anger or hatred can contribute to physical problems such as ulcers or colon problems. When the guilt of sin is removed by confession and forgiveness, a person may find there is physical healing as a side benefit.

PRAYER AND ANOINTING

It is normally in the context of the faith community that prayers are offered for physical healing by anointing of the sick with oil. Two passages in the New Testament refer to anointing with oil for healing. When Jesus sent out the Twelve in groups of two for ministry, Mark reports, "They drove out many demons and anointed many sick people with oil and healed them" (6:13). More familiar are James's instructions on healing.

> Is any one of you sick? He should call the elders of the church to pray over him and anoint him with oil in the name of the Lord. And the prayer offered in faith will make the sick person well; the Lord will raise him up. If he has sinned, he will be forgiven. Therefore confess your sins to each other and pray for each other so that you may be healed. The prayer of a righteous man is powerful and effective (James 5:14-16).

There are two metaphors here. "Oil, with soothing physical properties, has been used from time immemorial as a symbol of healing and consolation."[32] Anointing also involves the physical touch of the hand to apply the olive oil to the head. Jesus often healed by placing his hands on the person that was ill. The James passage links healing to the confession of sins and forgiveness. As a pastor I carried a small metal cylinder containing olive oil on my key ring in case someone desired to be anointed while I was calling in a home or hospital.

While it is certainly proper to anoint people for healing in a hospital, the preferred setting is a church service where the local Body of Believers has gathered. One of the most significant spiritual moments of my personal life took place nearly a year and a half after my wife's car accident mentioned earlier. One of her injuries was a broken and dislocated hip that made it difficult to walk, even though some healing had taken place. We felt led at that time to ask our pastor if we could have a healing service for my wife. The pastor anointed her the next Sunday evening, but when the service ended nothing happened, she was no different. We had felt so sure that this was God's directive. We stood together at the front of the sanctuary after most of the congregation had left.

Jackie said, "I know God can heal me."

I said, "Why don't we believe that he already has."

At that moment, in what I can only describe as a miracle, God did heal her. She began running up and down the side aisle, where before the service she struggled in pain to even sit down. The next day we visited our family doctor who had been at the church service the night before. Jackie did some deep knee bends for him. His mouth dropped open and he said, "Don't ever let anyone tell you that you did not receive a healing miracle from God." Although this took place many years ago, those who were there that night still talk about it. I have gained some insights from this experience:

There was a purpose behind the miracle.

The following weekend we both traveled to a church in another state where I spoke for a youth emphasis weekend. Two months later this church extended an invitation to come as their pastor. If the healing had not taken place, it was doubtful if my wife would be able to withstand the rigors of my being in full-time ministry. I would have had to reassess how to fulfill the calling I sensed God had given me.

No healing is guaranteed to last forever.

Even though Lazarus was raised from the dead by Jesus, he later died a second time. Seven or eight years later my wife developed arthritis where that hip bone had been broken. At first, we tried to deny the problem because we felt it was a lack of faith in God's earlier healing. We finally decided that God's reputation did not depend on our denying the problem, so we told our church.

God's healing can take many forms.

Later, Jackie underwent surgery for a total hip replacement. While God could have healed her instantaneously again, he worked through doctors using a surgical technique that was not available when the accident happened. God uses many ways to bring healing. No one method is superior or inferior. All healing ultimately has its source in God.

We should ask and not demand of God.

God's ways are higher than our ways. There have been many times when, if I were God, I would have brought healing to someone in response to anointing and prayer. But God chose not to heal. This is frankly a mystery that cannot be explained or understood. The Christian understanding of heaven leads us to believe that it is a place of final healing. Ultimately we must place our trust in God, whose knowledge is far greater than we can understand with our finite minds. And that confidence is sustained and encouraged within the community of faith—the church.

▶ COMFORT IN A HOSPITAL SETTING

Any pastor of a local church will quickly become very familiar with the hospital or hospitals in the community. Not only will you understand the layout of the physical plant, but you will increasingly understand how hospitals function.

There have been several changes in health care in recent years that affect the way pastoral care is shared with others. A major change is the shift to a shorter period of hospitalization. It was not uncommon fifty years ago for people to stay in the hospital for weeks, especially after surgery. Even in more recent times, surgical patients checked into the hospital the day before surgery to do testing. Today, tests for surgery are completed days before the actual date and the patient shows up at the hospital two hours before the surgery begins. In many cases, the person goes home the same day of surgery, returning at a later time to remove the stitches. One reason for this change is the great advances in medical technology. However, another factor driving change has been a desire to cut down the escalating cost of treatment. Same-day surgeries have made it difficult to find and minister to people who enter the hospital right before their procedure and leave quickly after the process is completed.

FROM CARE TO CURE

There has also been a shift in the focus or mission of hospitals. According to Kent Richmond and David Middleton, "Christians established the first hospitals primarily to *care* for the *incurably* diseased. Today, a hospital without a mission to *cure* is all but inconceivable."[33] From care to cure, the shift is subtle but significant. The first Christian hospital, created to help lepers, "was established in Caesarea in Cappadocia about 372 C.E. by Basil the Great, who was bishop of the area."[34] These very early Christian hospitals existed to compassionately care for those who would not be cured but needed people to help meet their physical and spiritual needs. There have been many medical advances in recent years that have shifted the focus to curing diseases. One problem facing medical professionals today is this: what do we do with those who cannot be cured?

One answer has been the hospice movement. Richmond and Middleton contend that "with the intense emphasis on cure, it became increasingly difficult to treat compassionately the incurable, dying patient. Therefore separate institutions and programs were established so that dying patients could be given compassionate care without the intense efforts to cure them. The hospices are in principle very much like the original hospital for lepers."[35] As hospitals have made this shift from care to cure, the role of pastoral caregivers providing comfort has become even more important. Hospice care can be a significant place of ministry for pastors and other Christian caregivers.

SCHEDULING VISITS

Who do pastors visit and comfort in the hospital? Obviously, the first on the list are those who are a part of your community of faith and their immediate families. But pastors should also include those who are new visitors to the church as well as people who claim no connection to the church. Also, pastors will be asked to visit friends or relatives of church members who are in a local hospital. Since some of these people may be unchurched, this can be a wonderful opportunity for ministry and evangelism.

Today, with many people entering the hospital for same-day surgeries, finding the time to meet with a patient before or immediately after the procedure can be a challenge. This is especially true if the surgery is scheduled later in the day. Surgery schedules become estimations as the day goes on. With the birth of a child, a pastor may not know the arrival time but will have an opportunity for visitation after the baby is born.

STRANGE ENVIRONMENT

People who are hospitalized find themselves in strange and unfamiliar surroundings and experience a variety of emotions. This uncertainty often leads to some form of fear. It may be the fear of separation from family and the familiarity of home. There are strange smells and sounds that can make it difficult to rest. The food will probably not be the same as home cooking. Strange people with uniforms enter the room unannounced and disturb normal sleep patterns. Doctors and nurses use medical terms that the patient does not fully understand. This deviation from one's normal patterns and surroundings can create a sense of uneasiness.

Patients also fear the loss of independence. Street clothes are replaced by ugly hospital gowns. Any sense of personal modesty in dress quickly evaporates as medical personnel prod and poke. A patient in a semiprivate room may not have control over when the television is on or what visitors come in the room. Patients may feel their personal privacy is constantly invaded. Closely related is the fear of having to be dependent on others. Questions abound. *Is the doctor who is doing my surgery really competent? Will the anesthesiologist give me the proper dose of medicine so I will wake up?* Following a surgery a patient may not be able to get up and walk and will be dependent on the nursing staff to bring a bedpan.

Perhaps the biggest fear when facing a serious surgery or dealing with a debilitating problem such as a stroke or heart attack is, *What will happen to me? Will I ever be well again? Can I handle the pain? If things don't go well, could I die?* Sometimes the patient wants to ask the pastor such questions. A pastor needs to be sensitive to the direction of the conversation. Sometimes it may be helpful to ask a leading question. "Do you have any concerns as you go into this surgery?" Another approach might be, "How can I best pray for you today?" Talking about fears can help the patient face up to his or her concerns and find ways to overcome worry.[36]

MAKING A PASTORAL VISIT SUCCESSFUL

What do you do on a pastoral visit in the hospital? One approach is simply to greet the patient and others in the room. After asking about the patient's condition, offer words of comfort and encouragement, closing with scripture and prayer. Introduce yourself if you are not well acquainted with those in the room. Try to keep the conversation positive. The patient should feel better because you have visited. It is important not to stay too long with a patient, especially one who is in a weakened physical state. Respect the patient's privacy and modesty. If the door is closed, knock softly before entering. If the patient is asleep, you will need to make a judgment about whether it is better to wake the person or let him or her sleep. If there is someone in the room, sitting with the patient, it may be better to talk to this person in the hall instead of waking the patient. If the person has been anticipating the pastor's visit, it may be better to wake the patient. Ask the person if he or she would like to have Scripture read. Focus on short, familiar Bible passages that will bring comfort. It is a good idea to ask for permission to pray with the patient, especially if you do not know the person well. A spirit of warmth, empathy, and hope in prayer is more important than the words we say. Try to voice the concerns the patient might have in this situation. Remember, prayer is always addressed to God, not to the person in the bed.

THE EMERGENCY ROOM

The emergency room (ER) can be a frightening, chaotic location for ministry during a medical emergency. A true-life ER experience may be totally unlike the carefully scripted program people are familiar with on television. The pastor who receives word of a medical emergency should get to the hospital as soon as possible.

The protocol of treatment for the medical team usually involves working with the most serious cases first. Thus a patient and the family may end up waiting for a long period of time before receiving treatment. Often the patient and the family may feel such stress because of the medical threat that they are unable to cope. While the pastor can do little to treat the medical problem, he or she can work with the patient and family to help make needed decisions. Be a good listener. Richmond says, "The pastor may often be the first person who is able to actively listen to the feelings of a patient or his/her family members."[37] If you are calm and sensitive, the patient and family will see you as someone they can trust.

THE INTENSIVE CARE UNIT

The intensive care unit (ICU) deserves special consideration. Usually the most seriously ill patients are found in this area of the hospital. The whole environment is sterile and somewhat impersonal. The air has a different antiseptic smell. Often the patient is hooked up with wires and tubes that prevent the person from moving or getting out of bed. Medical equipment whirrs and hums with lights flashing and information sent to the nurse's desk. Often the area is windowless, which can contribute to the patient's confusion over his or her location or whether it is day or night. Visitation is usually limited to family and clergy who are allowed into the unit for very brief periods of times. Some medical problems require anyone who enters the room to wear a sterile gown, don a mask, and put on gloves after scrubbing one's hands with an antiseptic solution. A visiting pastor needs to be considerate of the family who may have limited opportunity to see the patient themselves.

It is wise to stop first at the nurse's station to inquire how the patient is doing and if this is a good time to visit. While medical personnel usually understand the need for a pastoral visit, they are also concerned that the patient get medical attention when it is needed. Because patients are usually in serious condition in ICU, a pastoral visit should be very brief: five to seven minutes is sufficient. Speak words of affirmation, reassurance, and faith. Don't forget the importance of touch, even thought it may be more difficult with all the tubes and wires. "Family members are sometimes reluctant to touch a patient's hand for fear of hurting him/her. Such reluctance robs a patient of vital support. In addition, patients who have diseases such as cancer or AIDS quickly become aware of other people's fear of contracting the disease by touching them."[38]

One of the more difficult challenges is trying to minister to a person who is in a coma. This condition can be the result of a stroke or head trauma. One medical doctor told me that although the person may not respond, the person may be capable of hearing and understanding speech. Because this is true, a pastor needs to be very careful discussing the patient with doctors, nurses, and family when in the patient's room. Switzer writes, "I have heard a physician say that the last of the five senses to leave a person is that of touch and the last sense of touch to leave is that of the pads of the fingers. Touch is extremely important."[39] It is helpful to minister with the understanding that the unconscious patient can understand everything that is said. Take the patient's hand, assure the person that God would respond even though he or she cannot speak. Quote a short passage of Scripture and pray as if the patient were conscious. If the person is not a Christian, I have briefly presented the truths of the gospel and then prayed a prayer that the person could repeat to receive

Christ as Savior. While the patient may not offer any acknowledgment, God can respond to the cries of the heart.

CARE AFTER HOSPITALIZATION

People who have been released from the hospital often need to receive ongoing ministry from the church. This can be a wonderful opportunity for laypeople in the church to minister to the individual and the family. Churches can respond by bringing in food for a period of time or driving the person to doctor's appointments.

Some churches have developed a parish nurse program to care for the ongoing health needs of a local church. Parish nurses can provide preventative programs such as periodically taking blood pressure readings or giving nutritional information to the congregation. They can be observant of people who seem to need additional medical attention and make referrals for those who require medical help. Some parish nurses visit in homes and hospitals to see what additional volunteer help a parishioner may need. The growth of parish nurse ministries is a return to the Church's historic concern for the care of the physical needs of the community.

▶ COMFORTING MINISTRY

Some students and pastors may especially resonate with a ministry of comfort. There are many ways to fulfill God's call to minister with compassion to those who are ill. Some, as a part of their call to pastoral ministry, volunteer for community service with organizations such as hospice services, cancer survivor support groups, or helping in a senior adult care center. But there are also wonderful opportunities for full-time or part-time ministry as a chaplain.

Hospital chaplaincy provides an opportunity to demonstrate the love and compassion of God to those patients and families who are most in need of comfort. Lawrence Holst describes hospital chaplaincy as "a ministry of dialogue."[40] Chaplains not only talk and listen to patients and their families but also form an important link to the medical and service community of the hospital. They live and minister each day on the front line of pain and suffering as tangible representatives of Jesus.

Wherever you are called to serve, understand that an important part of pastoral care is an incarnational ministry with the comfort and concern that flows from the very heart of God. Paul is right. Because we have been comforted ourselves, we have the privilege and responsibility of showing that same comfort to others. In doing so, we become Jesus to them.

▶ QUESTIONS FOR REFLECTION

    ▷ Why is a proper understanding of the problem of suffering and evil so important to a pastor?

    ▷ What do you see as the three most difficult challenges to providing comfort in a pastoral context?

    ▷ How can a pastor involve laypeople in ministries of comfort both within and outside the church community?

FOURTEEN

THE PASTOR'S PRESENCE AMID DEATH AND THE DYING

When Kent Hammond left seminary to start a new church, he anticipated many challenges. Finding people to help in this church plant would not be easy. Yet God had helped him connect with a small number of passionate, committed believers who believed in this new congregation. The anticipated difficulties of finding a location and putting together a leadership team worked out without a hitch. The church, now in operation for sixteen months, was an exciting mix of young singles, newly married couples, a divorced mother with two toddlers, and some youngish middle-aged people with families. The one thing Kent never expected to face in this new congregation was a funeral. After all, no one was over fifty.

Shawn and Kate Paxton were one of the younger couples who had recently come to faith. They were so excited about the birth of their first child, a girl according to the ultrasound, that they had already named her a combination of their two names: Kashawna. Pastor Kent was a little surprised when Sue, Kate's Sunday School teacher and best friend, called to say that Kashawna had just been born. He thought she wasn't due for another few weeks. Kent was just about to breathe a prayer of thanksgiving when Sue said, "Pastor, I think you'd better get over to the hospital. There is something seriously wrong with the baby. The doctors are not sure that the baby is going to live more than a few hours."

Kent walked into the waiting area where Shawn's mother and Kate's parents sat off in a corner with Sue. While he paused a moment to meet the new grandparents, a nurse came over to them and said that Kate was being moved into a nearby hospital room and Shawn was with her. There was unmistakable tension as Kent went in with the grandparents and Sue to see Kate and Shawn. The young couple had expected this to be one of the happiest days of their lives, and now this. Shawn explained that Kashawna had some serious physical problems because she had been born so early. The medical team was working very hard, but there really wasn't much they could do. They didn't expect her to live more than a few hours.

Pastor Kent had everyone in the room gather around Kate's bed and join hands as he led them in a prayer for little Kashawna, asking God to bring healing to her tiny body. He also asked God to bring strength to Kate after her birth ordeal and encouragement to Shawn and the grandparents in the room.

After the prayer, Shawn whispered to Kent that he would like to talk to him out in the hall alone for a few minutes. As they walked down the long corridor to ward the coffee machine Shawn said, "I don't know what to do about this. I thought that when I became a Christian, God would handle these kinds of problems. It never entered my mind that we could be facing this type of complication."

Kent was about to reply when the doctor went by in the hall and motioned them to go back to Kate's room. It was obvious that the doctor was uncomfortable as everyone finally assembled again around the bed. He tried to be compassionate as he shared how the medical team had done everything possible, but the baby was not able to live. He asked if Shawn and Kate would like to hold the baby. When the couple nodded yes, he turned and left the room to make arrangements for the tiny infant's body to be brought to the room.

It was several hours before Kent finally arrived back home, exhausted. He had done his best to support Shawn, Kate, and the others in the room. And yet he wondered if his prayers and Scripture and hand-holding had done much of anything to take away the grief. This young couple had entered the hospital with such high hopes and dreams. Tomorrow they would be leaving the hospital empty-handed. He began to think about what his role was as pastor. What about the funeral? What kind of ceremony do you have for an infant a few hours old? How could he draw his small group of believers around Shawn and Kate to give them the love and support they would need both now and into the future? He remembered that Paul and Kay Roberts one day talked in their small group how they had lost a child in a late-term miscarriage—how it was so devastating. Perhaps they could be of help here. He was determined to be there for the Paxtons, wherever and whenever they needed him. But Kent wasn't sure where to start with the funeral and grief ministry.

▶ Helping to Mend a Broken Heart

Back in the 1970s the title of the most popular song of the singing group the Bee Gees was "How Can You Mend a Broken Heart?" While the song was probably addressing the heartbreak of lost love, the emotions of lost relationships through death would be very similar.

There is probably no more challenging and difficult task in pastoral care than helping people deal with their own imminent death or the death of a loved one. The process of final separation in this life evokes some of the deepest sorrow and loss humans can experience.

Death is the normal end to life here on earth. We all know intellectually that we are going to die, but for most of us it is out there in the nebulous future. Our society works hard to protect us from the reality of death. Norman Wright notes that we "criticize the Victorians because of their attitude toward sex, but they were very aware of and dealt openly with death. Today we have just the opposite attitudes. Our society is very open about sex but closed about death."[1] In earlier generations most people died at home, surrounded by family and friends. Today, many die in the sterile, impersonal atmosphere of a hospital. Older people often spend their final days on earth in a small room on a back hall of a nursing home, alone and forgotten.

Fear is one of the biggest reasons we try to avoid death. Many see it as the last unexplored frontier. We can probe the mysteries of the planet Mars and explore the composition of the atom, but we have yet to build a machine that can take one to the other side of death and back again. Today life expectancy is higher than ever before. Most people live more comfortably than previous generations because of medical advances and technological developments. But death is an inevitable consequence of human life. There is no fountain of eternal youth here on earth.

We not only fear what we do not understand but also fear what we will lose. In the past, when people were in bondage or facing difficult times, the only hope for deliverance was beyond death in heaven. One of the common themes of Negro spirituals during America's dark period of slavery was the ultimate victory of being in the eternal home on the other side. The hymnals printed the first half of the twentieth century contained many songs about heaven. We don't sing much about the subject today. In fact, a lot of churchgoers today have abandoned the Christian hope of heaven for a desperate attempt to create a heaven here on earth.

The Bible says a lot about God's view of death and heaven. Psalm 116:15 says, "Precious in the sight of the LORD is the death of his saints." Hebrews 9:27 speaks of the inevitability of death: "Just as man is destined to die once, and after that to face judgment." Jesus wasn't avoiding the subject when he promised his followers in John 14:2, "In my Father's house are many rooms; if it were not so, I would have told you. I am going there to prepare a place for you." John in Rev. 21:4 gives us a glimpse of the kind of place heaven will be: "He will wipe every tear from their eyes. There will be no more death or mourning or crying or pain, for the old order of things has passed away."

Yet, having a biblical understanding of death and heaven does not take away from the sense of grief and loss when the life of someone who is dear to us has been taken away. Wright describes bereavement as "the act of separation or loss that results in the experience of grief. . . . Mourning is the process following loss of which grief is a part, but extending beyond the first reactions into the period of reorganization of the new identity and reattachment to new interests and people."[2] Pastors need to understand that bereavement and mourning can provide a unique window of opportunity to do quality ministry that will make a real difference in people's lives. Thomas Oden writes, "The experienced minister knows that the times of approaching death and bereavement are exceptional opportunities for spiritual growth. . . . One's personal presence should be as open and outreaching as one's language is modest and self-limiting."[3] More than one person has said, after going through the grief recovery process, "I don't know how I would have made it without the support of my pastor." In the moments before and after death, a pastor can be God's agent sent to help mend a broken heart.

▶ CARING FOR THE DYING

The words of Fanny Crosby, although written more than a century and a quarter ago, is a reminder that the task of the church is to, "Rescue the perishing; / Care for the dying." But caring for the dying is more than simply caring about them. David Switzer says that this care is difficult because dying is usually complicated. "It is useful for us to keep in mind that dying is a psycho-social-biological process, and that for many if not most persons it is also a spiritual process."[4] While there are some situations such as massive heart attacks or fatal accidents when one has no time to prepare for death, it is very common for a person who has been ill to know when death is approaching. If we are going to provide the kind of care a person facing death needs, we need to try to understand what that person is experiencing in this process.

Elizabeth Kubler-Ross's monumental 1969 book *On Death and Dying* was one of the most significant studies of the twentieth century on how people cope with dying. Her studies led her to identify five stages in the dying process:

1. Denial—It's not me.

When a person receives the shock of the news, the first response is that it simply can't be true. The doctors must be wrong or the tests must have been mixed up. It's not just the dying person that is in denial, the family and close friends have a hard time accepting the diagnosis as well. When Jesus tried to tell his disciples he was going to die soon, they either wanted to argue with him or pledge to defend him to the end. Denial is not necessarily bad. It gives us time to begin to process reality in a way we can handle.

2. Anger—It's me, but why?

This is so unfair for me to have to face this when others seem to have no problems. Such anger can be directed at the medical personnel who cannot cure this process. People can become angry at God for not bringing healing and deliverance. It is important to understand that although this anger may be uncomfortable to accept, it is not necessarily sinful.

3. Bargaining—*It's me, but if you will do this, I will . . .*

In Ps. 39:13 David bargains with God, "Look away from me, that I may rejoice again before I depart and am no more." People sometimes bargain with God *If you would just lift this from me I will praise you and serve you with everything I have.* Or, a person may tell the doctor, "I really need to live until my fiftieth anniversary next summer." By bargaining people try to delay the inevitable.

4. Depression—*It's me, so what's the use?*

Because nothing else has been effective, nothing else can be done. Depression sets in. Wright says that there are two parts to this depression. "One is what is called reactive depression—thinking about past memories—and the other is called preparatory—thinking about impending losses. This is the time when the person needs to express sorrow, to pour it out."[5] Physical changes such as hair loss, loss of strength, or the loss of attractiveness can add to feelings of depression.

5. Acceptance—*It's me, and it's really happening.*

While some may think that acceptance brings happiness, in reality it is coming to terms with the fact that death is near, inevitable, and nothing else can be done about it. Some people at this stage begin to detach themselves from the people they love, and they lose interest in what is going on around them. This can be the time for family and friends to say those last-minute, important good-byes.

Elizabeth Kubler-Ross ends her stages here. However, Christian counselors and ministers append another stage.

6. Christian Hope—*It's not the end—there is the resurrection.*

One of the earliest leaders of the Christian Church, the apostle Paul, wrote his first book to believers in Thessalonica to encourage them to hold fast to the belief in Christ's resurrection. "Brothers, we do not want you to be ignorant about those who fall asleep, or to grieve like the rest of men, who have no hope" (1 Thess. 4:13). He goes on to say that when Jesus returns, the dead shall be raised and join those who are alive to be taken up to be with the Lord forever. He concludes with some powerful words of hope, "Therefore encourage each other with these words" (v. 18). The resurrection is a word of hope for any believer who is facing death. No more night, no more pain, no more sorrow, heaven will be eternal joy. The resurrection also brings to those who are left behind the hope of reunion again.

Elizabeth Kubler-Ross needs to be commended for her groundbreaking research, which has had a great impact in three areas:

- People dealing with grief need to address unfinished business before they can deal with death.
- Pastors need to be aware of the common experiences of dying people to help them identify the person's basic needs and give the needed support.
- Pastors need to learn from grievers to understand themselves and be more effective in ministry to the church.[6]

Since Kubler-Ross completed her study, there have been several studies that have looked at the issues of death and dying and have arrived at different conclusions. One of the problems of Kubler-Ross's early work was that people did not all flow neatly and in order through the five stages. Those who agree with her approach and try to categorize dying patients have a tendency to judge those who may revert back to an earlier stage as somehow "backsliding" in their progression. In actuality, it is hard to draw categorical conclusions about a person's stage because every individual is unique and will face death in a distinctive way, based on a multitude of personal experiences.

Another problem of thinking exclusively in stages is the tendency of caregivers to try to push the sufferer through the five stages, as though acceptance is the only goal. The truth is, dying is a series of experiences—and one's reactions may shift from anger one day to depression the next, and then back to denial. Some studies have shown that depression, anxiety, and even denial are evident throughout the dying process.[7] Leroy Joesten says, "If we look more closely at the five stages of Kubler-Ross, there really are only two, and they are not stages but reactions which remain in dynamic tension, namely, *resistance* and *acceptance.* Denial, anger, bargaining and depression are merely different expressions of resistance."[8]

How do we then view the work of Elizabeth Kubler-Ross? Switzer makes this personal observation. "Certainly, it is useful to think of dying as a complex process through which most people make some emotional, relational, and spiritual movement. The delineation and naming of stages which can account for the greatest number of occasions, however, still remains to be developed."[9] Perhaps the best way for someone providing pastoral care to understand the stages is to note that every emotion Kubler-Ross mentioned may be seen at some time in a person who is dying. These emotions are normal and expected. But to expect every person facing death to respond the same way is not realistic. A dying person's personality, life experiences, support system, length of the dying process, and even one's personal faith, all play a part in how one faces death.

▶ MEETING THE NEEDS OF THE DYING

Pastors and others from the church who provide care have a wonderful opportunity to minister with a uniquely Christian spirit to those facing death. There is a human tendency for some doctors, nurses, and even family members to begin pulling away from the dying person physically or emotionally. For those who see death on a daily basis in a medical facility it is hard to continually invest emotional energy. The alternative is to draw away, spending only what time is needed to care for the patient. This is why the pastor and church friends can be so important to the dying person. What are the special needs of people who are facing death?

They need someone who will be empathetic.

A pastor cannot presume to know exactly what the dying person is going through. There is the old spiritual "Jesus Walked This Lonesome Valley" that says, "We must walk this lonesome valley. / We have to walk it by ourselves." The song is not totally correct. David's familiar words might be more helpful to recall: "Even though I walk through the valley of the shadow of death, I will fear no evil, for you are with me; your rod and your staff, they comfort me."[10] While God may understand perfectly, humans can't.

What we can do is try putting ourselves in this person's position, and then imagine what this person must be experiencing. This is not complete understanding, but it goes a long way in saying, "I am trying my best to try to comprehend what you must be facing." What people don't need at this time are platitudes and clichés, such as, "This is all going to work out fine" or "This is God's plan for you." The dying person is not looking for answers as much as understanding.

They need people who will provide community.

Howard Clinebell says, "Dying is both a very private and intensely interpersonal experience. In our lonely society, the richness of one's interpersonal network makes a tremendous difference in the quality of one's dying."[11] When the person who is dying has been an active part of the local fellowship of believers, members of the congregation often gather around this person they love. That connective support may not be as strong if the person has outlived most friends or has been living in a nursing home for many years. It is most difficult if the individual did not attend church or lived in isolation from family and friends. Sometimes a pastor will be the only acquaintance the dying person may have. The saddest funerals I have conducted were attended by one or two distant relatives—no one else knew the person or cared enough to come

Mother Teresa established her ministry to the outcasts who were dying on the streets of Calcutta because she believed that no one should die alone without anyone present to care. The church should be a community for the dying as well as the living. When people are facing death in the face they need someone, or better yet, many, who will stand with them and be caring friends.

They need someone who will really listen.

Many dying people have questions or feelings of anger they need to voice to someone. "If I am God's child, why is he ignoring my prayers for healing?" Or, "I am in such pain. Why doesn't God just let me die and get this over with?" Those facing death need to have someone listen without judging them, even to the point of encouraging them to express their feelings. "Anger is a natural way for people to express self-concern. . . . They need permission to express all their feelings, so each one can be addressed in the open. After all, life does not seem fair; we don't always like what is going on either."[12] This person may want to reminisce about pleasant memories in the past as a way to temporarily escape the reality of the present. Reliving the past can be a way to tie life together and bring to completion one's personal narrative.

A good listener can provide a needed perspective if relationships need to be healed. It takes some time, more than a three-minute visit, to give a person permission to begin sharing from the heart. When the opportunity comes, pull up a chair and really listen, no matter how long it takes.

They need someone who will give spiritual guidance.

The moment of death represents a transition from the known to the unknown. Suddenly, spiritual issues that may not have been significant before, take on supreme importance. It is not uncommon for people to recall issues of the past that continue to make them feel guilty. In fact, they may feel that their present situation is God's vengeance or judgment for their bad actions. Guilt for sins does need to be confronted. But the good news of the gospel is that Christ has already died on the Cross so our sins can be forgiven and our hearts cleansed. Some may object that they have lived in sin so long, and they don't have any time to reform and live a godly life. The gospel is also a message of grace. The repentant thief on the cross received Christ's pardon even though he couldn't be baptized and serve God in the future. We have a wonderful message of hope, even for those who did not follow Christ during their lifetime. It is a great privilege to lead a person to faith in Jesus, even though the individual has only a brief time to live.

Even believers sometimes come to their time of death with feelings of guilt or deep regret. They may believe they could have done a better job raising their kids or spent more time serving in the church. No one goes through life performing perfectly in every single situation. Often the pastor has to help this person gain a different perspective of the situation, if the guilt is unjustified. Other times the pastor may bring together people who need to seek forgiveness of each other, and resolve the conflicts that have brought hurt. When a person has asked for forgiveness, a pastor can help this individual accept this forgiveness by declaring that the promise of God's Word in 1 John 1:9 is true. "If we confess our sins, he is faithful and just and will forgive us our sins and purify us from all unrighteousness."

We can provide real spiritual comfort to those who are dying by serving Communion, baptizing when appropriate, reading Scripture, having prayer, anointing, and assuring the individual that God is near. Pastors need to be careful not to offer philosophical and theological answers unless the person is ready and really needs to hear them. While we may not fully understand everything that will happen beyond the grave, we can confidently speak of the "blessed hope" of the Christian. Death is not the end. Jesus will return, the dead shall be raised, and those who have trusted in Christ for salvation will live with him forever in heaven. That hope can bring comfort to the one who is dying and the family who want to be united with him or her for eternity.

The personal memories of standing at my mother's bedside, joining hands with my family, singing hymns of faith and assurance, reading Scriptures, and offering prayers together, give me assurance, even today, that I will see her and know her again someday in the future. This is the reason believers love to sing Eliza Hewitt's words,

> When we all get to heaven,
> What a day of rejoicing that will be!
> When we all see Jesus,
> We'll sing and shout the victory.

▶ PASTORING THE FAMILY OF A DYING PERSON

The scope of ministry is not confined only to the person who is personally facing death. Pastoral care becomes a broader family concern. Pastor David Wiersbe says, "The family of a dying person begins their grieving the moment they hear the diagnosis. Their grief may be strong even before the patient shows signs of deteriorating. If death comes slowly, the family may grow tired of enduring the ordeal and express anger or frustration."[13]

My wife and I were visiting one day with a family friend whose husband was suffering with a long-term, debilitating disease that was very slowly taking his life. In the midst of the conversation she said, with a tone of frustration, "I don't understand why this is taking so long." Momentarily I was shocked by her forceful statement. It was so out of character with her personality. Then I began to understand the long road of caregiving she had already traveled, even though she had not been able to keep him in their home for several years. She visited with her husband daily at his care facility, while trying to fulfill her other responsibilities to her job and family. Our friend knew in her heart that her husband was never going to be better. And the stress of watching him die, inch by inch, over a long period of time was almost more than she could bear at times. Because of the constant pressure of anticipating death, it is not uncommon for family members to experience a sense of relief when the loved one dies. This can bring on guilt because they believe they shouldn't feel this way.

Family members sometimes take on the role of protecting the patient from the reality of death. They may have the mistaken belief that if Dad doesn't know he is dying, he will be happier. Often, withholding the truth about death is really a form of denial. This can put a pastor in a difficult predicament. Pastors may have had family members say to them in the hospital, "The doctors have said that Mom is not going to recover from her heart attack. We want you to promise that you will not say anything to her about her dying."

As a pastor I did not want to be restricted in what I could not say. If the patient would ask me directly if she was dying, I did not want to be put in the position of violating a promise on one hand or lying on behalf of the family. Most dying patients who are conscious and aware have a sense that they are going to die. It may come from the body language of the nurses and doctors or even from what family members are not saying. They may also have an inner sense that the problem they are facing will take their life. For this reason it is helpful for the pastor to work with the family to help them find an agreeable way to tell the loved one. Sometimes it can be helpful to request the doctor's assistance in working with the family. When death is near, family members need the chance to say important things to the dying person and give that person the opportunity to do the same. It is better to deal with unresolved conflict and misunderstandings during these last windows of opportunity before death comes.

▶ MINISTERING TO THE BEREAVED

Although family and friends may have time to accept that death is coming to their loved one, they really can't prepare fully for the finality of the moment when it happens. This is the moment of final separation here on earth. Several responses are common.

Shock

The news of death, especially an unexpected death, can bring on the numbing sensation like an anesthesia. People sometimes faint, stagger, or slump in a chair, trying to deal with what seems to be unbelievable news. The first response is that this must be a bad dream and not reality.

The role of the pastor at this point is to stand beside the person and be available to help. Sometimes holding the person's hand or getting a glass of water brings the most comfort in those first moments of shock. "The grief experienced by survivors, after a death has occurred, is similar to the grief experienced by the dying person prior to death. The survivors experience the wrenching pain between knowing one set of realities and yet craving another set. In other words, to know is not necessarily to accept."[14]

This is a protective process that helps a person finally deal with the shocking trauma that his or her loved one is dead. Often a person responds to the news of an unexpected death by saying, "This can't be true. You must have made a mistake. Maybe you have mixed my son up with someone else." Bereaved people have even been certain they saw the body in a casket move.

Crying

Tears are usually an involuntary emotional response to loss. Yet for some who come to comfort, tears may make them feel uneasy. Instead of discouraging crying, acknowledge that this is a normal way of expressing the grief and despair of loss.

When Jesus stood at the grave of his friend Lazarus, John used only two words to sum up the scene. "Jesus wept" (John 11:35). Tears are one way to let out all the complex emotions of love, abandonment, anger, sorrow, and loss that cannot even be put into words at that moment. As Ps. 42:3 expresses the emotions of the moment, "My tears have been my food day and night."

Assigning blame

In an attempt to make some sense of this death, people feel that someone must be responsible. Perhaps they could have done more to prevent this. This blame can be focused inward in guilt. A father will say, "If I had not given Mary the keys to the car tonight, she would have been home safe and the accident wouldn't have happened." Or, "If only I would have visited Dad more, I could have told him how much I loved him."

Sometimes there is justification for feeling guilty. A teenage girl babysitting a two-year-old boy by a swimming pool hears the phone ring and runs into the house to answer it. She is gone for what seems like only a minute. When she returns the young child is at the bottom of the pool and efforts to revive him are unsuccessful. It is natural for the teenager to feel guilt because she was negligent in her care. Whether the guilt is justified or false, it is important to listen, allow people to express their concerns, and experience God's forgiveness if that is needed.

Anger

At a time like this, hostility is an emotion that easily rises to the surface. A wife may feel angry toward her dead husband who has left her with a large debt and all the responsibilities of the family. More disconcerting to some pastors are expressions of anger toward God. "Why did you allow this to happen? Why didn't you do something to prevent this, God?" A pastor needs to understand that God wraps his arms around a person overwhelmed by bereavement and is absolutely unthreatened when that person beats his or her fist on God's chest in anger and frustration.

One of the most moving films dealing with the subject of death is *Shadowlands,* the story of C. S. Lewis's grief when his wife died of cancer. Near the close of the film Lewis sits down to talk to his stepson, Douglas. This youngster, struggling with his mother's death, expressed his anger by questioning God. "Jack, do you believe in heaven?" he asks Lewis, one of the most brilliant Christian thinkers of the twentieth century.

Lewis pauses for a moment, then answers, "Yes, I do."

The young lad, still obviously overwhelmed with grief, says, "I don't believe in heaven."

C. S. Lewis does not lecture or berate the boy. He simply says, "That's OK."

It is important not to stifle anger against God. A pastor can help people by encouraging them to express their anger or frustration as a natural part of the grieving process.

Pain

This process of mourning has been referred to in literature as "grief work." The one word that best describes it is *pain.* Because grief hurts so deeply, our culture has done much to help people avoid the pain of loss. Smith refers to our pastoral task as, "Ministering in a Grief-Lite Culture"[15] But avoiding grief is not an emotionally healthy trend. Joesten writes, "Unlike physical pain, someone in grief must be encouraged to endure the pain, to live with it."[16]

While others may say they understand, the pain of grief is something that is really felt only at a deeply personal level. Joesten continues, "For a time, the greatest comfort comes not in having their pain denied, or belittled, but by demonstrating through our physical presence a willingness to endure with them—as best we can—this devastating experience."[17]

How do we respond to people at those early moments of bereavement? Perhaps the most important first step is simply to be there with them. This can be a challenge, finding out where the family has gathered. Whether it is the hospital waiting room or a family member's home, a pastor needs to make the number one priority getting to the loved ones as soon as possible. If the family is scattered, find out when and where they will be meeting together. Pastoral presence means so much in those first moments of grief.

Bereaving people need someone with understanding. For some this may be their first experience with grief and they don't know what to expect. The pastoral role at a time like this is simply to be there to listen to them. Don't say, "I know what you are going through." You don't know, and even if you did, those words would not be comforting. Smith has learned to respond, "Of course I don't know what you're going through. But I never will if you don't tell me what it is like."[18] Our role is not dispensing advice but letting people talk to express their grief and gain some self-understanding.

Mourning people are also in need of our patience. Because they are experiencing a flood of emotions that may be entirely new to them, they cannot always be expected to respond in normal ways. There may be moments when they find it hard to make even a simple decision. It is not uncommon to see strong reactions of frustration and anger over even insignificant issues. The person in grief may not understand why these reactions come out, but they seem powerless to do anything about it. We need to be careful not to overreact when this person is just not acting "normally." In fact, we may take some of the pressure off their shoulders by anticipating some needs such as food or child care and call on people in the church to step in and help.

▶ PREPARING FOR THE FUNERAL

One of the significant roles for any pastor in dealing with a bereaved family is through the funeral. The funeral service itself serves several functions. It is a way to formally express our grief symbolically when words are inadequate. All the most important moments in life, such as birth, marriage, salvation, and death, have ceremonies for us to express their significance. Thus a baby dedication or baptism, a wedding ceremony or a funeral, is a form of enactment where we use our emotions, our physical bodies, our voices, every means available to express the importance of the moment.

The funeral is also a service of worship where we affirm our beliefs about God and our faith in God's provisions for our eternal future. This is our opportunity as a corporate Body of Believers to declare our faith as we sing hymns, read scriptures, pray, and preach. The service is not only about the deceased but also about God and our relationship to him and each other.

This service also provides the church with an opportunity to express our corporate grief, as well as our support, love, and encouragement to the mourning family. If the person who died was a part of the local Body of Christ, there is now a vacancy in the circle of believers. Even if the deceased was not known in the church, the congregation needs to show its care and concern to the family members who are part of the church.

The funeral is a significant moment in the life of a family that will be remembered for a long time. There have been people who have left a church because the pastor was insensitive or inattentive to the needs of the family in their time of crisis. On the other hand, there are pastors who are poor preachers or administrators but are dearly loved by members of the congregation for the way they cared for families in times of bereavement. An effective funeral demands careful preparation to meet the needs of those who mourn.

Contact the family

As pastor, do not assume you will have the leadership role in a funeral. There may be an old family friend or relative that will be asked to do the service. In such cases, be gracious and help facilitate the local planning of the funeral. People in moments of grief may not think, in their planning, about your connection to the person who has died. If the funeral is to be held in my church, I have sometimes asked if it would be OK for me to have a small part, such as reading a scripture or having a prayer, to represent the local congregation. On the other hand, the family may just assume you know that you will be doing the funeral, so it is good to be clear on the matter. Sometimes the funeral director can help shed light on the family's wishes.

Meet with the family

I have found that one of the most important moments in the process of planning a funeral has been assembling a family gathering, usually arranged a day or two before the funeral. As a pastor meets with the family, explain that it would be helpful to hear the family's remembrances about the person who has died. It normally does not take much urging to get the family to begin talking about their loved one. While they share, take notes. Explain that some material may be used in the service, if it is permissible with them. Also, ask them if the person had favorite scriptures, hymns, or other materials that could be used in the service. The conversations around that family circle can range from tender stories to hilarious incidents. Beyond the value of gaining valuable information about the deceased for the funeral, the laughter and the tears can be very therapeutic for the family. Often I have gone away from such gatherings feeling I have been honored to be allowed into the private, intimate interactions of this family for a brief period of time.

Work with the funeral director

There is a growing trend today for local funeral homes to be bought up by large corporations who may be more concerned with bottom-line profit than personal service. In this business climate, corporations sometimes question the need of personal funeral directors. Yet, for the pastor, a local funeral director can be an invaluable resource. These people know the community and its customs. This is especially helpful if you are new to the community or are doing a service away from your home. Funeral homes increase their business by having satisfied families return to the same home time and again. For this reason, the funeral home wants the pastor to have an effective service. If there are only one or two funeral homes that are used by most of the church family, get acquainted with the funeral home directors before the first funeral occurs. A good director will alert a pastor to any special needs or concerns a family has as they have worked out funeral details.

Plan ahead

As pastor, encourage the congregation to begin gathering material they would like to have as a part of their own funeral. Let people know that the funeral service is the final statement about the meaning of their life. Funerals communicate to people what was important and brought meaning to an individual's life. Encourage people to put those ideas down on paper, including favorite hymns and scriptures. Keep the file in a location others will be able to find, in the event of death. Family members may not know or remember those important details of life if they are not written down.

▶ MAKING THE RITUALS MEANINGFUL

While there are regional differences, most communities have some variation of these three rituals: one, the preservice ritual (calling hours, visitation, or wake); two, the funeral or memorial service; and three, the committal service at the graveside.

THE PRESERVICE GATHERING

A century ago in America, after the body was embalmed and placed in a casket, it was taken to the family home where people would drop by to pay their respects to both the dead person and the family. In more recent years this ritual has been moved to a funeral home. It is customary in many regions for the family to be at the funeral home for the entirety of the visitation time, talking with people as they come to view the body. Because many businesses no longer give employees time off for the funeral of anyone other than an immediate family member, these visiting hours have become a substitute for those who want to offer condolences to the mourning family. Others prefer attending the calling hours because there is more time to visit with the family than at the funeral service. Some people do not like funeral services with its more formal structure. With the time and travel difficulties of living in a large metropolitan area, many close friends will choose to attend either the visitation time or the funeral, not both.

As pastor, it is helpful to schedule to be present with the family prior to the visitation time when they first see the body. After the family has had sufficient time around the casket, gather the family members together for prayer, asking God to comfort and sustain them though the hours of visitation ahead. Local customs may dictate whether you are expected to be around for the entire time of visitation. In one region where I pastored, the whole concept of calling hours was not a part of their bereavement practice.

THE FUNERAL SERVICE

While the pastor does have a major role in the funeral service planning, today family members are taking more ownership in what takes place in the service. This can create problems when a family may request something that the pastor may feel is inappropriate for a Christian service in a church. While a pastor can be dogmatic and insist on having the sole power of decision making, a better approach might be to say, "Let's talk about it and see what we can work out." When the funeral is explained as a Christian worship service, family members are usually more open to finding appropriate compromises.

Pastors need keep a proper focus. Smith says, "The goal is not merely to 'do' a funeral ritual. The goal is to lead an assembled congregation—probably never to be together again—in a ritual that celebrates the life of the deceased and the life of Jesus Christ."[19] If the church was a meaningful part of the life of the deceased, the church building is an appropriate location for the funeral service of worship. However, many families choose to hold services in funeral homes, and increasingly, at beaches, country clubs, and ski lodges. Also, with the popularity of cremation on the rise, some people today prefer memorial services where there is no body present and no trip to the cemetery after the service. Without a body to bury, the service can be held weeks and even months after the person has died.

The funeral service should have some of the elements found in any Sunday worship service: music, Scripture, prayer, and preaching. To make the worship a corporate experience, many congregations participate by singing a hymn that affirms their common faith. If special music is used, it should also be compatible with a worship service. Read scriptures from both the Old and New Testament that offer comfort and confidence in our God. With more families actively involved in planning the service, is it now common to have one or more family members or friends give personal reflections or eulogies. The funeral can be a stressful time for the family, so it is good to encourage those who speak to write out their remarks and bring their notes to the podium.

The sermon should be brief. There are three appropriate approaches to developing a funeral sermon. First, it can be based on a scripture text with the illustrations coming from the life of the deceased. Second, it can be in the form of a eulogy that shows the person's life as reflecting the life of Christ. A third approach is to use the introduction as the eulogy of the person's life with the main body of the sermon as an exposition of the Scripture. One additional suggestion is to use the deceased person's name in the sermon and throughout the service to make it as personal as possible.

If the person who has died was not a Christian, do not try to preach the person into heaven. The sermon focus should be directed to offering Jesus Christ as the hope for living and comfort for those who are present. It is possible for the pastor to make positive references to the individual's interests at other places in the service without implying that doing good works will guarantee a place in heaven. If we are asked directly about a person who has not professed faith in Christ, we should answer that we need to place the person's future in the hands of a God who does all things well.

THE COMMITTAL SERVICE

In an earlier day, the body was taken from the funeral to the cemetery next door to the church or located on the edge of town. After the burial ritual was over, it was considered almost rude not to stay until the casket was lowered into the ground. The preacher sprinkled dirt into the grave, said "ashes to ashes, dust to dust," prayed, and dismissed the mourners. Then the family and friends went back to the church for a dinner of sliced ham, potato salad, and apple pie. While this custom is still practiced in many communities, committal services are more varied today. With families living great distances apart, the actual burial site may be in a family plot located in different state. If the body is cremated, the ashes are as likely to be scattered as buried. Some families prefer a private burial with only family present and then a memorial service later where the whole church is invited.

After the body arrives at the cemetery, the pastor has the responsibility of leading the casket from the hearse to the location where the body will be buried. As the mourners gather around the casket, the pastor customarily takes a position next to the head of the casket. Some cemeteries follow the burial custom of positioning the casket so the body is facing feet first toward the east, in anticipation of the resurrection. If you have a question where you should stand, speak privately with the funeral director beforehand. The committal service itself should be brief, with a few comments, a short scripture, and a prayer committing the body to the earth but trusting God for the hope of life eternal. After the benediction, it is appropriate to go to each of the immediate family members and personally offer your condolences with a handshake or a hug.

Harold Ivan Smith suggests a wonderful way to use anointing oil to minister to those who mourn. The Early Church used olive oil with the prayer of the elders for many needs. He suggests anointing grievers, after either the funeral or the committal service. At the funeral those who wish to be anointed could come forward. Another opportunity could be after the committal service. Instead of shaking hands, the pastor could anoint each person who desires, using the sign of the cross on the forehead with anointing oil. Smith suggests saying a paraphrase of Ps. 51:12 from *The Book of Common Prayer,* "Give me the joy of your saving help again," as you make the horizontal motion. Then say, "Sustain me with your bountiful Spirit" as you move vertically down the forehead. This could also be reinforced by reading or quoting Ps. 23, especially emphasizing "You anoint my head with oil" (v. 5).[20]

▶ Making Funerals Memorable

Many pastors feel inept at conducting funerals. Part of the reason is that they only lead funerals on an irregular basis. A pastor tends to work hard to improve the skill level of those things he or she does every week—preaching, administration, and leading worship. But there is no more opportune time to make an impact on people's lives than in the events surrounding a funeral.

One pastor of a large church developed a significant ministry to the people of his city by skillfully doing funerals. By the time he retired from that church he had conducted hundreds of funerals for people outside his church. Through this ministry he had the opportunity to lead many to Christ, some who later joined his church. This pastor found a way of making a funeral truly memorable.

To become an effective minister to people who are grieving, make a commitment to learn what makes funerals effective. Attend funeral services conducted by other pastors and observe what they do to minister to those who grieve. Ask funeral directors what they are observing in their work. These people attend funeral services almost daily. I have personally found that riding in the hearse with a funeral director to a cemetery provides a wonderful opportunity to discuss funerals. In the right sense of the word, a pastor is expected to be a professional in helping people during times of loss. Do your homework on the subject. For additional suggestions on funeral and committal planning, there are many good funeral manuals available with sample orders of service. These can be helpful when selecting scriptures and hymns as well as planning the committal service.

▶ AFTER THE CEMETERY

It's tempting to think our responsibility is completed with the grieving family, once the funeral dinner is over at the church. But for those grieving family members and friends, the slow process of rebuilding a new life without that loved one has just begun. Grief is a long, painful process that could be characterized as three steps forward, two steps back. And this process cannot be done by each individual alone. Those recovering from loss need others to stand with them—a caring community of supportive people—the church and pastor. There are three steps in this rebuilding process.

1. Accepting the past

In the days following the funeral, those in the immediate family—the spouse, the child, the parent, the sibling—try to deny, at some level, that things have really changed. It's just hard to believe that the loss is real. The denial can be quite subtle. For instance, a wife may refuse to give her late husband's tools to her sons who could use them. In her mind, her husband may be back and life will be normal again.

I visited a family one day and was being shown around their home. We came to one room and the couple said it was the bedroom of their son who had died. They opened the door and it looked like the boy had just stepped out for a minute. I asked them if it had been recently, the room looked so neat and clean. The woman sadly told me that their son had been gone for eight years. This family had created a shrine of their son's room, and that was keeping them living in the past rather than moving ahead.

On the other side, some want to run away from the pain associated with the location. It is not uncommon for a widow to want to immediately sell her house and move away after the funeral, because of all the memories that rattle around in the walls of the lonely home. Often people who make such quick decisions live to later regret their choices.

The major task for people at this stage of grieving is to begin to loosen the ties that anchor them to the deceased person and the life they had together. It is a challenge to face the reality of the past memories and slowly let them go as controlling issues. Norm Wright says, "This involves breaking the threads of shared experiences . . . and translating them into memories. Part of this involves learning to use the word 'I' in place of 'we.'"[21]

2. Adjusting to the present

The man who has lost his wife may need to learn to cook because no one is coming by every day to prepare the meals. The widow who never drove a car because her husband always did the driving is suddenly forced to take driving lessons or use public transportation. This adjustment period can change the relationship dynamics. The adult children are now stopping by to check on Dad more often because he is alone in the house. Maybe it will eventually mean having him move in with one of the kids. This current present is different from the old present the person was used to. A good sign of adjustment is when the individual is willing to tackle a new, challenging task, or go shopping alone for the first time.

3. Anticipating the future

At this stage a widow begins to live a new life without her spouse. The parents who lost a baby begin planning to have another child. It is a confident belief that there will be good things in the future, that the sun will shine again, that they will laugh and enjoy life without feeling guilty. For this reason, a person should not make those major commitments, such as remarriage or relocation, before arriving at this third step of rebuilding. A pastor can help discourage people from making life-changing decisions until they are really ready to anticipate a realistic future.

How long does the grieving process last? Wright has found that the feelings of grief are often quite intense for the first four months but then begin to subside some. However, as people approach the first anniversary of their loved one's death, the feelings of grief can intensify to a level as great as if the person had just died. I know of one pastor who goes to his date book after conducting a funeral and pencils in an appointment to see the grieving individuals one year later.

The period of recovery after the death of a spouse is about two years, but it can be longer. The violent death of a loved one usually means a longer period of recovery than for a natural death. Experts say that the death of a child has such an effect on parents that they never fully get over it. For that reason, in the majority of the marriages where a child dies, the couple ultimately ends up getting a divorce. With all grief recovery, things will never again be normal in the sense that circumstances will be the same as before death. However, people can experience a new normal. Life goes on without the loved one and people adjust to the new realities.

The pastor and the church can help the grief recovery by visiting and listening regularly. Be sensitive to feelings, but don't give false assurances that everything will be fine in a short time. Having people who stand by in the hard times can be the most valuable asset a rebuilding griever can have. That is an important role for any shepherd.

▶ QUESTIONS FOR REFLECTION

▷ What are the major challenges when attempting to minister to someone who is dying?

▷ Why is the prefuneral service family gathering important to the pastor and to the grieving family?

▷ What should be the pastor's goals for the funeral service?

THE PASTOR IS A PERSON

FIFTEEN

THE PASTOR'S CHARACTER
AND CONDUCT

Moving into the church parsonage was the easy part. Adjusting to life as a pastor and as a father at the same time, that was another matter. Kelly Springfield wasn't sure he was going to make it some days. It was a challenge learning the new names and strange customs of an area of the country far different from where he was raised. But the biggest adjustment was the new baby in their lives.

Kelly and Brenda had been excited throughout the pregnancy, even though they discovered that the due date was only eight weeks after they were to arrive at their first assignment. Because Brenda's pregnancy was not that easy, some of the women of the church helped them move in and get settled. Finally little Matthew was born, and Kelly assumed that life would get back to normal. But normal meant that Brenda had to get up several times every night for feeding and just to check that Matt was OK. Kelly knew that trying to get settled in their house as well as taking care of a baby had to be overwhelming for Brenda. He did what he could by fixing meals and doing laundry when he was home. Brenda complained that she felt continually exhausted—she just wasn't getting enough sleep. Well, with trying to take care of things at home and pastor a new church, Kelly was feeling pretty exhausted too.

Brenda had also gained quite a bit of weight during the pregnancy, and whenever she looked in the mirror she was convinced she was as big as a hippo. Kelly missed the times of physical intimacy with his wife since the baby had come. Her excuse was that she was always too tired or too unattractive, or the baby might wake up. Kelly knew she wouldn't always be like this, but it sure was creating a strain in their relationship right now.

Kelly was working in his office at the church one Tuesday morning when Denise Crawford stopped by to work in her Sunday School room. She asked if she could talk to him for a few minutes. Denise had been one of the women who had been so helpful during the move-in process. She had unloaded boxes and had stopped by two times since the baby had been born with a casserole and a pie. Other than that, Kelly really didn't know her very well.

Kelly stood and offered her the only chair on the other side of his desk. He went over to shut the door, but since there was no one else at the church, he decided to leave it open. As he walked by her he inhaled the unmistakable delicate scent of expensive perfume. That was nice, he thought.

She began talking about her family—her child in first grade, and her hus-band who was not a Christian and was gone a lot as a salesman. As Kelly listened his mind wandered from what Denise was saying to what she looked like. She was not strikingly beautiful, but there was something very sensual about her manner-isms. Denise was complaining about how her husband just seemed to ignore her. Kelly wondered how any husband could ignore a woman like this. Then she stood and extended her hand to Kelly. He felt uncomfortable because she held his hand just a little longer than necessary. She said she would like to come back again and talk because he was such a good listener.

After Denise left the office, Kelly slumped in his chair. She was an attractive woman, no doubt about that. Then he remembered the pledge that he had made to his college roommate Ron. Because they were both going into ministry they loved to talk about what it would be like as pastors. Several times they had talked about this very kind of temptation. Ron's former pastor at home had succumbed to sexual temptation. He had seen firsthand what could happen to a church when it had to deal with moral failure at the leadership level. Both he and Ron had pledged it would not happen to them.

Ron's words echoed in his mind, "If you are ever tempted, call me before you do anything stupid. I'll do the same with you."

Kelly had invested too much time and energy in preparation to serve God to throw it all away now. He really loved Brenda and little Matthew. And there was the commitment he had made to God to be a faithful shepherd. Kelly reached over, picked up the phone, and punched in the speed dial to Ron's study at his church five hundred miles away. Distance was not a factor when he and Ron got together elec-tronically to talk.

▸ THE RIGHT STUFF

The 1986 World Series was one of those great moments in sports. Boston Red Sox fans were hoping that they could finally climb to the pinnacle of achievement, winning Major League Baseball's Fall Classic after coming close and failing so many times. The Red Sox had a three-game to two edge over the New York Mets going into the sixth game. If they could win this game, they would be world champs.

It was the tenth inning and the frenzied fans were on their feet. Boston's Bob Stanley was within one pitch of retiring the Mets' batter, Mookie Wilson, and wrapping up the series. Wilson swung and hit a grounder to the Red Sox first baseman, Bill Buckner. Mets fans inwardly groaned—it was over. But somehow, this routine grounder mysteriously slipped under the glove and through the legs of Buckner, and Wilson was safe. That break gave life to the

Mets, who went on to win games six and seven—and the World Series Championship.

In many ways that missed grounder defined the career of Bill Buckner. Buckner was a very competent ball player; otherwise he wouldn't have been at first base in a World Series game. He could have made that play ninety-nine times out of a hundred. But all these years later, when Red Sox fans hear the name Bill Buckner, all they remember is the ball sliding under his glove, and the World Series slipping though their fingers.

Most baseball fans would like to think that character is an important part of baseball. Yet, there have been players, past and present, that may be lacking in personal character but perform well on the field. Buckner's personal character was never once called into question. That night in 1986 when the ball came across the infield toward him, the Red Sox fans' only concern was Buckner's hand-eye coordination to field the grounder and record the final out. In the final analysis, playing baseball is all about skill training and performance.

Pastoral ministry is just the opposite. It is all about personal character. Richard Gula writes, "We act the way we do largely because external conditions challenge us to reveal the habits we have formed, the beliefs we hold, the image we have of ourselves, the ideals we aspire to, and our perception of what is going on. In brief, we act the way we do more because of the character we have become than because of the principles we would apply."[1]

Ministry rises out of who we are as people, as Christians. What we are on the inside is more important than what we do on the outside. Because this is true, it is vitally important to know who we are at our very core. William Willimon says, "The pastor stands as priest, as mediator between people and God. The pastor serves the body and blood of Christ at the Lord's Table, holds the keys that bind and loose sin, and is steward of the mysteries of God. We must not let those who are ignorant of themselves be in the morally demanding role of pastor."[2]

Character is hard to quantify. It would be easier if we had a test for those entering ministry that could measure character on some kind of scale. We could determine a passing grade and eliminate anyone who didn't measure up. Or, one could pass a course on personal character just as one would complete a course in theology or preaching. But character doesn't lend itself to such an evaluation. It is something we can recognize when it is present, and we can certainly see the tragic result when it is absent. It is easy to identify character in people who have the courage of their convictions and are willing to stand by those beliefs, even when it is unpopular. We stand back and admire those who know who they are and what they believe and will not compromise even in the face of hardship or death.

I recently reconnected by e-mail with my best friend from childhood. We have not seen each other for probably forty years, so it was great catching up on what has happened in our adult lives. It caused me to reflect back on the importance of this childhood neighbor in my life. What I remember most about my friend was his strong character. Whatever the situation, I always knew Bill would make the right decision. If some activity was wrong, he would not go along with it, no matter what other people said. Bill always demonstrated the courage of his convictions. And from conversations with his mother, Bill's character from childhood has carried over into his adult life.

A study was begun in 1973 by the Association of Theological Schools in the United States and Canada to determine what churches were looking for when they called a minister. While skills to perform the tasks of ministry were important, churches seemed to be even more interested in the character traits the person possessed. The three most valued traits were: (1) a willingness to serve others without regard for public recognition, (2) personal integrity—a person who honors commitments and follows through on promises, and (3) a generous spirit—an example of Christian living others can respect.

At the other end of the scale, the three traits least desirable were: (1) a lack of self-discipline—including selfish behavior that would be offensive to others, (2) being self-absorbed—unwilling or unable to relate to other people, a critical, demeaning attitude, and (3) immaturity—unable to withstand the internal and external pressures of ministry. A 1987 follow-up study seemed to generally support the earlier findings.[3]

DEVELOPING CHARACTER

The question that naturally arises is this—how does one develop the kind of moral character that people value in a person they expect to shepherd them as their pastor? Gula says, "Character is caught as much as it is taught. Our natural inclinations, or sensitivities, are the raw material for developing character. These can be nurtured and directed toward the good, or restrained and distorted."[4] Many who were raised in good Christian homes may point to fathers or mothers who have shaped their character.

But those who may not have had the opportunity of a nurturing family can still develop strong character traits. Sometimes it is a teacher or a pastor that serves as a mentor and provides the motivation a person needs for character development. Of course, the most significant model is Jesus, who demonstrated how to live a life that is pleasing to God and provides grace for us to develop a Christlike character as we imitate him.

CHARACTER NEEDS COMPETENCE

It is not enough simply to have character, though. It needs to be combined with competence. There are wonderful ministers whose motives are sincere and whose character is above reproach. Yet as pastors they are mediocre at best. Willimon observes, "A person who desires to please God in ministry will desire to acquire those skills that make one an effective instrument for God. On the other hand, the skills required of ministry (like biblical interpretation, homiletical ability, pastoral care) reinforce our love of God and form us into more godly people."[5]

As a person who spends most of his time and energy training people for ministry, I think I have become a much better judge of who will finally end up in active ministry. I have been pleasantly surprised by some who, as they matured, suddenly saw their calling in a new light and began to apply themselves to the task of ministry. But most people who lack the motivation to develop their ministry skills drop out along the way, long before they arrive at their first church. Even the desire to develop those skills has its basis in one's character. Training, preparation, and study demand hard work. But being a pastor of a church is hard work as well, even if you are well prepared. That is why it is important to commit to become as competent as possible. Competency means preparation before entering ministry and lifelong learning while in ministry. Paul made this plain to Timothy, "Do your best to present yourself to God as one approved, a workman who does not need to be ashamed and who correctly handles the word of truth" (2 Tim. 2:15).

Inward character manifests itself in the choices we make. E. Stanley Jones often told audiences, "You can make your own choices; you cannot control the consequences of those choices."[6] A baseball pitcher, interviewed after a game he had lost, made this observation, "I only made two bad pitches in the whole game." Two bad pitches out of the approximate one hundred he threw—that meant 98 percent of his pitches were good. But the pitcher realized that both of those two pitches went for home runs and a total of five runs scored. That was enough to lose the game. Every pastor will make some wrong decisions in the course of doing ministry. A pastor choosing blue carpeting for a meeting room without consulting the proper committee may be making a poor decision, especially when the committee members prefer gray. That poor choice may not be significant to the church. But other choices of conduct could have broad ramifications for the pastor and the church.

▶ KEEPING CONFIDENCES

The whole issue of private information and confidentiality is a major issue in our society. Every time a financial institution develops a new method of safeguarding private electronic financial information, a dishonest computer hacker figures out a way to defeat the system. People have become aware of the potential danger of private information falling into the wrong hands. The danger exists elsewhere, such as in the field of medicine. Gaylord Noyce notes that anywhere from twenty-five to one hundred doctors could have access to the medical records of one person needing elective surgery. The opposite should define the ministry: "The privacy of conversation with mentor and confessor and pastor remains a precious commodity, not to be squandered. The information 'belongs' to the parishioner. One minister who spoke out of turn, indiscreetly imparting this kind of information, was sued for invasion of privacy."[7] While this subject has been mentioned in other chapters, it will now be examined in detail.

HIGH STANDARDS

Should pastors be held to the same high standard of confidentiality as other professions? The answer is a resounding yes! What are those standards? According to the American Medical Association policy, a physician may not divulge a confidence revealed in the course of medical treatment "unless he is required to do so by law or unless it becomes necessary in order to protect the welfare of the individual or of the society."[8] Margaret Battin states that "policies governing the practice of law have typically been more restrictive, permitting the attorney to divulge a client's confidences only when required by court order or to prevent a crime that involves the risk of death or serious bodily harm."[9] Psychologists and psychiatrists have similar restrictions in revealing confidential information, although the landmark *Tarasoff* court case in California in 1976 ruled that

> the duty of confidentiality in psychotherapy is outweighed by the duty to protect an identifiable victim from life-threatening danger. This duty can be discharged by warning the victim directly, informing others who can warn the victim, or notifying the police. That such a ruling had to be made at all shows that only with great reluctance should confidentiality be broken and then only in the face of clear and present danger.[10]

While most helping professions have clear guidelines for dealing with confidentiality, pastors are given more freedom to interpret what is indeed a confidential matter. In general terms, a matter is confidential if the person sharing information intends for that information to be kept as privileged, not to be shared with anyone else. "Confidentiality is how we exercise good stewardship of the power we have over others who make themselves vulnerable to us by their self-disclosure."[11]

WHAT IS PRIVILEGED?

But determining what is privileged and what can be shared with others can be very difficult. The fact that a person is a pastor may itself cause some people to speak more freely and honestly than they would with others. Noyce correctly observes, "When something is learned in true pastoral conversation, what might ordinarily be shared with others is not shared."[12] Gula says that a pastor needs to make a judgment "by reflecting on what is said, why it is said, the way it is said, and the context in which it is said."[13] He offers this general principle: "The more formal the process and private the context in which information is exchanged, the greater the weight given to it as confidential information."[14]

Perhaps the most obvious place for confidentiality is in the act of confession. The historic practice of Roman Catholic priests hearing confessions has helped to establish the legal precedence protecting clergy confidentiality. Battin writes, "In religious practice, it is *confession* that presents the most conspicuous dilemmas in confidentiality, since confession is a primary mode of conveying personal information about an individual to a religious professional."[15] Most people confessing a sin to a priest or pastor would do so believing that the minister is a representative of God. It is common practice for almost all religions. For this reason there are clergy-penitent laws of one type or another in virtually all states in the United States as well as many other countries.

LEGALITIES

These laws, with some variations, say that "the ordained minister 'shall not be allowed or compelled' to disclose a confession or confidence incurred in the line of professional work."[16] Many denominations also have statements in their constitutions requiring pastors to maintain in confidence private spiritual conversations. There have been cases when courts have tried to force pastors to reveal privileged information that would be crucial to a case. Battin says that various courts interpret confidential information differently. "However, some courts distinguish between communications that are penitential in character or which seek spiritual advice or absolution and those that merely convey information, protecting only the former."[17] Some pastors have even been held in contempt of court for refusing to divulge confidential information. Gula says, "Conflicts over confidentiality are in effect conflicts over power."[18] Does the state have the right to overrule in matters of religion? Ultimately, the legal principle of the sacredness of the confessional has been upheld repeatedly in the United States court system.

MORAL DILEMMAS

But confidentiality can bring moral dilemmas to a pastor. Most ministers at some time will have to make a difficult decision whether or not to divulge something told in confidence. As mentioned earlier, even doctors and lawyers have the responsibility of violating confidentiality responsibilities under certain circumstances. Noyce states, "The minister, like others is morally obligated to a concern for the safety of those he or she can protect. That moral claim, in this case, would override the importance of confidentiality."[19] It has already been mentioned that if a counselee threatens to do serious bodily harm, either personally or to others, the pastor needs to take action to provide safety for those who are threatened.

Providing for the safety of others is especially important for those who cannot adequately protect themselves—children, the elderly, and the mentally disabled. Many states require clergy, as well as people in other helping professions, to report any cases of suspected child abuse, especially sexual abuse. This can be very difficult when the person committing the abuse is a member of the church and confessing this in your office. However, the physical and mental health of this child is at stake. A pastor must insist that the guilty person seek help immediately. "Pastoral care in this case means avoiding the cheap grace of forgiveness without both repentance and therapeutic remedy. The same is true of pastoral care for the batterer."[20]

The dilemma of reporting some cases to authorities is that by doing so a pastor may be forcing people away from the help that clergy and other professionals can provide. Kathy Callahan-Howell mentions two other situations when it would be proper to divulge privileged information. (1) In cases of harmful intentions such as an underage teen girl who is pregnant, planning an abortion, and is requesting that you not tell her parents. (2) In cases of destructive patterns and addictions, such as a woman who is suicidal but does not want her husband to be told.[21]

If we must divulge privileged information, Gula suggests that we should meet the following criteria: "(a) reasonable efforts are made to elicit voluntary disclosure; (b) a high probability exists that harm will occur unless a disclosure is made (in this case, we can disclose without permission); (c) only those who have need to know are informed; and (d) only necessary information is disclosed in order to avert harm."[22]

SHARING WITH A SPOUSE

One further issue of confidentiality concerns sharing privileged information with a spouse. In one case the court ruled that because a pastor had shared confidential information with a spouse, the code of confidentiality had been broken and the pastor was forced to testify. Generally speaking, privileged information cannot be shared with anyone without permission. That is why I often asked if it would be permissible to share the information I had just received with my wife so we could pray for the situation together. I have also asked permission to share the need with other staff people. If the counselee would not give permission, then I was obligated not to tell anyone. As pastoral counselor Kathy Callahan-Howell states, "My understanding of marriage includes not keeping secrets from my husband that relate to our relationship. However, to be a pastor, or even a friend of integrity, I must be able to maintain the personal issues of others even from my spouse."[23]

One of the things I understood better the longer I pastored was the fact that there will be things I take to my grave that I can never tell anyone. This is one of the burdens of pastoral ministry.

▶ GOD'S UNDERSTANDING OF SEX

Anyone who studies culture will tell you that we live in a sex-saturated society. This is not to say that sex has been only recently discovered. The early chapters of Genesis tell us that God created humans as male and female. God performed the first wedding in the Garden of Eden so that Adam and Eve could enjoy sexual union within the protection of marriage. The Bible, from back to front, has always understood marriage in these terms. The Old Testament judges and prophets continually condemned the sexual worship of the Canaanite gods such as Baal and Asherah and warned the people of God not to participate. The New Testament churches repeatedly had to confront the sexual practices of idol worship as they evangelized in cities like Corinth and Ephesus.

MODERN SEXUAL ATTITUDES

Many in our current society seem to be reverting back to ancient attitudes of sexual looseness that were prevalent millennia ago. What has caused this shift in attitude? Gaylord Noyce lists several influences.

- *The psychological revolution* dating back to Sigmund Freud that encouraged people to talk about sexual matters much more openly.
- *The contraceptive revolution* that took away the fear of pregnancy and lowered the risks of promiscuity.

- *The media explosion,* including magazines like *Playboy,* television, movies, and Internet pornography, that promoted a shallow, cheapened view of sex as being only physical.[24]

All of these forces have caused our culture to separate love and marriage from sexual activity. Tina Turner's 1984 Grammy Award-winning song "What's Love Got to Do with It?" captures this split. A major male movie idol was interviewed about the breakup of his third marriage and his involvement with yet a new partner. The essence of his comment was that his last wife was a wonderful woman but no one stays with one person forever. In his mind, it was time to move on to someone else.

Pastors are continually confronted by people who have been wounded by sexual issues. Problems such as child sexual abuse, sexual promiscuity, teen pregnancy, abortion, AIDS, marital unfaithfulness, divorce, and people living together outside marriage are almost as common inside the Church as in society as a whole. The Church can no longer afford to simply ignore such issues in the hope that they will simply go away. Pastors have to be clear in their teaching and preaching that there are moral dimensions to the sexual issues people are facing. Churches need to partner with parents to provide sexual training, beginning with children and continuing through the teen years to the time people are preparing for marriage. Most importantly, churches need to help people regain a proper perspective of sex. E. Glenn Hinson writes, "You live in a culture that encourages self-indulgence, self-centeredness, and egoism. This culture uses sex to sell its products and to establish priorities. It demeans and distorts sex by promoting it as an end in itself rather than an expression of the highest form of love humans have for one another."[25]

DISTORTED VIEWS

Our society has had the distorted view that Christianity has always been and always will be against sex. There is an element of truth in this understanding. As early as the second century there were Church leaders that believed that sex was a marital duty for the sole purpose of producing children. For centuries this attitude dominated in the Roman Catholic Church. It promoted virginity and celibacy as spiritually superior to marriage, which was viewed as an accommodation to baser physical desires. A person could be closer to God and serve the Church more effectively by focusing on the spiritual dimension of existence and denying the physical desires of the body. To this day Roman Catholic priests and nuns are required to take the vow of celibacy when they enter their orders.

Simply viewing sex in terms of a physical act can lead to self-centered gratification with anyone at any time. But there is also a positive approach to understanding sex. If God created humans as male and female, there is a sense of the completion of God's intention when couples enjoy sex within marriage.

In Eph. 5 the apostle Paul explains the mystery of the love relationship between husbands and wives by comparing it to the relationship between Christ and the Church. He writes of the married couple becoming one flesh. Paul then summarizes by saying, "This is a profound mystery—but I am talking about Christ and the church. However, each one of you also must love his wife as he loves himself, and the wife must respect her husband" (vv. 32-33). Marriage, rather than being an accommodation to fleshly desires, is elevated to the highest visible expression of the Church in its relationship to God.

God is relational by nature. His purpose in creating humans was so he could love and have fellowship with them. God also created us so we could have friendships with other people. Hinson says, "God is love, and thus God reveals Godself in all forms of mutual attraction between human beings but especially in spiritual friendship. Equality, mutuality, and openness are marks of such a friendship."[26] If this is true, one of the ways we can know and love God is through human friendships. A spiritual relationship with God can be enhanced by a deep spiritual friendship with another human. Hinson concludes, "A healthy spiritual life should make you more sensitive, fully conscious, and tender in ways that would help you avoid abuse, diminish wrong attitudes and behavior, preserve sexual purity and enhance sexuality."[27]

▶ SEXUAL ISSUES AND THE MINISTRY

At one level it may be difficult to imagine why, if sex is such a beautiful expression of a married couple's affirmation of each other, it can also become a deadly force that can destroy a pastor's career if used wrongly. Yet sexual misconduct is one of the leading causes of pastoral failure.

To say it as clearly as possible, pastors should not take sexual advantage of other people in the congregation or allow themselves to be taken advantage of. It is totally out of character for one who has made a commitment to serve others in the name of God. As Richard Gula explains, "The imitation of the servant-leadership of Jesus calls us to be loving by having the best interest of others at heart, rather than to be self-seeking and gratifying our own needs."[28] As one who has been called to special service in God's kingdom, a pastor needs to be held to the highest level of behavior in one's personal life. Willimon says, "Often, when a pastor commits some public sin, there is someone around to trivialize the lapse by saying, 'Well, pastors are only human.' This is not only a curious abuse of the word *human,* but also a degradation of the ministerial vocation. Pastors are called to be more than human, as are all the baptized."[29]

WHY DO PASTORS GIVE IN?

There are many reasons that pastors succumb to sexual temptation. They may be in a vulnerable state. Perhaps they are not getting the fulfillment they need from their marriage. For women in ministry the sexual temptation may grow out of a close relationship where she is affirmed and appreciated. A male pastor with low self-esteem may find it very affirming to his ego when an attractive woman pays personal attention, compliments him, and perhaps touches him on the arm. It's not uncommon for women to come for pastoral help who are emotionally needy and who are seeking someone who will be willing to listen to their concerns. A woman like this may feel her husband pays little attention to what she is saying. Here is a man who will sit and focus on everything she is feeling as she talks. The pastor becomes the ideal husband. He is everything that her husband is not.

Temptation can become stronger when a pastor is spiritually, physically, and emotionally exhausted. The caution signals that normally go off in the brain can go unheeded because the will to resist is not as strong.

Sometimes temptation can come when people are together in a close working relationship. It is not uncommon for coworkers to spend more time together on the job than they do with their spouses. It is easy to develop emotional intimacy with someone of the opposite sex because you are sharing common goals as well as facing common challenges. Coworkers begin to share personal details of their lives that can make them more vulnerable to sexual intimacy. Noyce states, "There is a sexual dimension to all cross-gender relationships. We cannot chop up the human person by categories; there is no absolute line of demarcation between spiritual, intellectual, and physical attraction in human relationship."[30]

Human friendships are so important in our lives. Yet we need to be aware that there are potential temptations we must continuously guard against. We should be aware that no one is so removed from the world that temptation cannot strike. It calls for diligence on our part. Peter warns, "Be self-controlled and alert. Your enemy the devil prowls around like a roaring lion looking for someone to devour" (1 Pet. 5:8). Verse 9 gives the proper response, "Resist him, standing firm in the faith."

HOW TO RESPOND

How should we respond when sexual temptation occurs? Richard Gula gives a general principle that is foundational in human understanding. "In relationships where one party is stronger than the other, or more in control of the encounter, the greater burden of responsibility lies on the one with the greater power."[31]

Some localities in the United States have taken this principle as the basis for laws governing the conduct of professionals, including the clergy. It is assumed that the pastor is the person in the relationship with the greater power, and therefore it is the pastor who is held responsible when improper sexual behavior takes place. The penalties for such sexual misconduct can be very severe because this is considered a felony. The minister is charged with the responsibility of making sure nothing improper takes place of a sexual nature when dealing with parishioners.

TRANSFERENCE, COUNTERTRANSFERENCE

Pastors need to be aware of the danger of *transference*, where the counselee projects feelings and desires of a sexual nature into a counseling session. Often this person will seek constant help or contact with the pastor as a way to meet personal desires. If you sense there is a problem with transference, you need to take extra precautions rather than relaxing your personal conduct in the situation. Archibald Hart says, "The safest way to deal with transference is simply receive it as one would receive any feeling of a client. Help the client see that the feelings reside in him or her, not in the counselor."[32] If this cannot be done safely, it may be best to refer this person to another counseling professional.

Another similar problem is called *countertransference*. In this case the pastor feels feelings of sexual attraction to the person of the opposite sex in the counseling session. This can happen when the pastor looks forward to the counseling sessions with this person, extends the time of the sessions, or looks for ways to have contact between sessions. If a pastor recognizes the signs of countertransference, it is best to make a referral before the situation gets out of hand. While these two issues of *transference* and *countertransference* were addressed in an earlier chapter, they have specific relevance when dealing with sexual issues.

MARRIED AND SINGLE

For those who are married, one of the best safeguards against sexual infidelity is to strengthen the marriage and family relationship at home. Pastors face the same marriage and family problems everyone else does. People can get busy and not spend time together as husband and wife. Children get sick; they need transportation to school events; they make demands on the couple's time and energies. Pastors who are happy with their spouse and family are usually able to overcome temptations easier than those whose homelife leaves something to be desired. "There is an art as well as a discipline to tending our marriages, and learning the art is one of the joys of a good marriage."[33]

Single pastors need to face sexual temptation with different strategies. Sometimes unmarried clergy find their emotional needs met by developing a close relationship with one or two families in the church. These clergy may be invited over to family gatherings on holidays and other occasions. They may be unofficially adopted into these families and develop close ties to the children and extended family members.

Of course, the Church has long recognized that there are advantages to ministering as a single person. It gives one additional time and energy to engage in ministry, unhindered by marital and family demands. The apostle Paul recognized there were circumstances when one might choose not to be married. "Now to the unmarried and the widows I say: It is good for them to stay unmarried, as I am" (1 Cor. 7:8). However, because Paul acknowledged that some might find living a celibate life difficult, he added: "But if they cannot control themselves, they should marry, for it is better to marry than to burn with passion" (v. 9).

BUILDING SPIRITUAL VITALITY

There is close connection between a lowered spiritual vitality and a lowered resistance to sexual temptation. It is easy for a pastor to fall into the deception that simply being in ministry makes one immune to the devil's lies. Or, the pastor will begin to lie to others and even engage in self-deception in an attempt to justify actions that are improper. The next downward step is to try to be less then honest with God about this inner conflict of the heart.

To address the problem it is important to start with the spiritual dimension of our lives. Gula observes, "Given the link between the energies of spirituality and sexuality to strive towards wholeness and interpersonal communion, we ought to keep in mind the power of prayer and other spiritual disciplines to settle one's restless heart which yearns for communion and which will ultimately find full oneness only in God."[34] By spending time with God we can enjoy a closeness that can be like no other human relationship. When we know God intimately, we also have a greater capacity for intimacy in our human relationships, especially with a spouse.

▶ SETTING BOUNDARIES IN MINISTRY

One of the best protections against misconduct is to determine the outer limits of behavior, beyond which one will not go. This is referred to as *bound-*

ary-setting. While some may see erecting boundaries as being restrictive, maintaining boundaries actually brings us freedom.

Many years ago there was a study done on the importance of boundaries. An elementary school evaluated their grounds and decided that the fences around the playground restricted the students' freedom. Without the fences, they reasoned, the children will not feel hemmed in. They will be able to free their minds because they will not be fenced in like a herd of cattle. So, the fences came down and the teachers expected their students to begin expressing their new freedom in creative ways. What the adults observed as the students went out on the playground was the opposite of what they expected. Before the change, the children used every area of the playground, all the way up to the fence. But when the fences came down, they played only in the center of the play area. No one ventured out to the edges of the playground because it wasn't safe there anymore. In the end, the fences went back up. The children felt more free and safe when there were boundaries for their recess period.

Pastors also function better when they have predetermined limits or rules of conduct that govern daily practice. These boundaries provide protection and safety, both for the pastor and for the people who are part of the congregation. William Arnold says, "The safe place is the relationship itself, one in which the professional is aware of and respectful of the patient or parishioner's vulnerability."[35] Arnold, rather than trying to set a comprehensive code, has approached the issue of proper pastoral conduct by suggesting that a pastor determine certain boundaries, within which the pastor does ministry, especially counseling.

BOUNDARIES OF LOCATION

The place where personal counseling takes place sends a strong, unspoken message to the counselee. If a pastor sets a counseling session with someone of the opposite gender at a secluded restaurant, it may convey that there is another agenda at work. An office, on the other hand, gives an image of serious work. "When people come to the pastor's study, therefore, the place itself sets certain expectations and guidelines for behavior and subject matter. Those limits provide a sense of safety. That safety then provides freedom to explore sensitive matters with little fear or harm."[36] Every pastor will have people who will stop to talk in a hallway or on the street, but these times are not normally considered as formal counseling. Pastor Jim Smith says, "A formal counseling visit, with well-defined boundaries, creates a working environment for the counselee. There has been an appointment and an agreement to start on time and end on time. The counseling time is spent productively."[37]

There are some additional safeguards for counseling a person of the opposite gender in the office or pastor's study. It is important that someone else be present in the church and that the counselees be aware they are not alone with the pastor. If a secretary or janitor can remain in the building, it defuses the feeling that no one will know what happens. If no one else is available, a pastor could ask the spouse to come over to the church and be in the building during a counseling session. In addition, having a window in the office, even in the office door, reminds both pastor and counselee that someone could walk by at any time. If someone wants to counsel at the church and the pastor cannot find anyone to be in the building, it would be better to postpone the session until someone can be present and provide the needed protection.

Counseling in the pastor's home may sometimes be an alternative if the pastor does not have an office or no one can be at the church. It goes without saying that you should have your spouse or someone else present in the home, even if that person is not in the same room. If no other location is available, sometimes the only alternative is to meet in a public place. However, even a public venue can have pitfalls. We try to erect boundaries that will safeguard our reputation when we meet with a person of the opposite sex in a public setting. Most importantly, don't go to the home of the counselee without your spouse or a trusted friend accompanying you.

Arnold makes this additional suggestion. "Many female clergy find having lunch with a parishioner is a more private, less formal, time 'to talk.' If subjects arise that need more in-depth discussion, then a follow-up time can be arranged at the office."[38] Wherever you meet, it is a good idea to let someone— your secretary, a colleague, or your spouse—know who you are with and where you are meeting. This does provide protection if someone inquires about seeing the pastor with someone at a public location.

Setting boundaries of location is important, not only when meeting with adults of the opposite gender, but when meeting with children, teens, and even same-sex adults who may be dealing with sexual identity issues. It is always better to err on the side of caution. If someone accuses you of improper conduct, you may have no defense other than your own word if you have been totally alone with the other person.

BOUNDARIES OF CONTACT

Many people today are very sensitive about their personal space and what happens within that space. Austin Tucker observes about male pastors, "A generation ago, a pastor had to be very careful about showing affection to the ladies. He couldn't hold on too long when he was shaking a girl's hand. Now he is regarded with suspicion if he hugs other men or children of either sex."[39] Part of the problem stems from the growing suspicion toward the clergy as the result of publicity in the media over sexual misconduct. People question the motives of all pastors because of the misdeeds of a few. Also, the criteria for what constitutes sexual harassment can be vague. What a pastor may intend as a friendly pastoral hug can be misinterpreted as an unwanted sexual advance. Arnold says, "It is a shame that we need to be extra sensitive to matters of touching, but we live in a world in which touch is too often invasive instead of supportive. On the other hand, sensitivity to touch is a reminder of what a powerful and healing force it can be when offered with care."[40]

Touch is a way to affirm friendship and appreciation. A young person returns from serving in the military, and the reception area of the airport is lined with excited family and friends. There are hugs and tears at the welcome celebration. People hug at college reunions, funeral services, birthday parties, and wedding receptions. It is one physical expression people use to show their love and concern for one another. This might be the more contemporary equivalent of Paul's often expressed admonition in many of his letters, "Greet one another with a holy kiss" (Rom. 16:16).

The power of touch can be powerful when a pastor lays a hand on a dying person's arm in a hospital room. A touch on the shoulder of a grieving parent that has lost a child may speak more at that moment than any words you may say. But touch is also a means of communication with a sender, a recipient, and a message. Sometimes the issue is influenced by personality: some people are naturally huggers, and some are not. And because the message is nonverbal, the intent is not always clear. In our day, the interpretation of the message by the receiver is given higher credence than the intent of the sender. Your hug of support to a person of the opposite gender at the end of a counseling session may be read by the counselee as a sexual advance or invitation. In sexual harassment cases the victim is usually asked, "How did you feel?" rather than "What do you think the other person intended?" You need to be aware of the unintentional message you may be saying by your touch.

There are cultural differences to deal with too. When visiting in France, I noticed that all the people in the church kissed each other on both cheeks as a part of their normal greeting practice. This included people of the opposite sex and the same sex. On the other hand, other cultures have strong taboos on people touching one another.

A word of caution or restraint is in order for pastors. Remember, we may be sending an unintended message by our touch that the other person may find offensive. Ask yourself, "Why am I touching this person? Am I conveying the love of Christ, or does this create a sense of sensual excitement?" It is better to act with restraint than be put in a position of being misunderstood by your actions. Gary Collins says, "Even though touching can be an excellent way to make contact and give support, for any individual (including you) it should be guided by this general rule: if in doubt—don't!"[41]

BOUNDARIES OF EMOTION

We need to understand that as humans, our words and actions are closely tied to our emotions. Certain words or combinations of words have great emotional power. Think of the emotions that come at the mention of the words such as *mother, family, country,* or even *God.* This is the reason some people enjoy poetry. It can evoke powerful images that can bore to the core of the heart. *Love* can be one of those words. In the English language this one word can express how we feel about things ranging from pizza, to our spouse, and even to God. It is easy for our words to be misinterpreted emotionally by others. Arnold warns, "We may assure a person of our love and care only to discover later that our words were heard as a proposal or a more intimate relationship. Assurance to someone that he or she is 'special' to us may be interpreted as permission for them to call us and/or show up unannounced wherever we may be."[42]

We need to be candid about our own feelings as well. If we are honest with ourselves, we understand our great skill at self-deception. It is easy to deny that we feel any attraction to another individual. Yet, even though feelings may be pushed down below the surface, they are still alive and well. A better approach is to acknowledge that such feelings actually exist. At the same time we need to understand that we do not need to be ruled by our feelings or emotions. They can be controlled. We need to examine the consequences that following these temptations of emotion could have on our family, friends, and our reputation. What are the professional consequences of yielding to our emotions and losing the privilege of fulfilling our calling as ministers? Also, what would God think about our actions if we followed these wrong feelings?

Joseph in Gen. 39 must have understood the danger of responding to the emotions of another person. Potiphar's wife did her best to draw him into an illicit sexual relationship. He was a young, handsome man, and she found him attractive. One day she grabbed him by the clothes and again tried to entice him. Was he tempted emotionally and physically? Absolutely! But Joseph also knew it was wrong and realized that it could have devastating consequences. He made a decision and took immediate action. He "left his cloak in her hand and ran out of the house" (v. 12). Whenever we begin to near the boundary line of emotion, we need to face it, and, if necessary, we need to flee.

BOUNDARIES OF TIME

Members of the flock may feel that the pastor should be on duty twenty-four hours a day, seven days a week to help them with their needs. Because clergy generally do not charge for their time, some people think they have the right to unlimited pastoral access. Also, while pastors do need to spend time each week with the congregation and people in the community, they also need to have private time for prayer, Bible study, and sermon preparation. Every pastor has a responsibility, as a part of the spiritual commitment to a congregation, to be available in times of need. For some, this is a natural part of their personal makeup. They love being with people and could spend all their time in contact with others. Others may discover that providing personal care is somewhat unnatural and demands great effort, so they avoid it whenever possible.

Both positions, unavailability and total availability, are unhealthy if taken to extremes. Each pastor must come to a personal understanding of how much time each week should be devoted to the care of others, based on one's personal tendencies and the time needed to carry out the other responsibilities of the parish.

Having an awareness of time restraints is certainly important when it comes to the pastor's counseling load. Smith writes, "It's probably best for a pastor's mental health to devote no more than ten to twelve hours a week to counseling, unless this in one's primary responsibility."[43] Try to conduct counseling sessions during normal business hours if at all possible. While there are emergencies, generally people can make it to the right location at the time that will provide the best security for everyone. Most people don't quibble about an appointment time when they need to see a medical doctor for a serious physical need.

While we do need to be flexible when working with people's schedules, we also need to manage our own time. Often a pastor's time problem is not so much the lack of time but poor management of the time that is available. One can run from one activity to another from morning to night, keeping busy while neglecting the most important needs of the congregation. Because pastors care for others they can easily succumb to exhaustion and then discouragement. Noyce writes, "Burnout comes to the compassionate, pastoral person as readily as it does to the compassionate social activist."[44]

A key to developing time boundaries is to keep and manage a time schedule. And a part of the time in that weekly schedule needs to be reserved for your spouse and family. One of the best ways to protect family time is to actually pencil in those blocks of time you want as family time. If a person asks about an appointment at one of those times, you can honestly say that the time has been reserved. Pastors are the ones who ultimately decide how their time is used.

Each of us is given the same 168 hours each week. We can waste our time by sleeping late and quitting early. We can fret over the fact that we don't have enough time to get everything done. We can unwisely allot our time by neglecting to do the important things while spending our efforts on things that matter little in the long run. God gives us these 168 hours that, when gone, will never return again. How will we use those precious hours? As stewards of all God's blessings, including time, we need to use the moments he gives us wisely.

▶ LIVING WITH INTEGRITY

We all admire people of integrity. One person was elected to a very high, prestigious office in his denomination. He felt the pressure to accept the position because of the confidence people had placed in him. They were sure he could do the job. But this man was also a person of integrity. He had to know this was God's calling for his future. After praying and seeking God's direction, he returned to the body that had elected him and announced that he could not accept the honor and the office because he could not honestly say that God had released him from his current assignment. The crowd erupted in a standing ovation because they were in the presence of a man who put his integrity above his personal ego.

Integrity is more than what we do. It is who we are. Yet this inner integrity must ultimately drive our outward actions. Rick Ezell says, "A person of character is whole; his life is put together. People with integrity have nothing to hide and nothing to fear. Their lives are open books."[45]

Although integrity is highly valued, it is easily lost. While one can destroy a reputation in a single public act of wrongdoing, integrity can also be lost by a series of small, seemingly insignificant compromises over a period of time.

In Gen. 13 Abraham's nephew Lot was given the choice of grazing land, and he selected the fertile plain that included the region's Sin City capital—Sodom. At first he was attracted to the rich grasslands of the whole plain, but then slowly moved closer and closer to Sodom. He "pitched his tents near Sodom" (v. 12) and soon "he was living in Sodom" (Gen. 14:12). While Lot was disturbed by the lawless lifestyle of his neighbors (according to 2 Pet. 2:7), he became an elder of the city (Gen. 19). When God finally destroyed Sodom, Lot's wife died because she had become so attached to the lifestyle she couldn't bear to leave. Lot's loss of integrity also affected his two daughters who fled the city with him.

Our integrity shows when our outer lives authentically reflect who we are on the inside. We speak the truth and reject falsehoods. It used to be that a person's word was a person's bond. Now we need legal contracts just to make sure the parties do what they promise. One of the sad testimonials to our lack of integrity as a culture is the need for lie detector tests.

People of integrity take a stand for the right even when it is unpopular. Rick Ezell tells of a new surgeon who had a reputation for being rough on the nurses and others he worked with in surgery. At the end of his first day he was informed that although the surgical team had started with twelve sponges, they could only account for eleven. The doctor declared that he had removed all the sponges, but the nurse insisted they could count only eleven. In an authoritative tone the surgeon said he was going to suture the incision. Even though it could mean her job for insubordination, the nurse yelled for the surgeon to stop. That's when the surgeon moved his foot to reveal the twelfth sponge under his shoe. He smiled and said to her, "You'll do."[46] Integrity means both knowing what is right and doing it. Christians place a high premium on knowing that their pastor is, first and foremost, a person of high integrity.

▸ A GREAT CALLING

There is a temptation sometimes to look at the vocation of pastoral ministry and be overwhelmed. The expectations of the church are sometimes unclear. The tasks may be more than any one person can possibly perform. The needs of the people exceed the energies and abilities of even the best shepherd. The community places your importance in terms of influence just a little above the town dog catcher. The potential for growth seems almost nonexistent. The congregation doesn't seem to appreciate your efforts. The people you depend on to help you have serious flaws. And the list goes on and on. Who in the world would want to be a pastor? Sometimes all you have to hold to is the truth that God has called you.

Monday mornings can be especially brutal when you are emotionally drained from a busy Sunday. It's easiest to want to quit on Mondays. But then Tuesday comes and someone stops by with a sack of fresh corn and some juicy, ripe tomatoes "for the pastor's family." Wednesday afternoon you have a chance to help a young couple repair a marriage that seemed destined for the divorce court. You find yourself on Thursday morning getting so excited about the passage of Scripture for your sermon you simply can't write the ideas down fast enough. After school on Friday a teen from your church meets you for a soft drink and tells you that God is speaking about possibly going into pastoral ministry. You spend the next hour encouraging that young person to follow God's will. Saturday is a beautiful day and you spend the afternoon with your family on a picnic. The time is so relaxing it leaves you energized. And then it's Sunday morning. There is a new couple attending your young adult Sunday

School class. God's presence is so real as the congregation worships that you feel you could almost reach out and touch him. You are able to preach with a sense of freedom and anointing. The response of the people is overwhelming. You stand by the door as the last person finally leaves to go home and you say, "Wow! I wouldn't trade this job for anything. This was a great Sunday!"

Being a pastor has its high, ecstatic moments followed by dry discouraging times. It can be a roller-coaster existence. You know it and sometimes even the people in the congregation can see it. But most of them look below the surface to who you are. They are looking at your character. They ask themselves: Can we trust our pastor because he or she exhibits the characteristics we expect of a Christian? Does our pastor during the week live the kind of life he or she preaches about on Sunday?

What people want, more than anything else, is a pastor they can respect and follow—one whose character and conduct is above reproach.

▶ QUESTIONS FOR REFLECTION

▷ Why should parishioners have the right to know that their pastor will not share their story with others?

▷ What are some ways pastors can protect themselves from yielding to sexual temptation?

▷ How can a pastor demonstrate integrity in front of the congregation? Give some specific examples.

SIXTEEN

THE PASTOR'S PERSONAL LIFE

Two years into his first pastorate Darren Anderson had come to the end of his rope. It wasn't supposed to be like this. He had moved to this small community with some idealistic notions about the ministry, but he was unprepared for what he had experienced thus far.

Darren knew that he didn't fit the typical profile most churches were looking for in a pastor. For one thing, he wasn't married. He didn't think it was that big of an issue, but he discovered that a few women in the church felt that he didn't understand their viewpoint on some issues. Perhaps they were right. Maybe if he did have a wife he would have someone to talk to—someone who could listen to his frustrations and help him understand the feminine perspective.

Another thing he lacked was a background in denominational issues. Darren had become a Christian during his freshman year of college. No one in his family had ever attended any church with regularity, so he had known practically nothing about having a personal faith. He had chosen a Christian university because he had been offered a scholarship to play baseball. It was in the chapel services during his first semester that God not only changed his heart but called him to a new vocation—pastoral ministry.

During his senior year Darren had tried to learn everything he could from the pastor he worked with during his required internship, but there were many ministry issues he had never thought about until people were calling him pastor. Parishioners were constantly bringing up some unwritten rule or custom of church practice that everyone (but him) seemed to understand. How could he possibly know about all the intricacies of church culture and practice? They had never taught him these things in school.

Darren also struggled with his use of time. Several people in the church held the notion that because he was not married he didn't need a day off. For instance, he was expected to be at every committee meeting and the eight members of the senior adult Sunday School class made it clear that he needed to visit them in their homes at least once a month.

But Darren also contributed to the problem. He wanted so desperately to show his father that he was not a failure that he almost killed himself trying to be a success. On a light week he put in seventy-five hours. And it was not uncommon during a busy week for him to work ninety hours or more.

While Darren's emotional reserve tank was on the negative side of empty, he kept right on working, week after week, without a day off. How could he afford to take any time off when there was so much work to do and so few people willing to do their part.

If only he had just one person that he could talk to about ministry issues, it would help so much. But the closest colleague he really knew well and trusted lived four hours away in another state.

Darren wondered if his current lifestyle was normal for people in the ministry. Maybe he just didn't have what it took to be a pastor. If he just had someone he could talk to, just to get some perspective. But since there was no one around to help him, many days he thought seriously about quitting.

One Monday Darren was sitting down for breakfast at the local coffee shop, already dreading the full schedule ahead. Peg, the waitress who served him every day, said, "Pastor Darren, there's a man I'd like you to meet. He pastors over in the next town but often drives over here for a meal when he wants to get away for a few hours. Let me introduce you two. You may have a lot in common."

Jack Collins stood and gripped Darren with a warm handshake and invited him to join him at his table. In no time they both sensed a bond of friendship. Although they were from different theological backgrounds, and Jack was at least fifteen years older, Darren felt that here was a real brother—one who would understand him and give him some guidance. As Darren began to share some of his frustrations, Jack sensed that God had led him there that morning to be a mentor and friend to this young, inexperienced pastor.

Before they left the coffee shop that morning they made a covenant to meet every Monday morning for breakfast and conversation.

Darren found that Jack's experience as a pastor gave him a helpful pattern for reorganizing his work schedule and his priorities. Jack was also a safe confidant— someone who would not be judgmental when he vented his frustrations.

For Jack, seeing Darren's struggle and growth took him back to his early days of ministry as a staff member of a large church. The senior pastor had played racquetball with Jack every Wednesday noon and then took him to lunch where they talked. Jack now understood how important that relationship had been to him as he was starting out—with all of his questions and doubts. Since then Jack had wanted to be that kind of mentor/friend to someone else in ministry. And here was his opportunity: Darren, a young guy from a different denomination, pastoring in a different town.

God had brought them both together for a purpose. Now Darren could become more competent for ministry. As for Jack, God fulfilled his desire to become a mentor, like the apostle Paul, helping young Timothys starting out as pastors. Both found fulfillment and satisfaction from their relationship.

▶ Who, in the World, Am I?

We often get a clue to a person's identity by the kind of hat perched on top of the head. Sometimes it's the style of the hat. When I lived in the western United States and saw a person with a soiled and creased cowboy hat, I could assume that this person had actually spent time on a horse herding cattle. In the winter, certain types of knitted hats are associated with skiers and snowboarders. Some caps announce allegiance to a sports team or to a business. If one has a hat advertising a feed and seed store, there is a good chance the person is a farmer.

What kind of hat does a pastor wear? Speaking literally, while some religions may have specific head covering for their clergy on special occasions, in my culture there is no uniform headgear that would designate one as a pastor. However, the subject of clergy headgear gets a bit more complicated when we speak allegorically, because symbolically we wear many hats.

We put on our pastor hat when we take on that role while working in the church or representing Christ in the community. But we're not just pastors. As individuals we wear different hats—in other words, take on other roles—as a spouse, family member, friend, colleague, community leader, sports fan, neighbor, human being, and so on. Because of that, pastors sometimes struggle identifying what hat they should be wearing at a given moment.

Perhaps your ten-year-old daughter has won the spelling contest for her grade and has been invited to participate in the citywide spelling contest at 10 A.M. tomorrow. You look at your schedule and discover that an elderly saint in your church is going to have hip replacement surgery at the same time in a hospital forty miles away. Which role will you assume that morning: your pastor role or your parental responsibility?

Or, maybe you have been selected to be one of only a few clergy on an international denominational commission studying the future direction for the church. The joy of this honor is tempered because it conflicts with a gathering your spouse's family has been planning for the last two years to honor the ninetieth birthday of the family patriarch. Your kids want you to go to the family gathering because it is going to be held in a great vacation spot with lots of activities. However, the opportunity to serve on such a denominational commission may come along only once in a lifetime. Both are important activities—but you can only participate in one.

Actually, the bulk of ministry does not involve such momentous decisions. Instead, most weeks would be classified as rather ordinary. Pastors work hard during the week to prepare a sermon to preach or preparing for another role on Sunday. Then they start all over again, making the same preparation for the next week. People come to talk to us about their issues, and we discover, after a while, that we are hearing the same problems again and again. The people we pastor are, for the most part, the same people we met when we first moved to the church.

Pastoral ministry is much more about dealing with processes rather than completing tasks. Oh, there are the building dedications and the homegoing of saints whose race has been run; but it seems like much of the work of ministry is not the kind that can be finished in a week because it is ongoing in the lives of people. This can create frustration, because it is sometimes hard to know where one's private life ends and ministry begins.

Suppose you were out on a "date" with your spouse at a nice restaurant because you need time together to connect. As you are about to order, a couple from your church sees you and asks you if it is OK for them to join you at your table for dinner. You feel you can't say no even though you really need this time to be together as a couple. As your guests sit down at the other two chairs, your role shifts from being a spouse to being a pastor.

There are certainly rewards any pastor feels as parishioners grow and develop. It is humbling to know that we have had a part in the Spirit's maturing process. But pastors can also experience deep disappointment when people leave the congregation or, worse, fall away from the faith and become Kingdom casualties.

The frustration level increases when the demands of ministry seem to take all your time and energy. You are not sure that you are really qualified or gifted to do some of the tasks that fall on your shoulders simply because you are the pastor.

It's hard to walk on water when your feet are made of clay.

Maybe that is why Paul reminds us, "But we have this treasure in jars of clay to show that this all-surpassing power is from God and not from us" (2 Cor. 4:7). God knows we are human, and we need to learn to accept ourselves in the same way.

▶ UNDERSTANDING YOURSELF

If we as pastor-shepherds are going to be effective in helping others, we must first begin with an honest appraisal of our personal lives. This is easier said than done. While it seems obvious that we would know ourselves better than anyone else would know us, others see aspects of our lives that we may not observe.

Examining our own lives can be a painful process. One reason is that we can be clever at deceiving ourselves. We may create an image of what we would like to be without going to the effort of making the changes that are needed to become that person. At the core of our being we may be more concerned about our own self-interests, rather than the interests of others. Or, we may be so desirous of pleasing others that we cannot think about our own needs. The path to true self-discovery is sometimes easier with the help of another individual who can view us objectively. But it must begin with our willingness to take a realistic look at ourselves. Such a journey could begin by honestly answering the following questions.

Do I really desire to be like Jesus?

While this question may appear to be so basic that the answer is obvious, it is actually the central question of ministry. If our answer is yes, then it stands to reason that we must be willing to do all we can, by the grace of God, to become more Christlike. Our becoming more like Jesus comes out of the quality time we spend in relationship with him. But we can find it a challenge setting aside time to be with God. Richard Armstrong writes, "Nothing is more essential to your survival in ministry than your devotional life. . . . Some fail to begin because they think they don't have time to do what they'd really like to do. . . . If you haven't already opened your heart, soul, and mind to the presence of God, the time to do that is not later, but *now*."[1]

Find time each day for private prayer and the reading of the Word, as well as following other spiritual disciplines. You may have read about some saint of the past that arose at 4 A.M. to pray. You may be a night person who cannot think a coherent thought before 8 A.M. and you cannot imagine getting up regularly that early. If you're a morning person, you may read with wonder and amazement the accounts of Jesus spending the night in prayer, since you have trouble keeping your eyes open after 9 P.M. The time of day you spend with Jesus is not as important as developing the practice of having a daily appointment with him. How and when you practice your devotional habits should match your temperament and personality.

Also, don't let a particular method become a straitjacket, restricting the way God wants to interact with you. Some people like to pray on their knees for an hour. Others find great freedom walking and praying outdoors or in a church sanctuary. There are people who find it difficult to concentrate on any task for a long period and opt for two or three shorter devotional segments throughout the day. When I was in the pastorate, praying weekly with other local pastors helped keep me accountable for my spiritual development. Others prefer to meet periodically with a personal spiritual guide who will be objective about their spiritual progress. Keep experimenting until you find an approach that works effectively for you.

There has been a recent resurgence of interest in spiritual formation among Protestants. Authors such as Richard Foster, Dallas Willard, and others have helped us apply some of the ancient practices of the Church to our contemporary age. Pastors can take advantage of many excellent seminars, conferences, and retreats designed to help develop the interior life with God. With all the helps available, ignorance is no excuse. For each of us it comes down to the personal question—how much do I really want to be like Christ? The words of an old gospel song form a wonderful prayer:

> I have one deep, supreme desire
> That I may be like Jesus.
> To this I fervently aspire
> That I may be like Jesus.
> I want my heart his home to be
> So that a watching world may see
> His likeness shining forth in me.
> I want to be like Jesus.[2]

Am I willing to be an example to others?

Some pastors struggle with the idea that they should be expected to live at a higher level moral of conduct than their parishioners. Their argument is that pastors are humans, like everyone else. Since all believers are called to be like Christ, why should people in ministry be held to a higher standard of conduct than the laypeople in the pew. However, as William Willimon argues, being an example is one role a pastor cannot escape. "I think most of the ethical problems of pastors are not due to our forgetting that we are 'persons,' but rather when we forget that we are pastors. . . . Though pastors may chafe at the burden, there is no way to escape the truth that we are called to be 'examples to the flock,' as most of the rites of ordination put it, quoting 1 Peter 5:3."[3]

The apostle Paul certainly had no problem, as pastor, of taking on the role of modeling the faith before the congregation. He boldly proclaimed to the church in Corinth, "Follow my example, as I follow the example of Christ" (1 Cor. 11:1). When Paul left the church in Philippi, the first church he established on the European continent, he had no written manual of church conduct to leave behind. The only pattern for living was his own, and the lives of his companions, Silas and Luke. That is why he told this young church later in a letter, "Join with others in following my example, brothers, and take note of those who live according to the pattern we gave you" (Phil. 3:17). Paul complimented the Christians in Thessalonica when he wrote, "You became imitators of us and of the Lord; in spite of severe suffering, you welcomed the message with the joy given by the Holy Spirit. And so you became a model for all the believers in Macedonia and Achaia" (1 Thess. 1:6-7).

This idea of being an example flies in the face of the current culture's attitude of live and let live, with nonjudgmental acceptance. In the minds of many today, there are no objective standards of right or wrong conduct. Each person can determine a personal code of ethics. This is really a return to the amoral approach of Israel described during the period of the Judges. "In those days Israel had no king; everyone did as he saw fit" (Judg. 17:6).

Given the current climate in some denominations of tolerance and acceptance of activities that are clearly in opposition to biblical standards, many laypeople have been left confused and disillusioned. There are clergy today who not only do not want to declare any activity as sinful but also do not want to be held up as an example of moral living because that could be considered as condemning other viewpoints. Willimon counters this current attitude. "We are not being naively idealistic or demandingly realistic when we ask our leaders to be exemplary persons and, when they show that they are not, to ask them to remove themselves from positions of leadership. The needs of the community are superior to the needs of its leaders."[4]

Like it or not, pastors must be examples to believers. Paul deals with the practical application of being an example in 1 Cor. 8, when he discusses food sacrificed to idols. For Paul, these idols were not real gods. The food itself came from the Creator God, and Paul felt very comfortable eating this meat without any negative spiritual effect. But there were some new believers who had come out of that idol-worship culture. These people just couldn't bring themselves to eat such food. On the issue of personal rights and freedoms versus the destruction of a weaker person's faith, Paul's position was crystal clear. "Therefore, if what I eat causes my brother to fall into sin, I will never eat meat again, so that I will not cause him to fall" (1 Cor. 8:13).

Does this mean that the pastor needs to live up to the very highest standards of an extreme legalist? No! Paul would not submit to the opinions of the Judaizers, who insisted that Jewish Christians should not eat with Gentile Christians. He opposed Peter in Gal. 2 for allowing these legalists to take away Peter's freedom in Christ to treat all believers alike. Paul distinguishes between the needs of weak, immature Christians and the misinformed pressure of those who do not understand grace.

Because pastors are examples, we need to evaluate what we do, not only by our own understanding of God's will for our lives but also by how our actions will impact others in the church. Pastor Paul Cedar states the issue well, "I believe there are certain activities that Christian leaders simply cannot attend with integrity. I am not suggesting we establish legalistic standards, but I have seen many pastors and Christian leaders become involved in activities that are detrimental to them, their families, and the people they serve."[5] Cedar tells a personal account of a community dinner in Los Angeles where he was asked to pray the invocation. He was seated next to the chief of police, the speaker of the evening. The servers began to pour wine. On some other occasions he would simply let the person pour a glass rather than objecting, even though he had no intention of drinking the wine. However, that night he quietly asked the server to take away the wine glass. The next morning the picture on the front page of the *Los Angeles Times* showed Paul Cedar and the chief sitting together at the table. Cedar's wine glass was gone while the speaker's glass was full. "My first thought was how it would have appeared to some if I had allowed the waiter to leave a filled glass. That experience, among others, brought home to me the truth that when I'm on secular turf, my integrity is examined even more closely."[6]

Who am I trying to please?

Jesus said, "No one can serve two masters" (Matt. 6:24). Yet, if some pastors were asked who they answered to in ministry, they could give three dozen names. What are the expectations for a pastor, and who decides which expectations are valid? Some of these may be clearly delineated in a job description agreed upon when a new pastor arrives. Often this list of expectations is formed in the process of a church board seeking a new pastor. They begin asking themselves what they are looking for in a potential pastor—the skills a pastor should posses, the tasks a pastor should perform, and the list grows. It is an interesting experience to try to put a time allotment to each expectation. Usually, when the list is complete, more time would be needed to fulfill the tasks than there are hours in the week. The board or committee must then begin whittling down the list of expectations to reflect only the most important ones, agreed to by the majority.

But there may also be unwritten expectations that may not be verbalized but are recorded in the memory banks of some members. These may have their genesis in an activity, actual or imagined, that a beloved pastor in the past did well. A person may think, "I remember when Pastor Jones was here, he visited our house at least once a month." Actually, Pastor Jones may have been dead for thirty years, and when he was the pastor he only visited about once a year. Memories can be incomplete and selective at best.

Other hidden agendas may arise out of an individual's specific interest. A church member may be a part of the local Rotary Club and strongly believe that the pastor should join as well. This person may be very disappointed to discover that this pastor does not see being a Rotarian as high on the priority list.

Others view the pastor as the one who has the responsibility of introducing all new programs—plans to keep the youth interested or attract people from other churches or solve all the church's money problems. Some churches have an unwritten expectation that the pastor is to be a jack-of-all-trades. They want someone who can do everything for everybody. One pastor described the expectation in his congregation, "The pastor can pick up whatever church members do not want to do—teaching classes, filling in, janitorial work, secretarial work, lead the youth, be the errand boy!"[7]

For to many of us, our most demanding taskmaster is located six inches above our shoulders in our own brain. We think we should be able to evangelize like Billy Graham, lead like John Maxwell, write like Max Lucado, preach like Chuck Swindoll, counsel like James Dobson, or build the church like Rick Warren. And we are terribly disappointed when we don't measure up in even one of those areas. It is easy to then doubt our own God-given abilities and stop doing anything out of a fear of failure.

Expectations, no matter what the source, can be sometimes ambiguous and terribly unfair. We can find comfort from the concept that ultimately, there is only one person whose expectations are really important—one voice we listen to for affirmation. We are ministers of Jesus Christ, and his opinion of our work is the only one that really counts. Sometimes, though we do our best to please others, we can't meet their expectations. Often we disappoint ourselves because we fall short of what we believe we should have achieved. People may not always understand or agree with what we have done. But if our Heavenly Father says, "Well done, good and faithful servant," that should be all we need.

Do I work from my strengths?

The New Testament teaches that all believers are given spiritual gifts that enable them to contribute to the building up of the Body of Christ. As pastors, we are each gifted by God to provide a unique ministry for the Kingdom. In addition, we usually have developed some additional skills that contribute to our ministerial effectiveness. What is frustrating for some of us is the fact that God has not given us, or any pastor for that matter, all of the spiritual gifts or human talents. In fact, God has wired each one of us uniquely so we can serve a specific church with effectiveness at a particular moment in time.

Sometimes these spiritual gifts and natural talents can give us a sense of overconfidence. Jack Nicklaus, arguably the greatest professional golfer to ever play the game, was interviewed about his career and the sport he loved. Nicklaus burst on the golfing scene as a teenager from Ohio and soon began to win tournaments, including some Majors. After reaching a certain level of competence, he began to feel that he didn't have to practice as much. He could simply rely on his talent and experience. That led to a dry time in his career where he was not that successful in winning tournaments. What woke Jack Nicklaus up was the premature death of his father at fifty to pancreatic cancer. In his grief Nicklaus admitted to himself that he had not really given his best efforts to develop his golfing skills and had disappointed his father who had been so proud of his accomplishments. From that time on he dedicated his life to being the best golfer he could be, and by doing so, make his late father proud.

In 2005 I watched Jack Nicklaus play for perhaps the last time in his own Memorial Tournament in Dublin, Ohio. Since he was planning to retire from professional competition, it would have been understandable for him to simply coast along and enjoy the last season. After all, when he was in his prime he had been the best in the game. Instead, he was out on the course playing a practice round with Fred Couples. Also in the group was a third person, Jim Flick, one of the leading golf coaches in the world. At every tee, Nicklaus turned to the coach for advice and suggestions on his swing. As I watched I thought, *Jack Nicklaus, this gifted golfer who has won more tournaments and more major tournaments than anyone in golfing history, still seeks advice to improve his natural giftedness.* What does it say to us about improving our natural talents and utilizing our spiritual gifts for greater effectiveness?

There are preachers who are gifted communicators and rely on their natural abilities to impress crowds. Instead of doing the hard work of studying the text to preach the Bible, they weave together stories without a connection to the Scriptures they are supposed to explain. People go away entertained at the emotional level but hungry for spiritual sustenance. As I recently listened to a preacher follow this pattern, I thought how much more effective he could have been if he had really tried to expose the scriptural meaning of the text to his listeners. With gifting comes responsibility. When we fail to develop and utilize what God has given us, we become like the man in Jesus' parable who buried his master's money rather than investing it.

Our ministry will be most effective in those areas where we have our greatest gifting, abilities, and interest. Ben Patterson comments, "One thing that has stuck with me from the administrative books I read in my hopeful youth was a Peter Drucker maxim for the effective executive: we should determine the one or two things that only we can give to the organization, give it, and delegate everything else."[8] While that may be impossible, especially for the pastor of a small church, it affirms the truth that we should give the greatest energies to those top priority items we do well.

But, how do we deal with the things that must be done, yet hate the thought of doing? Our natural response is to procrastinate, hoping that the responsibility will go away or that Jesus will return again if we wait long enough. The problem with procrastination is the nagging guilt, the ought-to in the back of our minds that keeps us from enjoying life until we complete the task. Pastor Kent Hughes writes about his dislike of confronting people. "Nevertheless, when I must confront, I find it best to attend to the matter as soon as possible. If I procrastinate the situation only becomes worse, and since I'm not particularly gifted at it, the encounter also becomes worse."[9] My own experience has taught me that the possible scenarios I create in my head as I anticipate an unpleasant task are far worse than what really happens when I go ahead and do it.

How do I handle criticism?

It may seem strange, but there are some pastors who seem to actually thrive on controversy and conflict. With their combative personality, they enjoy confronting critics to prove that their position is superior. Usually these people do not last long in pastoral ministry. Lovers make better shepherds than fighters. And because most of us as pastors really do care about the people we serve, any personal criticism leveled against us is painful.

It hurts because we have made ourselves vulnerable by extending personal ministry. If you were in the tiger country of Africa, and a tiger attacked you, you would not be surprised. After all, attacking is natural to a wild tiger. But what if you had worked in a zoo with a tiger for years and developed a trust with this animal. If this tiger suddenly attacked without warning, you would feel the pain of disappointment as well as the physical wounds of the attack. Pastors understand that not everyone in the world is sympathetic to people who try to serve Jesus. But when pastors are personally attacked by a people in the church they have reached out to in loving ministry, the wounds go deep.

We begin to understand in a small way what Jesus must have felt on the Cross when the people for whom he was dying spat at him and yelled in derision. It is significant that Jesus at that moment cried out, "Father, forgive them, for they do not know what they are doing" (Luke 23:34). The truth is, sometimes people wound us without being aware that they are doing it. People can become so self-absorbed by their own pain that they do not think about the consequences of their words or actions upon others.

But some people can also be very aware of the hurt they are inflicting on others. They stick the proverbial knife between the ribs and then twist it. In those moments, when we are on the receiving end of a painful insult, it is particularly difficult to accept Jesus' words in the Sermon on the Mount: "Blessed are you when people insult you, persecute you and falsely say all kinds of evil against you because of me. Rejoice and be glad, because great is your reward in heaven, for in the same way they persecuted the prophets before you" (Matt. 5:11-12). The issue is not whether unjust criticism will come to us. It happens to anyone in leadership. The question is whether we have learned to deal with it constructively.

It is also possible for us to attract criticism by the way we handle an issue. Jay Kesler, retired president of Taylor University, wrote about the conflict he had with boards who acted as though he did not understand complex financial issues. "I eventually realized that my resentment was primarily due to ego, that I felt I needed to prove I was as smart as they were. Over time, however, I came to look at it more as the body of Christ functioning in all its parts."[10] I have observed pastors whose egos would not allow them to admit that they were wrong. It is hard, but necessary, to honestly ask ourselves when we are overly sensitive about an issue: *Why am I so insistent about having this decision go my way?* When we as pastors take the position that this resolution must go my way or else, we discourage others from freely expressing their own opinions on the matter.

There is wisdom in the counsel of other Christian leaders. Kesler says, "Another way to overcome resentment and deflect criticism is to not make decisions on your own. . . . Involve your board in the decision making process. You don't have to be smarter than everybody else, and you don't have to carry the load of making decisions alone."[11] When the Jerusalem Council came to an important decision regarding the Jews and Gentiles, they sought a consensus among the leaders. The Book of Acts confirms the unity of their decision when it says, "It seemed good to the Holy Spirit and to us."[12] Shared decisions usually result in consensus. The results provide enough praise to spread around when things work out well. It also defuses criticism if a decision turns out poorly.

It is important to remember that God has a way of taking hurtful situations and turning them around to bring glory to God. Joseph's response to his brother's cruelties is a model of forgiveness. "You intended to harm me, but God intended it for good to accomplish what is now being done, the saving of many lives" (Gen. 50:20). Forgiveness is not the normal response to criticism. It is a supernatural response. A. W. Tozer wrote of two kinds of hurts Christians may face: the pain of double-mindedness and the pain of the crucified self. "The pain of double-mindedness is like a toothache that lasts a lifetime . . . filling you with resentment, anger and envy. The pain of the crucified self, on the other hand, is a deep, terrible, surgical pain. But once it's over, it's over. It doesn't make you cry out anymore."[13]

▶ CARING FOR YOURSELF

When you become a pastor you do take on the responsibility of caring for the flock. If you are married and have children, you also have relational concerns for other members of your family. But as a person you also have a responsibility to take care of yourself. Richard Armstrong suggests that caring for oneself is a process of re-creation. "You must recreate for your own sanity, for your own physical, mental, emotional, and, yes, even spiritual well-being."[14]

You can't depend upon others to take care of you. You can't blame others for not watching out for your needs. Taking care of yourself is not an expression of selfishness. It is really a response of stewardship for all God has graciously given you. I can remember when I was a child, hearing preachers say, "I would rather burn out for Jesus, than rust out." I never really cared for either choice, although burning out sounded much more spiritual. But there is a third option—caring for yourself so you can be at maximum effectiveness for God throughout your life.

Pastors often choose a lopsided lifestyle. Some pour their energies into their pastoral responsibilities and totally neglect their physical bodies. Others are faithful to pump iron every day but never crack a book to improve their intellect. There are pastors who neglect the administrative responsibilities of the church because they are always drinking coffee with people at the local café. And still others seldom leave their computers to venture out into their communities. Often, when they see that life is out of balance, they totally shift their energies to another focus and go overboard with it. For them, life is like a pendulum, where life is centered only when it reaches the bottom of a swing on the way to another extreme. A better approach for self-care is to seek balance.

Have you ever watched a worker at an auto tire store install a tire on a rim? Logically, all he would need to do would be to get the tubeless tire inside the rim, inflate it with air so the tire makes an airtight seal against the rim, and then bolt it onto the car. After all, the rims are round and the tires are round because they are mass-produced at a factory. It should work perfectly. If the repairman simply put the tire on the rim, the tire would perform fine at slow speed—ten to twenty miles an hour. But when the speed reached fifty miles an hour, the wheel would begin to shake. The problem is that there are slight imperfections in both the rim and the tire. This is the reason the tire installer performs one additional step—balancing the tire. To find where there is an imbalance, the worker puts the mounted tire on a machine and spins it at high speed to identify the points where the imperfections make the tire vibrate. The tire is then balanced by putting precise weights to the edge of the rim so the wheel will be perfectly weighted and operate without wobbling or wearing unevenly. An out-of-balance tire may look good, but it will not perform well or last as long.

How does a pastor bring balance to a very busy, stressful, demanding life? Is it possible to function in our high-speed world without wobbling or wearing out? Wayne Schmidt observes, "Leaders continually pursue balance because life is always throwing individuals off balance. Realigning life is a continual process, requiring self-reflection and self-discipline"[15] Balance is difficult to maintain because our lives are constantly changing. People jokingly warn a couple expecting their first child that life will be different after the baby is born. The new parents quickly discover that getting a full night's sleep is out of the question. But as kids grow, parents have to adjust to new challenges: grade school, teen years, and then the empty nest as the children leave home. Just as family life moves through different stages, the church and your pastoral work in the church also changes. In order to stay in balance, you need to make adjustments based on your own understanding of your goals in ministry. "By continually clarifying one's life calling, a person can discern when the expectations of others are legitimate, while refraining from activities and commitments outside the zone."[16] There are several personal areas to consider in developing and maintaining a balanced life.

FIND A BALANCE IN YOUR WORK

For many people who work in retail or at a factory, when you work is never a question. You punch a clock when you start your shift and punch out when the required number of hours are over. They don't fasten a time clock to the wall outside a pastor's study. For most pastors, there is a job to do, a role to fill, and they keep working until the job is done. But that can become a problem. As our world has become more complex, so has the pastor's job description. A former colleague, Dr. Rick Ryding, found in a study he conducted that the average pastor worked over 62 hours a week to carry out 255 separate specific activities, each averaging 15 minutes in length.[17]

Too many in ministry feel like the proverbial cowboy who, when going to do his job, jumped on his horse and rode off in all directions at once.

Time management is always a challenge for pastors. The role we assume when we enter a ministry position implies that we are on duty all the time.

Emergencies do happen once in a while in the middle of the night after a busy day, and we respond. But those emergencies tend to be the exception rather than the norm. The truth is that pastors have more control over their time than they may realize. Dr. James McCord, retired president of Princeton Theological Seminary, told the story of a man who successfully completed thirty years of ministry at one parish. When asked how he managed to have such an effective, long-term pastorate, he replied, "I started off at a pace I could keep."[18] Being a good pastor means not only working hard but also working smart.

Many pastors try to evaluate their work schedule in terms of hours of the day or week. A more effective way may be to view each day in terms of three time periods: morning, afternoon, and evening. By developing such a schedule you can plan not to work through all three time periods every day of the week. If you are going to be working several hours in the evening, find some time in the morning or afternoon to rest or relax. It is helpful, before you begin a new week, to evaluate your work commitments for each three periods of each day of the week. Save your most productive periods for those activities that demand the highest level of creativity, such as sermon preparation. Blocking out periods in advance will allow you to work at a pace that is healthy and productive.

Scheduling time for study and sermon preparation is a special challenge for those who have weekly preaching responsibilities. Some pastors try to set aside three morning periods for study. My personal process involved blocking out Thursday morning and afternoon and Friday morning if necessary. Find a process that will keep you creative and alert.

Finding the right location for study can make those limited hours most productive. One problem with studying in the pastor's church office is that it is easy for people to come by and visit for a few moments. You can also find yourself distracted as you see a note to make a phone call or notice a half-finished letter. Some pastors who have solved this problem by having a study at home for sermon preparation. However, you may find that your children, or even your spouse, can unknowingly intrude on your time. An idea I personally found useful was doing my sermon work at the library of a local university. As well as being quiet, the library's resources are readily available. Search your community to find a place where you can be alone with God, your Bible, and your books as you prepare to preach. With conviction Paul Cedar writes, "The discipline of secluded study helps me fulfill my responsibility to nourish and feed people through teaching and preaching. It prevents a sloppiness that would have disastrous long-term effects on the lives of the people God has entrusted to my care."[19]

"UNSTRING THE BOW": KEEP THE SABBATH

An old American Indian adage says that if an archery bow is constantly strung, it loses its power. To keep the bow an effective weapon, you have to loosen the string when it is not in use. In the Creation narrative in Genesis, God developed a pattern of work and rest. He created the world in six time segments and rested on the seventh. From this came the practice of the Sabbath—work for six days and rest on the seventh day. One of the Ten Commandments speaks of keeping the Sabbath day holy.

Ask a group of pastors if they keep the Sabbath day, and most would affirmatively say they honor God on Sunday through the worship services. What they would fail to admit is that Sundays are usually the most exhausting day of their week. Darius Salter says, "I observe the pastor as the most likely person to neglect God's provision for one day of rest and recreation out of every seven. Keeping the Sabbath is God's design for continuing His creation in us (re-creation) and saving us from self-destruction."[20] Eugene Peterson defines it this way: "Sabbath means quit. Stop. Take a break. Cool it. The word itself had nothing devout or holy in it. It's a word about time, denoting our nonuse of it—what we usually call wasting time."[21] Having been raised in a parsonage himself, Daniel Spaite, M.D., voices a special concern for pastors who work seven days a week for months on end. "Keeping Sabbath means keeping the rhythm of God-created life. . . . A seven-day cycle involving work, worship, and rest protects spiritual and physical health. . . . Either you can give your body its Sabbaths, its time to cease and desist, or your body will take them back."[22]

Since Sundays are hardly a day of rest for pastors, it is your spiritual responsibility to schedule a weekly Sabbath into your week. Salter explains, "The Sabbath is a day devoted to playing and praying, activities that demand energy, investments with critical returns, emotionally and physically."[23] Some authors say that this is the same as a day off, while others think the Sabbath should be a separate day. The day of the week also varies from pastor to pastor. There are pastors who choose a specific day based on when the family can be together. While there are disadvantages to selecting Monday because of the exhaustion of Sunday, I personally found it suited me the best. I could begin Tuesday and work toward the following Sunday. In addition to a day of each week, one Christian leader takes a day each month as a one-day spiritual retreat for prayer and devotional reading.

We also need extended periods away from the job for recreation and restoration. I have heard pastors brag that they never took a vacation or never used all the time allotted to them. I want to ask them, "Why are you robbing yourself and your family of the time you need to re-create yourself?" I tried to take every day of vacation time allotted to me by the church. The old, tired argument that the church can't get along while you're gone is nothing more than an inflated estimation of your own importance. If you were to die tomorrow, they would have a funeral, return from the cemetery to eat ham and potato salad, and then select someone to succeed you. The church certainly can and will manage without you for a week or two at a time. In fact, they may be relieved that you are away from them for a few days. Vacations help us all to come back restored for more effective ministry.

Block out your days off, family activities, and vacations on your planning calendar. Do it as early as possible, because planning calendars have a way of filling up if you don't protect those special moments. If someone wants to schedule an appointment during your personal time, you can tell the person that the time they want is already scheduled. Taking weekly Sabbaths as well as vacations from the church needs to be a top priority. I jokingly tell my students that when they begin ministry, if I hear that they are not taking time away from their pastoral responsibilities, I will personally visit them and twist their arms until they promise to repent and do right. Remember, if you don't regularly unstring the bow, it will lose its strength and eventually even the string itself will probably snap.

FIND ACTIVITIES THAT CONTRAST WITH YOUR WORK

The weekday work of pastoral ministry usually involves a lot of sitting and standing, talking and listening, and little physical activity. Jesus and Paul did not need to go to the gym to work out because they got plenty of exercise walking between towns or rowing boats. A pastor's daily physical exercise may consist of no more than opening the car door a few times and walking down the hall of a hospital. Even Paul told his young pastor friend Timothy, "Physical training is of some value" (1 Tim. 4:8). Exercise will not get you into heaven, but if you don't do anything to keep in physical condition, you may be entering the pearly gates earlier than you planned.

Some pastors enjoy a game of tennis, basketball, racquetball, or golf to keep in shape. One pastor, who ran track in his younger years, tries to get out for a jog every chance he can. Another pastor showed me the new bike he plans to use to ride with his wife, so they can both get exercise. Even those who are not athletically inclined can go for a walk around the neighborhood. Physical exertion, rather than leaving you depleted, actually helps to elevate your emotional sense of well-being as well as your mental alertness.

Spend some time developing an interest or hobby away from the church. One pastor loves to spend hours alone in his garage restoring antique cars. Another pastoral couple go for long rides on their motorcycle. An evangelist is the national chaplain for a hot rod association. Salter offers this advice, "May I suggest that the pastor's family needs to be involved in activities outside the church: scouts, [the] orchestra, athletics, or whatever is in keeping with their aptitude. . . . This extramural (outside-the-wall) involvement allows for meaningful communication about what it means to be Christian in a pagan world."[24] I was an assistant Little League baseball coach when my son was young. One of the side benefits was the opportunity to meet a whole new group of parents I would never have known otherwise.

DON'T LET YOURSELF DIE ABOVE THE NECK

I never will forget a conversation I had with a younger pastor several years ago. In a moment of honesty he confessed that since he finished his schooling he had not read one book or written one original sermon. He had gone brain-dead even though he continued to try to function as a pastor.

Our intellect is a marvelous gift from God, and we honor him by using it. In our rapidly expanding world, if we are not constantly learning new things, we are falling behind. Using a computer analogy, if we fail to upgrade our software, the computer functions will become obsolete. Pastors who never think new thoughts slowly drift out-of-touch with the people in their congregations.

One of the obvious ways to stimulate our intellectual juices is to maintain the discipline of reading. Read books relating to your profession—theology, counseling, biblical studies, ministry practices, Christian education, church history, and evangelism. Broaden the scope of your reading beyond your specialization to include biographies, history, science, and current events. Subscribe to both the local newspaper and a national newsmagazine to keep abreast of current events and cultural changes. These can keep you informed about the world you live in and are a wonderful source for sermon illustrations.

Take advantage of opportunities for continuing education. This could involve formally pursuing advanced degrees or gaining informal training through conferences, seminars, and travel. Many local churches set aside funds to help meet the expenses of such training. In the master's program I coordinate I have a church executive from another denomination who is past sixty years of age, yet is busy pursuing an advanced degree. Many denominations have acknowledged the importance of ongoing learning by requiring ordained ministers to earn continuing education units each year to remain current in ministry.

To encourage longer pastoral tenure in a local church, many churches are encouraging their pastor to take a sabbatical leave. Most pastors become eligible for a sabbatical leave after seven years of service to that congregation. This leave may last from four to twelve weeks away from pastoral responsibilities. The church continues to pay the pastor's salary and benefits as well as the expenses that are incurred to fill the pastoral role. Some churches pay for the pastor's expenses for any training or conferences during this time. Most pastors design and submit an action plan for a sabbatical leave to the church board. These plans may include travel, reading, formal studies, observing successful churches, as well as activities designed to renew the pastor for future ministry. Denominational leaders can assist both pastors and churches in planning for a sabbatical for all pastoral staff members.

DEVELOP A CLOSE FRIENDSHIP

Every pastor needs a person to talk to, confide in, unload on, and be accountable to. For this friendship to really work, the pastor needs to be able to say anything without fear that the listener will either judge the pastor or say anything to anyone about their conversation. A true friend knows intuitively when to comfort and when to confront. London and Wiseman call this person a soul friend. "Ideally, a soul friend freely questions a pastor about his motives, his marriage and his ministry. The soul friend must be given permission to question a pastor about his relationship with God."[25]

While we may consciously set out to choose such a friend, often God has a way of bringing the right person to us. This person could be a part of the church, but usually it is better to have someone outside the congregation. This will allow the pastor to talk more frankly about troublesome church situations and the listener can be more objective. Although your spouse is your soul mate, you need someone else as your soul friend, because some subjects can be painful for your spouse as well. Soul friends can be fellow pastors or laypeople. They may be a part of your denomination or, as in the story at the beginning of the chapter, from another fellowship. Just as David treasured his friendship with Jonathan, a true friend can give us valuable counsel, encouragement, and accountability.

GUARD AGAINST BURNOUT

While we complain about the high-energy, frantic pace associated with living in our contemporary society, the truth is, many of us like it. In fact, we can become addicted to it. We enjoy the energy, the rush connected with starting a new project. We flock to theme parks to be thrilled and even frightened by the latest risky amusement ride that makes us feel we are flirting with death. When we gather with a group of friends, we brag to each other about how busy our lives have become and how much we have accomplished.

Our bodies respond to this excitement by producing adrenaline—that rush that makes our hearts flutter and our heads throb. It's that adrenaline that helps us maintain the frantic pace, juggle the multiple activities, or handle the difficult confrontations of modern life. When we don't feel we have enough energy, we stop by the local coffee stand for supersized latte with enough caffeine to keep the adrenaline levels high. And the end result is stress. Psychologist Archibald Hart says that stress "comes on when you've used too much adrenaline, when you've been too much on a high. Stress produces a state of emergency in the body—the body is, in effect in emergency mode."[26]

And the long-term result of a high-stressed lifestyle is burnout. Dr. Daniel Spaite asks, "What is this time bomb that ticks away with undetected certainty: It is the overworked, stressed-out lifestyle of the modern pastor. It is the work patterns and leisure deficits that leave a pastor spent with no backup for recovery. It is the contemporary anomaly called burnout."[27]

Jody Seymour warns that the result of burnout is "the emotional exhaustion resulting from the stress of interpersonal contact . . . in which helping professionals lose positive feelings, sympathy, and respect for their clients."[28] Hart distinguishes between stress and burnout. Stress has a biological basis while burnout is more of an emotional response. "In burnout, things are not going right. The resources aren't there. People are not affirming you and a state of demoralization sets in."[29] Burnout becomes more severe when you feel alone, without support. Your energy is gone. Your vision has been lost. Depression sets in and you just don't care anymore.

Jeremiah is a classic case of clergy burnout. He had a type-A personality and poured himself into his work with all he had. Although he really wanted to be liked, God gave him the task of pronouncing harsh judgment upon the nation. He preached the message God wanted, but instead of satisfaction, Jeremiah felt only weariness and loneliness. "What happens when we feel like God has led us to a dried-up brook? What happens when we need some water to put out the slow-burning fire within us that is burning us out?"[30] It's easy to feel, like Jeremiah, that we have been dropped into an empty cistern and nobody knows where we are, or even cares.

Is there any way out of a burnout situation? Hart says that the first step on the road to recovery is to face up to your situation.[31] Since burnout often occurs in isolation, you need to let people back into your situation. People suffering burnout sometimes feel like others are out to get them. The answer is to nurture human relationships. Spaite says, "Over and over the studies show that people with good social support systems have a decreased risk for disease . . . People without access to a support system increase their risk of developing a medical problem that could lead to death. . . . Part of the answer lies in the interaction between the immune system, stress, and emotional support from personal relationships."[32]

Another important step is to turn the situation over to Jesus. It is easy to feel that the success or failure of the church rests on our shoulders. "In fact, one of the major factors contributing to exhausted, burned-out Christian leaders is a failure to grasp the implications of the truth that the Church is not ours!"[33]

Finally then, go to your soul friend and share your situation. Hart writes, "It's absolutely essential to build an adequate support system, preferably with peers to whom you can turn to share your heart and, in bearing one another's burdens, to find the healing Christ can bring."[34]

▶ CARING FOR YOUR FAMILY

Although not everyone entering ministry will get married, many will eventually walk down the aisle. If you get married, it is quite likely you will have children, either by childbirth or adoption. For the pastor who is married, a big part of who you are as a person is connected in some way to your family.

There are stresses on today's marriages like never before. This is true for clergy marriages as well as for those laypeople who sit in the pews. In many cases, the pastoral spouses have not been called specifically to their unique role in the church. They are in the role because they married someone with a special calling.

The stresses of being a part of the pastoral family can bring resentment. Sometimes the church has an expectation that the spouse will become an unpaid assistant, devoting a major amount of time each week to the work of the church. Church people may expect the spouse to take personal criticism without feeling hurt. And what does the spouse do about a personal career when the pastor-spouse senses the need to move to a new church?

The pastoral couple may feel a lot of inner pressure to project an image of a perfect marriage to the congregation, even their marriage may be facing a great deal of inner turmoil. John Trent calls this image management. "There is a public self and a private self (which is normal, to a degree). The more our public self says one thing and our private self says something else, the more we have an image management problem."[35] One way of taking the pressure off is to reflect as realistic a picture of your marriage as possible, letting your congregation know that your marriage is not perfect. Also, you can be a buffer between your spouse and the congregation. Armstrong tells pastors, "You have a duty to protect him or her from unreasonably demanding, overly inquisitive, hypercritical parishioners. Interpret and defend the role he or she chooses to play in the congregation."[36]

Block out time to spend with your spouse to show her or him you value your time together. The ministry can even provide some unique opportunities for couple time. Try to attend conferences, conventions, and retreats together. If you need to visit someone at a hospital in another town, go over together as a couple and then take the opportunity eat dinner together before returning home.

Sometimes spouses and children feel like they are in competition with God for a pastor's time and attention. Children especially can feel that they are unspiritual when they wish to spend more time with their mom or dad. They may wonder how they can win in a contest with God, over their parent's attention. Now, there will be times when an emergency comes and we may need to postpone a family event. We can help our family understand our loyalty to them when we do not give the impression we are indispensable to the church functioning.

Let children be children. Don't expect them to behave as perfect little adults. Try to make being a P.K., a preacher's kid, an adventure. My daughter still talks as an adult today about the people she had opportunity to meet when they were guests in our home for dinner. It allowed her to see them as humans with their ties off, instead of people with titles. Emphasize the perks that go with being a part of the pastor's family. Both of our children reminisce about a time when they were young, traveling from the Midwest to attend a conference with us in Southern California. They had the opportunity of seeing all the tourist sites for the first time. Their comment later was, "We were lucky because none of the other kids from our church got to go."

We hear a lot these days about spending quality time with the family. Most children can identify what quality time means. Time is time to them. The more time you spend with your family, the better.

▶ PASTOR, YOU ARE A PERSON

Isn't it interesting that God would entrust the communication of the good news of salvation to humans? We are fallible, forgetful, and flawed. To paraphrase Paul, God entrusted the treasure of the gospel to be contained in a bunch of cracked pots (see 2 Cor. 4:7). No one could ever mistake the treasure for the clay. In the same way, God has also assigned the responsibility for the care and leadership of his followers, the Church, to other humans he has called pastors or shepherds. Angels might have been more dependable, but he chose us as humans to care for other humans. Since we have been called of God, we have the unique challenge to lead and love those other persons God has placed in our care. Don't hide your unique personhood. Instead, let God use you as a reflection, imperfect as it may be, of his divine love for all people. It is a great honor to be called *pastor*. It is a great calling to serve as a *shepherd*.

▶ QUESTIONS FOR REFLECTION

▷ Why is it difficult to really know who I am as a person?

▷ What do I perceive will be my greatest personal concerns as I enter pastoral ministry?

▷ How can I best care for myself so I can provide long-term effective service, knowing my personal tendencies as an individual?

Notes

CHAPTER 1

1. E. Glenn Wagner, *Escape from Church, Inc.: The Return of the Pastor-Shepherd* (Grand Rapids: Zondervan, 1999), 17.

2. David W. Wiersbe, *The Dynamics of Pastoral Care* (Grand Rapids: Baker, 2000), 34.

3. Thomas G. Oden, *Pastoral Theology: Essentials of Ministry* (San Francisco: HarperSanFrancisco, 1982), 59-60.

4. Robb Redman, "The Purpose of Pastoral Care," in *Leadership Handbook of Outreach and Care*, James D. Berkley, gen. ed. (Grand Rapids: Baker, 1994), 201.

5. Ibid., 203.

6. Ibid., 206.

7. D. Michael Henderson, *John Wesley's Class Meeting: A Model for Making Disciples* (Nappanee, IN: Evangel, 1997), 138.

8. Tom Albin interviewed by Tim Stafford, "Finding God in Small Groups," *Christianity Today*, August 2003, 43.

9. Thomas C. Oden, *Classical Pastoral Care*, vol. 1, *Becoming a Minister* (Grand Rapids: Baker, 1987), 5.

10. Michael Slaughter, *Out on the Edge: A Wake-up Call for Church Leaders on the Edge of the Media Reformation* (Nashville: Abingdon, 1998), 112.

11. Howard Clinebell, *Basic Types of Pastoral Care and Counseling* (Nashville: Abingdon, 1984), 26.

12. Slaughter, *Out on the Edge,* 93.

CHAPTER 2

1. John W. Frye, *Jesus the Pastor* (Grand Rapids,: Zondervan, 2000), 84-85.

2. Oden, *Pastoral Theology,* 186.

3. David G. Benner, *Care of Souls: Revisioning Christian Nurture and Counsel* (Grand Rapids: Baker, 1998), 23.

4. Ibid., 31-32. This information is taken from William Clebsch and Charles Jaekle, *Pastoral Care in Historical Perspective* (New York: Aronson, 1964).

5. Louis W. Bloede, *The Effective Pastor: A Guide to Successful Ministry* (Minneapolis: Fortress, 1996), 5. Bloede draws from the report of the Readiness for Ministry project, vol. 1, published in 1975 by the Association of Theological Schools.

6. Howard L. Rice, *The Pastor as Spiritual Guide* (Nashville: Upper Room Books, 1998), 35.

7. Ibid., 51-56; he discusses these disciplines in much greater detail in these pages. See also Richard Foster, *The Celebration of Discipline.*

8. Eugene H. Peterson, *Working the Angles: The Shape of Pastoral Integrity* (Grand Rapids: Eerdmans, 1987), 150.

9. Rice, *Spiritual Guide,* 61-62.

CHAPTER 3

1. Elton Trueblood, *Your Other Vocation* (New York: Harper and Brothers, 1952), 38.

2. Bruce Larson, Paul Anderson, and Doug Self, *Mastering Pastoral Care* (Sisters, OR: Multnomah, 1990), 27.

3. Dale Galloway, *Building Teams in Ministry* (Kansas City: Beacon Hill Press of Kansas City, 2000), 19.

4. William E. Diehl, *Ministry in Daily Life: A Practical Guide for Congregations* (Bethesda, MD: Alban Institute, 1996), 14.

5. Ibid., 15. Diehl raises the issue of Christians working in a grocery store that sells tobacco, saying that some areas in life are gray rather than black and white. Christians must prayerfully consider how to do ministry in these arenas.

6. Larson, et al., *Mastering Pastoral Care,* 30-33.

7. George G. Hunter III, *Church for the Unchurched* (Nashville: Abingdon, 1996), 124-27. Hunter gives a rather detailed description of methodology for promoting lay ministry in this church.

8. John Ed Mathison, "Niche-Pickin'—New Paradigm for Lay Ministry: The Frazer Church Volunteer Model," in Galloway, *Building Teams in Ministry,* 68.

9. In addition to printed materials, Elmer Towns has a free electronic Spiritual Gift Questionnaire evaluating nine spiritual gifts instantly. It can be found at his Web site <www.elmertowns.com>.

10. David Slamp, *Spiritual Growth Survey Questionnaire* © copyright 1997. Available through Church Growth Institute, P.O. Box 7, Elkton, MD 21922-0007. Orders: Box 9176, Oxnard, CA 93031-9176. Phone 1-800-553-4769 <www.churchgrowth.org>. For a free Spiritual Gifts Analysis visit <www.teamministry.com>.

11. Jim Garlow, "Purpose-Driven Lay Training: Equipping Christian Revolutionists" in Galloway, *Building Teams in Ministry,* 84.

12. George Barna, *The Habits of Highly Effective Churches* (Ventura, CA: Regal, 1999), 60-61.

13. Dennis E. Williams and Kenneth O. Gangel, *Volunteers for Today's Church: How to Recruit and Retain Workers* (Grand Rapids: Baker, 1993), 87.

14. Alan E. Nelson, *The New Thing: Cutting-Edge Ideas for 21st Century Ministry from Progressive Leaders in the Wesleyan Heritage* (Scottsdale, AZ: Southwest Center for Leadership, 1998), 53.

15. Douglas W. Johnson, *Empowering Lay Volunteers* (Nashville: Abingdon, 1991), 62.

CHAPTER 4

1. Hunter, *Church for the Unchurched,* 134.

2. Howard W. Stone, *The Caring Church: A Guide for Lay Pastoral Care* (New York: Harper and Row, 1983), 20.

3. Ibid., 19.

4. William Easum, *Dancing with Dinosaurs: Ministry in a Hostile and Hurting World* (Nashville: Abingdon, 1993), 77-78.

5. Rick Warren, *The Purpose-Driven Church: Growth Without Compromising Your Message and Mission* (Grand Rapids: Zondervan, 1995), 389.

6. Larson, et al., *Mastering Pastoral Care,* 114.

7. Ibid., 116.

8. Stanley J. Menking, *Helping Laity Help Others* (Philadelphia: Westminster, 1984), 26.

9. Gary R. Collins, *How to Be a People Helper* (Wheaton, IL: Tyndale, 1995), 23.

10. Leroy Howe, *A Pastor in Every Pew: Equipping Laity for Pastoral Care* (Valley Forge, PA: Judson, 2000), 25.

11. Ibid., 30.

12. Collins, *How to Be a People Helper,* 29.

13. Hunter, *Church for the Unchurched,* 12.

14. Collins, *How to Be a People Helper,* 3.

15. Gary R. Collins, *Innovative Approaches to Counseling: A How-To Approach* (Dallas: Word Publishing, 1986), 145-46.

16. Stone, *Caring Church,* 20; the passage gives an expanded explanation of the recruiting issues for lay training.

17. Collins, *How to Be a People Helper.* The original edition was published in 1976.

18. Stone, *Caring Church,* 29.

19. Collins, "Lay Counselors," *Leadership Handbook of Outreach and Care,* 286.

20. Menking, *Helping Laity,* 94.

21. Hunter, *Church for the Unchurched,* 136.

CHAPTER 5

1. Hunter, *Church for the Unchurched,* 82.

2. Henderson, *John Wesley's Class Meeting,* 93.

3. Tom Albin interviewed by Tim Stafford, "Finding God in Small Groups," *Christianity Today,* August 2003, 42. Albin did his doctoral research on the small groups of early Methodism.

4. Henderson, *John Wesley's Class Meeting,* 99.

5. Albin, "Small Groups," 43.

6. Henderson, *Class Meeting,* 121.

7. Albin, "Small Groups," 44.

8. Carl F. George, *Prepare Your Church for the Future* (Tarrytown, NY: Revell, 1991).

9. Ibid., 53.

10. Easum, *Dancing with Dinosaurs,* 60.

11. The program is explained in Dale Galloway, *20/20 Vision: How to Create a Successful Church* (Portland, OR: Scott Publishing, 1986).

12. Dale Galloway with Kathy Mills, *The Small Group Book: The Practical Guide for Nurturing Christians and Building Churches* (Tarrytown, NY: Revell, 1995), 9.

13. For an explanation of Saddleback's small-group ministry, see Hunter, *Church for the Unchurched,* 90-92.

14. Bill Donahue and Russ Robinson, *Building a Church of Small Groups: A Place Where Nobody Stands Alone* (Grand Rapids: Zondervan, 2001), 14.

15. Hunter, *Church for the Unchurched,* 93.

16. Donahue and Robinson, *Building a Church,* 207.

17. Ibid., 60.

18. Henderson, *Class Meeting,* 118-19.

19. Donahue and Robinson, *Building a Church,* 67.

20. Roger Razzari Elrod, "Study Groups," in *Leadership Handbook of Outreach and Care,* 258.

21. George, *Prepare Your Church,* 89.

22. For a more complete explanation see Galloway, *20/20 Vision.*

23. David Slamp, *CareRings: Sunday School and Small Groups Side by Side* (Wichita, KS: Vessel, 2004), 101-2. This book is a very practical guide for implementing a CareRing program in a local church. CareRings work equally well in smaller churches and larger churches.

24. Celebrate Recovery is a part of the ministry of Saddleback Church, Lake Forest, CA. For more information and materials, go to <www.saddleback.com>.

25. Donahue and Robinson, *Building a Church,* 149.

26. Easum, *Dancing with Dinosaurs,* 9. This statement came from an interview with Carl George at the Leadership Network gathering, August 1991, Denver.

27. Donahue and Robinson, *Building a Church,* 119.

CHAPTER 6

1. William Barclay, *The Gospel of John,* vol. 2 (Philadelphia: Westminster, 1955), 64-65.

2. Wiersbe, *Dynamics of Pastoral Care,* 27.

3. E. Glenn Wagner, *Escape from Church, Inc.: The Return of the Pastor-Shepherd* (Grand Rapids: Zondervan, 1999), 25.

4. Ibid., 27.

5. Joseph Stowell, quoted in Eric Reed and Collin Hansen, "How Pastors Rate as Leaders: *Leadership* Surveys Pastors and Their Congregations," *Leadership,* Fall 2003, vol. 24, no. 4, 32.

6. Linda Wilcox, *No More Front Porches: Rebuilding Community in Our Isolated Worlds* (Kansas City: Beacon Hill Press of Kansas City, 2002), 45.

7. Wagner, *Escape from Church,* 130.

8. Leith Anderson, quoted in "Called to What? A Leadership Forum," *Leadership,* Fall 2003, vol. 24, no. 4, 29.

9. Becky R. McMillan, "What do clergy do all week?" a study from the Pulpit and Pew Research on Pastoral Leadership project <www.pulpitandpew.duke.edu/clergyweek.html>.

10. Wagner, *Escape from Church,* 82.

11. Wilcox, *No More Front Porches,* 95.

12. Leonard Sweet, *Post-Modern Pilgrims: First Century Passion for the 21st Century Church* (Nashville: Broadman and Holman, 2000), 119.

13. Ibid., 119-20.

14. Oden, *Pastoral Theology,* 171.

15. Hunter, *Church for the Unchurched,* 120.

CHAPTER 7

1. James D. Hamilton, *The Ministry of Pastoral Counseling* (Kansas City: Beacon Hill Press of Kansas City, 1972), 13.

2. Ibid., 13-14.

3. Thomas C. Oden, *Classical Pastoral Care,* vol. 3, *Pastoral Counsel* (Grand Rapids: Baker, 1987), 14.

4. David G. Benner, *Strategic Pastoral Counseling* (Grand Rapids: Baker, 1992), 18.

5. Gary R. Collins, *Christian Counseling: A Comprehensive Guide* (Dallas: Word Publishing, 1988), 16.

6. William H. Willimon, *Pastor: The Theology and Practice of Ordained Ministry* (Nashville: Abingdon, 2002), 184.

7. Ibid., 185.

8. Collins, *Christian Counseling*, 43.

9. Benner, *Strategic Pastoral Counseling*, 20.

10. Collins, *Christian Counseling*, 41.

11. Ibid., 177.

12. Willimon, *Pastor*, 182.

13. Collins, *Christian Counseling*, 29.

14. Archibald D. Hart, "Counseling the Opposite Sex," in *Leadership Handbook of Outreach and Care*, 294.

15. H. B. London, "The Need to Flee," in *The Pastor's Guide to Effective Ministry* (Kansas City: Beacon Hill Press of Kansas City, 2002), 49.

CHAPTER 8

1. Taken from The Salvation Army Web site: www1.salvationarmy.org.

2. Robert Lewis, with Rob Wilkins, *The Church of Irresistible Influence* (Grand Rapids: Zondervan, 2001), 59.

3. Ram Cnaan, *The Invisible Caring Hand: American Congregations and the Provision of Welfare* (New York: New York University Press, 2002).

4. Marshall Shelly, "Secret Services," *Leadership Journal*, Spring 2003, 43.

5. Ram Cnaan, in an interview with Agnieszka Tennant, *Leadership Journal*, Spring 2003, 45.

6. Lewis, *Irresistible Influence*, 27.

7. Matt. 5:13.

8. Matt. 5:14.

9. William B. Oglesby Jr., *Referral in Pastoral Counseling* (Nashville: Abingdon, 1978), 29.

10. Jim Pettitt, "Fundamentals of Pastoral Counseling," in *Pastor's Guide to Effective Ministry*, 124.

11. David K. Switzer, *Pastoral Care Emergencies* (Minneapolis: Fortress, 2000), 180.

12. Ibid., 178.

13. Oglesby, *Referral in Pastoral Counseling*, 91.

14. Clinebell, *Basic Types of Pastoral Care*, 312.

15. Switzer, *Pastoral Care Emergencies*, 184.

16. Clinebell, *Basic Types*, 317.

17. Randy Christian, "Making Referrals," in *Leadership Handbook of Outreach and Care*, 300.

CHAPTER 9

1. Willimon, *Pastor*, 91.

2. Ralph L. Underwood, *Pastoral Care and the Means of Grace* (Minneapolis: Fortress, 1993), 7.

3. Ibid.

4. Randy L. Maddox, *Responsible Grace: John Wesley's Practical Theology* (Nashville: Abingdon, 1994), 193.

5. Ibid., 194.

6. Ibid., 196.

7. Acts 3:6.

8. Willimon, *Pastor*, 103.

9. William H. Willimon, *Worship as Pastoral Care* (Nashville: Abingdon, 1979), 31.

10. Darius L. Salter, *Prophetical-Priestly Ministry: The Biblical Mandate for the 21st Century Pastor* (Nappanee, IN: Evangel, 2002), 127.

11. Larson, et al., *Mastering Pastoral Care,* 39.

12. Galatians 6:2.

13. Willimon, *Pastor,* 106.

14. Larson, et al., *Mastering Pastoral Care,* 41.

15. The superscription says that David wrote this after he feigned insanity before Abimelech, who then drove him away.

16. Rice, *Pastor as Spiritual Guide,* 99.

17. Larson, et al., *Mastering Pastoral Care,* 43.

18. Willimon, *Pastor,* 93.

19. Ibid.

20. Thomas C. Oden, *Classical Pastoral Care,* vol. 2, *Ministry Through Word and Sacrament* (Grand Rapids: Baker, 1987), 36.

21. John Piper in Don Kestler, gen. ed., *Feed My Sheep: A Passionate Plea for Preaching* (Morgan, PA: Soli Deo Gloria Publications, 2002), 259.

22. Ibid., 260-62.

23. Donald Capps, *Pastoral Counseling and Preaching: A Quest for an Integrated Ministry* (Philadelphia: Westminster, 1980), 25.

24. Ibid., 26.

25. Michael Slaughter, "Preaching in a Postmodern Culture," in *Pastor's Guide to Effective Ministry,* 81-82.

26. Dan Kimball, *The Emerging Church: Vintage Christianity for New Generations* (Grand Rapids: Zondervan, 2003), 177.

27. Edward P. Wimberly, *Moving from Shame to Self-worth: Preaching and Pastoral Care* (Nashville: Abingdon, 1997), 14.

28. Ibid., 15.

29. Slaughter, *Pastor's Guide,* 81.

30. Underwood, *Means of Grace,* 51.

31. Ibid., 52.

32. Salter, *Prophetical-Priestly Ministry,* 123.

33. Ibid.

34. Underwood, *Means of Grace,* 59.

35. Edward P. Wimberly, *Using Scripture in Pastoral Counseling* (Nashville: Abingdon, 1994), 14-15.

36. Ibid., 31.

37. Donald Capps, *Biblical Approaches to Pastoral Counseling* (Philadelphia: Westminster, 1981), 23.

38. Wimberly, *Using Scripture,* 25.

39. Luther quoted in Oden, *Classical Pastoral Care,* vol. 2, 60.

40. Salter, *Prophetical-Priestly Ministry,* 124.

41. Rice, *Spiritual Guide,* 102.

42. Willimon, *Pastor,* 83.

43. Neil Wiseman, "New Paradigms for Pastoral Care," in *Pastor's Guide to Effective Ministry,* 117.

44. Maddox, *Responsible Grace,* 202.

45. Ibid., 203.

46. Willimon, *Pastor,* 87.

47. Ibid.

48. David Hansen, *The Art of Pastoring: Ministry Without All the Answers* (Downers Grove, IL: InterVarsity, 1994), 145.

49. Maddox, *Responsible Grace,* 205.

50. Ibid., 220.

51. Underwood, *Means of Grace,* 133.

52. Ibid., 86.

53. Gregory of Nyssa, quoted in Oden, *Classical Pastoral Care,* vol. 2, 128.

CHAPTER 10

1. Matt. 5:9.

2. L. Randolph Lowry and Richard W. Meyers, *Conflict Management and Counseling* (Dallas: Word Publishing, 1991), 24. The study was conducted for the Christian Conciliations Services of Orange County, California, surveying 135 respondents on the actual amount of time spent dealing with conflict.

3. Hugh F. Halverstadt, *Managing Church Conflict* (Louisville, KY: Westminster/John Knox, 1991), 6.

4. David W. Kale with Mel McCullough, *Managing Conflict in the Church* (Kansas City: Beacon Hill Press of Kansas City, 2003), 20.

5. Ibid., 21.

6. Ps. 133:1.

7. Lowry, *Conflict Management,* 49-50.

8. William Barclay, *The Gospel of Matthew,* vol. 2 (Philadelphia: Westminster, 1957), 206.

9. Keith Huttenlocker, *Conflict and Caring: Preventing, Managing, and Resolving Conflict in the Church* (Grand Rapids: Zondervan, 1988), 84-85.

10. Matt. 18:16.

11. Matt. 18:17*a.*

12. Lowry, *Conflict Management,* 59.

13. See 1 Cor. 5.

14. 1 Cor. 5:11*b.*

15. Lowry discusses the process of a Christian alternative to litigation in detail on pages 53-60.

16. 1 Cor. 3:3*b.*

17. Kale, *Managing Conflict,* 16.

18. Ibid., 37.

19. 1 Thess. 5:13*b.*

20. William H. Willimon, *Preaching About Conflict in the Local Church* (Philadelphia: Westminster, 1987), 15.

21. Ibid., 22.

22. Huttenlocker, *Conflict and Caring.* See pages 66-70 for a more complete explanation on the importance of communication.

23. Isa. 1:18.

24. Huttenlocker, *Conflict and Caring*, 72.

25. Kale, *Managing Conflict*, 88-89. He also describes several dirty fighting tactics to avoid in chapter 8.

26. Huttenlocker, *Conflict and Caring*, 57.

CHAPTER 11

1. Collins, *How to Be a People Helper*, 111.

2. Judson J. Swilhard and Gerald C. Richardson, *Counseling in Times of Crisis* (Dallas: Word Publishing, 1987), 16.

3. Clinebell, *Basic Types of Pastoral Care*, 187.

4. Howard W. Stone, *Crisis Counseling* (Philadelphia: Fortress, 1976), 5.

5. H. Norman Wright, *Crisis Counseling: What to Do and Say During the First 72 Hours* (Ventura, CA: Regal, 1993), 10.

6. Viktor Frankl, *Man's Search for Meaning* (New York: Washington Square, 1963), 121.

7. Stone, *Crisis Counseling*, 8.

8. Wright, *Crisis Counseling: What to Do*, 21.

9. Stone, *Crisis Counseling*, 13.

10. Wright, *Crisis Counseling: What to Do*, 22.

11. Stone, *Crisis Counseling*, 16.

12. This scale first appeared in the *Journal of Psychosomatic Research* 2 (1967), 213-18. It has been reproduced in Clinebell, *Basic Types of Pastoral Care*, 189-90.

13. Stone, *Crisis Counseling*, 19.

14. Ibid., 20.

15. Wright, *Crisis Counseling: What to Do*, 31-40. He has a very helpful chart of this crisis sequence on page 32.

16. Ibid., 34.

17. Ibid., 36.

18. Ibid., 37.

19. Stone, *Crisis Counseling*, 35.

20. Gary Gulbranson, "Emergency Calls," in *Leadership Handbook of Outreach and Care*, 226.

21. Collins, *How to Be a People Helper*, 121.

22. Wright, *Crisis Counseling: What to Do*, 97.

23. Stone, *Crisis Counseling*, 74.

CHAPTER 12

1. Aubrey Malphurs and Keith Willhite, eds., *A Contemporary Handbook for Weddings and Funerals and Other Occasions* (Grand Rapids: Kregel, 2003), 27.

2. Wiersbe, *Dynamics of Pastoral Care*, 119.

3. Les Parrott III and Leslie Parrott, *Saving Your Marriage Before It Starts: Seven Questions to Ask Before (and After) You Marry* (Grand Rapids: Zondervan, 1995), 12.

4. George Barna, *The Second Coming of the Church* (Nashville: Word Publishing, 1998), 6.

5. H. Norman Wright, *The Premarital Counseling Handbook* (Chicago: Moody, 1992), 8.

6. Matt. 19:6.

7. For further information and materials contact Covenant Marriage Movement at <www.covenantmarriage.com>.

8. James C. Dobson, *Love for a Lifetime: Building a Marriage That Will Go the Distance* (Sisters, OR: Multnomah, 1993), 20.

9. Ibid., 21-22.

10. T-JTA is published by Psychological Publications (5300 Hollywood Blvd., Los Angeles, CA 90027).

11. The test is developed by PREPARE/Enrich, P.O. Box 190, Minneapolis, MN 55440. Phone 1-800-331-1661 for information on training.

12. Wright, *Premarital Counseling Handbook,* 153.

13. Parrott and Parrott, *Saving Your Marriage,* 73.

14. Ibid., 75-79.

15. Ibid., 145.

16. H. Norman Wright, *Premarital Counseling* (Chicago: Moody, 1977). The book underwent a major revision in 1992 under a new title: *The Premarital Counseling Handbook,* also published by Moody Press.

17. Parrott and Parrott, *Saving Your Marriage Before It Starts.*

18. David L. Larsen, *Caring for the Flock: Pastoral Ministry in the Local Congregation* (Wheaton, IL: Crossway Books, 1991), 161.

19. Malphurs and Willhite, eds., *Contemporary Handbook,* 27. This book offers several wedding service options as well as sample wedding messages.

20. Larsen, *Caring for the Flock,* 163.

21. Robert E. Webber, "Eucharist Spirituality," *Authentic Worship: Hearing Scripture's Voice, Applying Its Truths,* Herbert W. Bateman IV, ed. (Grand Rapids: Kregel, 2002), 265.

22. Larsen, *Caring for the Flock,* 155.

23. Jeffrey D. Arthurs, "Communion with a Bread Machine," in Malphurs and Willhite, eds., *Contemporary Handbook,* 327.

24. Larsen, *Caring for the Flock,* 143.

25. *The Worship Sourcebook* (Grand Rapids: Baker, 2004), 249-50.

26. Franklin M. Segler, *Understanding, Preparing for, and Practicing Christian Worship,* 2nd ed. (Nashville: Broadman and Holman, 1996), 141.

27. Bruce L. Petersen, "The Significance of Dedication and Baptism," in *A Pastor's Worship Resource for Advent, Lent, and Other Occasions,* James R. Spruce, ed. (Kansas City: Beacon Hill Press of Kansas City, 1987), 149.

28. Wiersbe, *Dynamics of Pastoral Care,* 122.

29. Petersen, "Significance of Dedication," 153.

CHAPTER 13

1. From Isa. 40:1.
2. "God Rest You Merry, Gentlemen."
3. John 5:1-15.
4. John 8:11.
5. John 11:17-44.
6. John 19:26-27.
7. John 20:21.

8. Murray J. Harris, "2 Corinthians," *Expositor's Bible Commentary,* Frank E. Gaebelein, gen. ed. (Grand Rapids: Zondervan, 1976), 320.

9. Philip Yancey, *Disappointment with God* (Grand Rapids: Zondervan, 1997). Yancey deals with three questions people ask: Is God unfair? Is he silent? Is he hidden? This is a very personal sequel to his earlier book *Where Is God When It Hurts?* also published by Zondervan. (See note 14.)

10. Switzer, *Pastoral Care Emergencies,* 55.

11. Oden, *Pastoral Theology,* 223.

12. Ibid., 224-25.

13. Willimon, *Pastor,* 99.

14. Philip Yancey, *Where Is God When It Hurts?* (Grand Rapids: Zondervan, 1977), 67.

15. C. S. Lewis, *The Problem of Pain* (New York: Macmillan, 1962), 39.

16. Oden, *Pastoral Theology,* 231.

17. Ibid., 248.

18. Henri Nouwen, *The Wounded Healer* (Garden City, NY: Doubleday, 1972). In this simple book Nouwen analyzes suffering and how those who serve others can recognize suffering in their own lives as the starting point of providing comfort to others. He advocates ministry from woundedness and not from strength.

19. Michael Kirkindoll, *The Hospital Visit* (Nashville: Abingdon, 2001), 87.

20. Ibid., 88.

21. Ibid., 90.

22. Ibid., 91.

23. Switzer, *Pastoral Care Emergencies,* 49.

24. Eugene H. Peterson, *Five Smooth Stones for Pastoral Work* (Grand Rapids: Eerdmans, 1992), 141.

25. Switzer, *Pastoral Care Emergencies,* 69.

26. Oden, *Pastoral Theology,* 254.

27. Peterson, *Five Smooth Stones,* 144.

28. Willimon, *Pastor,* 106.

29. Peterson, *Five Smooth Stones,* 145.

30. Switzer, *Pastoral Care Emergencies,* 51.

31. Kirkindoll, *Hospital Visit,* 53.

32. Oden, *Pastoral Theology,* 259.

33. Kent D. Richmond and David L. Middleton, *The Pastor and the Patient: A Practical Guidebook for Hospital Visitation* (Nashville: Abingdon, 1992), 30.

34. Ibid.

35. Ibid., 31-32.

36. Kirkindoll gives a full treatment on patient fears and how to address them on pages 16-17.

37. Richmond and Middleton, *Pastor and the Patient,* 83.

38. Ibid., 86.

39. Switzer, *Pastoral Care Emergencies,* 65.

40. Lawrence E. Holst, ed., *Hospital Ministry: The Role of the Chaplain Today* (New York: Crossroad, 1985), xii.

CHAPTER 14

1. Wright, *Crisis Counseling: What to Do,* 152.

2. Ibid., 153.

3. Oden, *Pastoral Theology,* 297.

4. Switzer, *Pastoral Care Emergencies,* 82.

5. Wright, *Crisis Counseling: What to Do,* 175.

6. Harold Ivan Smith, *When Your People Are Grieving: Leading in Times of Loss* (Kansas City: Beacon Hill Press of Kansas City, 2001), 36. Smith gives an excellent argument for moving beyond the "stages thinking" to a more integrative approach. This book is one of the best ministry resources available for those who are dying and those who are grieving after death. It should be a part of every pastor's library.

7. Switzer, *Pastoral Care Emergencies,* 83.

8. Leroy B. Joesten, "The Voices of the Dying and the Bereaved: A Bridge Between Loss and Growth," in Holst, *Hospital Ministry,* 140.

9. Switzer, *Pastoral Care Emergencies,* 84.

10. Ps. 23:4.

11. Clinebell, *Basic Types of Pastoral Counseling,* 231.

12. Linwood H. Chamberlain, "Counseling People Who Are Dying," in *Leadership Handbook of Outreach,* 323.

13. Wiersbe, *Dynamics of Pastoral Care,* 102.

14. Joesten, "Voices of the Dying," 143.

15. Smith, *When Your People Are Grieving,* 46.

16. Joesten, "Voices of the Dying," 143.

17. Ibid.

18. Smith, *When Your People Are Grieving,* 53.

19. Ibid., 119.

20. See Smith, *When Your People Are Grieving,* page 106, for a more complete explanation of the use of anointing oil. Chapter 8 covers in detail the importance of the three rituals: viewing, funeral, and committal.

21. Wright, *Crisis Counseling: What to Do,* 160.

CHAPTER 15

1. Richard M. Gula, *Ethics in Pastoral Ministry* (New York: Paulist, 1996), 33.

2. William Willimon, *Calling and Character: Virtues of the Ordained Life* (Nashville: Abingdon, 2000), 37.

3. Study reported by Edward LeRoy Long Jr., *A Survey of Recent Christian Ethics* (New York: Oxford University Press, 1982), 151; cited in Gula, *Ethics in Pastoral Ministry,* 32.

4. Gula, *Ethics in Pastoral Ministry,* 35.

5. Willimon, *Calling and Character,* 41.

6. Quoted by Gordon MacDonald, *Rebuilding Your Broken World* (Nashville: Nelson, 1988), 32.

7. Gaylord Noyce, *Pastoral Ethics: Professional Responsibilities of the Clergy* (Nashville: Abingdon, 1988), 90.

8. Part of the AMA requirement of 1971, cited in Margaret P. Battin, *Ethics in the Sanctuary: Examining the Practices of Organized Religion* (New Haven, CT: Yale University Press, 1990), 24.

9. Battin, *Ethics in the Sanctuary,* 25.

10. Gula, *Ethics in Pastoral Ministry,* 132.

11. Ibid., 119.

12. Noyce, *Pastoral Ethics,* 91.

13. Gula, *Ethics in Pastoral Ministry,* 119.

14. Ibid.

15. Battin, *Ethics in the Sanctuary,* 26.

16. Noyce, *Pastoral Ethics,* 92.

17. Battin, *Ethics in the Sanctuary,* 35.

18. Gula, *Ethics in Pastoral Ministry,* 134.

19. Noyce, *Pastoral Ethics,* 94.

20. Ibid.

21. Kathy Callahan-Howell, "Strain of Confidentiality," *Leadership Journal,* Winter 2003, 40.

22. Gula, *Ethics in Pastoral Ministry,* 134.

23. Callahan-Howell, "Confidentiality," 40.

24. Gaylord Noyce, *The Minister as Moral Counselor* (Nashville: Abingdon, 1989), 92-93.

25. E. Glenn Hinson, *Spiritual Preparation for Christian Leadership* (Nashville: Upper Room, 1999), 122.

26. Ibid., 121.

27. Ibid.

28. Gula, *Ethics in Pastoral Ministry,* 104.

29. Willimon, *Pastor,* 299.

30. Noyce, *Pastoral Ethics,* 100-101.

31. Gula, *Ethics in Pastoral Ministry,* 105.

32. Hart, "Counseling the Opposite Sex," 194.

33. Noyce, *Pastoral Ethics,* 101.

34. Gula, *Ethics in Pastoral Ministry,* 110.

35. William V. Arnold, *Pastoral Responses to Sexual Issues* (Louisville, KY: Westminster/John Knox, 1993), 48.

36. Ibid., 49.

37. Jim Smith, "Boundaries and Safeguards," in *Leadership Handbook of Outreach,* 293.

38. Arnold, *Pastoral Responses,* 50.

39. Austin B. Tucker, *A Primer for Pastors: A Handbook for Strengthening Ministry Skills* (Grand Rapids: Kregel, 2004), 122.

40. Arnold, *Pastoral Responses,* 51.

41. Gary Collins, *Christian Counseling: A Comprehensive Guide* (Dallas: Word Publishing, 1988), 67.

42. Arnold, *Pastoral Responses,* 51.

43. Jim Smith, "Boundaries and Safeguards," 292.

44. Noyce, *Pastoral Ethics,* 77.

45. Rick Ezell, *Strengthening the Pastor's Soul: Developing Personal Authenticity for Pastoral Effectiveness* (Grand Rapids: Kregel, 1995), 84.

46. Ibid., 83-84.

CHAPTER 16

1. Richard Stoll Armstrong, with Kirk Walker Morledge, *Help! I'm a Pastor: A Guide to Parish Ministry* (Louisville, KY: Westminster/John Knox, 2005), 67.

2. "I Want to Be like Jesus," words by Thomas O. Chisholm, 1945; music by David Livingstone Ives, 1945, Lillenas Publishing, 1945, renewed 1973.

3. Willimon, *Calling and Character,* 44.

4. Ibid., 46-47.

5. Paul Cedar, "The Extra Mile of Pastoral Integrity," in *Mastering the Pastoral Role* (Sisters, OR: Multnomah, 1991), 125.

6. Ibid., 124-25.

7. Jay Kesler, *Being Holy, Being Human: Dealing with the Incredible Expectations and Pressures of Ministry* (Minneapolis: Bethany House, 1988), 69-70.

8. Ben Patterson, "Balancing Family, Church, and Personal Time," *Mastering the Pastoral Role,* 104.

9. Kent Hughes, "Working with My Weaknesses," *Mastering the Pastoral Role,* 82-83.

10. Kesler, *Being Holy,* 34.

11. Ibid.

12. Acts 15:28.

13. A. W. Tozer, referenced in Kesler, *Being Holy,* 36.

14. Armstrong, *Help! I'm a Pastor,* 90.

15. Wayne Schmidt, "The Pastor's Planner," in *Pastor's Guide to Effective Ministry,* 136.

16. Ibid., 137.

17. Cited in Daniel Spaite, M.D., *Time Bomb in the Church: Defusing Pastoral Burnout* (Kansas City: Beacon Hill Press of Kansas City, 1999), 71.

18. Cited by Armstrong, *Help! I'm a Pastor,* 100.

19. Cedar, "The Extra Mile," 122.

20. Darius Salter, "Physical and Emotional Health," in *Pastor's Guide to Effective Ministry,* 39.

21. Eugene Peterson, "The Pastor's Sabbath," in *Refresh, Renew, Revive,* H. B. London Jr., ed. (Colorado Springs: Focus on the Family, 1996), 82.

22. Spaite, *Time Bomb in the Church,* 67.

23. Salter, "Physical and Emotional Health," 40.

24. Ibid., 41.

25. H. B. London and Neil B. Wiseman, *The Heart of a Great Pastor* (Ventura, CA: Regal, 1994) 186-87.

26. Archibald Hart, "Stress and Burnout," in *Refresh, Renew, Revive,* 7.

27. Spaite, *Time Bomb in the Church,* 9.

28. Jody Seymour, *A Time for Healing: Overcoming the Perils of Ministry* (Valley Forge, PA: Judson, 1995), 31.

29. Hart, "Stress and Burnout," 7.

30. Seymour, *Time for Healing,* 33.

31. Hart, "Stress and Burnout," 9.

32. Spaite, *Time Bomb in the Church,* 84.

33. Ibid., 30.

34. Hart, "Stress and Burnout," 11.

35. John Trent, "Taking Care of Your Marriage," in *Refresh, Renew, Revive,* 53-54.

36. Armstrong, *Help! I'm a Pastor,* 43.

BIBLIOGRAPHY

Armstrong, Richard Stoll, with Kirk Walker Morledge. *Help! I'm a Pastor: A Guide to Parish Ministry.* Louisville, KY: Westminster/John Knox, 2005.

Arnold, William V. *Introduction to Pastoral Care.* Philadelphia: Westminster, 1982.

_____. *Pastoral Responses to Sexual Issues.* Louisville, KY: Westminster/John Knox, 1993.

Babb, Lynne M. *Beating Burnout in Congregations.* Bethesda, MD: Alban Institute, 2003.

Barna, George. *The Habits of Highly Effective Churches.* Ventura, CA: Regal, 1999.

_____. *The Second Coming of the Church.* Nashville: Word Publishing, 1998.

Battin, Margaret P. *Ethics in the Sanctuary: Examining the Practices of Organized Religion.* New Haven, CT: Yale University Press, 1990.

Benner, David G. *Care of Souls: Revisioning Christian Nurture and Counsel.* Grand Rapids: Baker, 1998

_____. *Strategic Pastoral Counseling: A Short-Term Structured Model.* Grand Rapids: Baker, 1992.

Berkley, James, ed. *Leadership Handbook of Outreach and Care.* Grand Rapids: Baker, 1994.

Biddle, Perry H., Jr. *A Marriage Manual.* Grand Rapids: Eerdmans, 1994.

Bloede, Louis W. *The Effective Pastor: A Guide to Successful Ministry.* Minneapolis: Fortress, 1996.

Brister, C. W. *Pastoral Care in the Church.* San Francisco: HarperCollins, 3rd ed., 1992.

Callahan-Howell, Kathy. "Strain of Confidentiality," *Leadership Journal.* Winter 2003.

Capps, Donald. *Biblical Approaches to Pastoral Counseling.* Philadelphia: Westminster, 1981.

_____. *Pastoral Counseling and Preaching: A Quest for Integrated Ministry.* Philadelphia: Westminster, 1980.

_____. *The Poet's Gift: Toward Renewal of Pastoral Care.* Louisville, KY: Westminster/John Knox, 1993.

Cedar, Paul, Kent Hughes, and Ben Patterson. *Mastering the Pastoral Role.* Sisters, OR: Multnomah, 1991.

Clebsch, William, and Charles Jaekle. *Pastoral Care in Historical Perspective.* New York: Aronson, 1964.

Clinebell, Howard. *Basic Types of Pastoral Care and Counseling: Resources for the Ministry of Healing and Growth (Revised and Enlarged).* Nashville: Abingdon, 1984.

Cnaan, Ram. *The Invisible Caring Hand: American Congregations and the Provision of Welfare.* New York: New York University Press, 2002.

Collins, Gary. *Biblical Basis of Christian Counseling for People Helpers.* Colorado Springs: NavPress, 1993.

_____. *Christian Counseling: A Comprehensive Guide,* rev. ed. Dallas: Word Publishing, 1988.

_____. *Effective Counseling,* Carol Stream, IL: Creation House, 1972.

_____. *How to Be a People Helper.* Wheaton, IL: Tyndale, Inc., 1995.

_____. *Innovative Approaches to Counseling: A How-To Approach.* Dallas: Word Publishing, 1986.

Diehl, William E. *Ministry in Daily Life: A Practical Guide for Congregations.* Bethesda, MD: Alban Institute, Inc. 1996.

Dobson, James. *Love for a Lifetime: Building a Marriage That Will Go the Distance.* Sisters, OR: Multnomah, 1993.

Donahue, Bill, and Russ Robinson. *Building a Church of Small Groups: A Place Where Nobody Stands Alone.* Grand Rapids: Zondervan, 2001.

Easum, William. *Dancing with Dinosaurs: Ministry in a Hostile and Hurting World.* Nashville: Abingdon, 1993.

Edwards, Gene, and Tom Brandon. *Preventing a Church Split.* Scarborough, MA: Christian Books, 1987.

Ezell, Rick. *Strengthening the Pastor's Soul: Developing Personal Authenticity for Pastoral Effectiveness.* Grand Rapids: Kregel, 1995.

Fisher, David. *The 21st Century Pastor: A Vision Based on the Ministry of Paul.* Grand Rapids: Zondervan, 1996.

Frankl, Viktor. *Man's Search for Meaning.* New York: Washington Square Press, 1963.

Frye, John W. *Jesus the Pastor.* Grand Rapids: Zondervan, 2000.

Furniss, George M. *The Social Context of Pastoral Care.* Louisville, KY: Westminster/John Knox, 1994.

Galloway, Dale E. *Building Teams in Ministry / Dale Galloway and Beeson Institute Colleagues.* Kansas City: Beacon Hill Press of Kansas City, 2000.

_____. *20/20 Vision: How to Create a Successful Church.* Portland: Scott Publishing, 1986.

Galloway, Dale, and Kathy Mills. *The Small Group Book: The Practical Guide for Nurturing Christians and Building Churches.* Grand Rapids: Revell, 1995.

Gangel, Kenneth O. *Feeding and Leading.* Wheaton, IL: Victor, 1989.

Gangel, Kenneth O., and Samuel L. Canine. *Communication and Conflict Management.* Nashville: Broadman, 1992.

Garlow, James L. *Partners in Ministry: Laity and Pastors Working Together.* Kansas City: Beacon Hill Press of Kansas City, 1981.

George, Carl. *Prepare Your Church for the Future.* Tarrytown, NY: Revell, 1991.

Gerkin, Charles V. *An Introduction to Pastoral Care.* Nashville: Abingdon, 1997.

Good Things Happen in Small Groups. Downers Grove, IL: InterVarsity, 1985.

Gould, J. Glenn. *Healing the Hurt of Man: A Study of John Wesley's "Cure of Souls."* Kansas City: Beacon Hill Press of Kansas City, 1971.

Gula, Richard M. *Ethics in Pastoral Ministry.* New York: Paulist, 1996.

Halverstadt, Hugh F. *Managing Church Conduct.* Louisville, KY: Westminster/John Knox, 1991.

Hamilton, James D. *The Ministry of Pastoral Counseling.* Kansas City: Beacon Hill Press of Kansas City, 1972.

Hansen, David. *The Art of Pastoring: Ministry Without All the Answers.* Downers Grove, IL: InterVarsity, 1994.

Harbaugh, Gary. *Caring for the Caregiver: Growth Models for Professional Leaders and Congregations.* Washington, D.C.: Alban Institute, 1992.

_____. *Pastor as Person.* Minneapolis: Augsburg, 1986.

Haugk, Kenneth C. *Antagonists in the Church: How to Identify and Deal with Destructive Conflict.* Minneapolis: Augsburg, 1988.

Henderson, D. Michael. *John Wesley's Class Meeting; A Model for Making Disciples.* Nappanee, IN: Evangel, 1997.

Hiltner, Seward. *The Christian Shepherd: Some Aspects of Pastoral Care.* Nashville: Abingdon, 1959.

Hinson, E. Glenn. *Spiritual Preparation for Christian Leadership.* Nashville: Upper Room, 1999.

Howe, Leroy. *A Pastor in Every Pew: Equipping Laity for Pastoral Care.* Valley Forge, PA: Judson, 2000.

Holst, Lawrence E., ed. *Hospital Ministry: The Role of the Chaplain Today.* New York: Crossroad, 1985.

Hunter, George G., III. *Church for the Unchurched.* Nashville: Abingdon, 1996.

Hurn, Raymond W. *Finding Your Ministry.* Kansas City: Beacon Hill Press of Kansas City, 1979.

Huttenlocker, Keith. *Conflict and Caring: Preventing, Managing and Resolving Conflict in the Church.* Grand Rapids: Zondervan, 1988.

Johnson, Douglas W. *The Care and Feeding of Volunteers.* Nashville: Abingdon, 1978.

_____. *Empowering Lay Volunteers.* Nashville: Abingdon, 1991.

Kale, David W., with Mel McCullough. *Managing Conflict in the Church.* Kansas City: Beacon Hill Press of Kansas City, 2003.

Kemp, Charles F. *The Caring Pastor: An Introduction to Pastoral Counseling in the Local Church.* Nashville: Abingdon, 1985.

Kesler, Jay. *Being Holy, Being Human: Dealing with the Incredible Expectations and Pressures of Ministry.* Minneapolis: Bethany House, 1988.

Kimball, Dan. *The Emerging Church: Vintage Christianity for New Generations.* Grand Rapids: Zondervan, 2003.

Kinghorn, Kenneth Cain. *Gifts of the Spirit.* Nashville: Abingdon, 1976.

Kirkindoll, Michael. *The Hospital Visit.* Nashville: Abingdon, 2001.

Kollar, Charles Allen. *Solution-Focused Pastoral Counseling.* Grand Rapids: Zondervan, 1997.

Langford, Andy. *Christian Weddings: Resources to Make Your Ceremony Unique.* Nashville: Abingdon, 1995.

Larsen, David L. *Caring for the Flock: Pastoral Ministry in the Local Congregation.* Wheaton, IL: Crossway, 1991.

Larson, Bruce, Paul Anderson, and Doug Self. *Mastering Pastoral Care.* Sisters, OR: Multnomah, 1990.

Lebacqz, Karen, and Joseph D. Driskill. *Ethics and Spiritual Care: A Guide for Pastors, Chaplains, and Spiritual Directors.* Nashville: Abingdon, 2000.

Lewis, C. S. *The Problem of Pain.* New York: Macmillan, 1962.

Lewis, Robert, with Rob Wilkins. *The Church of Irresistible Influence.* Grand Rapids: Zondervan, 2001.

London, H. B., gen. ed. *Refresh, Renew, Revive.* Colorado Springs: Focus on the Family Publishing, 1996.

London, H. B., and Neil B. Wiseman. *The Heart of a Great Pastor: Making the Most of the Unique Opportunities That Can Only Be Found Where God Has Planted You.* Ventura, CA: Regal, 1994.

_____. *They Call Me Pastor: How to Love the Ones You Lead.*

Lowry, L. Randolph, and Richard Meyers. *Conflict Management and Counseling.* Dallas: Word Publishing, 1991.

Maddox, Randy L. *Responsible Grace: John Wesley's Practical Theology.* Nashville: Abingdon Press, 1994.

Malphurs, Aubrey, and Keith Willhite. *A Contemporary Handbook for Weddings and Funerals and Other Occasions.* Grand Rapids: Kregel, 2003.

MacDonald, Gordon. *Rebuilding Your Broken World.* Nashville: Thomas Nelson, 1988.

McBurney, Louis. *Counseling Christian Workers.* Dallas: Word Publishing, 1986.

Menking, Stanley J. *Helping Laity Help Others.* Philadelphia: Westminster Press, 1984.

Mickey, Paul A., and Robert L. Wilson. *Conflict and Resolution.* Nashville: Abingdon, 1973.

Mohler, R. Albert, et al. *Feed My Sheep: A Passionate Plea for Preaching.* Morgan, PA: Soli Deo Gloria, 2002.

Morsch, Gary, and Eddy Hall. *Ministry: It's Not Just for Ministers.* Kansas City: Beacon Hill Press of Kansas City, 1993.

Morsch, Gary, and Dean Nelson. *Heart and Soul: Awakening Your Passion to Serve.* Kansas City: Beacon Hill Press of Kansas City, 1997.

Nelson, Alan E. *The New Thing: Cutting-Edge Ideas for 21st Century Ministry from Progressive Leaders in the Wesleyan Heritage.* Scottsdale, AZ: Southwest Center for Leadership, 1998.

Nouwen, Henri. *The Wounded Healer.* Garden City, NY: Doubleday, 1972.

Noyce, Gaylord. *The Minister as Moral Counselor.* Nashville: Abingdon, 1989.

_____. *Pastoral Ethics: Professional Responsibilities of the Clergy.* Nashville: Abingdon, 1988.

Oden, Thomas C. *Classical Pastoral Care,* vol. 1, *Becoming a Minister.* Grand Rapids: Baker, 1987.

_____. *Classical Pastoral Care,* vol. 2, *Ministry Through Word and Sacrament.* Grand Rapids: Baker, 1987.

_____. *Classical Pastoral Care,* vol. 3, *Pastoral Counsel.* Grand Rapids: Baker, 1987.

_____. *Pastoral Theology: Essentials of Ministry.* San Francisco: HarperCollins, 1982.

Oglesby, William B., Jr. *Biblical Themes for Pastoral Care.* Nashville: Abingdon, 1980.

_____. *Referral in Pastoral Counseling.* Nashville: Abingdon, 1978.

Oliver, Gary J., Monte Hasz, Matthew Richburg. *Promoting Change Through Brief Therapy in Christian Counseling.* Wheaton, IL: Tyndale, Inc., 1997.

Oswald, Roy. *How to Build a Support System for Your Ministry.* Washington, D.C.: Alban Institute, 1991.

Pappas, Anthony. *Pastoral Stress: Sources of Tension, Resources for Transformation.* Bethesda, MD: Alban Institute, 1995.

Parrott, Les, III, and Leslie Parrott. *Saving Your Marriage Before It Starts: Seven Questions to Ask Before (and After) You Marry.* Grand Rapids: Zondervan, 1995.

Peterson, Eugene H. *Five Smooth Stones for Pastoral Work.* Grand Rapids: Eerdmans, 1992.

_____. *Working the Angles: The Shape of Pastoral Integrity.* Grand Rapids: Eerdmans, 1987.

Rediger, G. Lloyd. *Fit to Be Pastor: A Call to Physical, Mental, and Spiritual Fitness.* Louisville, KY: Westminster/John Knox, 2000.

Rice, Howard. *The Pastor as Spiritual Guide.* Nashville: Upper Room Books, 1998.

Richmond, Kent D., and David L. Middleton. *The Pastor and the Patient: A Practical Guidebook for Hospital Visitation.* Nashville: Abingdon, 1992.

Salter, Darius L. *Prophetical-Priestly Ministry: The Biblical Mandate for the 21st Century Pastor.* Nappanee, IN: Evangel, 2002.

Sanford, John A. *Ministry Burnout.* Louisville, KY: Westminster/John Knox Press, 1982.

Segler, Franklin M. *Understanding, Preparing for, and Practicing Christian Worship. Second Edition.* Nashville: Broadman and Holman, 1996.

Seymour, Jody. *A Time for Healing: Overcoming the Perils of Ministry.* Valley Forge, PA: Judson, 1995.

Slamp, David. *CareRings: Sunday School and Small Groups Side by Side.* Wichita, KS: Vessel, 2004.

Slaughter, Michael. *Out on the Edge: A Wake-up Call for Church Leaders on the Edge of the Media Reformation.* Nashville: Abingdon, 1998.

Smith, Harold Ivan. *When Your People Are Grieving: Leading in Times of Loss.* Kansas City: Beacon Hill Press of Kansas City, 2001.

Spaite, Daniel, M.D. *Time Bomb in the Church: Defusing Pastoral Burnout.* Kansas City: Beacon Hill Press of Kansas City, 1999.

Spruce, James R., ed. *A Pastor's Worship Resource: For Advent, Lent, and Other Occasions.* Kansas City: Beacon Hill Press of Kansas City, 1987.

Stone, Howard W. *The Caring Church.* San Francisco: Harper and Row, 1983.

_____. *Crisis Counseling.* Philadelphia: Fortress, 1976.

_____. *Theological Context for Pastoral Caregiving.* New York: Haworth, 1996.

Stone, Howard W., and William M. Clements, eds. *Handbook for Basic Types of Pastoral Care and Counseling.* Nashville: Abingdon, 1991.

Stowe, Eugene L. *The Ministry of Shepherding: A Study of Pastoral Practice.* Kansas City: Beacon Hill Press of Kansas City, 1976.

Sweet, Leonard. *Post-Modern Pilgrims.* Nashville: Broadman and Holman, 2000.

Swilhart, Judson J., and Gerald C. Richardson. *Counseling in Times of Crisis.* Dallas: Word Publishing, 1987.

Switzer, David K. *Pastoral Care Emergencies.* Minneapolis: Fortress, 2000.

Toler, Stan. *The People Principle: Transforming Laypersons into Leaders.* Kansas City: Beacon Hill Press of Kansas City, 1997.

Towns, Elmer. *Ten of Today's Most Innovative Churches.* Ventura, CA: Regal, 1990.

Towns, Elmer, and Warren Bird. *Into the Future: Turning Today's Church Trends into Tomorrow's Opportunities.* Grand Rapids: Revell, 2000.

Trueblood, Elton. *Your Other Vocation.* New York: Harper and Brothers, 1952.

Tucker, Austin B. *A Primer for Pastors: A Handbook for Strengthening Ministry Skills.* Grand Rapids: Kregel, 2004.

Underwood, Ralph L. *Pastoral Care and the Means of Grace.* Minneapolis: Fortress, 1993.

Wagner, C. Peter. *Your Spiritual Gifts Can Help Your Church Grow.* Ventura, CA: Regal, 1979.

Wagner, E. Glenn. *Escape from Church, Inc.: The Return of the Pastor-Shepherd.* Grand Rapids: Zondervan, 1999.

Warren, Rick. *The Purpose-Driven Church: Growth Without Compromising Your Message and Mission.* Grand Rapids: Zondervan, 1995.

Webber, Robert E. *"Eucharist Spirituality," Authentic Worship: Hearing Scripture's Voice, Applying Its Truths,* Herbert W. Bateman IV, ed. Grand Rapids: Kregel, 2002.

Westberg, Granger E. *Good Grief.* Philadelphia: Fortress, 1971.

White, Peter. *The Effective Pastor: Get the Tools to Upgrade Your Ministry.* Great Britain: Christian Focus, 2000.

Wiersbe, David W. *The Dynamics of Pastoral Care.* Grand Rapids: Baker, 2000.

Wiersbe, Warren W., and David W. Wiersbe. *Ten Power Principles for Christian Service: Ministry Dynamics for a New Century.* Grand Rapids: Baker, 1997.

Wilcox, Linda. *No More Front Porches: Rebuilding Community in Our Isolated Worlds.* Kansas City: Beacon Hill Press of Kansas City, 2002.

Williams, Dennis E., and Kenneth O. Gangel. *"Volunteers for Today's Church: How to Recruit and Retain Workers.* Grand Rapids: Baker, 1993.

Willimon, William. *Calling and Character: Virtues of the Ordained Life.* Nashville: Abingdon, 2000.

_____. *Pastor: The Theology and Practice of Ordained Ministry.* Nashville: Abingdon, 2002.

_____. *Preaching About Conflict in the Local Church*. Philadelphia: Westminster, 1987.

_____. *Worship as Pastoral Care*. Nashville: Abingdon, 1979.

Willimon, William, et al. *The Pastor's Guide to Effective Ministry*. Kansas City: Beacon Hill Press of Kansas City, 2002.

Wimberly, Edward P. *Moving from Shame to Self-worth: Preaching and Pastoral Care*. Nashville: Abingdon, 1997.

_____. *Using Scripture in Pastoral Counseling*. Nashville: Abingdon, 1994.

Wright, H. Norman. *Crisis Counseling: What to Do During the First 72 Hours*. Ventura, CA: Regal, 1993.

_____. *Premarital Counseling*. Chicago: Moody, 1977.

_____. *The Premarital Counseling Handbook*. Chicago: Moody, 1992.

Yancey, Philip. *Disappointment with God*. Grand Rapids: Zondervan, 1997.

_____. *Where Is God When It Hurts?* Grand Rapids: Zondervan, 1977.

Yohn, Rick. *Discover Your Spiritual Gift and Use It*. Wheaton, IL: Tyndale, 1982.